People and Sustainable Organization

Tomaž Kern
Vladislav Rajkovič
(eds.)

# PEOPLE AND SUSTAINABLE ORGANIZATION

PETER LANG
Frankfurt am Main · Berlin · Bern · Bruxelles · New York · Oxford · Wien

**Bibliographic Information published by the Deutsche Nationalbibliothek**
The Deutsche Nationalbibliothek lists this publication in the Deutsche Nationalbibliografie; detailed bibliographic data is available in the internet at http://dnb.d-nb.de.



ISBN 978-3-631-62113-4



www.peterlang.de

# People and Sustainable Organization

## Preface

The world is boiling. Countries, with rare exemptions, are heavily indebted. Nations are on the streets. Unemployment is growing. Many companies are in trouble. Even the young and educated are without work. Pension funds are struggling to cope with the burden. The social rights of individuals are waning. Long-term security of people is uncertain. We are facing unhappiness on all sides of the world. Unhappiness with democracy, distribution of capital, chances and opportunities and last but not least survival in our environment.

What is wrong? What is happening to the world? How come the economic growth that seemed unstoppable only a few years ago has suddenly slowed down and in some cases collapsed into itself? Perhaps it has happened for only a moment and the world will rise to its former heights again? Perhaps, but there is no guarantee that things will go back to the way they were. In any case, we have received an obvious clue that the growth can stop. We have received a message that somewhere along the way we might have made a mistake! But do we know where? Do we know which the true causes for this situation are? Do we know what the solutions are? Do we know how to continue? Have we learned anything?

In 1974, Herbert Simon, winner of the Nobel prize for economy has already said: »There is only a model of reality«. But still, we learn from the models we have formed in the past. From experience we construct new ones, which will solve problems that we are facing.

Matters in the business world are all but simple. The times are disruptive. We cannot continue in the same manner. Solutions based on continuous and unlimited growth are less and less likely, because in their essence they are in all aspects limited with resources. Therefore it will not suffice to only amend the existing models. What we require the most are new, innovative models. How to get them?

Economic growth must be sustainable. We can and we must get out of recession, we must find a clear vision for development and clear answers. Luckily there are quite a few such answers. We have to pick out the right ones among many. There are a lot of new things. Technological solutions led by information and communication technology are no longer just an accessory, but dictate us how things are to be done, from science to art, from business world to the individual. Technology allows for new connections between people. It is about swift exchange of information around the world. This affects the values of people and enables new value connections. Simulation models allow studying of different scenarios and offer options in the context of risk management. Somehow these are gifts from the outside.

But inside the systems and business systems, we are still facing existing models and business models that no longer suit the modern man and the organization of society in which we are living. The need to change the business models and direction for sustainable development are mandatory for modern man. The gap occurs because relations between people and our perception of the world are catching up to technology with delay. In other words, man is falling behind technological innovations. Technological innovations are somehow happening outside us, while innovation of the business model is an inner thing of individual, company, institution or country.

We must internalise the changes and introduce them to our immediate surroundings. But because the changes are revolutionary, »cosmetic« changes alone will not do, revolutionary new, innovative business models have to be formed. The starting point for this is experience and especially new circumstances and needs. Yet we must not forget that the centre of business models is always the man and his knowledge, not technology.

The knowledge available today is so extensive, structured and accessible, that the path to innovative business models should not pose a problem. The problem lies in the human, his cognitive processes and values. We know that it is human to make mistakes and that many unnecessary mistakes result from that. We say that we overlook »the queen on the chessboard« even though we do not want to and that we have enough knowledge. But it is also true that human nature has great ability to adapt. We are talking about various tools and ways of solving problems, from simple reminders and checklists to knowing and understanding the underlying principles, to creativity and innovation.

In the presented monograph »People and sustainable organization«, contributions in which authors are trying to answer the questions raised above are collected. Researchers have utilized scientific methods of data gathering and prepared models and solutions based on analysis. The monograph is designed with knowledge that answers cannot be correct if problems are addressed from one perspective only. Therefore the ideas on how to form new and innovative business models and solutions are offered through the web and interweaving of different viewpoints.

In the monograph a lot of attention is devoted to learning and placement of learning and »people who are learning« into a learning organization. Models based on knowledge management are described. Several contributions touch the human resource management area. The influences of different forms of organizing, different ways of communication and different leadership approaches on effectiveness and success of systems are addressed. Regarding man and values, it is clear that there is no mechanism that would lead to optimal decisions without negotiation in the sense of finding a consensus with adaptation from all sides. When looking for the best solution among many, there is nothing wrong with thinking about ourselves first, but we must not forget others that our decision concerns. The monograph offers several new solutions at reforming business processes. It answers questions of gauging effectiveness and success, with very distinct organizations as subjects of analysis. Several researches deal with development of information systems. They are to be viewed as authors' contributions towards the search for new solutions at creating a lasting organization.

The message of the monograph could be condensed into a thought that despite all external influences and internal patterns in any system innovation is still the elixir of changes and the driving force of development. Innovation and the ability to implement new ideas is and will remain the domain of man. Our head cannot be innovative if it is empty. Therefore it is not an option to leave everything to technology while neglecting learning and thinking. Learning too is about new models of what and when to learn along with new technological options, to best utilize the »computer« between our two ears.

Tomaž Kern
Vladislav Rajkovič

## Thanks

We editors would like to thank the Faculty of Organizational Sciences, University of Maribor, which has made the preparation and release of presented monograph possible. Additional thanks go to Slovenian Book Agency for co-financing of the book. Special thanks go to prof. ddr. Björn Paape from the University of Aachen, who has helped with design and has given plenty of useful advice at devising the contributions. We would also like to thank all reviewers and of course our team of professional co-workers for fruitful collaboration and content contributions.

# Table of Contents

## IV. Information Systems

# Knowledge Management in Slovene Companies

***Janez Dekleva***

*janez.dekleva@cpu.si*

***Bojana Sever***

*bojana.sever@cpu.si*

***Goran Vukovič***

*goran.vukovic@fov.uni-mb.si*

## Abstract

Knowledge management is a sign of the implementation of new knowledge in a society and signifies both an advantage and a potential business opportunity. The concept of a learning organisation includes the process of development guidance, as well as the acquisition, implementation and measurement of knowledge with the aim of structuring the competitive advantages of a company and improving the performance of non-profit organisations. This chapter presents the results of research on the implementation of the concept of a learning organisation in Slovene companies. The research is focused on the assessment of the state of knowledge management and the state of promotion and transmission of new concepts of business success development in Slovene companies.

**Keywords**: knowledge management, knowledge, learning organisation

## 1. Introduction

A modern society is – regardless of any crises – defined as a society of learning and knowledge. It is in the very crises where we can find the opportunity to give knowledge and learning a strategic priority. Now is the urgent time for a national strategy to be shown as the foundation for a learning society and learning organisations. Naturally, mere delcarations or a conscientious accumulation of unused knowledge and the newest technologies will not suffice.

In Slovene companies, there are a set of reasons to implement knowledge management. The main one is to optimise the development and the usage of knowledge in the company's operating activities. In order to ensure that companies have the skills to utilise their competitive advantages, it is important to provide suitable and reasonable knowledge management. The establishment of companies' own know-how databases tends to lead to conditions in which employees can create innovative business decisions, which lead to innovations and business competitiveness.

Knowledge management is a foundation of business policies for a learning and knowledge-oriented organisation, in which managers must be familiar with and master all the processes of knowledge input and output. Knowledge management is the implementation of new knowledge in a society and signifies an advantage and a potential business opportunity. It is also the identification, measurement and evaluation of an intellectual capital in the business balance sheets, as well as the endeavour towards its own growth, compared to the material capital. Knowledge management is, therefore, a science encompassing people, processes and technologies.

When registering knowledge, we often use a classification defined by a Hungarian philosopher, economist and chemist, Michael Polany:

- Tacit Knowledge is knowledge that is individually treated and is very hard to be formalised and delivered. A person gains it directly from experience. Tacit knowledge is appreciated, as it is rooted in person's experiences, values and actions. This sort of knowledge is actually a generator of all kinds of ideas, solutions and new knowledge. The key to the creation of knowledge, thus supposedly lies in the activation and transformation of such knowledge.
- Explicit Knowledge is knowledge that is registered in a formal systemic language and is thus transferable. It originates from various types of documents (directions, pictures, videos etc.). This kind of knowledge stays within the organisation even when a person abandons it.

In Polany's opinion, tacit knowledge is more important for human development, as people and organisations gain knowledge especially through their experiences and their own existence. Knowledge that can be registered by means of letters and numbers is, according to Polany, only the tip of the iceberg. The goal and wish of any organisation that wants to manage knowledge is to document tacit knowledge, and thus transform it into the registered knowledge. Employees are generators of innovation, ideas and knowledge in the company. The task of knowledge management is to enable an increase in tacit knowledge and to document it as far as possible (Kop, 2001).

In the narrow sense of the phrase, the knowledge management model consists of five tasks or steps: the creation of knowledge, knowledge storage, knowledge protection, knowledge dissemination and knowledge application. In the primary phase, knowledge is created by means of the experience and skills of the employees. It is created when people define new ways of work and when they gain new experience. If there is no such cycle in the organisation, knowledge can be gained from external sources, such as various developments and research laboratories. Knowledge has to be available in useful formats to anyone within the organisation, whenever and wherever he or she needs it. The internet, intranet and other web technologies help spread knowledge.

All these processes have to be included in the overall operating activities of a company. They have to become a key element of the company knowledge culture and supported by suitable information technology. They have to be connected with proper human resource management policies as well as properly defined and implemented staff processes in the company.

The concept of human capital is further expanding on the so-called intellectual capital, which (in addition to knowledge, skills and abilities of individuals) includes the organisational structure of a company, customer relations and skills that ensure the market competitiveness to a company (Malačič, 2001). Intellectual capital is intangible and invisible, as it is not reflected in the balance sheet of the company (Maček, 2000, pp.38), but is presently becoming the most powerful competitive advantage. The concept of a 'community of practice' has assumed what seems to be a permanent, high place in management thinking (Steward, 2001, pp.2).

# 2. Purpose, Methodology and Implementation of Research

When evaluating the success of knowledge management, several points have to be continuously checked:

- whether a company or an organisation has an overview of available knowledge and employees possessing this knowledge.
- whether the knowledge stored in the suitable databases (treasuries of knowledge) is available to those needing it;

- whether evidence of realization of transmission of knowledge among co-workers is available;
- whether the whole process of knowledge management, knowledge monitoring and knowledge measurement is properly managed;
- whether the knowledge is appropriately protected;
- whether the velocity of knowledge transmission into the products and services is being measured;
- whether employees are kept informed about the successful results of knowledge usage and if they are appropriately rewarded.

The introduction of the concept of a learning organisation includes the process of development guidance, acquisition, implementation and (last but not least) the measurement of knowledge with the aim of structuring the competitive advantages of a company and improvement in the performance of non-profit organisations.

For the efficient implementation of the concept of a learning organisation, it is necessary to go through eight phases:
1. learning organisation level analysis,
2. project environment organisation and organisational restructuring,
3. strategic founding of the learning organisation, guidance styles, communication systems, teams etc.
4. involvement of employees – communication circles,
5. corporation culture strategic viewpoints,
6. project environment and knowledge management, innovation and internal entrepreneurship
7. evaluation and implementation of the learning organisation and
8. future development cycle learning organisation.

Accordingly, the main goals of the research are to:
- assess the state of knowledge management,
- assess the state of the promotion and transmission of new concepts of business success enhancements into Slovene companies
- and to develop and update learning organisation elements that would enable Slovene companies to have a more efficient adjustment to the globalisation challenges and more successful confrontation with global crises.

To accomplish the aims of the research, a survey has been conducted, based on the overall implementation of the concept of a learning organisation, which was developed in 2001 by the USP Institute and has been implemented as the first such model in practice in Slovene companies.

Research was conducted using the Delphi method. In the first round, the structured questionnaire with open questions was prepared and sent to 50 HR managers in companies from different branches to get feedback about important topics of in-company knowledge management to be used for the research.

Based on the a feedback, we compiled questionnaire, consisting of 51 open and closed questions divided into ten subjects: strategic aspect, management role, organisational culture, knowledge management, learning organisation, role of an individual, motivation, processes and systems, knowledge and employees satisfaction measurement and impacts of implementation of the concept of learning organisation on business performance. The questionnaire was sent to 500 major Slovene companies; 116 companies (23.2%) participated in the research.

The data collected with the questionnaire have been statistically analysed and broken down into the following segments:

- foundation for the implementation of a learning organisation and the role of management,
- organisational culture development triggers,
- knowledge acquisition and knowledge management,
- systems and
- results.

# 3. Research

## 3.1 Foundation for the Implementation of a Learning Organisation and the Role of Management

With the first segment of questions, we tried to establish whether organisations have the foundations for the implementation of the learning organisation concept and whether management is qualified to implement the concept.

The statistics of answers has shown that companies have:

- most frequently (82.7%) defined core values in written form for the achievement of strategic goals,
- in 56.9%, the learning organisation concept is already written in the strategic documents of a company and
- in 64.6%, the employees already follow the adopted Code of Conduct.

The success of an organisation, as well as the established changes, is largely dependent on its management. Its role in the learning organisation, however, differs from the role in the classic organisation. In the learning organisation, the managers are role models for their employees, their coaches and mentors. They are heads of the development of individuals and the teams of the organisation and its methods. They enjoy the strong support of their co-workers when making important decisions.

In the segment 'The role of management', the most frequently seen fact (70.7%) is that the head of the human resource management department is a member of a company's management board. In learning organisations, where people represent the core of competitive advantage, the responsibility for the human resource management should be entrusted the highest level of management.

## 3.2 Organisational Culture Development Triggers

An organisational culture of changes, innovation and entrepreneurship is a typical characteristic of learning organisations. Among the organisational culture factors of a learning organisation, there are:

- a written plan of changes in the company (83.6%) was the most common factor,
- the remaining three factors, such as responsibility of the employees for their own development, decision making and involvement of co-workers in problem-solving and decision-making and development planning and learning of both employees and management, are expressed in 71% of cases, in average.

Regarding the involvement of the employees in the company processes and their planned development, there are still opportunities for improvement among companies.

The field of innovative innovation activity (I&I):

- 58.6% of organisations have established a means of proper regulation,
- for the management of an I&I activity, 58.6% companies have also established an adequate service or named an accountable manager,
- in 60.0%, the effects of an I&I activity have been regularly monitored and evaluated,
- 14.6% of the employees have delivered at least one useful proposition per year.

The reason for such a poor state in the field of I&I activity lies in the indeterminate organisational systems and especially in an inadequate organisational culture, where management is one of the main generators of innovation.

## 3.3 Knowledge Acquisition and Knowledge Management

In learning organisations, learning is planned and addressed by all the employees in a continuous way and by means of efficient methods. An investment into knowledge is counted as efficient, when key knowledge arises from the strategic goals of a company.

Companies have identified key knowledge for the achievement of strategic goals in 62.9% of cases. The companies that were examined dedicate an average of 25 hours a year to the education and training of an employee.

Among the examined fields, acquisition of knowledge is most expressed, thus signifying that organisations, among all factors, pay most attention to their employees, acquisition of new knowledge. It is specifically for classic organizations that the knowledge is mostly obtained, whereas in learning organisations the aim is to make the newly-gained knowledge as efficient as possible, using planned and systematic knowledge management.

Investments in knowledge lead to new knowledge that increases the working capacity of an individual and consequently to increase in income and profit. So with investment in knowledge, we get new knowledge that increases the working possibilities of an individual and also facilitates higher returns (Keševljevič, 2004).

Acquired knowledge needs to be properly stored, organised and transferred to those needing it as quickly as possible or transformed into marketable and competitive products and services. Mutual trust and cooperation between employees increase the possibility that an individual will also participate in transfer and exchange of knowledge.

Knowledge transmission can be delivered interpersonally, whereby knowledge trustees can come useful. The companies in this study have an average of have 2.6 trustees per 100 of employees.

The most frequent forms of knowledge exchange among the teams and sectors are the meetings and regular gatherings, internet presentations, teamwork, project work, electronic mail and intranet.

A total of 61.2% of companies have key knowledge stored in an adequate knowledge database, whereby documentation archive, intranet, literature library, computer network knowledge database and personal folders of the employees are mostly used.

Companies can gain much knowledge and ideas from different forms of cooperation with their customers, which is used by 57.7% of the examined companies. Among all the examined fields, Slovene companies have most space for improvement in the efficiency of the knowledge management processes. Though it is improving, the exchange of knowledge with customers is still very poorly expressed.

Knowledge management must be conceived on the company level, in general, and must stay in that context under the responsibility of the highest management level (Čater, 2001). However, we must be aware of the fact that the accuracy life of knowledge is becoming shorter with rapid development; furthermore, as much as we are aware of growth of the needs of specific knowledge, we also must be aware of the risk that some knowledge and skills will be (or quickly become) obsolete. Skills obsolescence can occur in variety of ways. Technical skills obsolescence is due to changes originating in workers, while economic skills obsolescence is caused by changes in the job or work environment (Grip, Loo, Steur, 2001, pp. 122).

## 3.4 Systems

Learning organisations master internal processes and systems, signifying that they are in accordance with the strategy and the organisational structure, and that they are in tune with each other. Among systems, the information system and the motivation system are the most important for the development of the learning organisation concept.

The employees in the 75.8% of examined companies receive information on achieved goals of operating activities and financial results. According to 67.2% of the examined organisations, the information flow from the employees to the management is not as strongly expressed. The most frequent forms of informing employees are in written form, via electronic mail and intranet, information display, meetings, regular gatherings, presentations, board meetings and internal magazines.

Information systems are among most frequently expressed of the examined set of factors. Information flow is stronger downwards, while companies still have opportunities to improve the information flow in the upward direction.

In order to introduce changes in a company and to release creativity and innovation, it is necessary to establish an overall motivational environment, including both formal and informal ways of motivation. An important fact is that in 60.3% of cases, knowledge flow is supported by the reward system among the employees and that in 61.2% of cases all useful propositions and innovations of the employees are rewarded in accordance with the regulation. Among the ways of motivation, financial forms of rewards, such as the variable part of the payment and the payment for the conducted projects, especially stand out. The greatest room for improvement is in the practice of informal ways, such as various compliments, achievement acknowledgements, promotions of individuals, various bonuses etc.

New ways of learning by using high-level thinking processes change knowledge into the combination of information. Thus, knowledge in an old context is still a quantity of information, but in a new context is becoming the ability to combine data into new knowledge or solutions (Lipičnik, 2001, pp. 339).

## 3.5 Results

Due to the possibilities for the improving the achievement of planned goals, and investments into the employees, a learning organisation monitors, measures and evaluates the efficiency of knowledge investment, using selected criteria.

In the examined organisations, 62% systematically assess the quality of education that has been carried out. The most frequent ways of assessing the quality of education are surveying education and training participants, examining the knowledge at the end of education, and evaluation of education by a professional service.

Among the most frequently used indicators for measuring effects of investments in knowledge, companies do not mention the most appropriate instruments, such as BSC and Svelby. Of the examined organisations, 66.4% already systematically monitor the satisfaction of their employees, which they most frequently assess by means of interviews with the employees, measuring the organisation atmosphere and by means of a survey or annual evaluation interviews.

The field of result measurement is the most poorly expressed field in this research. As we can efficiently perform only that which we can measure, it would be logical to devote much more attention to this field and thus improve the efficiency of employee investments.

The significance of introducing changes in a company, such as the concept of a learning organisation, lies in the achievement of advanced business results, business excellence, public reputation and the appeal to investors.

The answers clearly reveal that introduction of the learning organisation concept has had positive effects on the success of a company. The most frequent positive effects of such a change have been better business results, greater flexibility of the employees and faster introduction of changes, higher motivation and satisfaction of the employees, greater work efficiency and higher quality of work done. From the effects that have been achieved, it can be seen that companies with better developed concepts of a learning organisation have more adequate and better expressed positive effects of introduction of the learning organisation concept.

From the results of the research on the presence of elements of the learning organisation concept in Slovene organisations, one can see a very slow growth of consciousness that employees are becoming increasingly important factor in the competitive advantage in the knowledge economy. This conclusion arises from the growth of employee investments, information system improvement as well as a gradually more expressed role of the employees in a company.

Demarest (1997) believes that innovation is strongly linked to the creation of new knowledge in the organisation. Each innovation begins with the creation of new knowledge.

There are not many companies in Slovenia that build their future on knowledge and innovation. We have established that there is quite a lot of space left for improvement in introducing the concept of a learning organisation in Slovene companies. We have found that there is most space in the field of indeterminate innovative innovation activity, in the development of management that has to accept new roles in the economy of knowledge (mentor, coach, role model, knowledge and creativeness motivator, protector etc.) as well as in the field of systematically formed process of knowledge management and the use of various instruments for the measurement of the effects of an investment.

The results of the research are useful for the companies that participated in the survey, since they can make a comparison of the situation on the field of knowledge management in their company with the situation on the national level, identify positive or negative deviations and consequently define areas where additional input or development activities are needed.

The results also show the need for specific measures on the area of education and training of HR managers and experts. In particular, it is necessary to emphasise or include topics that show the importance of co-oporative learning in the university and higher education professional programmes, as well as to provide existing HR managers and experts with an appropriate development paradigm in the form of continuous education and training courses with new contents and approaches that are emerging in practice. Investments in knowledge increase added-value employment and economic growth in the long term; thus, the active role of the state in this area is indispensable (Čater, 2004, pp.129).

# 4. Conclusion

The crucial success factors of the use of a knowledge management system are the motivation of the people, suitable information support and management interest.

Knowledge management systems are thus becoming generators of the knowledge revolution that has been affecting every part of society. The market and the needs for solutions in the field of knowledge management are also exponentially increasing due to increasingly larger mergers of communication systems, enabling simple access to enormous quantities of basically unstructured information. Globalisation, development, the dynamics of the modern economy and 24-hour activity force companies to face the fact that accurate and timely information is the ultimate key to success.

Knowledge management maintains the balance in a dynamic and open organisation, especially regarding the influences of the increasingly complex environment. The integration of internal levels of decision-making, management and production is no longer executed through the coordination and direct influence of managers and supervisory system, but through self-organisation and the connection of self-sustaining integral wholes. Naturally, the key problem is a cultural overlap in all spheres. The very flexibility and creativeness, connected to the concept of a learning organisation, establishes a 'new cultural environment' of an organisation.

In order to manage knowledge successfully, companies have to define roles in acquisition, flow and the usage of knowledge. Finally, it is the people who add value to data and information and transform them into knowledge.

## References


Bernik, M., Florjančič, J., Rajkovič, L. (2002): Upravljanje z znanjem in uporaba informacijskig tehnologij (Knowledge management and use of information technologies), *Organizacija*, Vol. 35, No. 8, pp. 473–477.

CEDEFOP (2010), *Access to success, Lifelong guidance for better learning and working in Europe*, Publications Office of the European Union, Luxembourg.

CEDEFOP (2010), *Better competences through better teaching and leading, Findings from study visits 2008/09*, Publications Office of the European Union, Luxembourg.

CEDEFOP (2010), *Employer-provided vocational training in Europe, Evaluation and interpretation of the third continuing vocational training survey*, Publications Office of the European Union, Luxembourg.

CEDEFOP (2009*), Future skill needs in Europe: medium-term forecast, Background technical report*, Publications Office of the European Union, Luxembourg.

CEDEFOP (2010), *Professional development opportunities for in-company trainers, a compilation of good practices*, Publications Office of the European Union, Luxembourg.

CEDEFOP (2009), *Professionalising career guidance, Practitioner competences and qualification routes in Europe*, Office for Official Publications of the European Communities, Luxembourg.

Common Competency Framework, Consolidated Report (2007), http://www.econ-it.com/ezines/cf_report_consolidated.pdf (Accessed 7 December 2009).

Čater, T. (2001): *Management znanja kot pripomoček za razvijanje konkurenčne prednosti podjetja* (Knowledge management as an instrument for development of competitive advantage), IB revija, Vol. 35, No. 1, pp. 76–85.

Čater, T. (2003): *Osnove konkurenčnih prednosti slovenskih podjetij*, doktorska disertacija (Basics of competitive advantages of Slovenian companies, doctoral thesis), University of Ljubljana, Faculty of Economics, Ljubljana.

Čater, T. (2004): *Pomen osnov konkurenčne prednosti podjetja v skladu s šolo na temelju virov* (Importance of basics of competitive advantages of the company in accordance with the school based on sources), *IB revija*, Vol. 38, No. 1 / 2, pp. 117–131.

Černelič, M. (2004): *Učeča se organizacija in ravnanje z znanjem v organizaciji, magistrsko delo* (Learning organization and knowledge management, master's thesis), University of Ljubljana, Faculty of Economics, Ljubljana.

Demarest, M. (1997): Understanding knowledge management, *Long-Range Planning*, Vol. 30, No. 3, pp.374–384.

Drucker, P. (1974): *Management: Tasks, Responsibilities, Practices*, Harper & Row, New York.

Florjančič, J., Kavran, D. (1992): Kadrovska funkcija – management (Human resources function – management), *Moderna organizacija*, Kranj.

Ferjan, M. (2003): Vplivni dejavniki napredovanj zaposlenih v Sloveniji (Factors influencing promotion of employees in Slovenia), *Organizacija*, Vol. 36, No. 7, pp. 469–476.

Ferjan, M., Jereb, E. (2004): Kadri in management (Human resources and management), *Moderna organizacija* pp. 124–137, Kranj.

Grip, D. A., Loo, V. J., Steur, M. (2001): Skill Obsolescence: Causes and Cures, *International Journal of Manpower*, Vol. 22, No. 1 / 2, pp. 121–137.

Gruban, B. (2002): Upravljanje človeškega kapitala podjetij (Management of human resources in companies), *ŠCID*, Vol. 2002, No. 8.

Gruban, B. (2000): Razlika med uspešnimi in neuspešnimi podjetji so ... ljudje (The difference between successful and unsuccessful companies is ... people), *ŠCID*, Vol. 2000, No. 4.

Kešeljević, A. (2004): *Sodobni vidiki razumevanja znanja v ekonomiji, doktorska disertacija* (Modern aspects of understanding knowledge in economy, doctoral thesis), University of Ljubljana, Faculty of Economics, Ljubljana.

Kešeljević, A. (2005): Pomembnost z znanjem neposredno povezanih procesov v organizaciji (The importance of knowledge directly related to processes in the organization), *Organizacija*, Vol. 38, No. 1, pp. 5–12.

Kaplan, R. S., Norton, D. P. (1996): *The Balanced Scorecard: Translating Strategy into Action*, Harvard Business School Press, Boston.

Kop, A., (2001): *Poslovodenje znanja*, Svetovalni dokument št. 15 (Knowledge management, Advising document No. 15), Združenje managerjev Slovenije

Leavy, F. (2010): How Technology Changes Demands for Human Skills, *OECD Education Working Papers*, No. 45, OECD Publishing.

Lipičnik, B. (2001): Učenje hitrejše od izobraževanja (Learning faster than education), *Organizacija*, Vol. 34, No.6, pp. 338–340.

Maček, M. (2000): Znanje je pogosto edina dodana vrednost izdelka (Knowledge is often the only added value to the product), *Marketing Magazine*, Vol. 20, No. 230, pp. 38–39.

Malačič, J. (2001): *Statistično upravljanje obsega človeškega kapitala, Novo tisočletje – pripravljenost statistike na razumevanje in merjenje novih pojavov*, Zbornik referatov 11. mednarodnega statističnega srečanja (Statistical management of human capital, New millennium – Preparedness of statistics to understand and measure new phenomena), Statistični urad RS, pp. 424–436, Ljubljana.

Molnar, M. (2010), Measuring Competition in Slovenian Industries: Estimation of mark-ups, *OECD Economics Department Working Papers*, No. 787, OECD Publishing.

Netteland, G. (2009), *E-learning for change: Competence development in work organization*, Development of Competences in the World of Work and Education: Conference Proceedings, Self-regulated network DECOWE.

Nonaka, I., Toyama, R., Konno, N. (2000), SECI, ba and leadership: a unified model of dynamic knowledge creation, *Long Range Planning*, Vol. 33 No. 1, pp. 5–34.

Polanyi, M. (1966): *The Tacit Dimension*, Doubleday & Company, Inc., New York

Quinn, J. B. (1992): *Intelligent Enterprise: A Knowledge and Service-Based Paradigm for Industry*, The Free Press, New York.

Senge. P. (1994): *The Fifth Discipline: The art and Practise of the Learning Organization*, Doubleday, New York.

Soliman. F. (1998): Optimum level of process mapping and least cost business process reengineering, *International Journal of Operations and Production Management*, Vol. 18, No. 9, pp. 810–816.

Suleman. F, Suleman, A. (2009), *Rating and ranking: A fuzzy approach to the individual bundle of competence*, Development of Competences in the World of Work and Education: Conference Proceedings, Self-regulated network DECOWE.

Steward, A. T. (2001): Intellectual capital: Ten Years Later, How Far We've Come, *Fortune*, http://money.cnn.com/magazines/fortune/fortune_archive/2001/05/28/303836/index.htm (Accessed 7 December 2009).

Sveiby, K. E. (1997): *The New Organizational Wealth: Managing & Measuring Knowledge-Based Assets*, Berrett-Koehler Publishers, Inc., San Francisco.

Vila, A. (1994): *Organizacija in organiziranje* (Organization and Organizing), Moderna organizacija, Kranj.

## About the Authors

**Janez Dekleva** is director of the Institute for Business Education at the Chamber of Commerce and Industry of Slovenia. His main research interests include the education system in Slovenia, adult education, labour market research and skills mismatches.

**Bojana Sever** is head of the department for international cooperation and projects at the Institute for Business Education at the Chamber of Commerce and Industry of Slovenia. Her main research interests include the areas of labour markets, human resources, vocational qualifications and competences.

**Goran Vukovič** is a full professor at the Faculty of Organizational Sciences, University of Maribor. His research interests include human resources and marketing. He is an experienced consultant in the areas of human resources and organisation in the profit and non-profit sectors of the economy.

# Study Progress of Classic and E-Learning Students at the DOBA Faculty of Applied Business and Social Sciences Maribor

***Alenka Gortan***

*alenka.gortan@guest.arnes.si*

***Eva Jereb***

*eva.jereb@fov.uni-mb.si*

## Abstract

This chapter deals with dropouts from traditional and e-learning academic courses and the reasons that lead students to either successfully complete their course or drop it. In the first part, the terminology dealing with traditional and e-education are presented. It concentrates on different interdependent factors: personal factors (motivation, effort, practice, aptitude, talent, time spent for studying, opportunities to study, previous education, age and gender), social factors (class, social stratum, education and occupation of parents, monthly income per a family member), organisation of a study process (number and series of courses, plan of exams, parallel/consequent way of study) and the quality of the study process (feedback, clarity of aims, expedients, methods and techniques, contents of materials, cooperation of a student with a professor) also considering the locus of control. In the second part, the results of the research that took place among 134 students of traditional and e-study programs at DOBA Faculty in Slovenia are presented. The results show that the main reasons that prevent students from dropping out from their academic courses are high levels of satisfaction with study programs and especially high levels of one's own success reflected in academic results.

**Key words:** traditional learning, e-learning, success factors, satisfaction

# 1. Introduction

We live in times when knowledge is not only the ultimate value but also the necessity that leads to the progress and development of society. More knowledge brings better jobs and enables us to live the lives we wish for.

E-study differs greatly from the traditional way of studying in classrooms. Students can study following their own rhythm anywhere at any time. They can cooperate with professors and tutors on a daily basis and can also communicate with other students through communication tools.

To research drop-out rates and study progress, it is vital to define the term 'drop-outs'. Levy (2003) offers an appropriate explanation of the term: these are students who deliberately decide to leave the course and take a financial penalty for doing so. Authors agree that dropping out is a complicated phenomenon (Billings, 1988; Parker, 1999; Volkwein and Lorang, 1995; Williamson and Crimer, 1988) that needs to be thoroughly studied in order to be able to define the factors that lead students to either dropping out or successfully completing the course. Administrators and teachers must define the causes and reasons for dropping out in order to lower the number of students who drop out (Xenos, 2002). Kember's model involves demographic factors, students' motivation, academic abilities and students' social factors as those that influence students' decision to drop out/successfully complete the course (Kember, 1989; see also Araque, 2009). Other authors believe that drop-out rate is not affected by demographic factors (Volkwein and Lorang, 1995; Williamson and Creamer, 1988). Dille and Mezack (1991) have come to the conclusion that not enough research has been done about personal characteristics that define each student. It is evident from their study that an important correlation is that between the age of a student and study progress. Older students and those that are employed are more likely to drop out than younger students (Levy, 2006). Levy's study shows that gender and family status do not affect the drop-out rate. As Jereb indicates, social class position presents a strong determinant of educational achievement out (Ferjan, Jereb, Šušteršič, 2008). The most important reason for dropping out/successfully completing the course is the satisfaction and dissatisfaction of students with study process (Chyung, Winiecki and Fenner, 1998; Jereb, 2010). Parker (1999) states that the main reason for progress in the study process is the locus of control as well as certain demographic factors like gender, age, and employment. An inner locus of control is developed by those students who believe in their academic achievements and take control, while the outer locus of control is developed by those who respond to fear of failure (Rotter, 1989). One of the key factors in study progress is students' satisfaction with the study process; 42% of students who dropped out were dissatisfied with the study environment (Chyung, 1998). The students who were highly satisfied with the study process and study environment aimed for better results. Surprisingly, older students expressed higher levels of satisfaction than younger students (Fredericksen et al., 2000; Jereb, Ferjan, Jesenko, 2009). Other research show interesting results: satisfaction with the study process is the key factor in study progress (Levy, 2000; Sachs and Hale, 2003), which leads faculties and educational institutions to emphasize students' satisfaction with the study course, which leads to study progress. Using electronic books in distance education is one of the factors that increases students' satisfaction (Jereb, Šmitek, 1999) and introducing multimedia instruction in e-learning is definitely more attractive to students and it heightens the motivation (Jereb, Šmitek, 2006). Methods of teaching and the development of study programs influence students' satisfaction (Shea, Pickett, Peltz, 2003). Their research shows that students' satisfaction greatly depends on precise and understandable instructions, organisation of academic topics, communication with professor/tutor, direct interaction with tutors who give instructions for current assignments and prompt feedback. Students who are offered on-line exams prove to be more satisfied with the study organisation than traditional students (Jereb, Bernik, 2006). Other studies involve social factors and co-operation with professor/tutor, because this co-operation is closely connected to academic achievements (Jereb, Ferjan, 2008). Better achievements make students more enthusiastic about further studies and towards better study progress (Richardson and Swan, 2003) and to life-long education (Jereb, Ferjan, 2005).

Next, the methodology and the results of the research that took place among 150 students of traditional and e-study programs are presented.

# 2. Methodology

## 2.1 Hypotheses

The following hypotheses were defined:

H1: *Female population of students is more successful at study than male population.*

H2: *E-students are on average younger than traditional students.*

H3: *E-students are more successful than those who study in a traditional way.*

H4: *E-students are more satisfied with study organisation than traditional students.*
H5: *E-students are more satisfied with their own academic performance than traditional students.*
H6: *E-students spend less time accomplishing their study assignments than traditional students.*
H7: *An important factor in taking up e-study is physical distance from academic centres.*
H8: *E-students have a higher monthly income than traditional students.*

## 2.2 Sample

A sample of 134 higher education students in Slovenia (36 males (27%) and 98 (73%) females) participated in this study. They came from various parts of Slovenia (Koper, Velenje, Maribor, Murska Sobota and Nova Gorica); 82 (61%) of them were traditional students (22 male and 60 female) and 52 (39%) students (14 male and 38 female) were e-students at DOBA Faculty. The DOBA Faculty of Applied Business and Social Sciences Maribor is a school with a modern, European vision, offering outstanding practice-oriented programmes and a flexible study system. It provides practice-oriented bachelor programmes in Business Management, Marketing and Business Administration, Organisation and Management of Social Activities and master programmes in International Business Management, Organisation and Management of Social Activities and Management of Lifelong Education. In both traditional and e-study, the female gender prevails, as seen in Table 1. Ages ranged from 20 to 61 years, with a mean of 32 years and 6 months.

*Table 1: Gender of students in e-study and traditional study*

| | | Type of study | | |
|---|---|---|---|---|
| | | traditional | e-study | total |
| Gender | Male | 22 | 14 | 36 |
| | Female | 60 | 38 | 98 |
| | Total | 82 | 52 | 134 |

## 2.3 Instrument

Two hundred and fifty questionnaires were distributed among the students of traditional and e-learning; 134 of them were returned. The questionnaire consisted of three parts.

The first part of the questionnaire contained nine questions in which we asked subjects about their demographic characteristics (gender, age, year of study, average academic grade on exams, previous education and the number of hours of studying weekly).

The second part of the questionnaire asked subjects to assess their motivation, effort, organisation of teaching-learning process, quality of a study, locus of control, and distance from the closest academic centre. A five-point scale was used from (1) 'I absolutely disagree' to (5) 'I absolutely agree'.

The third part referred to the social standards of a student's family and background. Subjects were asked to tell the level of parents' education, the employment of a student, parents and a partner (following Goldthorpe's (1980) scheme); the last question referred to the monthly family income.

# 3. Results

To test the first hypothesis, students were asked to answer the question 'What was the grade you achieved at your latest exam?' It can be seen in Table 2 that female students achieve higher grades (8.13) than male students (7.88). But the independent samples T-test shows that there is no statistically significant difference ($t = -1.350$; $\alpha=0.05$; $p_{\alpha}=0.179$) between male and female students in achieved grades (Table 3).

*Table 2: Average grade in male and female student populations*

| | Gender | N | Mean | Std. Deviation | Std. Error Mean |
|---|---|---|---|---|---|
| Average grade | Male | 36 | 7.88 | .858 | .143 |
| | Female | 98 | 8.13 | .972 | .098 |

*Table 3: Independent sample test of average grade in male and female student populations*

| | | Levene's Test for Equality of Variances | | t-test for Equality of Means | | | | |
|---|---|---|---|---|---|---|---|---|
| | | F | Sig. | t | df | Sig. (2-tailed) | Mean Difference | Std. Error Difference |
| Average grade | Equal variances assumed | .509 | .477 | -1.350 | 132 | .179 | -.248 | .184 |
| | Equal variances not assumed | | | -1.430 | 70.124 | .157 | -.248 | .173 |

The first hypothesis (H1) that female population of students is more successful at study than a male population was rejected.

The second hypothesis (H2) that e-students are on average younger than traditional students was also rejected. The average age of a traditional student is 32 years and of e-student is 34 years. E-students are slightly older than traditional students but the T-test showed ($t = -1.326$; $\alpha=0.05$; $p_\alpha=0,188$) that there is no statistically significant difference between traditional and e-students with regard to age.

The third hypothesis (H3) that e-students are more successful than traditional students was rejected as well.

E-students actually spend less time studying than traditional students, but their average grade is surprisingly higher. The average grade at e-study is 8.19 and at traditional study 7.98 as can be seen from Table 4.

*Table 4: Average grade of traditional and e-students*

| | Type of study | N | Mean | Std. Deviation | Std. Error Mean |
|---|---|---|---|---|---|
| Average grade | Traditional | 82 | 7.98 | .963 | .106 |
| | e-study | 52 | 8.19 | .912 | .127 |

Still, the T-test shows that the difference is not statistically significant ($t=-1.254$; $\alpha=0.05$; $p_\alpha=0.212$), which can be seen in Table 5.

*Table 5: T-test of average values for e-students and traditional students*

| | | Levene's Test for Equality of Variances | | t-test for Equality of Means | | | | |
|---|---|---|---|---|---|---|---|---|
| | | F | Sig. | t | df | Sig. (2-tailed) | Mean Difference | Std. Error Difference |
| Average grade | Equal variances assumed | .155 | .695 | -1.254 | 132 | .212 | -.210 | .167 |
| | Equal variances not assumed | | | -1.270 | 113.028 | .207 | -.210 | .165 |

The fourth hypothesis (H4) that e-students are more satisfied with the study organisation than traditional students was also rejected.

The changeable variable that was studied in this research is the level of satisfaction of traditional and e-students with regard to study organisation. The respondents were asked to mark the grade of satisfaction on a five-level scale, (1) meaning completely dissatisfied (nobody marked that possibility) and (5) meaning absolutely satisfied, as can be seen from Table 6. The hi-square test showed ($\chi 2 = 3.858$; $\alpha=0.05$; $p_{\alpha}=0{,}277$) that there is no statistically significant difference between traditional and e-students with regard to satisfaction with study organisation.

*Table 6: Satisfaction with study organisation among traditional and e-students*

| | | Type of study | | |
|---|---|---|---|---|
| | | traditional | e-study | Total |
| Satisfaction with study organisation | 2 | 4 | 2 | 6 |
| | 3 | 27 | 20 | 47 |
| | 4 | 35 | 13 | 48 |
| | 5 | 16 | 14 | 30 |
| | Total | 82 | 49 | 131 |

The fifth hypothesis (H5) that e-students are more satisfied with their own success than traditional students is rejected.

On the scale from 1 to 5, where 1 stands for totally dissatisfied and 5 stands for perfectly satisfied, the students marked their level of satisfaction with their study progress. The results can be seen in Table 7. There are no students who are totally dissatisfied and some students are really quite satisfied with their academic performance. The average value for the satisfaction was a little above 4.

*Table 7: Comparison of satisfaction with their own success of e-students and traditional students*

| | | Type of study | | |
|---|---|---|---|---|
| | | traditional | e-study | Total |
| Satisfaction with success | 2 | 3 | 1 | 4 |
| | 3 | 19 | 11 | 30 |
| | 4 | 36 | 20 | 56 |
| | 5 | 24 | 18 | 42 |
| | Total | 82 | 50 | 132 |

The hi-square test showed that the traditional and e-students do not differ significantly with regard to their satisfaction with their own success ($\chi2=0.855$; $\alpha=0.03$; $p_\alpha=0.836$).

The sixth hypothesis (H6) that e-students spend less time performing study tasks than traditional students was confirmed.

In this point, the e-students differ significantly from traditional students: the value of Pearson hi-square test is ($\chi2=36.035$; $\alpha=0.05$; $p_\alpha=0.045$).

The lower contingency table shows that e-students are the ones who dedicate less time to accomplishing study tasks. Almost 54% of e-students spend up to five hours a week studying (28 out of 52) while in traditional study only 7% of traditional students spends the same time studying (7 of 82). On average (with the same mean as before and the same weight), traditional students study 12.7 hours a week while the average in e-study is 7 hours a week, as can be seen in Table 8.

*Table 8: Comparison of hours of study in traditional and e-study*

| | | Type of study | | |
|---|---|---|---|---|
| | | traditional | e-study | Total |
| Hours of study per week | Up to 5 hours | 7 | 28 | 35 |
| | Up to 10 hours | 22 | 11 | 33 |
| | Up to 15 hours | 24 | 5 | 29 |
| | Up to 20 hours | 18 | 6 | 24 |
| | More than 20 hours | 11 | 2 | 13 |
| | Total | 82 | 52 | 134 |

The seventh hypothesis (H7), which claims that an important factor for taking up e-study is the distance from a study centre, is rejected.

Traditional and e-students do agree with this statement in a slightly different way but the t-test shows that the difference is not statistically significant ($t = 0.840$; $\alpha=0.05$; $p_\alpha=0.402$). Thus, we cannot confirm that the distance from a study centre significantly influences the decision which type of study one would take.

The eighth hypothesis (H8) that e-students have a higher monthly income per family member than traditional students is rejected as well.

The monthly income per family member is different between e-students and traditional students (Table 9). The Pearson's hi-square test ($\chi 2=17.9$; $\alpha=0.05$; $p_\alpha=0.001$) confirms that the difference in monthly income of e-student and traditional student is statistically significant.

*Table 9: Monthly income per family member with regard to type of study*

| | | Type of study | | |
|---|---|---|---|---|
| | | traditional | e-study | Total |
| Income per family member | Less than € 300 | 4 | 5 | 9 |
| | Up to € 400 | 4 | 12 | 16 |
| | Up to € 500 | 13 | 11 | 24 |
| | Up to € 600 | 28 | 15 | 43 |
| | Over € 600 | 32 | 7 | 39 |
| | Total | 81 | 50 | 131 |

Students with lower income are more inclined to take up e-study: the average income per family member is lower in a class of e-students (€475 per month per family member). More affluent students decide to take a regular traditional study; their average income is €603 per month per family member.

# 4. Discussion

Variables that influence the study progress in the present study carried out at the DOBA Faculty are personal (gender, age, intelligent quotient, motivation, effort, time devoted to studying), social (social class of a student, employment of a partner, employment of a mother, employment of a father, monthly income per family member). Variables that influence the quality of study process are explicitness of study materials, possibility of interaction with professor, modularity of a study process.

We have discovered that certain factors influence both traditional and e-students: gender, age, motivation, effort, satisfaction with one's own progress, social stratum, employment of one's partner, employment of one's mother, the education of parents.

Certain variables are more decisive: gender, age, motivation, effort, satisfaction with the study organisation, satisfaction with one's own success, social stratum. Among the variables that strongly influence the study progress in both traditional and e-students is social class, which is closely connected to the financial status of a student, the employment of one's mother and education of one's parents.

To stimulate study progress, we need to pay attention to motivation, satisfaction with one's own success, and study organisation. We also have the power to influence the possibility of interaction with a professor, as well as offering students a modular system of a study. We will increase the study progress in traditional students by concentrating on motivation, which is directly connected to one's own success. We also may have some influence over the organisation of the course that the students attend. However, we do not have much influence on social factors.

Age and gender are variables that have proved to be influential in study progress, but again we cannot influence that. The research shows that older students are more successful than younger ones and women get higher grades and are less inclined to drop out than men.

It was expected that the previous education (high school and vocational schools) would be quite decisive. The research shows that students who enter university programmes coming from high schools are not more successful in their studies than students who finished a vocational school.

Motivation is a strong positive and direct factor that influences study progress. Students emphasised that the highest form of motivating them is achieved by personal contact with a professor. In some faculties, professors or lecturers occasionally write students a motivation letter; the more the students are motivated, the better results they achieve. Their effort will grow along with the growing motivation; vice versa, the lower the motivation, the less effort will be put into studying. Consequently, the results will be worse.

E-students are inclined to the locus of control, while traditional students believe they got a good grade because they studied hard and not because the examiner was in a good mood or they had a lucky day. Traditional students trust their own judgement; they spend more time studying than e-students and their effort is repaid.

Previous studies show that an influential variable in study progress is the education and employment of one's father. Our study indicates that among the influential variable is an education of one's mother, not father. An important and decisive factor in taking either e-study of traditional study is one's partner's education and employment. Students with partners on a higher position and education take up e-study. The decision is closely connected to understanding the advantages of e-learning with regard to time and special flexibility.

Time spent on study is not always decisive in study progress. We have discovered that e-students spend less time on performing study obligations than traditional students. We understand that traditional students spend a certain amount of time in physical attendance at lectures. E-students are flexible in many aspects: they choose the time and place of studying, pace and contents as well. E-students use a virtual classroom, which is available at any time day or night wherever there is access to the internet. E-students spend their time on studying instead of travelling to school, looking for a parking space etc., which can be tiresome and expensive.

The satisfaction of students with their own success is one of the key factors that have a positive influence on study progress in both types of study: e-study and traditional study. Satisfaction is one of the most important motivators, but study organizers unfortunately do not have very much influence on that. However, we do have influence on the satisfaction of students with course organisation and the attitude of teachers towards students; these are strong motivators. Since these are the factors we have influence on, we should reconsider each and every aspect in these areas.

The satisfaction of students is also influenced by study materials. It is important to let a student know in advance which topics are to be studied and how to deal with materials. In recent years, we have discovered that even though there are a number of sources and types of access to information available, students seem to be less independent in looking for the information on their own. Searching for information presents a major problem for students. Only one third of students make their own notes; others get photocopied or borrowed notes, because they do not try hard enough to make their own notes.

E-students have a higher monthly income per a family member. The research also indicates that those students with better financial means have better grades and their study progress is faster. In the past, well-off students used to study longer, they could afford to entertain themselves and indulge themselves in other activities. The students from families with lower standards of living studied hard and rapidly to get a degree as soon as possible and to get a job, in order to improve their financial situation. At present, these students study longer because they need to take care of their own existence besides studying. Social factors cannot be influenced by a course organizer; the state should reconsider their financial policy with regard to students from lower class families, offering them scholarships and grants.

## References

Araque, F., Roldan, C., Salguero, A. (2009): Factors influencing university drop out rates, *Computers & Education*, Vol. 53, No. 3, pp. 563–574.

Billings, D.M. (1988): A conceptual model of correspondence course completion, *American Journal of Distance Education*, Vol. 2, No. 2, pp. 23–25.

Chyung, Y., Winiecki, D.J., Fenner, J.A. (1998): *A Case Study: IncreasetEnrolment by ReducingtDropout rates in Adult Distant Education*, Proceedings of the annual conference on distance teaching and learning, Madsison, WI.

Dille,B., Mezack, M. (1991): Identifying predictors of high risk among community college telecourse students, *The American Journal of Distance Education*, Vol. 5, No. 1, pp. 24–35.

Ferjan, M., Jereb, E., Šušteršič, O. (2008): Social class position as a determinant of educational achievement, *Društvena istraživanja*, Vol. 17, No. 4/5, pp. 869–886.

Goldthorpe, J. (1980): *Social Mobility and Class Structure in Modern Britain*, Oxford: Clarendon Press.

Jereb, E., Šmitek, B. (1999): Using an electronic book in distance education, *Informatica*, Vol. 23, No. 4, pp. 483–486.

Jereb, E., Bernik, I., (2006): Elektronsko preverjanje znanja, pripravljenost študentov, *Organizacija*, Vol.39, No.4, pp. 273–277.

Jereb, E., Šmitek, B. (2006): Applying mutimedia instruction in e-learning, *Innovations in Education and Teaching International*, Vol.43, No.1, pp 15–27.

Jereb, E., Ferjan, I. (2008): Social classes and social mobility in Slovenia and Europe, *Organizacija*, Vol.41, No.6, pp.197–206.

Jereb, E., Ferjan, M., Jesenko, J. (2009): Conceptual model of study progress in higher education. *Didactica - Pedagoška obzorja*, 2009, Vol. 24, No. 1, pp. 168–184.

Jereb, E. (2010): Elements influencing study success, *Organizacija*, Vol. 43, No.1, pp. 9–20.

Kember, D. (1996): A longitudinal process model of drop out from distance education, *Journal of Higher Education*, Vol. 60, No. 3, pp. 287–301.

Levy, Y. (2003): A study of learners' perceived value and satisfaction fordimplied effectiveness of on-line learning system, Dissertation *Abstracts International*, Vol. 65, No. 3, Locke & Latham.

Parker, A. (1999): A study of variables that predict dropout from distance education, *International Journal of Education and technology*, Vol. 1, No. 2, pp. 1–12.

Richardson, J.C., Swan, K. (2003): Examening social presence in on-line courses in relation to students' perceived learning and satisfaction, *Journal of Asynchronous Learning Networks*, Vol. 7, No. 1, pp. 68–88.

Sachs, D., Halle, N. (2003): Pace university's focus on student satisfaction with student services in on-line education, *Journal of Asynchronous Learning Networks*, Vol. 7, No. 2, pp. 36–42.

Shea, P.J., Pickett, A.M., Pelz, W.E. (2003): A follow up investigation of teaching presence in the SUNY Learning Network, *Journal of Asynchronous Learning Networks*, Vol. 7, No. 2, pp. 61–80.

Volkwein, J.F., Lorang, W.G. (1995): Characteristic of extenders: full time students who take light credit loads and graduate in more than four years, In *Association for Industrial Research Annual Forum*, Boston, M.A.

Williamson, D.R., Creamer, D.G. (1998): Student attribution in two and four year colleges: Application of a theoretical model, *Journal of College Students' Development*, Vol. 29, No. 3, pp. 210–217.

Xenos, M. (2002): A survey on student dropout rates and causes concerning the students in the course of informatics of the Hellenic Open University, *Computers/Education*, Vol. 39, No. 4, pp. 361–377.

## About the Authors

**Alenka Gortan** is a teacher of English and Spanish at Velenje High School and a lecturer at the Business College in Maribor. Her field of interest is defining causes and reasons for dropping out of e-learning courses and factors that influence study progress.

**Eva Jereb** is a full professor in the Department of Education – Personnel and Information Science at the Faculty of Organisational Sciences, University of Maribor, Slovenia. She is currently researching personnel expert systems, education and distance education (particularly e-learning and e-examination), office automation and the phenomenon of telework.

# Web 2.0 and Open Educational Resources as a Foundation of Organisational Learning

***Tanja Arh***

*tanja@e5.ijs.si*

***Dejan Dinevski***

*dejan.dinevski@uni-mb.si*

## Abstract

Nowadays, Web 2.0 technologies and e-learning are easing access to a wide range of different sources of knowledge. Mastering this knowledge is becoming crucial for successful working and is an important source of competitive advantages in companies. In this context, open educational software and resources are a future source and the foundation of organisational learning. This chapter focuses on the presentation of Web 2.0 technologies, organisational learning and open educational resources. Some ideas and existing initiatives are presented and a vision of the future of open educational resources is introduced.

**Keywords**: Web 2.0, e-learning, organisational learning, open educational resources

## 1. Introduction

Success in a highly dynamic environment requires a more efficient responsive from the side of organizations to their customers, more flexible approaches in facing their daily business processes and more focus on employees' competencies. Employees' knowledge and competencies significantly contributes to the companies' ability to react to the requirements of rapidly changing markets, customer's needs and successful business processes. To perform this approach effectively, employees and all members of the organisation are expected to continuously refresh and enhance their skills and knowledge. As human capital replaces physical capital as the source of competitive advantage, organisational learning has emerged as a key enabler of success. Only by making learning a truly strategic investment can an organisation ensure that every person in it is fully enabled to perform effectively and meet constantly changing demands. The study of organisational learning is relevant, as it seeks to respond to the challenges that arise in a constantly changing business environment and can help companies to confront their long-term survival difficulties (Lei, Slocum & Pitts, 1999). Organisational learning thus represents a source of heterogeneity and of potentially sustainable competitive advantages, because of the companies' different capabilities for learning and absorbing knowledge (Easterby-Smith, Crossan & Nicolini, 2000).

When companies plan in their strategies to acquire knowledge by educating their employees, they can find most suitable solutions in e-learning and Web 2.0 technologies (Zhang, 2002; 2003). With the recent development of Web 2.0 and social software, e-learning is moving beyond utilisation of the internet for knowledge management, as a store of information, or for course management. Instead, the internet may be used for participation, communication, sharing and collaboration. The term Web 2.0 was coined by O'Reilly (2005) as a common denominator for recent trends heading towards the 'Read-Write Web', allowing everyone to publish resources on the web using simple and open, personal and collaborative publishing tools known as social software: blogs, wikis, social bookmarking systems, podcasts etc. The main features of these tools are their **dynamism, openness and free availability**. According to MacManus and Porter (2005), the power of social software lies in content personalisation and remixing with other data to create much more useful information and knowledge.

While open software has both historical and philosophical roots within universities, e-learning was not one of the major focus areas of the early open source software movement. The early development of e-learning technology was based on the rise of the web and the widespread adoption of e-learning software and courses, especially learning management systems such as WebCT and Blackboard in the education sector, and Saba, Click2Learn, and others in corporate training. However, there are early attempts to create open standards for e-learning software and content, driven by specification organisations such as IMS Global Learning Consortium, AICC and ADL, and relevant committees of international standards bodies such as the IEEE LTSC. Despite the potential relevance of these open standards for the proprietary e-learning systems, the consistent adoption of e-learning standards by LMS vendors was slow, particularly in the education sector.

When advocating OS in e-learning applications, most readers will search for the benefits of the end users instead those of developers. What is the main advantage that the OS applications bring to the educational and training institutions? Generally, the benefits of open source in e-learning are (Dooly, 2005): low initial cost, flexibility and customisability, extensive active user communities, multi-platform capabilities, adherence to standards and a tendency to use and link to other open source software.

Within organisations aspiring to become development organisations, open e-learning and Web 2.0 technologies and tools offer a series of opportunities for creating informal learning environments in which organisational learning and development are integrated parts of a continuous organisational practice.

## 2. E-Learning and Web 2.0 Technologies

E-learning is a term introduced along with the introduction of information and communication technology for educational purposes (Arh, Kokalj, Dinevski & Jerman-Blažič, 2008). Definitions of e-learning are various, diverse and lack unity; consequently, it is of outmost importance to provide precise definitions of it and its related notions. In this chapter, we are referring to the process of studying and teaching as e-learning when it includes information and communication technology, regardless of the mode or the scope of its use (Henry, 2001).

Kirschner and Paas (2001) defined e-learning as a learning process in which the internet plays the key role in the presentation, support, management and assessment of learning. Rosenberg (2001) defines e-learning as a learning process in which information technology partially or fully undertakes the role of a mediator between different stakeholders involved in the learning process. We refer to the process of studying and teaching as 'e-learning', when it includes information and communication technology, regardless of the mode or the scope of its use (Henry, 2001; Dinevski & Plenković, 2002).

E-learning extends the company out to ever-widening circles of impact. Companies are participating in a radical redefinition of industries, markets and of the global economy itself. Today, organisations are making great efforts to properly adjust to the changing business environment to enhance their competitiveness. In step with the development of information technology and the internet, many businesses are replacing traditional vocational training with e-learning to better manage their workforce. However, it is questionable whether training programs actually change employee behaviour after implementation. In the case of US companies, only 10–15 % of training is applied to work (Sevilla & Wells, 1988).

When discussing e-learning, we cannot overlook the impact that Web 2.0 technologies brings to the process of e-learning. Web 2.0 technologies are changing the way messages spread across the web; a number of online tools and platforms are now defining how people share their perspectives, opinions, thoughts and experiences. Web 2.0 tools such as instant messaging systems, blogs, RSS, video casting, social bookmarking, social networking, podcasts and picture sharing sites are becoming increasingly popular. One major advantage of Web 2.0 tools is that the majority of them are free. Of the great number of these tools, some of the more popular ones are instant messaging systems, blogs, video wiki services, XO-WIKI, Doodle, podcasting and RSS.

## 2.1 Instant Messaging Systems (IMS)

The need for communication tools in the learning process is often underestimated by educators, especially those who feel comfortable with the traditional, instructive way of teaching. However, even with their traditional approach, learners need to communicate with each other when working together. At the beginning of the 1990s, digital communication tools were rather limited; apart from direct face-to-face meetings, the main way to communicate was using a fixed-line telephone. Sharing course materials was possible only by using a copier or a fax machine. However, these devices were quite rare in ordinary households (Dulik, 2008). The only barriers to communication that exist today are a lack of skills needed to operate new technologies. This barrier is not even noticed by most younger people, who have grown up as 'digital natives', rarely pulling themselves away from their computers (even outdoors they have mobile phones in their pockets), but it definitely still is a serious obstacle for many educators.

However, the new technologies are inevitably filtering down into daily practice; in 2010, it is probably not necessary to explain what the purpose of instant messaging is. The top 10 instant messaging systems number of users in the world according to statistics from Wikipedia (2008) is counted in hundreds of millions of users, e.g., QQ: 783 million total, 317.9 million active. 40.3 million peak online (mostly in China), MSN: 294 million active: Yahoo: 248 million active; Skype: 309 million total, 12 million speaking online etc. The most important decisive factor for an ordinary user when choosing an instant messaging system is the recommendation of a friend (most people start out using the same system that the majority of their friends are already using). The IMs are used for any kind of information exchange including communication between employees, students regarding their study or learning environment. For that reason, this practice is included in the technology that contributes to the personalized learning environment.

## 2.2 Blogs

A blog is a type of web site in which entries are made as in a journal or diary, and are displayed in reverse chronological order (Väljataga, 2008). Basically, an individual maintains his or her own blog, and it functions as a sort of online personal diary. Regular entries, such as comments, descriptions of events, or other types of materials combined with text, images, and links to other weblogs and websites are the typical ingredients of weblogs. Blogs have gained much attention in educational circles, where they are experienced as tools that support several pedagogical aims and scenarios, ranging from individual knowledge management and competence development to group-based learning activities. Therefore, blogs have become an important educational tool in recent years, providing an opportunity for both facilitators and employees to publish their ideas, essays or simply as a space to reflect upon their particular learning process and reading material. In the context of teaching and learning, blogs can do much more than just deliver instructions or course news items to employees. They can be an interesting collaboration tool for employees who can join a relevant community and find people to collaborate with, and give feedback to management and others.

The most frequent use of blogs in a learning environment is the publishing and sharing content with others. Blog technology can be improved by plug-ins such as the FeedBack tool used to track and integrate the content of other authors within one blog. FeedBack is a standard plug-in piece of code developed within the framework of the iCamp project (www.icamp-project.eu). In a simple way, it is used to enable blog users to subscribe to each others' blogs. Blogging technology, in combination with innovations such as the FeedBack specification, definitely has great potential to be considered as a powerful tool for learning with others (Väljataga, 2008).

## 2.3 Video-Wiki and Xo-Wiki

Publishing or presenting someone's thoughts online usually means writing some text and illustrating it with pictures (Cibulskis, 2008). Still, the most natural form of communication for humans is face to face and, for most people, the majority of information is presented orally, directly facing the presenter; his or her non-verbal information is often even more important than their actual words. Video could serve as a replacement for face-to-face presentation, since it is able to convey visible behaviour and important non-verbal information. In the past, recording a video and getting it to the target audience was quite a challenge. Depending on the number of intended users, TV broadcasts or video tapes could be used. Employees, taking part in an e-learning course work in groups are urged to form groups by getting to know each other and by discovering some common topic. The mentor/tutor usually gets use of a videowiki to record some short self-introduction videos in which employees are presenting their background, explaining what their expectations are regarding some specific topic for the group assignment. Videowikis are based on the Red5 open-source Flash server, written in Java and Flash, allowing video recording, searching and playback through the main system webpage or via standard URL links. Videowiki services also provide RSS feeds for each author, and videos can be embedded on any webpage using special code (Cibulskis, 2008). Collaborative creation and maintenance of knowledge artefacts is one of the emerging phenomena of online internet communities; prominent examples include Wikipedia.org, MediaWiki.org, LyricWiki.org, Microformats.org and Wikitravel.org.

Furthermore, a collection of webpages (a so-called wiki) can be very useful for teaching and learning purposes, for instance, if learners need to collaborate to work on certain topics, or if facilitators wish to develop and share their learning content with others. Consequently, a contemporary approach to e-learning requires tools that can enable learners to work on artefacts collaboratively, either by allowing them to publish small posts which can be reused and combined with others (see the blog-based solution presented in the previous section) or by providing real wiki functionality.

XoWiki is one such wiki implementation, realized as a component of OpenACS (Open Architecture Community System), a framework for building scalable, community-oriented web applications. XoWiki includes a rich text editor for easily creating and editing wiki pages and provides features for structuring, commenting, tagging and visualizing wiki-based content (Cibulskis, 2008).

## 2.4 Doodle

When employees are working on a project together, they need to divide tasks among the members of a group and monitor the progress of the project. This requires them to engage in collaboration, discussion and decision-making processes. In the context of bringing different cultures, educational systems, and levels of teaching, languages and technology skills into a common virtual learning space, planning a series of meetings several weeks in advance may very simply not work. Taking this into account, employees must adopt a simple solution to meet their needs. There are plenty of solutions that can help to make project to run smoothly. One of them is Doodle, which can simply be described as a web-based tool for finding suitable dates for appointments with other people. Doodle allows employees to plan their meetings with partners, suppliers and other employees. In addition to time management, it can be used to vote for any other issue that arises as part of the distance learning process, for example, the literature that needs to be selected and analysed in order to complete a particular task.

### 2.5 Searching the Net: ObjectSpot

ObjectSpot is a meta-search engine designed to facilitate different types of research. It can be used to find publications and other learning resources on the web. ObjectSpot realizes federated searches over an ever-increasing number of digital libraries and learning-object repositories. It provides access to more than 10 million learning objects spread across famous libraries such as the Directory of Open Access Journals (DOAJ), OAIster, EBSCO, ACM, CiteBase and IEEE (Drbalek, Dulik & Koblischke, 2008). Some of these repositories are open access, whilst others require registration or a subscription.

## 3. Organisational Learning

In recent years, the concept of organisational learning has enjoyed a renaissance among both academics and practitioners seeking to improve organisations. Early proponents (e.g., Argyris & Schön, 1978) found their ideas largely confined to the periphery of management thought during the 1980s, but the 1990s witnessed a rebirth of interest. The current renaissance is evident in the creation of a journal about organisational learning (*The Learning Organization*) as well as in the devotion of special issues of several journals to the topic (e.g., *Organization Science*, 1991; *Organizational Dynamics*, 1993; *Accounting, Management and Information Technologies,* 1995; *Journal of Organizational Change Management*, 1996). The appearance of several major review articles is testimony to organisational learning's growing stature in the research community (see Crossan, Lane & White,

1999; Dodgson, 1993; Fiol & Lyles, 1985; Huber, 1991; Jones, 2000; Levitt & March, 1998; Miner & Mezias, 1996). Moreover, a large number of articles in professional periodicals describing the design and management of learning organisations attest to the popularity of organisational learning and knowledge management among practitioners. New theories of knowledge creation have become prominent (Nonaka, 1994; Raelin, 1997), and formal knowledge management programs have been undertaken in many companies (Davenport, De Long & Beers, 1998).

Therefore, as we move forward in the twenty-first century, organisational learning promises to be a dominant perspective with influence on both organisational research and management practice (Argyris & Schön, 1996).

## 3.1 Defining Organisational Learning

Organisational learning is defined in numerous ways and approached from different perspectives. The pioneers (Argyris, & Schön, 1996; Senge, 1990) defined organisational learning as an individual's acquisition of information and knowledge, and development of analytical and communicational skills. Understanding organisational learning as a process, which can take up different levels of development and makes the learning organisational structure an ideal form of organisation that can only be achieved once the process of organisational learning is fully optimised and the organisation is viewed as a system (Senge, 1990).

Jones (2000) emphasizes importance of organisational learning for organisational performance defining it as "a process through which managers try to increase organisational members' capabilities in order to understand better and manage with organisation and its' environment to accept decisions that increase organisational performance on a continuous basis".

The aforementioned statements regarding the lack of unity of organisational learning definitions are also supported by the findings of Shrivastava (1983) and Dimovski (1994). The former states that extensive research carried out in the field of organisational learning has mostly been fragmented, while the latter adds the fragmentation has lead to the multitude of definitions (e.g., Nonaka & Takeuchi, 1996; Wall, 1998), differing according to the criteria of inclusion, scope and focus (Škerlavaj, 2003). Dimovski (1994) and Dimovski & Colnar (1999) provided an overview of previous research and identified four varying perspectives on organisational learning. Their model managed to merge informational, interpretational, strategic and behavioural approaches to organisational learning and defined it as a process of information acquisition, information interpretation and resulting behavioural and cognitive changes.

The study of organisational learning is relevant as it seeks to respond to the challenges that arise in a constantly changing business environment and can help companies to confront their long-term survival difficulties (Lei, Slocum & Pitts, 1999). Organisational learning thus represents a source of heterogeneity and of potentially sustainable competitive advantages, because of the companies' different capabilities for learning and absorbing knowledge (Easterby-Smith, Crossan & Nicolini, 2000).

# 4. Impact of E-Learning and Web 2.0 Technologies on Organisational Learning

Findings based on a rather wide overview and systematisation of literature have shown that we can expect positive impact of e-learning and Web 2.0 technologies on organisational learning. Robey et al. (2000) do warn that e-learning and Web 2.0 technologies may take the role of a promoter of organisational learning, so we proposed the following hypothesis: $H_1$: *E-learning and Web 2.0 technologies have positive impact on organisational learning.*

## 4.1 Development of the Research Instrument

The questionnaire used in our study has been in a process of constant development and validation for more than 10 years (Dimovski, 1994; Arh, Dimovski, Jerman-Blažič, 2008). For this study, the operationalisation of e-learning and Web 2.0 technologies and organisational learning was improved and applied on a sample of Slovene firms, each with more than 50 employees. The reason to include smaller companies is to improve the generalisability of the research findings. The measurement instrument used in this study has 22 items for the e-learning and Web 2.0 technologies construct and 29 items for the organisational-learning construct. Pretesting procedures were conducted in the form of interviews and the studies with managers, focus groups with research and academic colleagues. Table 1 presents the constructs, indicators used for construct assessment, number of items totalled to give the value of an indicator and the theory or empirical research on the basis of which the measurement items were developed.

*Table 1: Operationalisation of constructs*

| Latent Variables (constructs) | Indicators and Number of Items from Questionnaire | Theoretical Grounds, Research, Authors |
|---|---|---|
| **Technology-Enhanced Learning (TEL)** | • Information and Comm. Infrastructure (ICI) – 9 items<br>• Education Technology (ET) – 10 items<br>• Learning Contents (LC) – 3 items | • Kirschner in Paas (2001)<br>• Rosenberg (2001)<br>• Gold, Malhotra, & Segars (2001)<br>• Leonard-Barton (1995)<br>• Arh, Dimovski, Jerman-Blažič (2008) |
| **Organisational Learning (OL)** | • Knowledge Acquisition (KAC) – 9 items<br>• Knowledge Transmission (KTR) – 10 items<br>• Use of Knowledge (UoK) – 10 items | • Dimovski (1994)<br>• DiBella, Nevis (1998) |

In short, the hypothesized model shall be composed of four constructs and six indicators, and will be of recursive nature, meaning that there shall be no cases of two variables appearing simultaneously, i.e., as a cause and a consequence to one another.

## 4.2 Research Procedure

The methodology applied to test our research model was structural equation modelling (SEM). This involves a combination of confirmatory factor analysis (CFA) and econometric modelling, which aims to analyse hypothesised relationships among the latent constructs, measured with observed indicators (measurement variables).

## 4.3 Data Gathering and sample

Based on the model's conceptualisation, a questionnaire was developed and sent in June 2007 to the CEOs or board members of all Slovene companies with more than 50 employees, which totalled 1215 companies; 356 completed questionnaires were returned, five of which were excluded from further analysis due to missing values. The response rate was 29.7 %, which can be considered successful in the Slovene context.

### 4.4 Parameter Value Estimates

The results of structural equation analysis by LISREL were utilized to test the proposed hypotheses in this study. As discussed in the previous section, the relationships between the constructs were examined based on t-values associated with the path coefficients between the constructs. If an estimated t-value is greater than a certain critical value ($p < .05$, t-value = 1.96) (Mueller, 1996), the null hypothesis that the associated estimated parameter is equal to 0 was rejected. Subsequently, the hypothesized relationship was supported.

### 4.5 Results of the Study

The results of the survey prove a statistically significant, strong and positive impact of e-learning and Web 2.0 technologies on organisational learning (t-value = 6.54, $p < .05$). Those companies that systematically incorporated e-learning, Web 2.0 technologies, various advanced educational tools and systems into their daily work and ensured high quality equipment with information and communication technologies recognized the importance of the achievement of organisational learning as the most effective process for the production, dissemination and application of knowledge.

## 5. Open Educational Resources

The term 'open educational resources' (OER) has been introduced and promoted in the context of UNESCO's aim to provide free access to educational resources on a global scale. The term was first adopted by UNESCO in 2002 in the final report of the Forum on the Impact of Open Courseware for Higher Education in Developing Countries, to refer to 'the open provision of educational resources, enabled by information and communication technologies, for consultation, use and adaptation by a community of users for non-commercial purposes' (UNESCO, 2002).

With regard to this definition, it is important to note that 'resources' are not limited to content, but comprise 'three major areas of activity: the creation of open source software and development tools, the creation and provision of open course content, and the development of standards and licensing tools. The outputs of all three may be grouped together under the term "Open Educational Resources (OER)".' There are also much broader interpretations OER. For example, the OECD's Centre for Educational Research and Innovation (CERI) states on the webpage of their OER survey that this would comprise 'Open courseware and content; Open software tools; Open material for e-learning capacity building of faculty staff; Repositories of learning objects; Free educational courses.'OER have (Gesser, 2007) the following core attributes:

- that access to open content (including metadata) is provided free of charge for educational institutions, content services, and the end-users such as teachers, students and lifelong learners;
- that the content is liberally licensed for re-use in educational activities, favourably free from restrictions to modify, combine and repurpose the content; consequently, that the content should ideally be designed for easy re-use in that open content standards and formats are being employed;
- that for educational systems/tools software is used for which the source code is available (i.e., open source software) and that there are open application programming interfaces (open APIs) and authorisations to re-use web-based services as well as resources (e.g., for educational content RSS feeds).

It is obvious that a particular pedagogical model is not a key point in OER, as such. The discussion of OER has often been dominated by technical and management considerations rather than the perspectives of educational practitioners. To achieve the ambitious goals of the presented lifelong learning philosophy, didactics and pedagogy must be deeply involved in practical solutions. This subject requires a wide and integral approach that exceeds the scope of this paper. Obviously, serious research will have to be invested in the direction of pedagogical models in lifelong learning.

## 5.1 Open Educational Resources Idea and Initiatives

With reference to the OER movement, the William and Flora Hewlett Foundation justifies their investment in it as follows: 'At the heart of the movement toward Open Educational Resources is the simple and powerful idea that the world's knowledge is a public good and that technology in general and the internet in particular provide an extraordinary opportunity for everyone to share, use, and re-use knowledge. OER are the parts of that knowledge that comprise the fundamental components of education – content and tools for teaching, learning and research.'There is an established understanding that easy access to educational resources is required to promote lifelong learning by active learners of all ages. Also, the role of such access in reducing social inequalities, fostering social inclusion of migrants, and supporting education in developing countries is often acknowledged (Halimi 2005). No doubt that open access to resources is an important element in educational innovation; in contrast, it is also clear that it does not solve all the problems. The decisive factor is that open educational practices are fostered by the appropriate institutional culture and mindset and supportive environment, including easily accessible and shareable tools, services and content.

There are a variety of open questions on this subject, among which the most important is: Who (and why) will create and provide educational content? The answer to this question is not easy. Probably the public and politicians must answer it (and not the publishers). Today, one can find several repositories of learning and teaching resources that are freely accessible by anybody. There are of several kinds but mostly project based with a lot of volunteer work invested. The amount of the learning material is usually very low and the diversity is limited.

Another type of repository is in a way public, but not free for all. The most important are those initiated by national Ministries of Education or other political initiatives. The European SchoolNet (EUN) has a special place as a collaboration of ministry departments and national educational networks throughout Europe. The initial idea of the EUN, which was started in 1996, was a 'bottom-up' process with the EUN as a central access point to educational resources from the national and regional networks. This included the idea that in the emerging digital environment educators would themselves increasingly create and provide content to a common pool of teaching and learning materials. Over the following years, the EUN and the national educational networks learned that there are considerable barriers to the effective participation of educators in pooling educational resources. Consequently, the approach shifted towards a more 'top-down' approach, which has been massively supported through project-based EU funding over the years. Today, the core longer-term initiative of the EUN is the European Learning Resource Exchange (LRE), which will be accessible to all interested Ministries of Education participating in the EUN and other public and private sector owners of educational content repositories. Important ongoing work is the creation of the LRE Application Profile, which provides a set of metadata elements and vocabularies that are to be used by all participating learning object repositories.

The MIT Open Courseware initiative, started in early 2001, was one of the first and the most well-known all over the world as a single institution effort for open content (in March 2006, about two thirds of MIT professors had their courses online).

In the higher education, the 'MIT broadened' Open Courseware Consortium with over a 100 participating universities from all over the world seems to have a critical mass for a serious breakthrough. There are also several other excellent repositories initiatives, like the US-based Connexions platform which has about 200,000 unique visitors per month from over 150 countries.

The special place among the 'big plans' is held by the Google Print Library Project, which has the ambitious aim of digitally scanning millions of books from the collections of major American libraries and making them searchable online via Google's search engine. On a global level, an encouraging example is the recent establishment of the Global Learning Objects Brokered Exchange (GLOBE) initiative, which is a collaboration of ARIADNE (Europe), Education.au (Australia), eduSource Canada, MERLOT (USA) and NIME (Japan).

To arrive at a point when large repositories of high quality content will be free for all, many questions still have to be answered; finding answers to them will be one of the major research trends in lifelong learning and e-learning in the following years. Clearly, open content itself (though high quality and even localized for the end user) is not enough for effective lifelong learning. Before addressing useful open content, tools and licenses, one must consider the pedagogical approaches in which these resources could make a difference, i.e., by being used in innovative forms of teaching and learning.

## 5.2 The Nature of Open Content

Open digital content has some fundamental differences in comparison to published commercial content (Dinevski, Fošnarič & Arh, 2010). The roles of all the stakeholders in learning processes are different when open content is used as a learning material. Though there are several licensing, accessibility and copyright solutions for open content, we can draw some general principles of its lifecycle (creating, using, modifying, sharing, licensing, controlling quality and managing). Open content obviously has many authors, including professional authors, teachers and also learners and is, therefore, in the constant improvement process. Open content quality control is in the hands of learners and teachers (and is conducted simultaneously with the learning process) instead of instructional experts. The learning units are constantly evolving with various granularities of interlinked material, a variety of micro-content from different content feeds is present and updates are frequent. Wikis, weblogs, RSS feeds and aggregators are the authoring tools together with content acquisition and creativity tools, which results in different formats and usually poor metadata structures. The creation of rich metadata will remain costly and OER initiatives will need to strike the right balance between the achievable richness of metadata and the costs they incur (e.g., due to the need to employ skilled personnel).

Open content licensing is a separate story, where the leading role is that of Creative Commons (CC). As a response to 'open-content-unfriendly' commercial 'all rights reserved' licenses, the non-profit organisation Creative Commons provides an easy-to-use mechanism for choosing and attaching to a creative work one of six standardized CC licenses from the most liberal 'Attribution' to more restrictive (but still open) 'Attribution–Non Commercial–No Derivatives'. Creative Commons licenses have already been 'ported' into several legal jurisdictions around the world and are in the process of integration into many others (http://creativecommons.org/worldwide).

## 6. Conclusion

E-learning and Web 2.0 technologies, as a way of knowledge and competence acquisition, have been widely adopted as a promising solution by many companies to offer learning-on-demand opportunities to individual employees in order to reduce training time and cost. E-learning, referring to learning via the internet has become a major phenomenon in recent years. Through the e-learning and Web 2.0 technologies, workers have access to various on-line databases, tools and e-services that help them find solutions for work-related problem. The authors believe that one of the most important e-learning development directions, in order to come to the lifelong learning reality, are open access to learning, open source software, open standards, and open educational resources. Clearly open content itself (though of high quality and even localized for the end user) is not enough for effective lifelong learning. Before addressing useful open content, tools and licenses, one must consider the pedagogical approaches in which these resources could make a difference, i.e., by being used in innovative forms of teaching and learning.

The results of the presented survey have shown the strong and positive impact of e-learning and Web 2.0 technologies on organisational learning. Those companies that systematically incorporated e-learning, Web 2.0 technologies, various advanced educational tools and systems into their daily work and ensured high quality equipment with information and communication technologies recognized the importance of the achievement of organisational learning as the most effective process for the production, dissemination and application of knowledge.

## References

Argyris C. & Schön D. A. (1978). *Organizational Learning: A Theory of Action Perspective*. Reading, MA: Addison-Wesley.

Argyris, C. & Schön, D. A. (1996). *Organizational Learning II: Theory, Method and Practice*. Reading, MA: Addison-Wesley.

Arh, T., Dimovski, V., Jerman-Blažič, B. (2008). *Model of impact of technology-enhanced organizational learning on business performance*. In P. Cunningham, M. Cunningham (ed.), Collaboration and the knowledge economy: issues, applications, case studies, (pp. 1521–1528). Netherlands: IOS Press.

Arh, T., Kokalj, R., Dinevski, D. & Jerman-Blažič, B. (2008). Pregled stanja na področju e-izobraževanja v Sloveniji. *Organizacija*, *41*(3), 155–167.

Barnes, P., Bollier, D., Rowe, J. (2006). The Commons Rising. Tomales Bay Institute. http://onthecommons.org/files/Commons_Rising_06.pdf (Accessed 11April 2009)Cibulskis, G. (2008). VideoWiki. In K. Grodecka, F. Wild & B. Kieslinger: *How to use social software in higher education* (pp. 24–28). A handbook from the iCamp project.

Collins, C. J. & Smith, K. G. (2006). Knowledge exchange and combination: the role of human resource practices in the performance of high-technology firms. *Academy of Management Journal*, 49(3), 544–560.

Crossan, M., Lane, H. W. & White, R. E. (1999). An organizational learning framework: from intuition to institution. *The Academy of Management Review*, 24(3), 522–537.

Dimovski, V. & Colnar, T. (1999). Organizacijsko učenje. *Teorija in praksa*, 5(36), 701–722.

Dimovski, V. (1994). *Organisational learning and competitive advantage*. Unpublished doctoral dissertation, Cleveland State University.

Dinevski, D., Brodnik, A. (2005). *Lifelong learning technology innovations for efficient adult education*. Florjančič, J. and Paape, B. W., editors. Personnel and Management: Selected Topics. Frankfurt am Main: P. Lang, pp. 135-144.

Dinevski, D., Fošnarič, S., Arh, T. (2010). Open educational resources in e-learning. *Organizacija* (Kranj), 2010, vol. 43, no. 1, 4–8.

Dodgson, M. (1993). Organizational learning: a review of some literatures. *Organization Studies*, 14(3), 375–394.

Dooly, B. J. (2005). *Open Source E-Learning: Alternatives to Proprietary Tools, Systems, and Courseware*. Brandon Hall Research, Sunnyvale, CA.

Drbálek, Z., Dulík, T. & Koblischke, R. (2008). Developing components for distributed search engine ObjectSpot. *Proceedings of the 8th WSEAS International Conference on Distance Learning and Web Engineering* (pp. 82–85). Santander: Spain.

Dulik, T. (2008). *Communication*. In K. Grodecka, F. Wild & B. Kieslinger: How to use social software in higher education (pp. 14–18). A handbook from the iCamp project.Easterby-Smith, M., Crossan, M. and Nicolini, D. Organizational Learning: Debates Past, Present and Future, *Journal of Management Studies* 37(6), 2000, pp. 783–96.

Fiol, C. M., & Lyles, M. A. (1985). Organizational learning. *Academy of Management Review*, 10(4), 803–813.

Gesser, G., ed. (2007). *Open Educational Practices and Resources*. Published by the 'Open e-Learning Content Observatory Services' project, Salzburg, Austria, ISBN 3-902448-08-3.

Halimi, Suzy (2005). *Lifelong learning for equity and social cohesion: A new challenge for Higher Education*. In: McIntosh, Christopher (ed.): Lifelong Learning and Distance Higher Education. Commonwealth of Learning /UNESCO 2005, pp. 11–22.

Henry, P (2001). E-learning technology, content and services. *Education + Training*, 43(4), 251–259.

Huber, G. P. (1991). Organizational Learning: The Contributing Processes and the Literatures. *Organization Science*, 2(1), 88–115.

Jones, G. R. (2000). *Organizational Theory*. (3rd ed.) New York: Prentice Hall.

Kirchner, P. A. & Pass, F. (2001). Web-enhanced higher education: a Tower of Babel. *Computers in human behaviour*, 17(4), 347–353.

Lei, D., Slocum, J. W., & Pitts, R. A. Designing organizations for competitive advantage: The power of unlearning and learning. *Organizational Dynamics*, 27(3), 1999, pp. 24–38.

Levitt, B. & March, J. G. (1998). Organizational learning. *Annual Review of Sociology*, 14, 319–340.

MacManus, R. & Porter, J. (2005): *Web 2.0 for design: bootstrapping the social web*. http://www.digital-web.com/articles/web_2_for_designers (Accessed 15 April 2008).

MacManus, R. & Porter, J. (2005): *Web 2.0 for design: bootstrapping the social web*. http://www.digital-web.com/articles/web_2_for_designers (Accessed 15 April 2008).Miner, A. S. & Mezias, S. J. (1996). Ugly duckling no more: pasts and futures of organizational learning research. *Organization Science*, 7(1), 88–99.

Mueller, R. O. (1996). *Basic Principles of Structural Equation Modeling: An Introduction to Lisrel and EQS*. New York: Springer.

Nonaka, I. (1994). A dynamic theory of organizational knowledge creation. *Organization Science*, 5(1), 14–37.

O'Reilly, T. (2005). *What Is Web 2.0. Design Patterns and Business Models for the Next Generation of Software*. Retrieved November 10, 2009, from http://oreilly.com/web2/archive/what-is-web-20.html

Raelin, J. A. (1997). A model of work-based learning. *Organization Science*, 8(6), 563–578.

Rosenberg, M. (2001). *E-Learning, Strategies for Developing Knowledge in the Digital Age*. NewYork: McGraw-Hill.

Senge, P. M. (1990). *The Fifth Discipline: Art and Practice of the Learning Organization*. New York: Doubleday.

Sevilla, C. & Wells, T. D. (1988). Contracting to ensure training transfer. *Training & Development*, 6(1), 10–11.

Shrivastava, P. A. (1983). Typology of Organizational Learning Systems. *Journal of Management Studies*, 20, 1–28.

UNESCO. (2002). *Forum on the impact of Open Courseware for higher education in developing countries*. Final report. Paris: UNESCO.

Väljataga, T. (2008). *Blogs*. In K. Grodecka, F. Wild & B. Kieslinger: How to use social software in higher education (pp. 20–24). A handbook from the iCamp project.Zhang, D. (2002). *Media structuration – Towards an integrated approach to interactive multimedia-based E-Learning*. Ph.D. dissertation, The University of ArizonaZhang, D., & Nunamaker, J. F. (2003). Powering e-learning in the new millennium: an overview of e-learning and enabling technology. *Information Systems Frontiers*, 5(2), 207–218.

## About the Authors

**Tanja Arh, PhD,** obtained a bachelor's degree in Computer Science at the Faculty of Organizational Sciences, University of Maribor. She obtained her Master's degree at the Faculty of Organizational Sciences, University of Maribor and PhD degree at the Faculty of Economics, University of Ljubljana. She works in the Laboratory for Open Systems and Networks at the Jožef Stefan Institute as a researcher in the field of e-learning and organisational learning. Her current research work is performed mostly for European-wide research programmes (GLOBAL, e4VET etc.) with a focus on application of information and communication technology in education, standardization of e-learning and organizational learning. She is member of Executive Board of the Slovenian Project Management Association and technical editor of the scientific journal Project Management Review.

**Dejan Dinevski, PhD.,** is an associate professor at the Faculty of Education and Faculty of Medicine, University of Maribor. He has coordinated several international and national projects in the wider area of e-learning. He is an author of several publications on e-learning, including scientific articles and books.

# Competency Management in the Czech Republic and Slovenia: A Comparison of Two Different Development Trends

***Jürgen Mühlbacher***

*juergen.muehlbacher@wu.ac.at*

***Michaela Nettekoven***

*michaela.nettekoven@wu.ac.at*

***Jure Kovač***

*jure.kovac@fov.uni-mb.si*

***Anna Putnová***

*putnova@fbm.vutbr.cz*

## Abstract

The transition processes in central and Eastern Europe (CEE) have entered their second phase. During the first phase, the emphasis was on constructing the market economy institutions, the rule of law and integration with different international organisations. The current period puts forth the construction of a globally competitive economic structure and increased efficiency of the rule of law. An important element of the competitiveness of companies is individual competency management. Human resources are becoming a key element in the competitiveness of companies, and not only in CEE. This chapter presents contemporary studies in the field of competency management researched in two CEE countries – the Czech Republic and Slovenia – from the point of view of drivers of change to competency management.

**Keywords**: competency management, Czech Republic, human resources, transformation economies, Slovenia

# 1. Introduction

A core element of restructuring the economic apparatus in transition countries falls under the study of management. Managers were particularly exposed to the processes of reorganising economic structures. Due to the privatisation processes and the current consolidation processes of ownership structures, managers in the transition environment have frequently found themselves taking key initiatives in directing the development of their organisations. We often denote them as 'change agents' or accelerators of business transformation processes (Lang et al., 2000, pp.201).

Focusing on managers and their roles in transition countries has shown that their competencies have become not merely a fashionable trend, but a necessary, integral part of the strategic planning for the sustained development of the organisation. Individual competency management occupies a special place in the building of competitive capacities of the organisation. Especially in transformation economies like the Czech Republic or Slovenia, human resources have to be regarded as a key factor for the present and future success of the economy.

# 2. Competency Management

Competency management is a holistic field of research ranging from strategic to organisational and individual competencies (for a more detailed overview, see Elliot & Dweck, 2005; Tidd, 2006; Mühlbacher, 2007). The following focuses on the definition of individual competency and the development of competency classes, both of which are needed to answer our research question: *Which management competencies do Czech and Slovene managers have and how are these competencies influenced by external and internal drivers of change?* Due to the limited space of this chapter, a number of interesting aspects will have to be omitted here and left to future research.

Recent work on individual competency management (e.g., Probst et al., 2000; Sarges, 2002, pp. 258ff; Erpenbeck & von Rosenstiel 2007, pp. Xi ff; Johannes & Kauffeld, 2009, pp. 126) mainly emphasises the fact that competencies are strongly oriented towards the future. This enables a person to tackle upcoming challenges, whose nature cannot be predicted or determined, in a self-organised manner. Thus, discussions regarding competencies are of importance whenever strategic personnel planning and development take centre stage in times of great uncertainty.

This requires a change in perspective within human resource management. Both the current requirements and the competencies necessary in the future have to become the focal point of the analysis and must be seen as a strategic competitive advantage for the company (McCall, 1998; Nahapiet & Sumantra, 1998, pp. 242ff). From this point of view, the question of in which specific competencies a company should invest in order to realise value added in the future – in the sense of return on investment – at first remains unanswered. Only the answer to this question, however, makes it possible to use further education as a strategic instrument of management development.

Particularly regarding anticipated competencies, one should keep in mind that this data – in accordance with a delphi study – are explorative prognoses. Therefore, apart from the comparison of the current distribution of competencies, this study can only serve the function of generating hypotheses.

## 2.1 Definition of Competency

The definition of competency changes with each theory used, i.e., it has a fixed meaning only within the specific construct of a particular competency theory. Competencies in a narrow sense are dispositions of self-organised actions. As they are internal, unobservable dispositions, competencies are always subjective characteristics, attributed on the basis of problem and solution orientation, by informing a person of an objective – without a specific solution – and then measuring the degree to which the objective was achieved. Competency is defined here as accomplishing or even exceeding a set objective (Erpenbeck/von Rosenstiel, 2007, pp. xvii). The most important objectives of professional competency development are the establishment and promotion of professional action competency. Here, the integration of cognitive, emotional-motivational, volitional and social aspects of human behaviour in work situations is the main focus of interest (Heyse, 1997).

## 2.2 Classes of Competencies

An early differentiation of competencies was made by Jacobs (1989, pp. 36), who distinguishes between 'hard and soft competencies'. Hard competencies refer (among others) to analytical and organisational capabilities, while creativity and sensitivity are soft competencies. From this, Jacobs develops the argument that hard competencies result in observable behaviour, with the invisible, but dominant soft competencies underlying them. The principles of this conviction, though conceivable, are difficult to prove and thus this conception has been classified as an artificial differentiation with low explanatory potential in the theoretical discussion (Woodruffe, 1993, pp. 34).

To avoid this criticism, a categorisation of knowledge, capabilities, properties and abilities required has prevailed, first consisting of three (still without the category of self- and personal competency) (Sloane, 1998, pp. 100)) and then later four areas of competency, which meets both the theoretical and pragmatic requirements (Heyse, 1997, p. 6). A clearer description of these four classes of competencies can be found in Sonntag and Schaper (1999, pp. 411ff.).

All these categorisations have been reworked. In newer classifications, for instance, functional and methodological competencies are combined because of their proximity and the desired generation of a general competency model, which separates self-dispositive actions from personal dispositions and introduces a new class: leadership competency. As a result, the following five classes of competencies can be distinguished (Kasper et al., 2000, pp. 261):

- Self-dispositive competencies, which represent the self-organised use of one's own resources (time, know-how etc.)
- Methodological competencies, comprising all analytical and solution-oriented behaviours
- Social-communicative competencies, covering the area of social interaction (excluding leadership)
- Leadership competencies, including the full range of leadership, motivation and personnel development
- Personal competencies, mainly manifesting themselves in extraordinary personality traits

Based on this classification, the empirical data are coded and then, in a second step, analyzed with regard to the influence of the external and the internal environment, in order to answer the research question.

# 3. Empirical Analysis

## 3.1 Field of Research

Historically, Czech management has to be seen as proud and also a little bit selfish. Czech managers react relatively sensitively to external pressure if it is perceived as a threat. In particular, personal efforts and leadership skills are reduced in this case. This also means that although the basic work is being done, no highly motivated or innovative results beyond the normal can be expected if economic pressure is exerted. As a result, managers bide their time. Changes resulting from social or technological developments, but also a clear and motivating corporate strategy, are perceived very positively and involve great individual effort. This can at least partly be explained by the tradition of a communist economy of scarcity (Schuh & Ploszajski, 2008, pp. 65), when time, innovative behaviour and personal effort were necessary to improve the situation.

Geographically, historically and economically, Slovenia occupies a unique position. Slovenia fought for and won its special economic position in non-aligned, Tito-ist Yugoslavia. With the restrictively regulated allowance of private property, the idea of self-management was developed up to the point at which the government was unable to rule the country centrally (Hösler, 2006, pp. 192), which brought special benefits to the Slovene economy.

Decentralisation efforts and private self-interest are the basis for central managerial competencies, such as cooperative management and goal-orientation. Regarding the former skill, Slovenia differs, historically and politically, from the more authoritarian management style present in the Czech Republic.

The current pace of closing Slovenia's economic gap with better developed economies seeks to fulfil the chief economic objective of the Slovene development strategy, which is to achieve the average stage of development among EU countries by 2013. According to the first Eurostat estimate, the gross domestic product in 2007 reached 89% of the EU average. With respect to these indicators, all new EU member states have a lower stage of development, as do Cyprus and Portugal among the older member states as well. Between 2004 and 2007, the growth rate in Slovenia was at 4%. Six new member states (Estonia, Latvia, Slovakia, Lithuania, Romania, and the Czech Republic) were more successful than Slovenia in eliminating their economic development shortfall; one state was equally successful (Bulgaria), whereas in the remaining new member states the pace of convergence in the years that followed their accession to the EU was slower than in Slovenia (Zupančič, 2008). The positive development of economic competitiveness is shown in the latest report of the international institution IMD, according to which Slovenia took 32nd place among 55 countries in the ranking of countries' competitiveness, thus improving its rank by eight places, compared to 2007 (Statistical Office of the Republic of Slovenia, 2009; Eurostat, 2008). Nevertheless, according to the 2010 IMD ranking, Slovenia did not succeed in sustaining its economic growth and therefore to maintain the competitive position (Slovenia recorded a drop of 20 places in the year 2010 in comparison with the year 2009). Slovenia's slip was also bigger than the average drop of the EU. The reason for Slovenia's lower ranking, in terms of the IMD's methodology, can be explained due to the movement of gross domestic product (GDP), GDP per capita and drop in investments, which corresponds to the global economic crisis.

According to the European Economy News (2007), the Czech Republic has one of the most developed and prosperous economies (characterised by strong growth, low inflation and continued heavy inflows of foreign investment) of the mainly central and eastern European countries that joined the EU in May 2004.

In attempting to accelerate economic growth, the Czech Republic established the Economic Growth Strategy (EGS). The proposed EGS is prepared by a country that treasures European values and is aware of the fact that EU membership has contributed to its competitiveness and improved its position in the global economy. One of the main objectives proposed in the strategy was to attain the average level of EU development by 2013. The growth of GDP is an ambitious objective for Czech Republic; according to Eurostat (2009) GDP reached 82% of the EU average in the year 2007. In order to analyse the behaviour of economies over time, one needs to use volume changes (percentage change on previous year of GDP volume growth). Annual growth rate in the Czech Republic declined to 2.5% in 2008, after growth rates of 6.1% in 2007 as well as 6.8% in 2006. Both the EU and the euro area experienced an economic slowdown in 2008 as well. However, estimated for the year 2009, the gross domestic product (GDP) in Czech Republic contracted at an annual rate of 4.3 percent, which is mainly due to slower growth affected by the global financial and economic cisis.

Modern economies place increasing emphasis on adding value by means of better use of knowledge and innovation. Permanent regeneration of competitiveness in production and services constitutes the fundamental condition underlying economic growth; it requires continuous preparation and implementation of technical, technological, organisational, commercial and other innovations of all types. According to the EGS, these can only originate in adequately structured and sufficiently financed research and development (R&D) favouring innovation. Government support for R&D represented 0.8% of GDP in the EU-27 in 2006, with the shares around 0.6% in the case of the Czech Republic. Gross domestic expenditure on research and development in terms of percentage of GDP was approximately 0.7% in the year 2006 (in comparison to the EU-27 average of 0.9%). Positive developments in the Czech economy are also closely linked to investment, including foreign direct investment (FDI). The Czech Republic reached a relatively high level of inward FDI in the year 2007 (expressed in EUR, the value of inward FDI for the Czech Republic is at the top among the new EU members) (Eurostat, 2009).

## 3.2 Methodology and Sample

To detect the different developments in the Czech Republic and Slovenia, we conducted a survey and collected data concerning the currently needed and expected needs for the competencies of more than 200 top and middle managers in both countries. We used open questions and the answers were coded with a theoretically based category scheme (see Mühlbacher, 2007, pp. 129) and statistically analysed.

Questionnaires were collected at the beginning of the financial crisis, from the second half of 2008 until the first half of 2009, from:

- 107 participants in four Executive MBA classes of the University of Technology in Brno, Czech Republic and
- 105 participants of numerous executive management courses of the University of Maribor in Kranj, Slovenia.

The sample comprises 36 top managers and 71 middle managers from the Czech Republic and 34 top managers and 71 middle managers from Slovenia. Both hierarchical groups are thus in the representative range. The sectoral and functional breakdown of the interviewees reflects well the economic situations of both countries. Although the sample is not representative from the perspective of the Czech and Slovene population of active companies, the following description of the sample shows a satisfying variety of data that can offer information on the desired connections between the phenomena studied. The results demonstrate the appropriate representativeness of the phenomena studied.

In this specific case, the starting point for the dependency analyses was the correlation matrix of the five competency classes and the external or internal drivers of change. Since, due to the form of survey selected (i.e., open questions with the possibility of multiple answers and subsequent coding), only an ordinal scale level is given for the drivers of change and no normal distribution can be assumed; the matrix was created on the basis of the non-parameter correlation coefficients (Spearman-Rho). Only the directed connections between the competency classes and the internal and external drivers for change were adopted, as only these have a direct influence on the target values (see Jammernegg & Kischka, 2005, pp. 419f).

The model thus derived was tested with the help of the computer program AMOS 5.0. The program was selected because it makes possible a combination of multivariate regression and ANOVA analyses, which can also be used with ordinally scaled data and do not require a strict normal distribution. The parameters of the models were estimated using the maximum-likelihood method.

## 3.3 The Case of the Czech Republic

The Czech ranking of the individual competency classes shows a clear predominance of methodological competencies, followed by social-communicative competencies and leadership competencies, and, clearly behind, personal and self-dispositive competencies. Regarding future expectations this ranking also looks very similar. The professional-methodological competency class even gains in importance. Social-communicative competencies and leadership competencies switch their positions and – almost identically – also their value. The table (Table 1) for self-dispositive competencies increases slightly, whereas personal competencies clearly lose value (see here and in the following also Mühlbacher et al., 2009, pp.15ff)

When analyzing the differences between the assessments of competencies currently required and anticipated for the future, weakly significant differences in the composition of competency classes can be discerned. Here the sample size must be taken into consideration, which in an extension planned for the future certainly will result in stronger significances. In general, the T-test with paired samples already shows that personal competencies significantly lose in importance; social-communicative competencies are also slightly reduced, while the other three competency classes gain importance, with the rise of the methodological competencies particularly attracting attention.

*Table 1: Changes in relevance of competency classes over time – Czech Republic*

| Competency classes | Mean Value | T | Sig. (2-sided) |
|---|---|---|---|
| Methodological competencies – present | 30.8119 | -1.688 | 0.095 |
| Methodological competencies – future | 35.4455 | | |
| Social-communicative competencies – present | 16.3861 | 1.862 | 0.065 |
| Social-communicative competencies – future | 12.8713 | | |
| Leadership competencies – present | 13.3168 | -1.440 | 0.153 |
| Leadership competencies – future | 16.3366 | | |
| Personal competencies – present | 8.2178 | 2.391 | 0.019 |
| Personal competencies – future | 3.9604 | | |
| Self-dispositive competencies – present | 7.3564 | -1.119 | 0.266 |
| Self-dispositive competencies – future | 9.5545 | | |

## 3.4 Causal Model of the Czech Sample

Having established the general changes, the impact of drivers of change on the individual competency classes is to be determined. The illustration of the model (Table 1) shows the significant external and internal drivers of change on the left, and the individual competency classes on the right. The arrows represent the causal relations tested, with the first value showing the regression coefficient and the value in brackets showing the standardised β-coefficient. The value in the upper-left corner of each variable is $R^2$ and states the percentage of the variance measured that can be explained by the model regarding the respective competency class.

*Fig. 1: Causal model of drivers of change and their effects on the competency classes – Czech Republic*

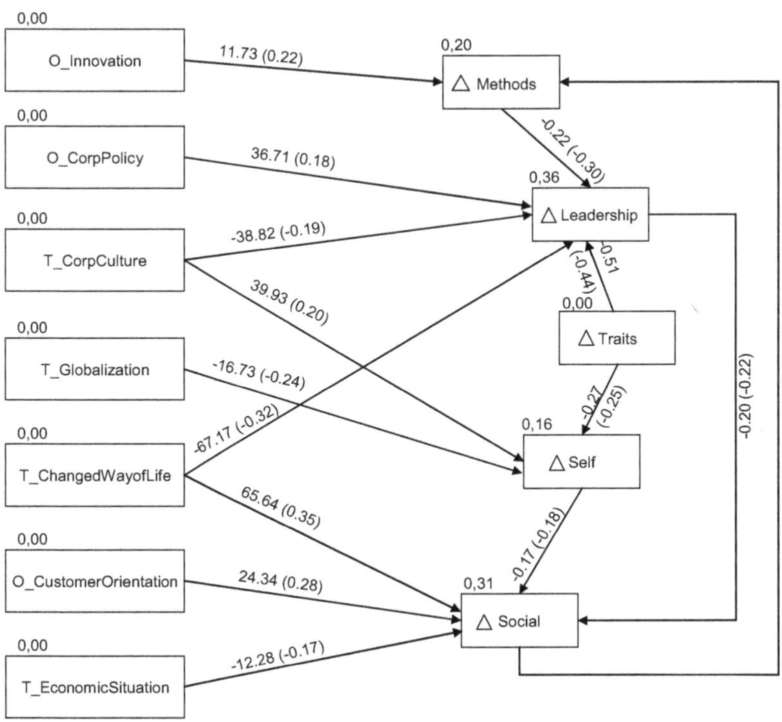


*(n = 101; O= Opportunity; T=Threat)*

The methodological competencies show the highest absolute increase. Interestingly, this is due to only two factors. First, the positive connotation of innovations as external driver of change results in an increase of 11.73 points (β = 0.22); secondly, there is an inverse relationship between the decreasing social-communicative and the methodological competencies of -0.66 points (β = -0.45). What is surprising is the connection between innovation and methodological competencies, as creativity is supposed to be a self-dispositive competency. The long tradition in mathematics and natural science in Eastern Europe makes this easier to understand. Accordingly, innovation is here – not only within the TIPS concept developed in Russia – seen as a systematic-analytic activity, and not intuition, as is commonly believed in Western Europe and North America. Innovation as a positively perceived driver of change explains, together with the decrease in social-communicative competencies, at least 20% of the variance of the professional-methodological competencies (= $R^2$ at the upper left hand corner of the competency class).

Leadership competencies rise second-fastest and react particularly sensitively to two external and one internal drivers of change. A negatively perceived change in values or a new way of life results in a decrease in the value of leadership competencies by -67.17 percentage points (β = -0.32) and the negatively perceived corporate culture also results in a decrease of -38.82 points (β = -0.19). Only a positively evaluated group or company policy increases leadership competencies by 36.71 points (β = 0.18). Thus, negatively perceived external circumstances mainly result in a reduction of leadership tasks with Czech managers. Corporate cultures or lifestyles can thus hardly be transferred from outside the Czech Republic, but have to be adapted to local circumstances. For this reason, ethnocentric approaches of multinational companies stand little chance of realisation. If adaptation takes place, however, and managers identify with the new group or company policy, this leads to an effective implementation in leadership matters.

The inverse relationship with methodological competencies of -0.22 points (β = -0.30) can be explained by the preferred non-bureaucratic and flexible leadership style of the new generation of Czech managers. There is also an inverse relationship to personal competencies (or traits) of -0.51 points (β = -0.44). Together, these factors of influence explain 36% of the variance of leadership competency.

The self-dispositive competencies increase by 39.93 points (β = 0.20) with the negative perception of the corporate culture. This turns out to be a kind of stabilisation valve for the reduction in leadership competencies also caused by this driver of change. The dissatisfaction with corporate culture not only results in a withdrawal from the leadership function, but also to an adaptation of a person's own behaviour. Czech managers, therefore, turn out to be very adaptable, though high performance is only to be expected in a suitable environment. If globalisation is seen as a threat, however, self-dispositive competencies fall by -16.73 points (β = -0.24). The inverse influence of personal competencies of -0.27 points (β =

-0.25). Altogether, these three factors can explain 16% of the variance of the self-dispositive competencies.

The analysis of social-communicative competencies confirms the negative development trend of this competency class, as it can be seen that each mention of the business cycle as an external threat potential reduces it by -12.28 points (β = -0.17). This suggests that external economic crises mainly result in a fall in social competencies in the Czech Republic. A similar phenomenon can be detected in the Austrian data when changes in the services offered are perceived as a threat. While in the Czech Republic innovations are seen as something very positive, in Austria there is often a decrease in the willingness to communicate and interact in order not to endanger one's own job. (Mühlbacher, 2007, pp. 266ff) Such restrictive behaviour is often self-fulfilling, actually generating the crisis people are afraid of. Generally, therefore, in crisis situations mainly encouraging an open communication policy should be on the managers' agenda.

The positive evaluation of customer orientation and the change in values and way of life that is seen as a threat both result in an increase in social-communicative competencies, which is a logical adaptation of a person's own social behaviour to the new external circumstances – in the first case by 24.34 points (β = 0.28), in the second even by 65.64 points (β = 0.35). All three drivers of change explain, together with the inverse exchange effects between the competency classes – -0.20 points (β = -0.22) with an increase in leadership competencies and -0.17 points (β = -0.18) with an increase in self-dispositive competencies –0.31% of the variance of social-communicative competencies.

Yet the strongest decrease in importance takes place with personal competencies (traits). The independence of this competency class indicates the high stability of character traits that was surveyed here. There is an inverse relationship to leadership competency of -0.51 points (β = -0.44) and self-dispositive competencies of -0.27 points (β = -0.25). Both can be explained by the heavy fall in the personal competency of dominance, which has a positive effect on a more participatory leadership style and the self-dispositive ability to cooperate.

To prove the validity of the model described above, the following test has been calculated: The $\chi^2$ test, which due to its high sensitivity to sample size and its intolerance in connection with deviations from a normal distribution is often criticised, also provides conditional proof of the model. The $\chi^2$ value, for instance, is at 1.090 ($C_{min}$ = 55.582 with 51 degrees of freedom) and thus far below the required limit of 2 with P = 0.306. (Backhaus et al., 2000) Arbuckle and Wothke (2003) in this context refer explicitly to the high sensitivity of this value regarding sample size and the unrealistic assumption of a 'Perfect Fit'. In addition, the independent model produces a much worse relation of $\chi^2 = 2.870$ ($C_{min} = 189.445$ with 66 degrees of freedom).

Because of the criticism of the classic $\chi^2$ test, variants of this analysis were calculated in order to evaluate the overall quality of the model; these variants are relatively independent of the sample size and resilient to breaches in the assumption of a normal distribution. The Goodness-of-Fit-Index (GFI) states that the model can explain 91.6% of the variances of the empirical data. Taking into account the degrees of freedom, the Adjusted-Goodness-of-Fit-Index (AGFI) confirms that 87.9% of the variance is still explained by the model, which is slightly below the recommended critical value of 90%, but still acceptable.

## 3.5 The Case of Slovenia

The Slovene ranking of competency classes also shows also a clear predominance of methodological competencies, followed by leadership and social-communicative competencies, and again, clearly behind, personal and self-dispositive competencies. Future rankings are also expected to look very similar. The methodological competency class looses in importance, but remains in first place. Leadership competencies drop slightly, but remain in second place. Social-communicative competencies remain stable, while personal and self-dispositive competencies both increase significantly in value (See Table 2).

*Table 2: Changes in relevance of competency classes over time – Slovenia*

| Competency classes | Mean Value | T | Sig. (2-sided) |
|---|---|---|---|
| Methodological competencies – present | 41.2793 | -1.940 | 0.055 |
| Methodological competencies – future | 36.4595 | | |
| Leadership competencies – present | 15.7477 | -1.312 | 0.192 |
| Leadership competencies – future | 13.8108 | | |
| Social-communicative competencies – present | 13.7477 | -0.406 | 0.686 |
| Social-communicative competencies – future | 13.0405 | | |
| Personal competencies – present | 7.4955 | 2.320 | 0.022 |
| Personal competencies – future | 11.1937 | | |
| Self-dispositive competencies – present | 6.9550 | 2.314 | 0.023 |
| Self-dispositive competencies – future | 10.1802 | | |

Again, as with the Czech sample, sample size has to be taken into account. However, the T-test with paired samples already shows that personal competencies and self-dispositive competencies significantly gain in importance; social-communicative competencies are nearly stable, while the other two classes of competency classes lose importance.

## 3.6 Causal Model of the Slovene Sample

As before, Figure 2 shows the significant drivers of change on the left, and the individual competency classes on the right.

*Fig. 2: Causal model of the drivers of change and their effects on the competency classes – Slovenia*

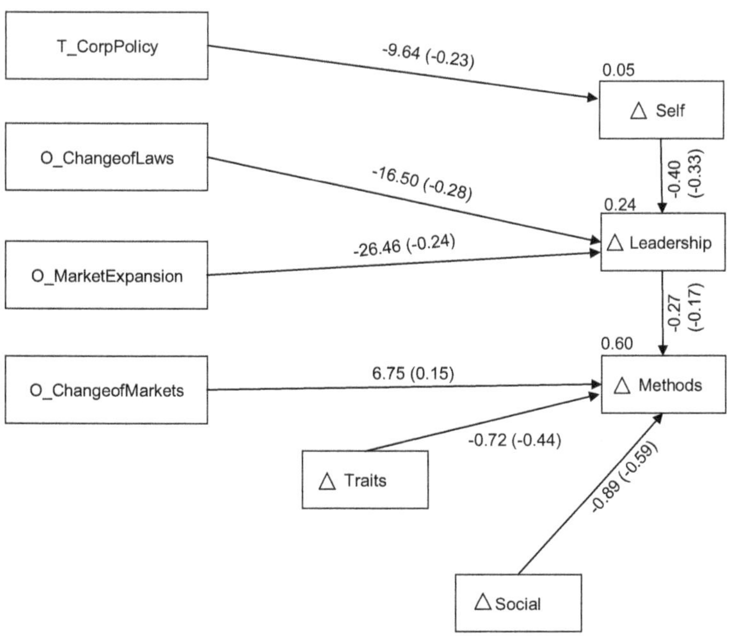

At first glance, it is evident that, unlike similar analyses in Austria (Mühlbacher, 2007, pp. 231) and the Czech Republic (Mühlbacher et al., 2009, pp. 22), the development of qualification is influenced merely by external driving forces of changes.

It is paradoxical that the significant increase in self-dispositive competencies cannot be found here. In fact, the analyses shows only a strong decrease caused by the perception of one company's policy by -9.64 percentage points ($\beta$ = -0.23). This also shows a relatively small influence with $R^2$ = 5%.

The intermittent category of leadership competencies, which decreased by 0.40 points ($\beta$ = -0.33) with the increase of self-dispositive competencies, also bears a negative effect on methodical competencies with -0.27 points ($\beta$ = -0.17). This category is influenced externally by a positively perceived change of legal norms with -16.50 points ($\beta$ = -0.28) and negatively by the expansion, particularly to the eastern neighbour countries, with -26.46 points ($\beta$ = -0.24). Direct individual leadership is thus evidently more often replaced by structural management, or rather delegation. These influences explain 24% of the variance between the current and expected demands.

As the sole external driving force of changes in methodical competencies, the analysis showed a positive perception of market changes and restructuring. Here, the growth led to an increase of 6.75 points ($\beta$ = 0.15). The decline in the sum of this qualification category can be explained with a growing significance of personal competencies (traits) with -0.72 points ($\beta$ = -0.44), the influence of relatively stable social-communicative competencies with -0.89 points ($\beta$ = -0.59), and the already-explained negative impact of leadership competencies. The decline of the latter has a positive effect because of this inverse relation, which can again be explained with the growth of self-dispositive competencies. The variance of this qualification category can be explained with the help of all these factors up to as much as 60%.

Although the significance of personal competencies increases the most, this cannot be explained by using any internal or external driving force of changes. This is also logical as it involves stable personal characteristics. These are first developed in one's youth and are then formed into a self-image, which is questioned only in crisis situations. The growing significance can, however, be explained by a generation renewal in Slovene management.

After all, the social-communicative competencies also remain without internal and external weighting factors. This can be explained with a stable value of this competency class.

Analyses of the development of competency classes and the influence of internal and external driving forces of changes are thus considered extremely contradictory. In attempting to explain this, we can state that there is a current generation renewal. The renewal was the reason why insufficiently qualified managers were offered their positions. This is balanced by a high personal use of self-dispositive competency. At the same time, the external driving forces of change, such as positively perceived factors like market changes and restructuring, changes of the legal framework, economic expansion towards the East, and a company's policy all call for a greater professionalisation of management. This paradox currently represents the greatest challenge to the Slovene economy.

To prove the validity of the model: the $\chi^2$ value is at 1.549 ($C_{min}$ = 43.377 with 28 degrees of freedom) and the independent model produces a much worse relation of $\chi^2 = 4.037$ ($C_{min}$ = 145.327 with 36 degrees of freedom). The Goodness-of-Fit-Index (GFI) states that the model explains 91.2% of the variances of the data and the Adjusted-Goodness-of-Fit-Index (AGFI) confirm that 85.9% of the variance is still explained by the model.

# 4. Conclusion and Limitations

Although the changes of the competency classes seem to prove a similar development of competencies in the Czech Republic and Slovenia, the causal models and the individual competencies shows a completely different picture. The causal model the Czech Republic is much more complex and indicates a very sensitive management, whereas the Slovene data are very clear and show a decrease of the high value of methodological competencies in favour of self-dispositive competencies.

The individual competencies of Czech managers show a typical development of transformation economies, whereas the Slovene data are more similar to the Austrian development (see Mühlbacher, 2007, pp. 231ff) and indicate high adaptability, as well as a decrease in core management competencies in the future.

Finally, as the results show, research into and the practice of individual competency management are still in their early days. A common understanding regarding the competency class terminology is developing only slowly. Still, it can be seen that internal and external drivers of change have a significant influence on the competency requirements of companies. This makes it more important to address the topic of competency management in a focused and methodical manner. Individual and isolated measures of personnel development and change management, which so far have dominated organisations, do not reach far enough. In order to maintain competitiveness, it is not only necessary for management to rethink matters, but also to integrate corporate strategy into the operational human resource management. Personnel development should not merely focus on adapting employees to the system, but also emphasise the ability of the whole organisation to strategically renew itself and innovate.

Regarding this explorative model, a point of self-criticism has to be made in that the causalities shown cannot be fully grounded in theory, but are based on the subjective experience of the persons interviewed. Still, they provide an inter-subjectively comprehensible picture of the reality of Czech and Slovene managers. The high residual values and the still unexplained share in the variances can equally be criticised, as they point to further factors of influence. The aim of this analysis, however, is to create a general model of the changes in individual competency classes and the factors influencing them that are statistically verifiable.

## References

Arbuckle, J. L., Wothke, W. (2003): *AMOS 4.0 User's Guide*. 7th Print, Small Waters, Chicago.

Elliot, A. J., Dweck, C. S. (editors.) (2005): *Handbook of Competency and Motivation*, Guilford, New York.

Eurostat regional yearbook (2008): http://bookshop.europa.eu/eubookshop/download.action?fileName=KSHA08001ENC_002.pdf&eubphfUid=625601&catalogNbr=KS-HA-08-001-FR-C (Accessed on 2 March, 2009).Eurostat regional yearbook (2009): http://epp.eurostat.ec.europa.eu/cache/ITY_OFFPUB/KS-HA-09-001/EN/KS-HA-09-001-EN.PDF (Accessed on 10 March, 2010)European Economy News (2007): No. 8, October 2007, http://ec.europa.eu/economy_finance/een/008/article_6172_en.htm (Accessed on 10 March, 2010).

Erpenbeck, J., von Rosenstiel, L. (editors) (2003): *Handbuch Kompetenzmessung*, pp. IX-XL, Schäffer-Poeschel, Stuttgart.

Hösler, J. ( 2006): *Slowenien, Vom Mittelalter bis zur Gegenwart*. Pustet, Regensburg.

Jacobs, R. (1989): Getting the Measure of Managerial Competency *Personnel Management*, Vol. 21, No. 6, pp. 32–37.

Jammernegg, W., Kischka, P. (2005): Dynamic, Customer-oriented Improvement of Supply Networks, *European Journal of Operational Research*, Vol. 17, No. 2, pp. 413–426.

Johannes, C., Kauffeld, S. (2009): *Führung als Hebel zur Steigerung der Vertriebsleistung: Das Cohen-Brown-Vertiebstraining* in Kauffeld, S, Grote, S., Frieling, E. , Handbuch Kompetenzentwicklung, Schäffer-Poeschel Verlag, Stuttgart.

IMD World Competitiveness Yearbook 2009 (2009): http://www.promexico.gob.mx/work/sites/Promexico/resources/LocalContent/1092/2/scoreboard.pdf (Accessed on 19 July 2010).

IMD World Competitiveness Yearbook 2010 (2010): http://www.imd.ch/research/publications/wcy/upload/PressRelease.pdf (Accessed on 19 July 2010)

Kasper, H., Mühlbacher, J., von Rosenstiel, L. (2005): Manager-Kompetenzen im Wandel *Führung + Organization*, Vol. 74, No. 5, pp. 260–264.

Lang, R., Kovač, J., Bernik, M. (eds.) (2000): *Management in Transition Process* (Management v tranzicijskih procesih), Moderna organizacija, Kranj.

McCall, M. W. (1998): *High Flyers, Developing the Next Generation of Leaders*, Harvard Business School Press, Boston.

Mühlbacher, J. (2007): *Kompetenzmanagement als Grundlage strategischer Wettbewerbsvorteile*, Linde, Vienna.

Mühlbacher, J., Nettekoven, M., Putnová, A. (2009): Drivers of Change and Competency Management in the Czech Republic, *Journal of Global Business and Technology*, Vol. 5, No. 1, pp. 15–27.

Nahapiet, J., Sumantra, G. (1998): Social Capital, Intellectual Capital, and the Organizational Advantage, *Academy of Management Review*, Vol. 23, No. 2, pp. 242–266.

Probst, G. J. B., Deussen, A., Eppler, M. J., Raub, St. P. (2000): *Kompetenz-Management. Wie Individuen und Organizationen Kompetenz entwickeln.* Gabler, Wiesbaden.

Sarges, W. (2002): *Competencies statt Anforderungen – nur alter Wein in neuen Schläuchen?* Strategien der Personalentwicklung, pp. 258–300, Gabler, Wiesbaden.

Schuh, A., Ploszajski, P. (2008): *What the West can learn from the East* Grow East, pp. 62–69, Linde, Vienna.

Sloane, P. F. E. (1998): *Funktionen im Wandel: Das neue Verhältnis von Arbeiten und Lernen in einer wissensstrukturierten Praxis* Innovationsforschung und Technologiemanagement, pp. 89–104, Springer, Berlin/Heidelberg.

Sonntag, K., Schaper, N. (1999): *Förderung beruflicher Handlungskompetenz* Personalentwicklung in Organizationen, 2nd Edition, pp. 211–244, Hogrefe, Göttingen.

Statistical Office of the Republic of Slovenia (2009): *The average age of Slovenian top managers in year 2000 and 2008*. Special report, Ljubljana.

Tidd, J. (ed.) (2006): *From knowledge management to strategic competency: Measuring technological, market and organisational innovation*, World Scientific, London.

Woodruffe, C. (1993): "What is Meant by a Competency?" Leadership & *Organization Development Journal*, Vol. 14, No. 1, pp. 29–36.

Zupančič, K. R. (ed.) (2008): Entwicklungbericht 2008. http://www.umar.gov.si/fileadmin/user_upload/publikacije/pr/2008/PoR_08.pdf#K (Accessed on 2 March 2009).

## About the Authors

**Jürgen Mühlbacher** is an associate professor at the Institute for Change Management and Management Development, WU Vienna University of Economics and Business. His research interests are strategic management, organizational design, knowledge and competence management, leadership and emerging markets.

**Michaela Nettekoven** is an associate professor at the Institute for Operations Research, WU Vienna University of Economics and Business. Her research interests are finance, quantitative methods and decision theory.

**Jure Kovač** is a full professor of Organization and Management at Faculty of Organizational Sciences, University of Maribor. His research interests are organization theory, organization design and management development.

**Anna Putnová** is a senior lecturer of economics and management at Faculty of Business and Management Technical University in Brno, lecturing in management and business ethics. She is a member of the board of The Association for Ethics and Economics and is a member of ARARE (Academic Response to Anti-Semitism and Racism in Europe).

# Managing with Power in the Organisation to Achieve Common Progress

***Miha Marič***

*miha.maric@fov.uni-mb.si*

***Marko Ferjan***

*marko.ferjan@fov.uni-mb.si*

## Abstract

This chapter examines how individuals' perceptions of managing with power on the personal level affect their perceptions of their organisations' progress and its care for sustainable development. The study was based on theoretical definitions of the concepts of power, managing with power, an organisation's progress and sustainable development. A total of 305 people from Slovenia participated in the study. We recognised a certain influence of the perceptions of managing with power and the perceptions of having power on the perceptions of an organisation's progress and its care for sustainable development. The main predictor of the perception of an organisation's progress is how individuals perceive their recognition of various networks among their co-workers in the organisation. The main predictor of the perception of an organisation's care for sustainable development is how well individuals perceive their knowledge of co-workers' points of view on various topics. The perception of an individual's own power is relevant compared to an organisation's progress as to how its care for sustainable development is perceived. The difference between this study and other studies of power is in the fact that we have conducted this study quantitatively.

**Keywords**: power, organisation, management, progress

# 1. Introduction

Power, politics and conflict in organisations can increase productivity and efficiency or reduce them substantially (Wagner & Hollenbeck, 2010, pp. 215), which is why power is considered one of the most important factors in an organisation.

Pfeffer (2009, pp. 17) states that power, except for occasional discussion of the bases of power, was largely missing from management textbooks and also from the research literature on organisations and management. This can be attributed to the fact that power has a bad reputation (Wisse & Van Knippenberg, 2009, pp. 55), because it has traditionally been considered a destructive force in organisations, corrupting those with power and demoralising those without it (Tjosvold & Wu, 2009, pp. 83).

Organisational development is not unbiased and nor is it always for the common good. It may promote the interests of some social or organisational groups and perhaps impede those of others depending on the conditions and situations under which it is implemented. Power is an essential part of interpersonal processes in an organisation (Moorhead & Griffin, 2009) and getting things done simply requires power (Pfeffer, 1992, pp. 343).

We believe that individual's perceptions of managing with power on a personal level affect their perceptions of organisation's progress and its care for sustainable development.

# 2. Power

Power is a vital part of our lives, personal and organisational, and basically represents the ability to implement one's will. The expanded definition of power is that it is the ability to influence various outcomes by mobilising resources (human and material) to get things done within the web of relations (Rees, 1999) and to resist unwanted influence in return (Wagner & Hollenbeck, 2010, pp. 215). It is often the case that individuals who have power also have it in their organisational as personal lives. Power and its use often have a negative connotation; this is sometimes (but not always) justified.

An individual's power in organisations can be best assessed with observation (Finn, 1995). However, this is a long process, sometimes even subjective, and would take much time and effort to implement on a larger sample. That is why the power-evaluating process takes part only on smaller samples; for instance, one company or one branch of a company at a time. Robbins (quoted in: Senior, 2002, pp. 351) argues that power has been described as the last dirty word and that those who have it deny it; others who want it try not to appear to be seeking it, and those who are good at getting it are secretive about how they got it.

Power is also very relative; one could have it one day and lose it on another (Mintzberg, 1983). Or one could have power in one group, and simultaneously have none in another group of people. Power is difficult to measure, since it can only be perceived. From the social-psychological perspective, a person's behaviour is affected by his or her behavioural intentions, which are in turn influenced by an attitude and set of perceptions. Behavioural intention is regarded as a key antecedent in determining one's future behaviour (Wu et al., 2008). It could be said that power concerns the capacity of individuals to exert their will over others. While formal power is defined, the informal power that is in many cases even more important is not so well defined. It could be said that informal power comes from the authenticity that one has (Dimovski et al., 2009).In a company or in an organisation, there are basically two kinds of power: formal and informal power (Mintzberg, 1983). Formal power comes from one's place in the hierarchy, one's duties and position, and is well defined. Informal power, however, is less defined and often more important. It is both connected to formal power, but also affected with the interpersonal connections with other employees and even the outside world. Hierarchical levels are adjusted to convey the relative authority of employees (Rosenbaum, 1980, pp. 2).The need for power represents the desire to have influence and to control others. This is learned during childhood and adolescence (Wagner & Hollenbeck, 2010). Individuals with such needs enjoy their 'responsibilities', seek influence over others, are preferably placed at competitive and status-oriented positions, are often more concerned with reputation and gaining influence over others (Langton & Robbins, 2006, pp. 110), are in favour of joining different groups (Wagner & Hollenbeck, 2010, pp. 215) and are likely to be effective managers. Of course, all of this is in addition to their own desire to achieve power.

It is one thing to understand power – how to diagnose it, what its sources are, what the strategies and tactics for its use are, and how it is lost. It is quite another thing to use that knowledge in the world at large (Pfeffer, 1992).

## 3. Managing with Power

Organisational development is not unbiased and not always for the common good. It may promote the interests of some social or organisational groups and perhaps impede those of others, depending on the conditions and situations under which it is implemented (Finn, 1995). In many relationships, one party often has power over the other (Afuah, 2004, pp. 1234). Therefore, understanding power relations is essential in understanding omnipresent hierarchies, and diagnosing how dominance and influence are both acquired and used (Pfeffer, 2009).

Putting the knowledge of power and influence into action – managing with power – is essential for those who seek to accomplished things (Pfeffer, 1992). Managers work toward various goals (Moorhead & Griffin, 2009) and getting things done requires power (Pfeffer, 1992). That is the reason managers find it important to manage with power in organisations.

Pfeffer (1992) distinguishes four parts of managing with power:

- recognising that there are varying interests in almost every organisation;
- figuring out what point of view these various individuals and sub-units have on issues of concern to us;
- understanding that to get things done, you need power – more power than those whose opposition you must overcome;
- understanding the strategies and tactics through which power is developed and used in organisations.

However, managing with power means more than knowing the ideas discussed above (Pfeffer, 1992), some people simply 'have it' and others do not. We will be discussing power on the 'personal' or 'micro' level.

## 4. Organisation's Progress

Progress is defined as a forward movement towards a destination; development towards a better, more complete, or more modern condition (AskOxford, 2010); advancement in general; growth or development; continuous improvement; the development of an individual or society in a direction considered more beneficial than and superior to the previous level; forward or onward movement (Free Online Dictionary, 2010).

Based on this definition of progress, we can conclude that an organisation's progress is defined first by the ability to achieve its goals and second by the ability to further develop and advance its current state. An organisation's goals are included in its mission and vision statements. Organisations achieve progress by effectively transitioning from one state to a more desirable one.

Progress is achieved through change and adaptation to the surrounding; perhaps the most important element of change is power. Effectively managing with power in times of change can mean the difference between a successful organisation and one that will soon cease to exist.

We can relate the perception of organisation's progress to organisation development which is based on the behavioural sciences disciplines of psychology, sociology, organisational behaviour and management, with a specific focus on the human side of organisations (Parsch & Baughman, 2010).

# 5. Sustainable Development

Sustainable development is defined as a development that minimises the risk of creating new or exacerbating existing problems, as 'a development that meets the needs of the present without compromising the ability of future generations to meet their own needs' (de Graaf et al., 1996, pp. 205). Sustainable development means 'different things to different people in different contexts' (Laine, 2005, pp. 395) and is considered depending on the context, specific aspects of which differ within different contexts (Karakosta et al., 2010).

Hall et al. (2010, pp. 1) claim that sustainable development has emerged as an influential, albeit controversial, concept for business and policy, and that there is growing recognition that a fundamental transformation is needed to reduce detrimental environmental and societal impacts created by our currently unsustainable business practices. Sustainable development is viewed in terms of realising economic growth that is forceful and at the same time socially and environmentally sustainable (Kolk & van Tulder, 2010, pp. 2).

Sustainable development is nowadays the goal – in words at least – of most politicians and decision makers (Andriantiatsaholiniaina et al., 2004, pp. 149). It is constructed as a win-win concept; however, behind the usual business rhetoric there is very little evidence of anyone actually walking this talk (Laine, 2005, pp. 395).

Managing for sustainability is considered to be critical to the development of corporate sustainability, and is fundamentally about strategic organisational development and change (Holton, Glass, Price, 2010). Any complete strategy for reaching sustainable development should be able to consider all possible activities and all their side-effects; it should also be effective (de Graaf et al., 1996). Principles of development (increasing well-being and equity) as well as sustainability (preserving natural and man-made capital) should be included (Gudmundsson & Höjer, 1996, pp. 269).

# 6. Methodology

## 6.1 Hypotheses

Below, we explore the influence of managing with power with respect to perceptions of progress and the care for sustainable development in the organisation.

The use of power has its purpose, as does managing with power. Based on our theoretical background, we believe that the perception of managing with power on a personal level (of the variables used to measure managing with power: the recognition of various interests among co-workers in the organisation, the recognition of various networks among co-workers in the organisation, knowing co-workers' points of view on various topics, understanding co-workers' points of view on various topics, knowing how to get things done in the organisation, ability to overcome the interests of co-workers in the organisation and knowing how to accumulate more power in the organisation) also affects the perceptions of the organisation's progress and its care for sustainable development. That brings us to our first two hypotheses.

*H1: The perception of an organisation's progress depends on the perceptions of managing with power.*
*H2: The perception of an organisation's care for sustainable development depends on the perceptions of managing with power.*

Information is one of many sources of power. Based on that fact, we believe that people who perceive themselves as having power are also better informed and can affect their organisation's outcomes; therefore, they should also have higher perceptions of their organisation's progress and its care for sustainable development, which brings us to our second set of hypotheses.

*H3: The perception of high personal power has a positive correlation with the belief of organisation's progress.*
*H4: The perception of high personal power has a positive correlation with the belief that the organisation cares for sustainable development.*

## 6.2 Instrument and Variables

We prepared a questionnaire to acquire the data required for our study. The questionnaire was of a closed type and contained two questions (A and B) referring to the data on the respondents and 10 questions (C to L) referring to the respondent's perceptions of managing with power, progress, sustainable development and power. Respondent's perceptions were measured on a scale ranging from 1 to 5 where: 1 – always false; 2 – mostly false; 3 – nor true, nor false; 4 – mostly true; 5 – always true.

General data

A. *Age (individuals were asked about their age)*
B. *Gender (individuals were asked about their gender)*

Managing with power

*Varying interests*

C. *Recognition of various interests among co-workers in the organisation (individuals were asked to rate how well they recognise various interests among their co-workers in the organisation on a scale from 1 to 5)*
D. *Recognition of various networks among co-workers in the organisation (individuals were asked to rate how well they recognise various networks among their co-workers in the organisation on a scale from 1 to 5)*

*Points of view*

E. *Knowing co-workers' points of view on various topics (individuals were asked to rate how well they know their co-workers' points of view on various topics on a scale from 1 to 5)*
F. *Understanding co-workers' points of view on various topics (individuals were asked to rate how well they understand their co-workers' points of view on various topics on a scale from 1 to 5)*

*Getting things done*

G. *Knowing how to get thing done in the organisation (individuals were asked to rate their knowledge of getting things done in the organisation on a scale from 1 to 5)*
H. *Ability to overcome the interests of co-workers in the organisation (individuals were asked to rate their ability to overcome the interests of co-workers in the organisation on a scale from 1 to 5)*

*Developing power*

I. *Knowing how to accumulate more power in the organisation (individuals were asked to rate their knowledge on how to accumulate more power in the organisation on a scale from 1 to 5)*

*Organisation's progress*

J. *Organisation's progress (individuals were asked to rate their organisation's progress on a scale from 1 to 5)*

*Organisation's care for sustainable development*

K. *Organisation's care for sustainable development (individuals were asked to rate their organisation's care for sustainable development on a scale from 1 to 5)*

*Power*

L. *Power (individuals were asked to rate their power in the organisation on a scale from 1 to 5)*

## 6.3 Sample

Participants in this study were selected randomly and participation was voluntary. The study was conducted in February 2010 in all districts of Slovenia using a prepared questionnaire. A total of 305 complete responses were obtained.

The sample consisted of 120 men and 185 women (n=305). The age range of the respondents was between 20 and 61 years. The average age of the respondents was 34.62 years.For questions C to L, we calculated Cronbach's alpha coefficient. The value calculated is 0.745, which indicates great reliability of measurement. With regard to the composition and characteristics of the sample, we believe that it is representative.

## 6.4 Results

We begin by constructing the frequency tables for the variables that we have used in our research.

*Table 1: Frequency tables for the variables*

| | n=305 | | Mean | Median | Std. Dev. | Min | Max |
|---|---|---|---|---|---|---|---|
| | Valid | Missing | | | | | |
| Varying interests | | | | | | | |
| C | 305 | 0 | 3.80 | 4 | 0.726 | 1 | 5 |
| D | 305 | 0 | 3.72 | 4 | 0.780 | 1 | 5 |
| Points of view | | | | | | | |
| E | 305 | 0 | 3.56 | 4 | 0.805 | 1 | 5 |
| F | 305 | 0 | 3.60 | 4 | 0.785 | 1 | 5 |
| Getting things done | | | | | | | |
| G | 305 | 0 | 3.54 | 4 | 0.850 | 1 | 5 |
| H | 305 | 0 | 2.96 | 3 | 0.908 | 1 | 5 |
| Developing power | | | | | | | |
| I | 305 | 0 | 3.26 | 3 | 0.890 | 1 | 5 |
| Organisation's progress | | | | | | | |
| J | 305 | 0 | 3.70 | 4 | 0.840 | 1 | 5 |
| Organisation's care for sustainable development | | | | | | | |
| K | 305 | 0 | 3.68 | 4 | 0.911 | 1 | 5 |
| Power | | | | | | | |
| L | 305 | 0 | 3.15 | 3 | 0.998 | 1 | 5 |

*Table 2: Pearson r Correlation Coefficients [n=305]*

| | C | D | E | F | G | H | I | J | K |
|---|---|---|---|---|---|---|---|---|---|
| D | .346** | | | | | | | | |
| E | .279** | .498** | | | | | | | |
| F | .201** | .328** | .499** | | | | | | |
| G | .204** | .318** | .351** | .311** | | | | | |
| H | .067 | .123* | .195** | .077 | .388** | | | | |
| I | .059 | .089 | .109 | .037 | .468** | .421** | | | |
| J | .086 | .219** | .212** | .114* | .242** | .212** | .180** | | |
| K | .144* | .154** | .230** | .179** | .128* | .135* | .114* | .515** | |
| L | .164** | .138* | .177** | .212** | .377** | .348** | .311** | .164** | .133* |

*. *Correlation is significant at the 0.05 level (2-tailed).*

**. *Correlation is significant at the 0.01 level (2-tailed).*

We can see in Table 2 that there are positive correlations between all of the variables. All the variables were measured on an increasing scale.

*Table 3: regression analysis for the dependent variable Oorgaaisation's progress "and independent variables representing 'Managing with power" (n=305)*

*R=0.325; $R^2$=0.106; Δ $R^2$=0.085*

| Predicators | Non-standardised Coefficients | | Standardised Coefficients | t | Sig. |
|---|---|---|---|---|---|
| | B | Std. Error | Beta | | |
| (Constant) | 2.087 | .351 | | 5.945 | .000 |
| Recognition of various interests among co-workers in the organisation | -.017 | .068 | -.015 | -.245 | .806 |
| Recognition of various networks among co-workers in the organisation | .141 | .071 | .131 | 1.973 | .049 |
| Knowing co-workers' points of view on various topics | .098 | .074 | .094 | 1.326 | .186 |
| Understanding co-workers' points of view on various topics | -.016 | .069 | -.015 | -.234 | .815 |
| Knowing how to get thing done in the organisation | .099 | .069 | .101 | 1.439 | .151 |
| Ability to overcome the interests of co-workers in the organisation | .105 | .058 | .113 | 1.809 | .071 |
| Knowing how to accumulate more power in the organisation | .061 | .062 | .065 | .985 | .325 |

*Dependent Variable: Organisation's progress.*

With the predictors that we have used to describe 'managing with power', the 8.5% variance of the variable 'organisation's progress' is explained. 'Recognition of various networks among co-workers in the organisation' ($\beta$=0.131, p=0.049) has the most influence. Individuals who are good at recognising various networks among their co-workers perceive that their organisations are progressing.

*Table 4: Regression analysis for the dependent variable 'organisation's care for sustainable development' and independent variables representing 'managing with power' (n=305)*

*$R=0.278$; $R^2=0.077$; $\Delta R^2=0.055$*

| Predicators | Non-standardised Coefficients | | Standardised Coefficients | t | Sig. |
|---|---|---|---|---|---|
| | B | Std. Error | Beta | | |
| (Constant) | 1.943 | .387 | | 5.022 | .000 |
| Recognition of various interests among co-workers in the organisation | .095 | .075 | .076 | 1.265 | .207 |
| Recognition of various networks among co-workers in the organisation | .027 | .079 | .023 | .344 | .731 |
| Knowing co-workers' points of view on various topics | .163 | .081 | .144 | 2.005 | .046 |
| Understanding co-workers' points of view on various topics | .100 | .077 | .087 | 1.311 | .191 |
| Knowing how to get thing done in the organisation | -.039 | .076 | -.036 | -.508 | .612 |
| Ability to overcome the interests of co-workers in the organisation | .075 | .064 | .075 | 1.174 | .241 |
| Knowing how to accumulate more power in the organisation | .076 | .068 | .074 | 1.114 | .266 |

*Dependent Variable: Care for sustainable development.*

With the predictors that we have used to describe 'managing with power', a 5.5% variance of the variable 'organisation's care for sustainable development' is explained. 'Knowing co-workers' points of view on various topics' ($\beta=0.144$, $p=0.046$) has the most influence. Individuals who have better knowledge of their co-workers' points of view on various topics perceive that their organisation cares for sustainable development.

Since we are researching managing with power, we also wanted to see how an employee perceives his/her organisation's progress compared to the perception of his/her own personal power.In the tables below, we can see that individuals who perceive themselves to have more power also better perceive their organisation's progress and the organisation's care for sustainable development.

*Table 5: An individual's own perception of power compared to an individual's perception of organisation's progress (n=305)*

| 1 | | Organisation's progress | | | | | |
|---|---|---|---|---|---|---|---|
| | | 2 | 3 | 4 | 5 | | Total |
| Power | 1 | | 25.0% | 41.7% | 25.0% | 8.3% | 100.0% |
| | 2 | | 9.0% | 22.4% | 59.7% | 9.0% | 100.0% |
| | 3 | 0.8% | 7.6% | 28.0% | 55.1% | 8.5% | 100.0% |
| | 4 | | 10.1% | 26.6% | 43.0% | 20.3% | 100.0% |
| | 5 | | 3.4% | 20.7% | 34.5% | 41.4% | 100.0% |
| | Total | 0.3% | 8.9% | 26.2% | 49.8% | 14.8% | 100.0% |

*Table 6: An individual's own perception of power compared to an individual's perception of organisation's care for sustainable development (n=305)*

| 1 | | Organisation's care for sustainable development | | | | | |
|---|---|---|---|---|---|---|---|
| | | 2 | 3 | 4 | 5 | | Total |
| Power | 1 | 8.3% | 16.7% | 41.7% | 16.7% | 16.7% | 100.0% |
| | 2 | 1.5% | 4.5% | 28.4% | 50.7% | 14.9% | 100.0% |
| | 3 | 1.7% | 6.8% | 36.4% | 44.9% | 10.2% | 100.0% |
| | 4 | 1.3% | 7.6% | 27.8% | 36.7% | 26.6% | 100.0% |
| | 5 | 3.4% | 3.4% | 17.2% | 41.4% | 34.5% | 100.0% |
| | Total | 2.0% | 6.6% | 30.8% | 42.6% | 18.0% | 100.0% |

## 6.5 Discussion

Our research confirmed the H1 hypothesis that the variable representing the perception of organisation's progress depends on the variables representing perceptions of managing with power; 8.5% variance of the variable 'organisation's progress' is explained using the predictors to describe 'managing with power'.

We confirmed the H2 hypothesis that the variable representing the perception of organisation's care for sustainable development is dependent on the variables representing perceptions of managing with power; the 5.5% variance of the variable 'organisation's care for sustainable development' is explained using the predictors to describe 'managing with power'.

In addition, we confirmed the H3 hypothesis that the variable representing the perception of high personal power has a positive correlation with the variable representing organisation's progress (r=0.311, p=0.000) and the H4 hypothesis that the variable representing the perception of high personal power has a positive correlation with the variable representing 'organisation's care for sustainable development' (r=0.181, p=0.002).

Several limitations of this study need to be considered before interpretations of the results can be explored. First, the discussed findings and implications were obtained from a single study; generalising the results should be done with caution. Second, the research was focused mostly on how managing with power on a personal level affects the perceptions of organisation's progress and its care for sustainable development. When we were defining the goal of the study, we did so in the knowledge that it is relatively simple with a concept that is influenced by many other variables that are not included in this study. We also suggested that power is to be measured with observations and not with questionnaires. Thus, this was, in essence, an attempt to measure it in a new way.Another very important point to add here is that the respondents answered the questionnaire about the way that they perceive that their surrounding perceives them; it would be better if it would have been constructed from observations of others. However, in this case using this method of an open random survey is impossible. The problem with these answers is that one often better perceives oneself than co-workers etc. perceive one's self-image (Cialdini. 2001).

The difference between this study and other studies of power is that we have conducted this study quantitatively where as it is mostly performed qualitatively, i.e., from the researchers' subjective points of view. In our study, we acknowledge the fact that respondents gave their answers from their own subjective point of view, which does not present a problem, because power is subjective and thereby relative depending on the surroundings.

Power makes it possible to accomplish what individuals cannot; yet it can be just as easily destructive (Winter, 2009, pp. 33). That is why we have to claim good power while protecting ourselves from the bad.

# 7. Conclusion

Managing with power has been and will be essential in organisations as long as there are people working in them, because power is an essential part of interpersonal processes. The use of power has its purpose; it can be either competitive or collaborative. By managing with power, we can achieve much more than one person as an individual ever could. This study provides insights into the connections between managing with power on a personal level and the perceptions of organisation's progress and its care for sustainable development.

We mentioned that the purpose of power is to achieve a goal through its use. An organisation's progress and its care for sustainable development are two goals that cannot be achieved by one person alone. By having and using power over co-workers in an organisation, an individual is enabled to achieve goals that could never have been achieved without having power.The goal that we were testing was common progress by managing with power. Through our research, we learned that managing with power does contribute to the perception of organisation's progress and organisation's care for sustainable development, and that individuals who have more power are more inclined to believe that the organisation is progressing. We can conclude that of all the activities that we have used to construct managing with power, the part that best explains the perceptions of organisation's progress and its care for sustainable development is knowing co-workers' points of view on various topics.

We attribute our findings to the fact that people who are better at managing with power and have more power feel better about themselves and also have a better image of their surroundings.

## References

Afuah, A. (2004): Does a focal firm's technology entry timing depend on the impact of the technology on co-opetitors?, *Research Policy*, Vol. 33, pp. 1231–1246.

Andriantiatsaholiniaina, L. A., Kouikoglou, V. S., Phillis, Y. A. (2004): Evaluating strategies for sustainable development: fuzzy logic reasoning and sensitivity analysis, *Ecological Economics*, Vol. 48, pp. 149–172.AskOxford.com: Search Results, available at: http://www.askoxford.com/results/?view=dev_dict&field-12668446=progress&branch=13842570&textsearchtype=exact&sortorder=score%2Cname (Accessed 1 March 2010).

Cialdini, R. (2001): *Influence: Science and Practice* ($4^{th}$ ed.), Allyn and Bacon, Boston.

de Graaf, H. J., Musters, C. J. M., ter Keurs, W. J. (1996): Sustainable development: looking for new strategies, *Ecological Economics*, Vol. 16, pp. 205–216.

Dimovski, V., Penger, S., Peterlin, J. (2009): *Avtentično vodenje v učeči se organizaciji*, Planet GV, Ljubljana.

Finn, B. (1995): *Organization, Power and Change*, Handelshøjskolens Forlag, Copenhagen.

Free Online Dictionary – definition of progress, available from: http://www.thefreedictionary.com/progress (Accessed 1 March 2010).

Gudmundsson, H., Höjer, M, (1996): Sustainable development principles and their implications for transport, *Ecological Economics*, Vol. 19, pp. 269–282.

Hall, J. K, Daneke, G. A., Lenox, M. J. (2010): Sustainable development and entrepreneurship: Past contributions and future directions, *Journal of Business Venturing*, preprint.

Holton, I., Glass, J., Price, A. D. F. (2010): Managing for sustainability: findings from four company case studies in the UK precast concrete industry, *Journal of Cleaner Production*, Vol. 18, pp. 152–160.

Karakosta, C., Doukas, H., Psarras, J. (2009): Directing clean development mechanism towards developing counties' sustainable development priorities, *Energy for Sustainable Development*, Vol. 13, pp. 77–84.

Kolk, A., van Tulder, R., (2010): International business, corporate social responsibility and sustainable development, *International Business Review*, preprint.

Laine, M., (2005): Meanings of the term sustainable development in Finnish corporate disclosures, *Accounting Forum*, Vol. 29, pp. 395–413.

Langton, N., Robbins, S. P. (2006): *Fundamentals of Organizational Behaviour*, (Third Canadian Edition), Pearson Education Canada, Canada.

Mintzberg, H. (1983): *Power In and Around Organizations*, Prentice Hall, Englewood Cliffs.

Moorhead, G., Griffin, R. W. (2009): *Organizational Behavior: Managing People and Organizations*, (9th ed.), Cengage Learning, South-Western.

Parsch, J. H., Baughman, M. S. (2010): Towards Healthy Organizations: The Use of Organization Development in Academic Libraries, *The Journal of Academic Librarianship*, Vol. 36, No. 1, pp. 3–19.

Pfeffer, J. (1992): *Managing with Power*, Harvard Business School Press, Boston.

Pfeffer, J., (2009): Understanding power in organizations, in *Power and Interdependence in Organizations*, Edited by V D. Tjosvold & B. Wisse, Cambridge University Press, Cambridge.

Rees, R. (1999): Power: an example of its changing nature, *The Canadian Journal of Higher Education*, Vol. 29, No. 1, pp. 27–46.

Rosenbaum, J. E. (1980): Hierarchical and Individual Effects on Earnings, *Industrial Relations*, Vol. 19, No. 1, pp. 1–14.

Senior, B. (2002): *Organisational Change*, (2nd ed.), Prentice Hall, Harlow.

Tjosvold, D., Wu, P., (2009): Power in cooperation and competition: Understanding the positive and negative faces of power, in *Power and Interdependence in Organizations*, Edited by V D. Tjosvold & B. Wisse, Cambridge University Press, Cambridge.

Wagner, J. A. III, Hollenbeck, J. R. (2010): *Organizational Behavior: securing Competitive Advantage*, Rutledge, New York.

Winter, D. G., (2009): *How can Power be Tamed? Power and Interdependence in Organizations*, Edited by V D. Tjosvold & B. Wisse, Cambridge University Press, Cambridge.

Wisse, B., Van Knippenberg, D. (2009): Power and self-constructual: How the self affects power processes. *Power and Interdependence in Organizations*, V D. Tjosvold & B. Wisse, (Editor), Cambridge University Press, Cambridge.

Wu, W., Chang, H. P. & Guo, C. J. (2008): An Empirical Assessment of Science Teachers' Intentions toward Technology Integration, *The Journal of Computers in Mathematics and Science Teaching*, Vol. 27, No. 4, pp. 499–520.

## About the Authors

**Miha Marič** graduated in 2006 and in the following year (2007) received his master's degree at the University of Ljubljana's Faculty of Economics. He is currently employed as an assistant at the University of Maribor's Faculty of Organizational Sciences and is a doctoral student at the Faculty of Economics, University of Ljubljana.

**Marko Ferjan** is a full professor at the Faculty of Organizational Sciences, University of Maribor. He received his master's degree and doctorate at the University of Maribor. His areas of research include HRM, communication processes in organisations and educational planning. Currently, he is the dean of the University of Maribor's Faculty of Organizational Sciences.

# Usage of Work Systematisation in Slovene Organizations


***Dunja Labović***

*dunja.labovic@fov.uni-mb.si*

***Janez Mayer***

*janez.mayer@fov.uni-mb.si*

***Neja Zupan***

*neja.zupan@bisernica.si*


## Abstract


There are different perceptions of work systematisation in practice, the comprehension of which depends on the purpose served. Because of the lack of expertise, employees often do not recognise all of its purposes and benefits. Organisational development requires constant adaptation and moderation of work processes and, thus, work systematisation. The following research analyses the use of work systematisation in Slovene organisations. By law, all organisations with more than ten employees must have an arranged systematisation of work. We have researched which elements of systematisation are included in systematisation of work and if successful organisations have better systematisation than others. On the basis of the research results, we have made proposals for the quality systematisation of work as a basic organisational tool. Specifically, we treated the concept and importance of work systematisation, its components and characteristics, its formation and change. The correlation between the quality of work systematisation and the success of Slovene organisations and achieving EFQM (European Foundation for Quality Management) business excellence round model is considered. One hundred and four Slovene organisations were included in the research. The results show that there are important differences between successful and unsuccessful organisations concerning work systematisation quality and its use. An important factor is the inclusion of the concept of competence in systemisation. Organisations that have determined the key competences for the competitiveness of organisation have a larger market share of successfully initiated products/services.



**Key words:** systematisation of work, organisation, efficiency, competence, the EFQM excellence model

# 1. Introduction

In practice, the systematisation of work is understood in several ways. Understanding depends on the purpose of its usage. Because of the lack of the expertise, organisations' managers are often unfamiliar with all the objectives and advantages of systematisation of work. Due to the internationalisation of human development, work and working environment, constant adaptations and changes in both the work process and (consequently) the components of systematisation of work are needed.

In this chapter, practical application of the systematisation of work in Slovene organisations has been analysed. The elements of it are: a job title, job description, required qualifications, efforts (physical, intellectual, social), working conditions, means and objects of work, work objectives, scope of work, work basics, authorities, responsibilities, psychophysical performance, skills, functional knowledge, ethical requirements, work basis (instructions), work experience and competences. The aim of the study was to discover which of the elements are included in the systematisation of work of individual Slovene organisations and what the aim of the classification is.

This is a current concern in Slovenia, since the organisations with more than ten employees are legally required to have systematisation of work. If it is done only because it is required by law, it is very often incomplete and consequently unable to fulfil its numerous possible goals. The question has been raised whether Slovene organisations really use the systematisation of work adequately or only in order to satisfy formal legal obligations. This issue is closely connected with the fact that the number of Slovene organisations that want to achieve business excellence is increasing, but at the same time this cannot be achieved without basic organisation tools. Another point of interest is also whether Slovene organisations that have already achieved business excellence have good quality systematisation of work and whether they use it adequately. The concept 'organisation' in this chapter is applied through two terms: one is 'organisation as an institution' and the other is 'organisation as a combination of relationships between people'.

# 2. Systematisation of Work

'Systematisation of work is a method of categorising jobs in the working process, defining the role of employees in achieving the goals of the organisation and defining the personnel administration requirements. Actual work in the organisation is defined by the written description of the tasks, duties and responsibilities of a certain post or field of work. This is an illustration of its actual content which defines criteria for work evaluation' (Kejžar, 2001, 37).

'Systematisation of work is an act by which an organisation or an employer defines the place of employment, arranges compensation classification rates and collects all the necessary information for job vacancies and job evaluation by using a chosen method' (Jurančič, 1995, 14). It represents a stage in the process where problems are systematically divided into smaller units (Prasad, 2001, p. 523).

'Systematisation of work is an important basic personnel administration tool and thus the basis for all the human resource activities in the organisation: for choosing the most appropriate employees, education and training, remuneration and promotion' (Hopp, Iravani, Yuen, 2007).

'The main objectives of the systematisation of work are: Identification of the tasks that constitute the working process, programmes and organisational units, Work reorganisation, Defining the classification grade, Business process reengineering, Defining work results and Implementation of the human resource processes' (Mayer, 2008).

The aim of the systematisation of work is to ensure an appropriate and adequately paid job that also has a social value. However, expanded systematisation of work in the social sector and dominant marketing ethics can lead to intellectual overwork, which demands more and more individual work and can consequently lead to social isolation (Tsukamoto, 2007, 199).

In organisations, systematisation of work should achieve basic aims and objectives:

- organisation and division of work; If the work is classified, all the tasks are described in the systematisation. Organisations can benefit tremendously from well-organised work, since it is much more effective and faster. Also, problems can be solved faster since qualified workers can solve them alone and thus faster than they would have, if they had to contact management first (Benders et al., 2006, pp. 246–249). The systematisation of work has to be designed according to basic principles. It has to consist of the description of the tasks and assignments that an employee is expected to perform. The description has to be clear and concise so that an employee knows exactly what, when and how he or she is expected to do the job (Vieira, Ribas, 2008). 'Merely subjective evaluation of the work efficiency is insufficient for existence and development of interpersonal relations in complex organised societies' (Novak, 2008, p. 149). 'Systematisation of work is the cornerstone of all the subsequent work with employees. Time spent on designing it is repaid when designing competent profiles, evaluation and remuneration systems, when planning employee's career, reorganisation, organisation takeover etc.' (Kanetani, 2002).

- enter into contracts of employment; 'Systematisation of work plays an important role for workers, especially for reasons of protection and transparency of their individual employment rights. The systematisation of work aims to ensure a certain level of protection for workers, since it defines their duties upon which the employment contract has been signed. It guarantees that a worker perform tasks and assignments that are in accordance with his or her education and qualifications during employment relationship. That is why each individual legal action, which was based on inadequate systematisation of work, was judged in favour of a worker who was considered as "a weaker party" in the process' (Vukasović Žontar, Sevšek, 2006, pp. 9–10).
- design jobs, education, professional development and promotion of workers; Systematisation of work is a means of informing employees that work accomplishments will be rewarded and 'thus higher level of loyalty can be achieved since they will use their potential, abilities, knowledge and experiences for the benefit of the organisation' (Mantura, 2008, p. 577). Furthermore, systematisation of work is a classification system of all the work within an organisation that consists of assigned information for performing the tasks and enables evaluation of their level of difficulty (Kravaris, Mousavere, 2007). 'Variations in the task performing difficulty level are reflected in money' (Teppo et al., 2009). Day (2007) believes that employees who actively work on the tasks described in the systematisation of work more easily demonstrate their potential to promote to more demanding (leading) positions.
- determining the basic salaries of workers; 'The 1960s marked a change in an attitude towards payment policy. It was understood that the salary of the employees has to be commensurate with their knowledge, skills and experience. Such a work evaluation is appropriate only if a system for remunerating the worker's efficiency is established. Systematisation of work ensures a worker that the organisation has defined characteristics that are needed for him or her to achieve a certain salary level (e.g., upgrade functional knowledge and skills) and on the other hand provides satisfactory explanation in case of lower salary. Well-defined systematisation of work can hence also represent an important motivation factor for more efficient work' (Hickman, Lawler, 2000, pp. 52–54). Systematisation of work establishes order within the organisation and equality between the workers in terms of workload and appropriate payment in relation to classification grade and working results.

Systematisation of work describes all potential factors of the employees' satisfaction which is the key to success in each organisation. It enables employees to compare their goals with goals of the organisation, it provides insight into work content, the level of autonomy, working conditions, basic salary, professional and business relations, management techniques and work organisation. Systematisation of work is an important means of organisation for organisations that are not only aware of constant human resource formation but also of the fact that there is a strong correlation between the efficiency of the employees and the organisation's performance. Shaw et al. (2009, p. 1018) claim that '[T]he equity of the systems within organisations is difficult to identify.' Systematisation of work provides a comprehensive overview of the working processes, their altering and development, the structure and planning of employees, goals, visions etc.

A broader aim of the systematisation of work is that employees would contribute to good organisation's performance, with appropriate efficiency.

# 3. Correlation between the Systematisation of Work and BUSINEss Excellence

Systematisation of work closely correlates with the business excellence. 'With self-assessment and expert assessment based on the EFQM Excellence Model, organisations get a powerful tool for establishing the process of continuous quality improvement, managing human resources, providing internal communications, revealing irregularities and deficiencies, dealing with the needs and requests of employees and clients and nevertheless with the effects on social atmosphere and business results" (Kern, Leon, 2004). Self-assessment provides insight into the current level of quality within the whole organisation and within individual segments. It enables determination of the level of quality of the organisation and suggests which segments would need priority improvement. Systematisation of work can be made, altered and upgraded only on the basis of the content analysis and on the basis of analysis of the classification grade, which forms the core of the organisation quality. Further connection between systematisation of work and business excellence are competences that require constant learning and development of new skills, which ensure individual's efficiency. The higher the competence of the employees, the more competitive is an organisation and also closer to the business excellence.

The EFQM Excellence Model provides an overview of the quality of the production factors, processes and results, learning process and constant improvement process, which are all closely connected with the systematisation of work.

1. **Leadership:** Systematisation of work instructs the managers in developing and achieving the mission and the vision of the organisation. An orderly arrangement provides rapid insight into all working processes, management and decisions taken. It enables both the transparency of authorisations and the responsibilities of an individual. It provides a list of competences that are needed for a future leader to acquire.

2. **Business policy and strategy:** A strategic starting point is a mission, a vision, a strategy and a business culture of the organisation. Systematisation of work defines the central figure in the strategic directions of the organisation and how strategic goals are set and achieved. This enables the organisation to reconcile business tasks and more easily plan the operation of the organisation.

3. **Employees:** Systematisation of work on the both provides insight into the employment policy of the organisation and how it manages, develops and releases the capital of its employees and also enables employees to define their current role in the organisation and define their future career prospects.

4. **Partnerships and resources:** Systematisation of work provides information on how and to which extent an organisation connects with its business partners in business and proprietary networks.

5. **Processes:** Systematisation of work describes all the activities that arise from working processes in the organisation and are divided into several individual jobs. This is the basis for establishing required competences and comparing them with the actual competences of employees or candidates for the job as well as for determining individual personal and professional development.

6. **Results concerning employees:** Results show the level of the employees' satisfaction considering their expectations and future career prospects. This has a direct impact on employees' motivation.

7. **Key operational results:** Economic indicators are no longer considered as the only indicator for successful organisation. Nowadays, satisfied customers and business partners, employees as well as those that live nearby and are therefore directly affected by the organisation are considered equally important. Success indicators are adequately balanced (Kaplan, 2006). As the basis of some indicators, quality systematisation of work influences the results of the organisation's operation.

Business excellence is based on evaluation of quality factors, processes and results and, furthermore, on the quality of learning and constant improvements. A detailed analysis of the quality of the composing elements needs to be conducted by the organisation. Systematisation of work forms an integral part of the composition and cannot be ignored when planning and aiming to achieve business excellence.

Systematisation of work already plays an important role when assessing the elements, for example 'an employee'. 'The way an employee is engaged in arranging disposable resources, defines the organisation's performance. Showing respect, maintaining dialogue, giving authorities and ensuring safe and healthy working environment are key elements in winning employees' loyalty and engagement in achieving business excellence' (Kern Pipan et al., 2007). Systematisation of work forms a link between an employee and an organisation. It describes the means of interpersonal cooperation among employees and of managing disposable resources, which define the performance of an organisation and lead it towards business excellence. Furthermore, systematisation of work also describes working conditions.

The EFQM Excellence Model enables the assessment and evaluation of the following segments of systemisation of work:

1. Transparency of the employment scheme, which is developed and run in accordance with the strategy and planning:
   - Quality human resources (employment, allocation, development) enable accomplishing the tasks and balance of the tasks and responsibilities. Systematisation of work defines which qualities an employee needs to possess in order to efficiently complete the tasks (e.g., level of education and branch, functional knowledge, competences, working experience etc.)
   - A clear policy with objective criteria in terms of employment, promotion, remuneration and granting managing functions. Systematisation of work determines job requirements and helps with employing appropriate workers. It also provides an overview of the promotion possibilities of employees and influences development of the remuneration system.
   - Ensuring quality working conditions and providing health and safety at work. Systematisation of work includes all elements that describe the working environment and conditions and presents possible dangers, such as exposure to noise, vibration, gases, pollution, toxic substances, infections, illnesses and accidents.
   - Employment and promotion management by ensuring objectivity, fairness and equal possibilities for all without prejudice to sex, sexual orientation, disabilities, age, race or religion. Systematisation of work is based on qualifications not personal characteristics of individuals and is, therefore, a measure of fairness and equality for all employees.

2. Identification, development and use of employees' competences by coordinating goals of individuals and organisation goals:
   - Identification of currently accomplished competences in comparison to desired ones. Systematisation of work includes competent profiles that enable comparison between the profiles of employees and job candidates.
   - Support and assistance for new employees (mentoring, coaching and guidance). Systematisation of work enables new employees to acclimatise faster to new environment, since it describes their working tasks, goals, expectations, authorisations and responsibilities.

Evaluation according to the EFQM Excellence Model relates to key processes in an organisation and gives an overview of:

3. Identification, projection, management and improvement of the processes:
   - Continuous identification, description and dossiers on key processes. Systematisation of work describes tasks performed at workplace that constitute working process. This enables checking the actual processes and the projection of changes and improvements.
   - Process coordination. Systematisation of work offers insight into which working places or processes are connected and coordinated and by which means.
   - Measuring and examining the level of effectiveness of the process changes and comparison with other processes that play an important role for improvements. Systematisation of work illustrates the current state of the processes in organisation. By changing the systematisation of work elements, processes also change and vice versa. Since changes are recorded, subsequent assessment of the changes can be made and consequences can be identified.

4. Development and provision of products and services
   - Provision of all available adequate and reliable data. Systematisation of work describes all job elements and provides an insight into database.
   - Development of well-designed systems and procedures for responding to requests and dealing with complaints. A systematisation of work database enables the rapid handling of complaints (of employees), since classification is considered legal act.

5. Innovating processes, in which costumers are included:
   - An inclusion of the parties in innovating processes. An organisation with the help of competences encourages employees to be creative and innovative and thus contributes to the progress of the organisation.
   - Provision of necessary resources for innovating processes. Since systematisation of work provides clear insight into the processes in an organisa-

tion, deficiencies that interfere with the processes can be found. Furthermore, it also provides an overview of the resources that can be used for higher efficiency. With systematisation of work, it is easier to plan and ensure resources.

Quality systematisation of work influences the factors that are evaluated with the EFQM Excellence Model, which provides an insight into the current situation in an organisation and enables less complicated revealing of undesired incidents. 'The excellence model is a systematic quality management approach to gain competitive advantage' (Moeller, 2001).

In systematisation of work, competences are assessed by the EFQM Excellence Model; this is how business excellence is influenced. To ensure higher quality by using the EFQM Excellence Model, engagement of the entire staff needs to be provided. The EFQM Excellence Model not only aims to achieve higher level of competitiveness, but also to improve abilities, knowledge and competence of the staff. 'Competences relate to knowledge and ability' (Ormerod 2008, 1435).

'Education, engagement, selection and flexibility at work influence the knowledge, abilities, skills and motivation of the staff. In such a way, employees develop competences and prepare themselves to start using the EFQM Excellence Model' (Combs et al, 2006). Competences are the key factor in introducing the EFQM Excellence Model. 'They represent the abilities, knowledge, skills, perspectives, self-images, motivations, social roles, views and reactions of each individual in a certain situation' (Bezjak 2008, 46). Competences help achieve business excellence and are therefore the key element in introducing the EFQM Excellence Model. Table 1 indicates connection between the EFQM Excellence Model, competences and work evaluation.

*Table 1: Connection between the EFQM Excellence Model, competences and work quality evaluation*

| Competences | Evaluated factors | Perspective adopted for evaluating work quality |
|---|---|---|
| Leadership ability | Employees | Costumers' results |
| Knowledge on the policy and strategies | Processes | Employees' results |
| | Partnerships and resources | Results of the society |
| | | Key performance results |

The ability of effective leadership, knowledge of policy and strategies are competences that are needed in order to accomplish business excellence. These competences are very important. Without them, the EFQM Excellence Model would have no effect, since we would not know how to approach the staff and they would be lost in a chaotic situation. Employees, processes, partnerships and resources are being evaluated by the management of the organisation. Work quality evaluation is based on the results of the costumers, employees and society and is done by the management of the organisation or by the evaluation committee, if the organisation participates in the competition for The Business Excellence Award of Republic of Slovenia.

'An organisation needs to achieve results that fulfil the expectations of the customers, employees and society. It has to create sustainable value for the costumer. Evaluation is essential, if we want to know whether this is the right way to achieve business excellence. It is necessary to investigate quality by using the EFQM Excellence Model and its evaluation. Of great importance are also development and maintenance of the value-driven approach to partnerships in several different processes, especially with the help of the employees' (Oakland, 2003). All the criteria of the EFQM Excellence Model can be linked to the competences and work evaluation perspectives, since all the criteria need to be measured. 'The meaning of employees can be seen in two criteria of the EFQM Excellence Model (employees and employees' results). The knowledge on how the criteria "qualifications" and "employees results" are connected is still poor' (Eskildsen, Dahlgaard, 2000). It is reasonable to assume that there is a certain degree of connection since all qualification criteria: leadership, policy and strategies, employees, partnerships and resources and nevertheless processes influence the results of the employees. 'Job satisfaction and work motivation are the result criteria of the EFQM-Model for Excellence' (Ehrlich, 2006).

The EFQM Excellence Model is connected with the competences that are included in the modern systematisation of work. Competences play an important role in evaluating jobs and in payment policy, in educating staff, in their promotion, remuneration and performance efficiency evaluation. Competences are also a means of evaluating creativity of the employees.

By changing environment and working processes which are shaped by people, systematisation and its elements also change. In the modern systematisation that we are aiming at, some elements can be replaced by competences.

*Table 2: Connection between systematisation of work and the EFQM Excellence Model through competences*

| Systematisation element | Competences |
|---|---|
| Mental effort | Learning ability |
| | Strategic thinking ability |
| | Analytical thinking and expressions |
| | Creative thinking and expressions |
| | Ability of discovering and responding to opportunities |
| Ethical requirements | Rigour, honesty, responsibility |
| | Being a role model |
| Functional knowledge | Project management skills |
| | Interpersonal communication skills |
| | Public speaking skills |
| | Skills in dealing with people |
| | Conflict management skills |
| | Negotiation skills |
| | Assigning tasks and setting the goal |
| | Recognising competences of the employees |
| | Knowledge on business processes |
| Knowledge | Application of functional knowledge and experiences |
| | Positive attitude towards changes and continuous learning |
| Expected results | Timely execution of tasks in accordance with the superior's instructions |
| | Time and work management |
| | Compliance with quality standards |
| Connection with other functions, areas, units, institutions | Team work ability |

# 4. Case Study

The aim of this study was to analyse which elements of the systematisation are in practice included in the systematisation of work and, by comparing individual organisations, ascertain whether successful organisations also have good systematisation. This is the basis of the actual role of systematisation and its key elements. The research question is the following: 'Are there important differences between successful and unsuccessful organisations in terms of systematisation of work quality and efficiency of its use?'

A survey was conducted in order to define which factors in connection to systematisation positively or negatively influence the organisation's development. We were interested in the effect of including competences in the systematisation of work and thus in the shift of the concept of thinking regarding job difficulty. We investigated the connection between the systematisation of work and business excellence, since we believe that well-designed and modern systematisation represents an important move in achieving business excellence.

## 4.1 Reference Group

Analysis was made in form of a questionnaire. The survey included 104 randomly chosen Slovene organisations (business and public sector) that were willing to participate. The public sector organisations operate mostly in the areas of energy, trade, construction, insurance, tourism, telecommunications, rubber, food, clothing and footwear, while the business organisations operate mostly in the areas of trade, construction, tourism, printing, chemicals and food. The questionnaire was handed in directly. It was completed mostly by experts or people in management positions (executives, managers, human resource management experts), i.e., 74% of respondents, while 26% of respondents perform other tasks. Their answers confirmed our hypothesis that specialised experts are needed in order to design effective systematisation of work. Table 3 and Table 4 show the basic characteristics of the reference group: total number of employees and number of employees in the Human Resource Management department.

*Table 3: Characteristics of organisations participating in the survey – total number of employees*

| **Total number of employees** | Up to 30 | 31 - 50 | 51 - 80 | 81 - 100 | 101 - 200 | 201 - 300 | 301 - 700 | 701 - 1000 | More than 1000 |
|---|---|---|---|---|---|---|---|---|---|
| **Number of organisations** | 13 | 15 | 19 | 3 | 14 | 16 | 18 | 2 | 3 |

*Table 4: Characteristics of organisations participating in the survey – number of employees in the Human Resource Management (HRS) department*

| **Number of employees in HRS department** | 0 | 1 | 2 | 3 | 4 | 5 | 6 | 8 | 14 | 15 | 16 | 18 |
|---|---|---|---|---|---|---|---|---|---|---|---|---|
| **Number of organisations** | 2 | 35 | 17 | 12 | 7 | 1 | 1 | 1 | 1 | 1 | 1 | 1 |

Survey respondents evaluated the organisation's performance in the light of their budget, since it represents 'a means of understanding how individuals understand costs and incomes in accordance with the goals of the organisation' (Beautement, Sasse, Wonham 2009, p. 47). In the survey, a rating scale was used: 1 – yes (consistent); 2 – partially; 3 – no (inconsistent). Table 5 indicates that the mean value is 1.38, which means that organisations are mainly successful in the light of consistency with the budget; more precisely 67 organisations, or 64.4% of the respondents, consider their organisations to be successful in the light of consistency with the budget, 30 or 28.8% consider them to be partially consistent and only four organisations or 3.8% of the respondents consider them to be inconsistent with the budget. This question is very important for our research, since their business performance was assessed on the basis of consistency with the budget. Organisations that answered 'yes' were included in the category of highly successful organisations; those that answered 'partially' or 'no' fall into the category of less successful organisations.

*Table 5: Characteristics of organisations participating in the survey – Consistency with the budget*

| | **No. of organisations** | **Mean value** | **Standard deviation** |
|---|---|---|---|
| **Consistency of performance and budget** | 101 | 1.38 | 0.563 |
| Share of successfully introduced products/services | 96 | 1.97 | 1.051 |

When evaluating business excellence with the EFQM Excellence Model, the share of the successfully introduced products/services is also considered. A rating scale was used to assess the share: 1–more than 50 %; 2–between 30% and 50%; 3–between 10% and 30%; 4–less than 10%. The mean value is 1.97, which is very close to answer No.2, which means that percentage of successfully introduced products/services in organisations is mainly above 50%, or in any case well above 30% (Table 5).

## 4.2 Results Analysis

*Hypothesis 1: Successful organisations have good quality systematisation of work.*

The level of success of organisations was defined according to the consistency with the budget. While highly successful organisations are completely consistent, less successful organisations are only partially or not at all consistent with the budget. Our sample included 67 highly successful and 34 less successful organisations. To determine the variables (components of a systemisation) according to their importance on a systemisation list, the Thurston method was used. The following elements were proved to be the most important on the systemisation list: job description, required qualification, job title, competences, responsibilities and work objectives. Among less important variables, ethical requirements, work basis, scope of work and working conditions were listed. Then we compared variables (components of a systemisation) among two groups with a T-test (Table 6).

*Table 6: A t-test for checking the differences between an average of answers about the data importance on the systematisation checklist between the groups of highly successful and less successful organisations*

| | Levene's test of equality of variances | | T-test of equality of the arithmetic means | | | | | | |
|---|---|---|---|---|---|---|---|---|---|
| Level of importance: | F | Statistical significance of the F-test of equality of variances | t | df | Statistical significance of the difference between the arithmetic means | The difference between arithmetic means | Standard error of the differences | 95% confidence interval lower limit | upper limit |
| Job title | 0.49 | 0.48 | 0.00 | 99.00 | 1.00 | 0.00 | 0.23 | -0.47 | 0.47 |
| | | | 0.00 | 58.81 | 1.00 | 0.00 | 0.25 | -0.49 | 0.49 |
| Job description | 0.06 | 0.80 | -0.12 | 99.00 | 0.91 | -0.02 | 0.20 | -0.42 | 0.37 |
| | | | -0.11 | 53.51 | 0.91 | -0.02 | 0.22 | -0.46 | 0.41 |
| Required qualifications | 0.20 | 0.65 | 0.67 | 98.00 | 0.50 | 0.14 | 0.20 | -0.26 | 0.54 |
| | | | 0.61 | 51.47 | 0.54 | 0.14 | 0.22 | -0.31 | 0.58 |
| Effort | 6.01 | 0.02 | 1.16 | 92.00 | 0.25 | 0.31 | 0.27 | -0.22 | 0.84 |
| | | | 1.06 | 52.35 | 0.29 | 0.31 | 0.29 | -0.28 | 0.89 |
| Working conditions | **13.67** | **0.00** | **2.73** | **90.00** | **0.01** | **0.77** | **0.28** | **0.21** | **1.33** |
| | | | 2.44 | 48.53 | 0.02 | **0.77** | **0.32** | **0.14** | **1.41** |

| | Levene's test of equality of variances | | T-test of equality of the arithmetic means | | | | | | |
|---|---|---|---|---|---|---|---|---|---|
| Means and subjects of work | 0.36 | 0.55 | 0.90 | 92.00 | 0.37 | 0.23 | 0.25 | -0.27 | 0.72 |
| | | | 0.87 | 60.19 | 0.39 | 0.23 | 0.26 | -0.30 | 0.75 |
| Work objectives | **22.19** | **0.00** | **2.80** | **85.00** | **0.01** | **0.89** | **0.32** | **0.26** | **1.52** |
| | | | 2.48 | 45.43 | 0.02 | **0.89** | **0.36** | **0.17** | **1.61** |
| Scope of work | **20.80** | **0.00** | **3.25** | **85.00** | **0.00** | **0.98** | **0.30** | **0.38** | **1.58** |
| | | | 2.92 | 48.11 | 0.01 | **0.98** | **0.33** | **0.31** | **1.65** |
| Work basics | **1.78** | **0.19** | **3.25** | **89.00** | **0.00** | **0.84** | **0.26** | **0.33** | **1.36** |
| | | | 2.98 | 52.54 | 0.00 | **0.84** | **0.28** | **0.28** | **1.41** |
| Responsibilities | 0.01 | 0.92 | 0.93 | 97.00 | 0.35 | 0.20 | 0.22 | -0.23 | 0.63 |
| | | | 0.87 | 55.47 | 0.39 | 0.20 | 0.23 | -0.26 | 0.66 |
| Psychophysical performance | 3.02 | 0.09 | 0.44 | 92.00 | 0.66 | 0.11 | 0.24 | -0.38 | 0.59 |
| | | | 0.40 | 50.90 | 0.69 | 0.11 | 0.27 | -0.43 | 0.64 |

| | Levene's test of equality of variances | | T-test of equality of the arithmetic means | | | | | | |
|---|---|---|---|---|---|---|---|---|---|
| Skills | **7.68** | **0.01** | **3.02** | **95.00** | **0.00** | **0.66** | **0.22** | **0.23** | **1.09** |
| | | | 2.57 | 44.27 | 0.01 | **0.66** | **0.26** | **0.14** | **1.18** |
| Functional knowledge | **16.11** | **0.00** | **2.74** | **95.00** | **0.01** | **0.60** | **0.22** | **0.16** | **1.03** |
| | | | 2.33 | 44.22 | 0.02 | **0.60** | **0.26** | **0.08** | **1.12** |
| Ethical re-quirements | **5.93** | **0.02** | **3.71** | **76.00** | **0.00** | **0.95** | **0.26** | **0.44** | **1.45** |
| | | | 3.52 | 54.32 | 0.00 | **0.95** | **0.27** | **0.41** | **1.48** |
| Work experi-ences | 0.22 | 0.64 | -0.28 | 98.00 | 0.78 | -0.06 | 0.22 | -0.51 | 0.38 |
| | | | -0.25 | 53.17 | 0.80 | -0.06 | 0.24 | -0.55 | 0.43 |
| Competences | **22.02** | **0.00** | **3.77** | **93.00** | **0.00** | **0.98** | **0.26** | **0.46** | **1.49** |
| | | | 3.18 | 42.74 | 0.00 | **0.98** | **0.31** | **0.36** | **1.60** |

By analysing the data from Table 6, the following was ascertained:

On average, highly successful organisations (M=3.45, SE=0.14) consider inclusion of information on 'working conditions' in the systematisation checklist more important than less successful organisations (M=2.68, SE=0.29). This difference is statistically significant t(90)=0.01, p<0.05. The hypothesis is confirmed, which means that we managed to prove the difference between the use of the information 'working conditions' in highly successful and less successful organisations.

On average, highly successful organisations (M=4.04, SE=0.14) consider the inclusion of information on 'work objectives' in the systematisation checklist more important than less successful organisations (M=3.15, SE=0.33). This difference is statistically significant t(85)=0.01, p<0.05. The hypothesis is confirmed, which means that we managed to prove the difference between the use of the information 'work objectives' in highly successful and less successful organisations.

On average, highly successful organisations (M=3.57, SE=0.14) consider the inclusion of information on 'scope of work' in the systematisation checklist more important than less successful organisations (M=2.59, SE=0.30). This difference is statistically significant t(85)=0.00, p<0.05. The hypothesis is confirmed, which means that we managed to prove the difference between the use of the information 'scope of work' in highly successful and less successful organisations.

On average, highly successful organisations (M=3.49, SE=0.14) consider the inclusion of information on 'work basics' in the systematisation checklist more important than less successful organisations (M=2.65, SE=0.25). This difference is statistically significant t(89)=0.00, p<0.05. The hypothesis is confirmed, which means that we managed to prove the difference between the use of the information 'work basics' in highly successful and less successful organisations.

On average, highly successful organisations (M = 3.78, SE = 0.10) consider the inclusion of information on 'skills' in the systematisation checklist more important than less successful organisations (M = 3.12, SE = 0.24). This difference is statistically significant t(95)=0.00, p< 0.05. The hypothesis is confirmed, which means that we managed to prove the difference between the use of the information 'skills' in highly successful and less successful organisations.

On average, highly successful organisations (M=3.95, SE=0.10) consider the inclusion of information on 'functional knowledge' in the systematisation checklist more important than less successful organisations (M=3.35, SE=0.24). This difference is statistically significant t(95)=0.01, p<0.05. The hypothesis is confirmed, which means that we managed to prove the difference between the use of the information 'functional knowledge' in highly successful and less successful organisations.

On average, highly successful organisations ($M=3.39$, $SE=0.13$) consider the inclusion of information on 'ethical requirements' in the systematisation checklist more important than less successful organisations ($M=2.44$, $SE=0.23$). This difference is statistically significant $t(76)=0.00$, $p<0.05$. The hypothesis is confirmed, which means that we managed to prove the difference between the use of the information 'ethical requirements' in highly successful and less successful organisations.

On average, highly successful organisations ($M = 4.07$, $SE = 0.11$) consider the inclusion of information on 'competences' in the systematisation checklist more important than less successful organisations ($M=3.09$, $SE=0.29$). This difference is statistically significant $t(93)=0.00$, $p<0.05$. The hypothesis is confirmed, which means that we managed to prove the difference between the use of the information 'competences' in highly successful and less successful organisations.

The results show that highly successful organisations consider more elements of the systemisation of work as more important than less successful organisations. Highly successful organisations are aware of the importance and advantages that good quality work systematisation brings. It has also been proven that highly successful organisations include information on 'competences' in their systematisation checklists and thus complete systematisation with new concepts. Through competences, organisations encourage employees to be creative and innovative and thus aim to achieve progress of the personnel and the whole organisation. If systematisation is used at annual interviews and at remuneration policy, it represents evaluation of work in relation to job position requirements. It enables employees to present additional or new competences and innovations or creativity, since systematisation defines what is expected from an employee. Competences automatically encourage an employee to think and therefore encourage creativity, which justifies the presence of an employee at an organisation.

A statistically significant difference in systematisation quality in the interest of more successful organisations has been proved in the following categories: working conditions, work objectives, scope of work, work basics, skills, functional knowledge, ethical requirements and competences. The survey has proved that highly successful organisations effectively use these data.

Highly successful organisations consider more than a half of information listed in the systematisation checklist statistically significantly more important than less successful organisations. That is why we can conclude that successful organisations have good quality systematisation of work. **The hypothesis is confirmed.**

*Hypothesis 2: Organisations with specified key competences for organisation competitiveness have larger share of successfully introduced products/services into the market.*

To assess the share of successfully introduced products/services into the market a rating scale with the following categories was used in the survey: 1–more than 50%; 2–between 30% and 50%; 3–between 10% and 30%; 4–less than 10%.

Table 7 indicates quantitative terms divided into groups or descriptive statistics. It can be inferred that our sample includes the same number of organisations that possess key competences for organisational competitiveness and those that do not, i.e., 47. The mean value of the successfully introduced products/services into the market for organisations with defined key competences for organisation competitiveness is 1.72 and for other organisations it is 2.17. Both are close to Answer 2, which says that the share of successfully introduced products/services into the market is between 30 % and 50 %. For organisations with defined key competences for organisation competitiveness, the mean value is 0.800; for others, it is 1.204. The last column indicates the standard deviation of the mean value. Because the standard deviation is relatively small in comparison with the size of mean value, it can be claimed that our sample is representative.

*Table 7: Quantitative terms divided into groups (key competences for organisation competitiveness – the share of successfully introduced products/services into the market)*

| | **Key competences for competitiveness are defined** | **No. of organisations** | **The mean value** | **Standard deviation** | **Standard error** |
|---|---|---|---|---|---|
| **The share of successfully introduced products/services into the market** | yes | 47 | 1.72 | 0.8 | 0.117 |
| | no | 47 | 2.17 | 1.204 | 0.176 |

Table 8 indicates Levene's test of equality of variances and a t-test of equality of the arithmetic means.

*Table 8: A t-test for checking the differences between averages of answers of successfully introduced products/services into the market between the groups of organisations that have defined competences for organisation competitiveness and those that do not.*

| | Levene's test of equality of variances | | T-test of equality of the arithmetic means | | | | | | |
|---|---|---|---|---|---|---|---|---|---|
| | F | Statistical significance of the F-test of equality of variances | t | df | Statistical significance of the difference between the arithmetic means | The difference between arithmetic means | Standard error of the differences | 95% confidence interval lower limit | upper limit |
| The share of successfully introduced products/ Services into the market | 10.231 | 0.002 | -2.12 | 92 | 0.037 | -0.447 | 0.211 | -0.865 | -0.028 |
| | | | -2.12 | 80 | 0.037 | -0.447 | 0.211 | -0.866 | -0.027 |

According to the analysed data presented above, the following can be inferred:

On average, organisations with defined key competences of the employees for organisation competitiveness have a larger share of successfully introduced products/services into the market (M=1.72, SE=0.117) than organisations that do not have these key competences defined (M=2.17, SE=0.176). This difference is statistically significant $t(92)=-2.120$, $p<0.05$.

According to the share of successfully introduced products/services, the business excellence of the organisation is evaluated with the EFQM Excellence Model. The results show that there is a statistically significant difference in favour of organisations with defined key competences of their employees for an organisation to be competitive on the market as opposed to those organisations that do not have these competences defined. These results confirm our hypothesis that, next to other factors, competences and thus well arranged systematisation are positively connected with the business success and excellence of the organisation.

**The hypothesis is confirmed:** Organisations with specified key employee competences for organisation competitiveness have a larger share of successfully introduced products/services into the market.

# 5. Discussion

On the basis of the analysed data results from 104 Slovene organisations, it has been determined that successful organisations use better quality systematisation than less successful ones. Our basic research question can therefore be confirmed: there are significant differences between successful and unsuccessful organisations in relation to the quality of systematisation and its application. We can agree with that systematisation of work brings several advantages to each and every organisation, but it is up to individual organisations as to whether these advantages are recognised and benefited from. In order to be able to do that, knowledge in the field of systematisation of work is needed.

Regarding the importance of the information included on the systematisation checklist, the following has been ascertained: highly successful organisation more often use information on the factors of 'working conditions', 'work objectives', 'scope of work', 'work basics', 'skills', 'functional knowledge', 'ethical requirements' and 'competences' than less successful organisations. Furthermore, it is necessary to state that it is not reasonable to specify too many details on the systemisation checklist; otherwise, it will very quickly become obsolete and useless.

This means that the quality of systematisation of work in our research sample depends on these data.

It has also been ascertained that the importance and application of the information on 'competences' on the systematisation checklist affects the business performance of an organisation; in other words, highly successful organisations included information on 'competences' in their systematisation checklist. Smith (2008, p. 52) claims that 'competences refer to the organisation's ability to constantly improve its efficiency.' How important the concept of competences is can also be proved by providing the finding that organisations with defined key competences of the employees for organisation competitiveness have larger market share of successfully introduced products/services. Although the costs for special experts in the field of HRM employee may not be affordable in smaller organisations, it would be necessary, as one of the professional tasks, to assign HRM tasks to someone else; for example, the executive secretary.

All of our findings are related to our theoretical presumptions about the influence of systematisation of work on the business excellence of the organisation. The quality of performance of an organisation was defined according to organisation's consistency with the budget and according to the market share of successfully introduced products/services. Both performance indicators have been taken into account when assessing business excellence. We have connected them with systematisation and competences and proved that, *inter alia*, good quality systematisation of work which includes information on 'key competences for competitiveness' has an impact on business excellence of an organisation.

Good systematisation is of great advantage in competitive environments. By including competences into systematisation, critiques about the importance of the systematisation of work and its insufficient use have began, which is the consequence of lack of knowledge of the topic. Morrell (2008) claims that the creation and development of systematisation of work is a great challenge or a project for organisations. Palacios et al. (2009) note that management knowledge is needed to create and develop systematisation of work since 'organisation skills are based on strategic skills' Dhillon (2008, p. 297).

"[The] ability to learn and knowledge are essential for innovation" (Akgun et al. 2007, p. 503), which is the key element of systematisation of work. Innovation is changing knowledge into business. It is a process of discovering, learning and applying new technologies and techniques from many different resources. 'It is an important motive power for productivity and economic growth and final improvement of standard of living,' claims Tang (2005, p. 68). Dragoni et al. (2009) state that managers who continuously learn perform development tasks in organisations and also have higher employment possibilities. Ellonen et al. (2009) believe that organisations with relatively high dynamic abilities in terms of discovering, reshaping and creating innovations combine their existing knowledge with new knowledge, which results in creating a new market niche and revolutionary changes. Organisations want to gain additional knowledge in the field of systematisation of work, since quality systematisation of work is a popular topic in the business sphere and also open for development.

On the basis of the survey, our presumption that the systematisation of work is an important source of management information has been confirmed. Systematisation of work serves as a basic means for human resource management and ensures the principle of equal treatment and fairness when distributing the workload and evaluating work effects. The time of construction of the new systemisation or its renewal is the perfect moment to reform the organisation structure, which is a tool of management to achieve business goals.

The primary interest of every organisation is financial success, which both ensures its commercial viability and also gives meaning to business life of its employees. Both can be achieved only on the basis of quality working processes, which are largely a result of good quality systematisation of work that needs to be adequately developed and used. Systematisation of work is therefore 'a theoretical basis for an insight into work and future development of organisation' (Leleur 2008, p. 67).

Systematisation of work cannot be considered as a static document which is updated from time to time, but as a process which is constantly changing, parallel to the contents and structure of work. The classic concept of systematisation cannot follow these changes. Modern organisation has become a result of employees' competences and not of work characteristics. By adapting systematisation to the needs of employees and working processes, their actual value and role in organisation is shown. That is how we encourage them on the way to business success and excellence.

Parallel to the development of society and thus of organisations, the systematisation of work is also developing and is considered increasingly important. 'Long experience and successfully performed tasks increase and gain knowledge' (Teerajetgul et al. 2009, p. 834); employees also develop their abilities in the field of systematisation of work. On the basis of the survey, it can be concluded that systematisation of work is an essential means of organisation, which enables good quality human resource and process management.

## References

Akgun, A., Keskin, H., Byrne, J., Aren, S. (2007): Emotional and learning capability and their impact on product innovativeness and firm performance, *Technovation*, Vol. 27, pp. 501–513.

Beautement, A., Sasse, M.A., Wonham, M. (2009): The compliance budget: managing security behaviour in organisations, *New Security Paradigms Workshop*, Vol. 3, pp. 47–58.

Benders, J., Hoeken, P., Batenburg, R., Schouteten, R. (2006): First organise, then automate: a modern socio – technical view on ERP systems and teamworking, *New Technology, Work and Employment*, Vol. 21, No. 3, pp. 242–251.

Bezjak, M. I. (2008): *Zaposleni največji capital 21. stoletja*, Založba Pro Andy, Ljubljana.

Combs, J., Yongmei, L., Hall, A., Ketchen, D. (2006): How much do high performance work practices matter? A meta-analysis of their effects on organizational performance, *Personnel Psychology*, Vol. 59, pp. 501–528.

Day, D.V. (2007): *Developing Leadership Talent: a guide for succession planning and development*, Alexandria, VA: Society for Human Resource Development.

Dhillon, G. (2008): Organizational competence for harnessing IT: A case study, *Information & Management*, Vol. 45, pp. 297–303.

Dragoni, L., Tesluk, E.P., Oh, I.S. (2009): Understanding managerial development: integrating developmental assignments, learning orientation, and access to developmental opportunities in predicting managerial competencies, *Academy of Management Journal*, Vol. 52, No. 4, pp. 731–743.

Ehrlich, C. (2006): The EFQM model and work motivation, *Total Quality Management & Business Excellence*, Vol. 17, No. 2, pp. 131–140.

Ellonen, H.K., Wikstrom, P., Jantaunen, A. (2009): Linking dynamic-capability portfolios and innovation outcomes, *Technovation*, Vol. 29, No. 11, pp. 753–762.

Eskildsen, D. (2000): A causal model for employee satisfaction, *Total Quality Management*, Vol. 11, No. 8, pp. 1081–1094.

Hickman, E.S., Lawler, E. (2000): Pay the person, not the job, *Training & Development*, Vol.54, No. 10, pp. 52–57.

Hopp, W.J., Iravani, S.M.R., Yuen, G.Y. (2007): Operations systems with discretionary task completion, *Management Science*, Vol. 53, No. 1, pp. 61–77.

Jurančič, I. (1995): *Plače v gospodarstvu: Sistemizacija delovnih mest, metode za vrednotenje dela in merila za ugotavljanje delovne uspešnosti*, Založba ČZ Uradni list RS

Kanetani, Y. (2002): Simulation model for work systematization, *Agriculture and Horticulture*, Vol. 77, No. 2, pp. 233–238.

Kaplan, R.S., Norton, D.P. (2006): *Using the Balanced Scorecard to Create Corporate Synergies*, Harvard Business School Press, Boston.

Kejžar, I. (2001): Oblikovanje sistemizacije delovnih mest v podporo razvoju kadrov. Management in globalizacija, 20. znanstveno posvetovanje o razvoju organizacijskih ved, Portorož, 28.-30. marec 2001, pp. 33–44, *Moderna organizacija*, Kranj

Kern, K., Leon, L. (2004): Rezultati uvajanja modela odličnosti EFQM v Sloveniji v primerjavi z Evropo, Management, znanje in EU – Kranj: *Moderna organizacija*, Kranj.

Kern Pipan, K., Kovač, P., Vraber, E., Žurga, G. (2007): *Skupni ocenjevalni okvir za organizacije v javnem sektorju: CAF 2006*, Ministrstvo za javno upravo republike Slovenije, Ljubljana.

Kravaris, C., Mousavere, D. (2007): ISE-optimal non-minimum-phase compensation for nonlinear processes, *Journal of Process Control*, Vol. 17, No. 5, pp. 453–461.

Leleur, S. (2008): Systems science and complexity: some proposals for future development, *System Research and Behavioral Science*, Vol. 25. No. 1, pp. 67–79.

Mantura, W. (2008): Human factors in quality management, *Human Factors and Ergonomics in Manufacturing*, Vol. 18, No. 5, pp. 565–579.

Mayer, J. (2008): Univerza v Mariboru. Fakulteta za organizacijske vede, *Sistematizacija dela, SVD3-sistemizacija dela*, http://www1.fov.uni-mb.si/mayer/SVD/SVD-3-Sistemizacija%20dela.ppt (Accessed on 18 June, 2008).

Moeller, J. (2001): The EFQM excellence model. German experiences with the EFQM approach in health care, *International Journal for Quality in Health Care*, Vol. 13, No. 1, pp. 45–49.

Morrel, K. (2008): The Narrative of 'Evidence-Based' Management: A Polemic, *Journal of Management Studies*, Vol. 45, No. 3, pp. 613–635.

Novak, M. (2008): Problems of Data Evaluation in the Frame of Processes of their Data Mapping, *Atlantic*, Vol. 18, pp. 149–156.

Oakland, S.J. (2003): *TQM: Text with cases*, Third edition, Elsevier Science, Great Britain.

Ormerod, R.J. (2008): The transformation competence perspective, *Journal of the Operational Research Society*, Vol. 59, pp. 1435–1448.

Palacios, D., Gil, I., Garrigos, F. (2009): The impact of knowledge management on innovation and entrepreneurship in the biotechnology and telecommunications industries, *Small Business Economics*, Vol. 32, No. 3, pp. 291–301.

Prasad, B. (2001): Product, process and methodology systematization to handle structional and computational complexity in product realization, *Systems Research and Behavioral Science*, Vol. 18, No. 6, pp. 523–543.

Shaw, D. J., Dineen, B. R., Vellella, R. F. (2009): Employee-organization exchange relationships, HRM practices, and quit rates of good and poor performers, *Academy of Management Journal*, Vol. 52, No. 5, pp. 1016–1033.

Smith, R. (2008): Harnessing competencies, capabilities and resources. *Research Technology Management*, Vol. 51, No. 5, pp. 47–53.

Tang, J. (2005): Competition and innovation behaviour, *Research Policy*, Vol. 35, No. 1, pp. 68–82.

Teerajetgul, W., Chareonngam, C., Wethyavivorn, P. (2009): Key knowledge factors in Thai construction practice, *International Journal of Project Management*, Vol. 27, No. 8, pp. 833–839.

Teppo, F., Nicolai, J. F. (2009): Organizational routines and capabilities: Historical drift and a course-correction toward microfoundations, *Scandinavian Journal of Management*, Vol. 25, pp. 157–167

Tsukamoto, N. (2007): Social consequences of diversified employment: From a perspective of work and society, *Asian Business & Management*, Vol. 6, No. 2, pp. 199–218.

Vieira, G.E., Ribas, P.C. (2008): Fractional factorial analysis to the configuration of simulated annealing applied to the multi-objective optimization of master production scheduling problems, International Journal of Production Research, Vol. 46, No. 11, pp. 3007–3026.

Vukasović Žontar, M., Sevšek, M. (2006): *Opisi delovnih mest in akt o sistematizaciji: Najnovejši vzorci, modeli in pojasnila za delovna mesta v različnih dejavnostih*, Založba Forum Media d.o.o., Maribor.

## About the Authors

**Dunja Labović** is a research assistant in the field of the human resource management. She is currently working on organisational anthropology, systematisation of work and evaluation, methods of choosing employees and on the competency models.

**Janez Mayer,** PhD, assistant professor at the University of Maribor, Faculty of Organisational Sciences is a doctor of psychology. He is the author of a special assessment procedure for measurements of intellectual potential of most promising people in organisations.

**Neja Zupan,** PhD, is a director of the Bisernica Institute, an institute for the development of creativity and personal growth. She is an internationally recognised NLP trainer and NLP coach. She has a doctorate in organisational sciences. She is involved in the development of individuals and groups, so they find their way to success, satisfaction and health in a challenging environment. She is the author of many national and international professional and scientific papers.

# Internal Communication and Its Importance for Company Management

*Jana Holá*

*jana.hola@upce.cz*

## Abstract

Recent studies provide strong evidence that effective internal communication contributes significantly to the success of the company. Internal communication is directly related to higher employee engagement. The engagement of employees is based on their satisfaction, their motivation and the meaningfulness of their work, aw well as on trust in the organisation and its activities. The internal communication process directly influences employees' working attitudes and the building of mutual relations between the company (management) and its employees. Unfortunately, the importance of internal communication is not sufficiently understood in managerial practice. This chapter is an overview of internal communication and its meaning. It clarifies the internal communication within the context of personal, marketing and other areas of the company control process. It describes the synergy that can be created by proper utilisation of managers' abilities and skills, and the use of information and communication technology tools. The chapter also includes selected results of the field research and the current status and trends of managers' views on the issue of internal communication. The research shows that internal communication is in many cases underestimated.

**Keywords:** internal communication research, management, communication strategy, internal marketing.

## 1. The Concept of the Company Communication

Communication is a basis of cooperation in the company as well as in the personal life of each person. Communication is not easy to define; it is a term of with many definitions. Table 1 shows how each way of thinking about communication might be put into play in the organisational context. There are a great many communication issues that show the diversity and complexity of communication in an organisation.

The wide scope in defining communication shows the notion that *communication is a process* that is continuous and complex and cannot be arbitrarily isolated. Communication unfolds over time. This corresponds to the idea popularised by David Berlo (1960) over 40 years ago: 'If we accept the concept of process, we view events and relationships as dynamic, on-going, ever-changing, continuous. When we label something as a process we also mean that it does not have a beginning, an end, and a fixed sequence of events. It is not static, at rest. It is moving. The ingredients within a process interact; each affects all others.' Lewis (1963) defined the process of communication this way: 'Communication is a process by which a person reduces the uncertainty about some state of affairs by the detection of cues which seems to him to be relevant to that state of affairs.'

*Table 1: Approaches the Concept of Communication source; adapted from Craig R.T. (1999)*

| | Communication Theorised as: | Possible Use in the Organisational Context: |
|---|---|---|
| Rhetorical | The practical art of discourse | Considering the communication strategies of organisational leaders during times of crisis |
| Semiotic | Intersubjective mediation by signs | Studying the ways that organisations create and sustain identity through corporate symbols |
| Phenomenological | Experience of otherness; dialogue | Using dialogue to mediate conflict between two employees |
| Cybernetic | Information processing | Finding optimal ways to set up communication network system for employees who telecommute |
| Sociopsychological | Expression, interaction and influence | Using knowledge about personality and intersection style to improve conflict management programs |
| Sociocultural | (Re)production of social order | Looking at intersection of organisational, national, and ethnic cultures in multinational organisations |
| Critical | Discursive reflection | Confronting the issues of sexual harassment in the workplace through programs designed to shift beliefs about gender and power |

Some other theories state that *communication is transactional.* Such theories deal with the following activities: transmission of messages from source to receiver, or audience including social context, social interaction and personal identity that create very complicated information transfer. (Miller, 2005)

A third area of conceptualisations of communication is the belief that *communication is symbolic*. The concept of sign is the core of marketing communication. These issues more elaborate (e.g., Leeds-Hurewitz (1993), De Pelsmacker (2003), Kottler (2008), Horáková (2008)).

The above-mentioned theories illustrate how difficult the perception and application of communication is. Communication within a company is very complicated, but communication is essential to the functioning of the organisation. Effective internal communication is a major challenge for management.

Every company needs sufficient information from its surroundings to survive in a highly competitive market. Information from both micro- and macro-surroundings helps fulfil the company's targets. According to market information, the company analyses the market opportunities and threats, and considers all the possibilities to determinate the company's strategy. In contrast, the information from the company to the market ensures the success of the company's products or services on the market. The external information stream between the company and the broad surroundings in which the company offers its own products or services is a basic condition of effective working. The internal information and its implementation are necessary for the company and market success as well. The communication process inside the company is as important as external information; sometimes, in special situations, it could be even more important.

It is necessary to realise that the main task of internal communication is satisfying the information needs of all people in the company. At first, they need basic information for managing their job duties. Information regarding the company's targets and strategies helps to foster the employees' trust and loyalty.

The company's communication is involved in all management activities, and it is the main element that connects and coordinates all activities in the company through managing people. In this context, we can understand the communication process as a process of giving, exchanging and receiving information, which must be based on understanding and feedback (e.g., Jackson (1987), Ramsey (2002)).

Mostly, we can see the meaning of communication in these activities:

- transfer (giving) of news, information and decisions;
- clarifying situations and states of current affairs of the company;
- persuasion and influence.

However, the broader understanding of communication can also include working with the information summarised in these activities:

- monitoring: searching for and understanding content, collecting; recording and saving of information;
- interpretation: providing the information with its intended purpose;
- distribution: providing the information effectively according to its value;
- sharing: understanding the meaning of information by all members of the team;
- realisation: practical implementation and use the information for setting of the processes and standards in the company.(Chauder,2004)

The managers are also responsible for prevention of miscommunication. They should prevent the creation of information noise and vacuum, which lowers the effectiveness of the control and functioning of the company, in general. The results of miscommunication have far reaching effects on the team and each member's activities and behaviour; for example:

- decrease of motivation;
- indecision, i.e., decrease of ability to make a decision;
- passivity;
- frustration.

These deficiencies could result in:

- high rate of employee turnover (fluctuation);
- ineffective coordination of all activities of the company;
- failing to reach the company's target;
- ineffective target and strategy;
- ineffectiveness in marketing;
- inability to compete.(Koubek,2004)

All these results of miscommunication show the necessity and importance of the correct setting of information channels and the setting of the company's standard communication processes. The company's communications channels are based on using information and communication technology (ICT) utilities and systems, and also on the company's strategy.

For setting the correct function of internal communication, it is very important to understand internal communication as an everyday priority of a manager's activity. Communication is essential if employees are to work effectively. Such communication is a basis for every activity and especially for managers directing of people. To understand communication means to realise that communication is focused on the recipient who receives some information; therefore, the communication process must involve enough space for feedback. It is very important to understand communication as an instrument of corporate culture, company processes and information, and communication technologies. The company's communication is designed by the synergy of the owners' vision, personal and marketing management, managers' communication competences, and personal communication of each member of the company.

## 2. Communications – Way to Achieving Goals

According to various research papers of managers' views, 60% of problems in the organisation are caused by incorrect communication. Watson Wyatt's latest research (Yates, 2006) has found convincing evidence that the companies with highly effective internal communication practices produce superior financial results and enjoy greater organisational stability. This study provided proof of the strong correlation between communication effectiveness, organisational turnover, and financial performance on the basis of a survey and analysis of responses from 335 participants (260 U.S and 75 Canadian companies). Figure 1 shows the relationships between internal communication and financial performance and organisational stability.

*Figure 1: Communication Effectiveness Drives Superior Financial Performance* (Yates, 2006)

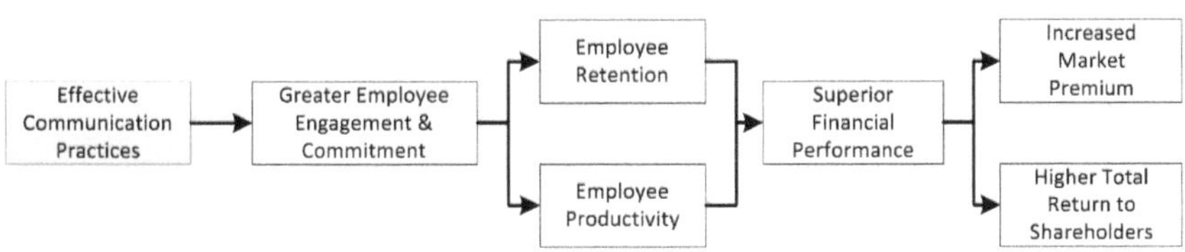


Watson Wyatt (Yates, 2006) calls the effective communication practices the 'Hierarchy of Effective Communication', as shown in Figure 2. The effect of each communication practice on market premium is also shown. Significantly, research shows that the companies can reach a 19.4% higher market premium, by using effective communications. These companies are able to drive behavioural change in their employees: change that produces positive business and financial results. Watson Wyatt defines a basis of the effective communication organisation in eight areas:

- organisational culture and values;
- understanding the business;

- customer needs;
- financial information and objectives;
- information of total rewards programs;
- promoting of new programs and policies;
- integrating new employee;
- strong leadership.(Yates, 2006)

*Figure 2: Hierarchy of Effective Communication and Impact of communication Practices on Market Premium* (Yates, 2006)

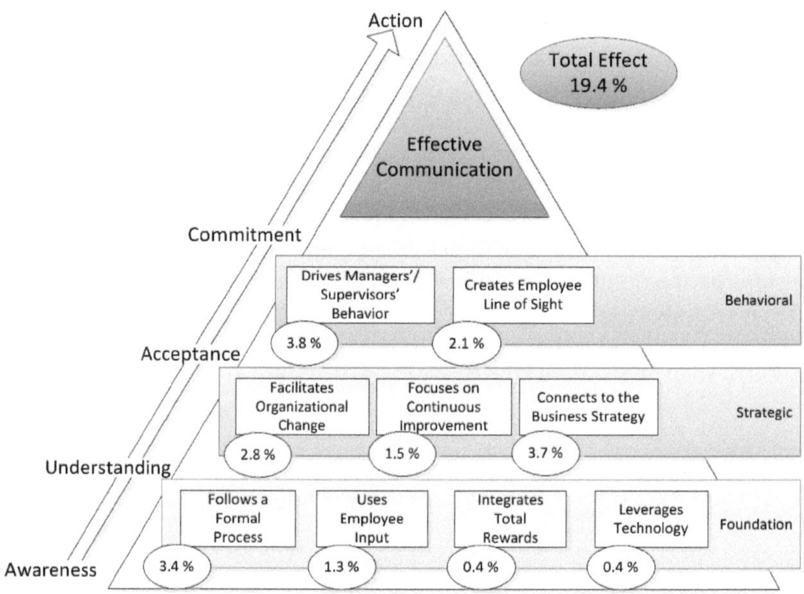


Another interesting study, the European Survey of Enterprises on New and Emerging Risks of European Agency for Safety and Health at Work, showed that ineffective communication is a factor that contributes to emerging psychosocial risks. Psychosocial risks are risks that are linked to the way work is designed, organised and managed, as well as to the economic and social context of work, resulting in an increased level of stress and potentially leading to serious deterioration of mental and physical health. Poor communication between management and staff and poor cooperation between colleagues were identified as problems by more than one quarter of respondents (http://osha.europa.eu/en).

The two above-mentioned studies confirm that communication is a strong motivational factor and that strong tools of leadership are important factors in creating basic working conditions.

All recent authors agree that the comprehensive content of internal communication is realised within leadership, e.g., Wright et al. (2009). The main challenge of leadership is to achieve mutual benefit for the company and its employees. The fulfilling of mutual expectation (company's employees' results requirements as well as the employees' requirements) is a very important premise, which leads to overall company prosperity. When employees' work results or their work behaviour and attitudes are not in accordance with the company's aims, management can find reasons in three categories of problem areas:

1. they do not know what course of action to take due to a lack of information;
2. they cannot achieve the company's goals because of their lack of skills or because the workplace conditions are inadequate;
3. they do not deliver because they are not motivated enough to achieve the work target. (Holá, 2005)

Only open and effective communication leads to the prevention and detection of the sources of these issues, to problem definition and its subsequent solution. The basis of the prevention and solution of first-category issues is providing information for daily management. Examples of suitable communication tools are internal workshops, clarifying and setting of tasks, making regular appraisals of work performance and sufficient, up-to-date and relevant information necessary for employees work performance.

Human resources management can prevent second-category problems. The job description including work requirements creates a good framework for an effective recruitment process. The personnel management sets a basic frame to meet the requirement of mutual understanding. (Armstrong, 2008)

The most demanding solution is required for problems of the third category, which can be described as 'employees do not want to…' This issue involves the overall company culture (including internal communication), teambuilding, partnerships between the company and its employees, an employee motivation program, formal and informal relations, managerial styles and communication abilities and skills.

From the above-mentioned, the main objectives of internal communication can be summarised:

1. information and motivation connection;
2. mutual understanding and cooperation;

3. forming desired working positions (of performance and behaviour);
4. effective feedback for continuous evaluation.

After defining the main objectives, the content (tasks) of internal communication can be determined:

- providing information for employees' needs (information necessary for job duties);
- internal marketing, e.g., public relations (communication necessary for employees' work behaviour and attitudes);
- consolidation of employees' stability and loyalty (communication necessary for company activities coordination, processing, standards, building of company culture);
- set up of feedback.

Internal communication penetrates the whole organisation. The process of internal communication involves personal management, internal marketing, managerial communication abilities and skills, and (finally) company information and communication infrastructure. Only the synergy of all of the above-mentioned activities can guarantee effective internal communication as the basis of company management.

## 3. Selected Results of Internal Company Research in Reference Files

In the years 2005–2006, an initial investigative communication research was carried out in approximately 800 Czech enterprises. During the years 2007–2009, subsequent internal communication research was carried out in 50 enterprises and three case studies were done (analysis and new set up of internal communication) by the author. Both parts of research were focused on views of the board of managers and the employees. The agreed-upon statements were selected. The questionnaire was designed with a social-survey methodology (Easterby-Smith, 2008). The second part of the research was based on findings from the first part of the survey. The questionnaire was similar, only simplified and focused on selected issues. The difference between the results of the first and second research projects was not statistically significant; therefore, all results were processed together. In summary, 850 companies participated in the survey, but complete results were obtained from only 453 companies; 722 responders participated in the survey designed for the employees. Companies that participated were chosen regardless of their size and business field. Their common features were: minimum of five employees, the company was connection to and using the internet, and the willingness to cooperate in the survey. Contacting the companies was conducted by using practices and professional activities of the author.

Case studies were conducted in three different types of organisations: a small firm of 23 employees dealing with beverage machines, a firm of 120 employees operating six e-shops, and a state-owned hospital with 600 employees. The main objective of the each case study was set to a higher level of efficiency of internal communication. The initial qualitative survey with management was conducted to show the status of internal communication and the main issues in the organisation. Quantitative results of all employees' research and statistical testing of hypotheses verified the original assumptions.

## 3.1 Research Methods

The obtained material served as the data of the managers' views and the company's solution of the internal communication process. This was based on choosing answers that were set according to personal theoretical knowledge and practical experience, e.g., Walker (2009). Another survey was carried out from employee's perspective in three case studies (total almost 400 respondents). The questionnaires were focused on managerial communication and levels of internal communication within a specific organisation. The open-source software phpESP[1] was modified for purpose of the research and the questionnaire was accessible via the internet to provide anonymity and to increase the respondents' comfort. The results of the research were processed by common statistical methods of nominal categories. The field research was focused on proving the assumptions of several following areas:

- The meaning of internal company communication is not really sufficiently comprehended in managerial practice.
- The internal communication process is not considered and solved systematically in small companies of up to 25 employees. An active management organisation in the internal communication process is connected with an increase in the number of employees.
- In most cases, the meaning of internal communication is not well understood by management. The managers do not comprehend the complexity of the internal communication process. The companies prefer external partners and do not appreciate their internal partners (employees). The managers often focus

1 phpESP is Easy Survey Package, http://www.butterfat.net/wiki/Projects/phpESP/

on the technical solutions of communication and the information and communication infrastructure.

- Influence of internal communication on work performance and behaviour of employees.
- Managerial communications.
- The level of internal communications within the organisation from the perspective of employees.

## 3.2 Testing Selected Hypothesis

Table 2 contains the selected hypothesis, testing results and, if accepted, alternative hypotheses. To test the hypothesis, a chi-square test was selected, because categorical variables and chi-square test are used for testing associations in contingency table of nominal category. For objective assessment of the results, a statistical analysis was used to test the equality of parameters of alternative distribution. The level of significance is the traditionally determined value of 0.05. (Easterby-Smith, 2008)

*Table 2: Defining a research hypothesis to tested*

| | *Null hypothesis H0 testing at 5% level of significance* | *Accepted/ rejected* | *Acceptance of the alternative hypothesis HA* |
|---|---|---|---|
| 1. | Company size has no impact on internal communication system solution | rejected | Company size has an impact on internal communication system solution. |
| 2. | Companies use the internet for external and internal communication as well. | rejected | Companies use the internet more for external than internal communication. |
| 3. | Company size does not affect the use of the intranet portal. | accepted | |
| 4. | Managers often do not concentrate on technical solutions to internal communications. | rejected | Managers most often concentrate on technical solutions to internal communications. |
| 5. | Companies are investing in internal communications in different ways equally. | rejected | Companies are investing in the internal communication through capital assets of ICT predominantly. |

| | | | |
|---|---|---|---|
| 6. | Internal communication has no impact on job performance and work behaviour of employees. | rejected | Internal communication has an impact on job performance and work behaviour of employees. |
| 7. | Internal communication does not affect cooperation in business. | rejected | Internal communication affects cooperation in business |
| 8. | Internal communication does not affect mutual trust. | rejected | Internal communication affects cooperation in business. |
| 9. | Managerial communication does not affect relationships in the work team. | rejected | Managerial communication affects relationships in the work team. |
| 10. | Managerial communication does not affect the team collaboration. | rejected | Managerial communication affects team collaboration. |
| 11. | Managerial communication does not affect employee's feeling of a job well done. | rejected | Managerial communication affects employee's feeling of a job well done. |

The next step was testing the statistical significance of employees' responses. Again, this was tested at a significance level of 5% (Pecáková, 1998). Statistical significance was confirmed at selected frequencies above 50% of the responses related to managerial communication:

- Managers do not communicate openly with employees (60%).
- Managers do not motivate employees, do not adequately assess employees' contribution and do not share the company's goals and direction (72%).
- Managers ignore critical voices (65%).
- Managers create an atmosphere of fear in which employees are afraid to communicate openly (52%).
- 80% of employees agree with the statement that internal communication significantly affects their job performance and behaviour.

## 3.3 The Most Important Results

Hypotheses are based on the views of managers and information provided by firms in the statistical sample; therefore, the accepted hypotheses reflect the situation and may lead to certain conclusions. The accepted hypotheses are:

*Company size has an impact on internal communication system solution.*

Figure 3 shows the overview of using communication system solution in individual groups according to the number of employees. The figure depicts an increasing number of employees' urgent need of a communication system solution. Unfortunately, when the conditions of a small organisation make it easier to set a system solution, the management does do that and decides to implement a system solution after the communication problems occur.

The intranet could be a very suitable tool for company internal communication. The range of intranet usage is wide: it can be only a notice board for information, but it can also be a full-value communication portal, which makes the internal communication process more effective. Figure 4 shows how the intranet is used in companies that currently use the internet. This figure confirms the fact that companies are more interested in external communication. It also confirms the companies' poor attitude towards internal communication.

*Figure 3: Percentage of using communication system solution in individual groups according to number of employees*

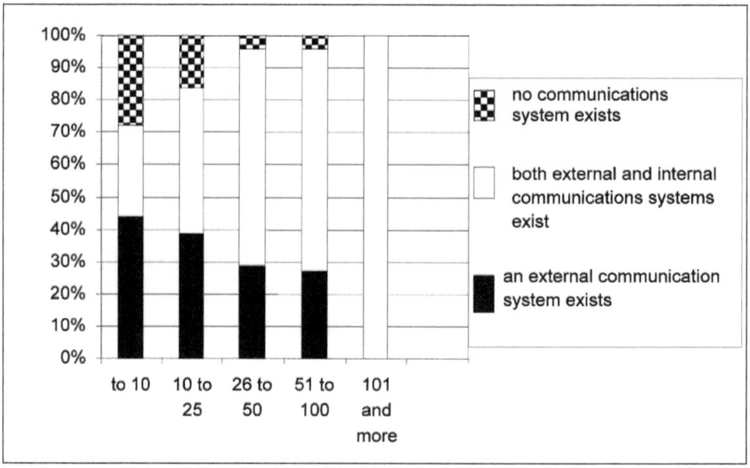

*Figure 4: Percentage using intranet in individual groups according to number of employees*

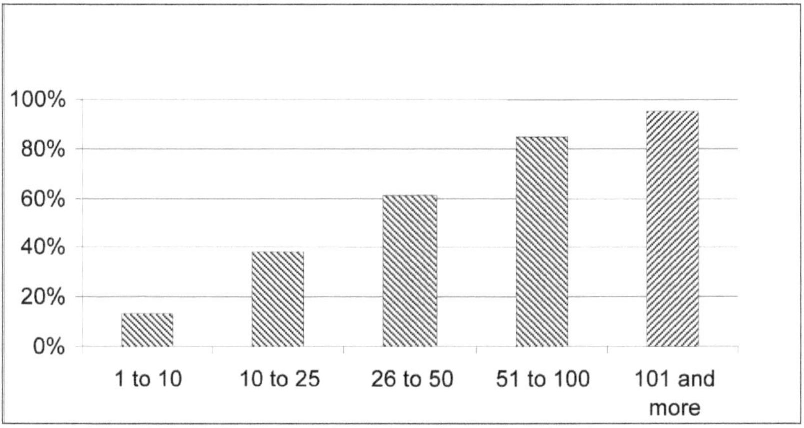


*Companies use the internet more for external than internal communication.*

Only 46% companies use an intranet portal; the companies mostly use the internet as tool for:

- e-mail (100%);
- website for company PR (87%);
- direct e-mail (65%);
- marketing campaigns and advertisements (45%).

*Company size does not affect the use of the intranet portal.*

No correlation exists between company size and the use of intranet portal.

*Managers most often concentrate on technical solutions to internal communications.*

Fifty-five percent of managers in the survey reported that their company will concentrate on communication with customers; only 30% of the managers said that communication systemically solves focuses on all stakeholders, including employees.

*Companies are investing in their internal communication predominantly through capital assets of ICT.*

Figure 5 illustrates how the companies invest in internal communication and - what possibilities (investments) they use. All companies use ICT more frequently than any other possibilities. It is easier to install or upgrade ICT than to improve managerial communication or create an effective company communication strategy.

*Figure 5: Percentage of improving internal communication possibilities in companies*

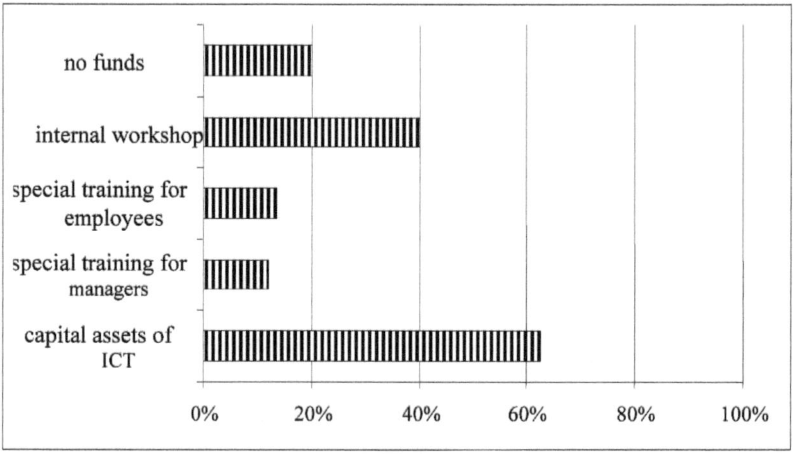


*Internal communication has an impact on job performance and work behaviour of employees.*

- 80% employees agree with the statement that the internal communication significantly affects their job performance and behaviour.

*Internal communication affects cooperation in business.*

- 80% of managers and 65% of employees agree with the statement that internal communication affects cooperation in business.

*Managerial communication affects relationships in the work team.*

- 55% of employees agree with the statement that managerial communication affects relationships in the work team.

*Managerial communication affects team collaboration.*

- 55% of employees agree with the statement that managerial communication affects team collaboration.

*Managerial communication affects employee's feeling of a job well done.*

- 85% of employees agree with the statement that managerial communication affects employee's feeling of a job well done.

Eighty percent of employees agree with the statement that the internal communication significantly affects their job performance and behaviour. The association between the level of internal communication and employee's loyalty is statistically significant. Employees often cited the cause of failed communication as unwillingness and lack of time. An inadequate explanation and lack of space for discussion are the most frequently reported weaknesses of internal communication. From employees' perspective, managers often make these communication errors.

- Managers do not communicate openly with employees (60%).
- Managers do not motivate employees, do not adequately assess employees' contribution and do not share the company's goals and direction (72%).
- Managers ignore critical voices (65%).
- Managers create atmosphere of fear in which employees are afraid to communicate openly (52%).

All figures confirm that management often underestimates the importance of internal communication. Mostly, management is not familiar with the main content of internal communication and the most important communication tools. Managers acknowledge that company internal communication needs improving, and they also consider the internal communication process very important for the company's effectiveness. However, they also indicate a shortage of time as the main barrier of internal communication. The numbers in Figure 6 show the barriers of internal communication as defined by the managers. A shortage of time means that the internal communication is not a priority area of management. This fact again confirms that the internal communication is mostly underestimated.

The research shows that there is a deep misunderstanding between managers and employees, but that only the management can improve internal communication. Management has to pay attention to employees' concerns and to address them.

*Figure 6: Percentage of the most frequent internal communication barriers according managers views*

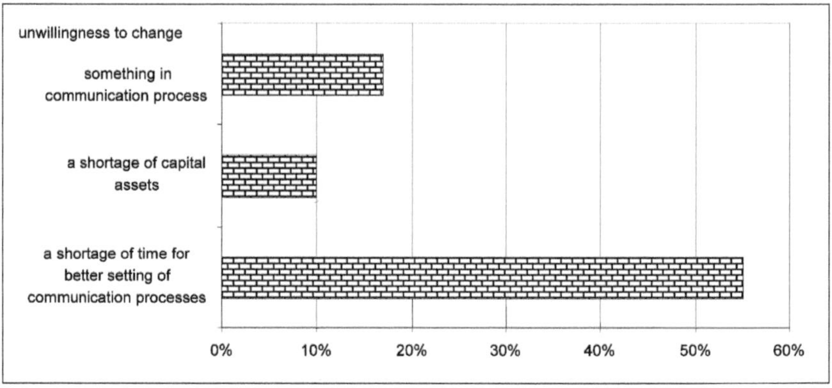


These results can be summarised on the basis of accepted and rejected hypothesis:

- Management mostly underestimates the meaning of internal communication.
- The managers do not want to accept the responsibility for understanding.
    - The process of internal communication develops according to company growth.
- The managers prefer external communication.
- The management prefers technical solutions.

# 4. Discussion: Internal Communication Set Up

All managers who were included in the investigative survey agreed about the importance of internal communication. They would like to improve their company's internal communication but lack the competence and leadership skills to do so. Managers often do not know the content of internal communications and do not develop their competencies in this area. Leaders who understand their responsibility for effective communication want to set up new internal communication. The research and next the studies shows that the new set up of higher level of internal communication is implementation based on rules and principles.

1. It is necessary to clarify what effective communication means in order to improve it. The measurement of effective communication by management must be indentified and a communication framework must be developed.
2. This process must begin with the setting of clearly stated and achievable objectives. The objectives can be the main objectives of internal communication or specific goals of improving or achieving the desired conditions).

3. The research of internal communication statue must be carried out and the results must be the basis for improvement. The result must be published, including the proposals for improvement. The research should include a qualitative part (the main issues are determined and the main objective is stated) and a quantitative part (statistically significant data for confirmation of issues and for comparison in the future).
4. Setting of necessary premises of internal communication.
5. Setting of processes and standards ('golden opportunity', daily business management, personal work, internal marketing)
6. Settings of communication channels and tools, ICT infrastructure
7. Verification via feedback
8. Evaluation

A similar process (the first three points) is also recommended by Wright (2008).

## 4.1 The Necessary Premises of Correct Communication

Effective internal communication proceeds in a company environment that is determined by concrete conditions. These conditions are the premise of effective communication.

- A corporate culture based on ethics and morale values.
- Full management responsibility. A unified management team must be engaged in the new set up.
- Communication strategy.
- Defined work organisation and organisational structure.
- Personnel policy based on mutual respect between company and employee.
- Effective internal marketing, mainly internal public relations.
- The communication abilities and skills (competencies) of the managers.
- Open communication, including feedback.
- Leveraging of technology.

Some authors mainly recommend setting a suitable social context in organisation as first step to built internal communication (Quirke, 2008; Miller, 2009). However, the company management must first accept the responsibility for correct internal communication process (e.g., Sims 2002; Ramsey, 2002). The level of internal communication can be improved by setting corporate culture (based on rightful social context and strong leadership) and then communication standards, internal marketing and the use of information and communication technologies. Also, Watson Wyatt's research defines an effective communication in similar areas (Yates, 2006).

Communication strategy is a very important driver of organisational communication. Unfortunately, many small businesses do not create either a business strategy or a communication strategy. A communication strategy is considered by many authors to be the basis of communication. Experience shows that if communication strategy is set, the effective internal communication is on a higher level. A communication strategy is based on company strategy and is a mean for its fulfilment (see Horáková, 2008 for an example). Communication strategies are understood as a summary of the fundamental objectives and means of achieving them. Table 3 summarises the examples of basic communication strategies.

*Table 3: The examples of communication strategy creation*

| **Partner** | **Target** | **Means (via)** | **Tools** | **Measurability** |
|---|---|---|---|---|
| Existing customers | Loyalty, turnover and gross profit | Customer satisfaction with products and provided services | CRM systems, regular meetings, product training, regular visits | Regular purchase, annual sales, gross profit, customers' feedback |
| Potential customers | Arouse interest in the products and services | Desired image and reputation of companies, products and services | Means of marketing communication mix | Number of new customers and their turnover |
| Employees | Positive relation to the company, forming the desired working positions (of performance and behavior), reinforcing loyalty to spread the reputation of the company, to meet the information needs of work, coordination of work, teamwork | Satisfaction, a high degree of self-motivation, belief in the prospect of the company and in his own career in the company | Internal PR, management of work performance (e.g., regular evaluation), the fulfillment of information needs (internal workshops, intranet, meetings), communication standards at the beginning of the new workers, functioning feedback | Performing the tasks, the achievement of the objectives, specific performance, turnover, satisfaction measurable shifts in time series (anonymous surveys and evaluation) |

| Partner | Target | Means (via) | Tools | Measurability |
|---|---|---|---|---|
| Associated companies | Beneficial co-operation with serious and necessary partners, building the company's reputation and desirability of permanent trade relations (suppliers, banks, freight forwarding companies, agencies, offices, etc.) | Serious and professional approach to the partnership based on moral principles, trust and respect of partners, mutual satisfaction, in cooperation | Providing information about the company (website, printed company profile) regular contact , extract application and regular meetings, additional PR activities | Cost of services and quality of services (price / performance ratio), payments and economic indicators of trade relations |
| Other public, media, competitors, population | Building a desirable image and reputation, the spread of reputation, offer the potential cooperation partners and employees | Desirable image and reputation of company, products and services | Public Relations, behavior of company (management), spread of reputation by staff | Monitoring of views and attitudes regarding public image and reputation of the company |

Over the previous decade, employers have changed how they think about internal communication; they want people to be involved and engaged; therefore, they call a new type of professional: the communication expert (communicators).

These communicators help develop managers' communication competencies. The communication competencies (skills, knowledge and experience) of the managers and communicators are very good (as described by Dewhurst & Fitzpatrick (2009). These competencies are defined as concrete behaviours from the basic 1st level to higher 3rd level and may provide development plans for managers. For managers, it is very important to be good communicators but there also needs to be a good corporate culture and other premises for the application of communication competencies.

The organisation should set the 'golden opportunity' as standards to help create the basic frame of communication process in organisation. The golden opportunity is extremely important for internal communication to be the greatest influence in forming the work performance and attitudes of employees. These opportunities arise in each organisation. It would be a mistake not to utilise this opportunity as the consequences are detrimental to the company's future. These opportunities are:

- time period for adaptation and orientation in the company;
- performance management, assessment and development of career;
- internal workshops to increase knowledge and skills (not only for competencies, but also for the sharing of know-how and the adoption of changes in organisation and business processes).

Coming back to the beginning, top management has to set the framework of internal communication and must accept responsibility for its operation. Small and middle-size companies do not tend to systematically deal with internal communications. Thus, the management is not aware of the most important function of effective internal communication, which is essential for knowledge management, reengineering and the prosperity of the company. Without effective internal communication, the company does not take full advantage of its resources. Effective internal communication improves the work environment climate while increasing awareness among employees of company's activity and plans. Management gets to hear suggestions about the company's plans and policies from its employees through effective feedback mechanisms. Thus the company is able to use fully the accumulated experience of all its employees. Effective internal communication enhances the role of the managers and enables more positive attitude to change within the company. It also allows opportunities to solve problems before they become crises. It creates and sustains employee commitment and concentrates effort on the task on hand while achieving the company's objectives.

# 5. Conclusion

Finally, it should be emphasised that internal communication has a significant impact on company operations, job performance, and work behaviour and attitudes of employees. In the questionnaires, 80% employees agree with the statement that the internal communication significantly affects their job performance and behaviour. The association between the level of internal communication and employee loyalty exists.

All employees, including managers, need enough information and communication for better identification of the corporate objectives; such communication builds confidence in the company and convinces them of the meaningfulness of their specific work in the functioning of the company. Sophisticated internal communication uses suitable tools that can affect the staff working morale and the relationship between the employees and company. This also builds the company's good reputation. Good internal communication is based on the principle that there is a need to treat employees as internal partners (i.e., internal customers) who should meet their own needs associated with the global company performance and lead them to the common goals.

It is important that the company management be constantly working on creating and maintaining positive employee relations. People in business are the most important assets for the company. The aim of any management is for the employees to be effective, productive and loyal. It is very difficult to achieve this goal. It is not difficult to teach the employees what to do and how to do it; however, it may be challenging for any management to motivate them.

## References

Armstrong, M. (2008): *Human Capital Management: Achieving Added Value Through People*, Kogan Page, London.

Berlo, D.K. (1960): *The Proces of Communication.* New York: Holt, Rinehart&Winston.

Craig, R.T (1999): Communication as theory as a field. *Communication Theory*, 9 , pp. 119–161

Chauder, A. (2004): Successful communication, *SuperVision*, 11, pp. 7.

De Pelsmacker, P., Geuens, M., Bergh, J. (2003) *Marketing Communication, Grada Publishing*, Prague.

Dewhurst&Fitzpatrick (2009): *What makes a Competent Communicator*? In Wright, M (eds.), Gower Handbook of Internal Communication, Gower Publishing Limited, Farnham

Easterby-Smith, M., Thorpe, R., Jackson, P.R. (2008): *Management Research*, Sage Publication, London.

Holá, J. (2005): *Internal Communication within Firm* (original in Czech) Computer Press, Brno.

Horáková, I., Stejskalová, D., Škapová, H. (2008): *Company Communication Strategy* (original in Czech), Management Press, Prague.

Jackson, P. (1987) *Corporate Communication for Managers*, Pitman, London.

Kottler, P., Keller, K. L. (2008): *Marketing Management*, Pearson Education, London.

Koubek, J. :( 2004): *Performance Management* (original in Czech), Management Press, Prague.

Leeds-Hurwitz, W. (1993): *Semiotics and Communication: Signs, codes, cultures*. Hillsdale, NJ: Lawrence Erlbaum.

Meffert, H. (1996): *Marketing Management*, Grada Publishing, Prague.

Miller, K. (2005): *Communiation Theories*, McGraw-Hill, New York.

Miller, K. (2009): *Communication Theories*: Approaches and Processes, Wadsworth Cengage Learning, Boston.

Pecáková, I., Novák, I., Herzmann, J., (1998): *Acquisition and data analysis in opinion polls* (original in Czech), VŠE, Prague.

Ramsey, R. D. (2002): 20 ways to be better communicator. *SuperVision*, 1/2002, pp. 10–20.

Sims, R. (2002): *Managing Organizational Behavior*, Quorum Books, Westport.

Quirke, B (2009): *Leadership and Engagement*. In Wright, M (eds.), Gower Handbook of Internal Communication, Gower Publishing Limited, Farnham

Walker,S.(2009): *Measurement*. In Wright, M (eds.), Gower Handbook of Internal Communication, Gower Publishing Limited, Farnham

Yates, K. (2006): Internal Communication Effectiveness Enhances Bottom-Line Results, *Journal of Organizational Excellence*, 25(3), pp.71–79.

## About the Author

**Jana Holá** studied economics and management at the Technical University of Liberec, Czech Republic. She received her Ph.D. in 2005 and is now Head of the Department of Healthcare Informatics and the Management at Faculty of Health Studies, University of Pardubice, Czech Republic. Her fields of research are company communication and business informatics.

# Organisation and Motivation of Researchers in an Interdisciplinary Research Team

***Borut Likar***

*borut.likar1@guest.arnes.si*

***Damijan Miklavčič***

*damijan.miklavcic@fe.uni-lj.si*

## Abstract

Research and development is performed in laboratories in academic and industrial settings by highly educated, skilled and, most of all, motivated researchers. They are willing to invest extra hours into their work. Since they are expected to work approximately forty years (or more) of our life, it is difficult to imagine that a researcher would be permanently willing to sacrifice his/her private life for the sake of his/her work, although at least in some periods of professional life this seems inevitable.

In our study, we investigated the relations between R&D efficiency and various influencing factors, as well as the burnout syndrome of researchers in one of the best performing research teams in Slovenia. The pilot study encompassed two levels: the organisational aspects at the research unit level and at the individual one. The study indicates that the extension of the working day is a part of life in the analysed successful research team. The results show that the researchers' satisfaction is closely related to systemic organisational activities, which should be focused on building a common team vision, relations among co-workers and with management, flexibility of work, creative and enjoyable work resulting in success, personal development, acknowledgment and respect. In contrast, the negative effect of stress influenced by deadlines, uninteresting work, simultaneous work on various unrelated projects, unpleasant personal relations and extraneous additional work should be avoided.

**Keywords**: R&D, systemic aspects, efficiency, organisation, motivation, burnout, stress

# 1. Introduction

Researchers are people who love their work and are dedicated to it, probably more than in many other professions. They are frequently willing to sacrifice their private life for the sake of their work. Is this only a matching and overlaying of the profession and hobby? This was probably so in the times of Leonardo da Vinci and perhaps also some decades ago. We also believe it remains true to a certain extent nowadays. However, researchers are more and more integrated into the global economical and political dynamics. Why? The time has passed when responsibility for seeking an opportunity to improve the economic situation of the country could be left to the economy itself. The need for an efficient integrating of R&D results into commercial products has become an absolute necessity. In addition, the Lisbon aims require overcoming the innovation gap between the academic sphere and the economy (Likar, 2009). Furthermore, the forthcoming EU strategy represents the continuation of the Lisbon process in which the exit from the current crisis should be the point of entry into a new sustainable social market economy, a smarter, greener economy in which our prosperity will result from innovation and from using resources better, and where knowledge will be the key input (European Commission, 2010). It is related to increased dynamics in the academic sphere as well. If the extension of the researcher's working day (based on the nature of scientific work itself) is augmented with the additional pressure of research requirements, projects, cooperation, publications, deadlines and teaching, appropriate conditions for the stress are established. The logical question is whether such work can be sustained over a long period of time. What is the motivation of a researcher? Does he/she go by without reward and compensations by the employer? What organisational and systemic conditions should be established to minimise excess pressure and at the same time carry on outstanding performance?

The literature addresses leadership and related organisational aspects of companies and other institutions as well as motivational aspects (Chandler et al., 2008) in detail. There is also a significant number of scientific publications tackling leadership and related organisational aspects within the academic environment. The properties of high-performing R&D teams (Vaill, 1982) operating much better than others have some common characteristics: 1) clarity of purposes and near-term objectives, 2) commitment to purposes, 3) teamwork focused on the task at hand, 4) strong and clear leadership, and 5) generation of inventions and new methods. Carayannis and Laget (2004) showed that team-based research is one of major forms of research activity in the international scientific community. Additionally, they emphasised the importance of successful R&D groups consisting of various nationalities. Morgan et al. (1976) showed that in more effective teams, members experience more satisfaction of their professional needs, are more attached to their teams and perceive their teams to be more willing to take risks based on knowledge. In general, more effective teams are also more homogeneous than the less effective teams.

Additionally, stress and its resulting burnout syndrome are well investigated and described. However, there is only a small number of publications focused on stress in the research environment. One of those showed that academic stress is associated with a variety of negative outcomes, such as physical illness and deteriorating mental health. The results showed that robustness was negatively associated with both academic stress and the number of health complaints, and showed that robustness moderated the association between academic stress and health (Hystad, S.W. et al., 2009). Sheard and Golby (2007) found an association between robustness and academic achievement. They collected data on robustness at the beginning of students' second academic year and subsequently monitored their academic performance. Upon degree completion, the results showed that students with high levels of robustness achieved a higher mean dissertation mark than students with low levels, and that students scoring high on the commitment facet had a higher second-year grade point average.

We also believe that the issue of burnout syndrome is becoming increasingly important. As to the reduction of burnout, there are two primary approaches to intervention programs: trying to change individual employees and trying to change the organisation (Ross and Altmaier, 1994; Schaufeli and Buunk, 2002). Programmes that seek to change individuals have been more prominent, both in research and in practice, perhaps because of a belief that burnout is due to personal issues or an assumption that it is easier to change individuals than to change an organisation (Maslach and Goldberg, 1998). When taking into account the specifics of research units in the academic sphere, we realise they are most often relatively small. Therefore, organisational aspects can also be managed more easily as well as changed. This is the reason we focused on both in our research: the individual and the organisational levels.

## 1.1 Introduction of the Pilot Research Group – Laboratory of Biocybernetics

The research group, the Laboratory of Biocybernetics, is composed of 27 members and five associate members. Most of them have an electrical engineering background, but there are biologists, microbiologists, chemists and physicists among them. The interdisciplinary composition of research group, i.e., blending, is one of the keys to the success this group has had over the previous 15 years. The Laboratory of Biocybernetics has been involved in three European framework programme projects: Cliniporator, Esope and Angioskin (www.cliniporator.com). The first two projects were dedicated to the development of a clinical device and protocols for electrochemotherapy and gene electrotransfer in tumors (Marty et al., 2006, Miklavčič et al., 2006, Andre et al., 2008), whereas the third project was aiming at the development of gene transfection by means of electroporation to skin (Pavšelj and Preat, 2005, Pavšelj et al., 2007). The group was thus involved in an intense international collaboration from 2000 to 2009. The Laboratory of Biocybernetics research team has also been involved in numerous bilateral projects with teams from Argentina, Austria, Croatia, Germany, France, Poland, Romania and the USA.

In Slovenia, researchers and research groups are regularly evaluated on the quality and relevance of their work with respect to the number of published research papers in peer-reviewed journals, the number of citations that their papers received and the amount of grant money that researchers are able to obtain from EU Framework Programmes and with respect to direct contracts with the end users (Javna agencija za raziskovalno dejavnost RS, 2009a). Similarly, all calls for proposals and (co)financing of research activities by Slovenian Research Agency consider the quality of the researcher according to the methodology that takes into account the scientific excellence of the proposer by evaluating the researcher's publications, patents, citations and contracts with end users (Javna agencija za raziskovalno dejavnost RS, 2009b).

According to these evaluations and also according to the general peer review exercise of research programmes (research programmes being the form of core long-term funding of the best performing research teams in Slovenia) that was carried out in 2008, the Laboratory of Biocybernetics (research identification no. 1538-004) has been listed among the top 25% in Slovenia. According to the information database system of research in Slovenia, the SICRIS database (http://sicris.izum.si/search/grp.aspx?lang=slv&id=2170), this research group published 97 original research papers in peer-reviewed journals, 13 chapters in books and received three US patents in the period from 2005 to 2010. Their papers received 1,713 citations (self-citations excluded) in the period from 2000 to 2010.

The research group that we investigated is managed by the Head of the Laboratory of Biocybernetics. Although the Laboratory of Biocybernetics (according to the organisational structure) is a member of the Department of Biomedical Engineering at the Faculty of Electrical Engineering, University of Ljubljana, and is thus subject to institutional rules, there is some liberty in terms of the management of research and researchers. In particular, this research group has regular weekly meetings every Friday, and has seminars in which individual members of the team present their research results or project results. Furthermore, progress on research projects is reported and discussed. In addition, each member of the team has his/her own mentor/supervisor with whom he/she has regular individual meetings. These individual meetings are more frequent for PhD students (on a weekly basis) and are less frequent for post-doctoral research associates, and research and teaching assistants (on a roughly monthly basis). Individual annual reports and plans are discussed once per year in an annual personal growth interview with the immediately superior team member. All the annual plans are kept and reviewed against the performance report the following year. In this way, planning is coordinated with team plans and is kept realistic.

Team vision is shared and built on seminars during the planning of new projects and following project realisation. Team building is performed twice per year on a regular basis for this purpose. Social events outside university premises are organised: in summer a picnic with sports activities and in early December dinner party. These social activities occur during regular working hours in order to avoid conflict with family obligations whenever possible.

# 2. Methodology

The research was performed as a pilot study in one of the best performing research teams in Slovenia, i.e., the Laboratory of Biocybernetics. The employees of this research team formed our target group. The total number of respondents was 20 researchers, two technicians and the head of the Laboratory of Biocybernetics. Others were not available at the time this study was conducted. The study was performed in the following steps:

1. Preparation of the concept and the questionnaire
   A combination of open questions and some closed ones was selected.
   The questionnaire followed the basic idea, i.e., searching for connection among personal satisfaction, work organisation, personal attitude/competencies, burnout syndrome and research results, was prepared. The questionnaire addressed two levels: the organisational aspects at the research unit level and individual one. Even though the study of the R&D results did not form the main focus, we wanted to study the basic properties of the results as well (see also Table 9).

2. Presentation of the questionnaire to the target group
   It is worth mentioning that the pilot research group is focused on technical and natural sciences/biomedical engineering; therefore, the employees' research methodology differs from the methodologies applied in the social sciences. As a result, we organised an explanatory session, presenting the questionnaire and its background in detail. The event also offered an opportunity to respond to some of the questions posed.

3. Research and the results' analysis
   The respondents had only a few days to complete the questionnaire. We received 22 questionnaires in total and performed the statistical analysis. First, the answers concerning open questions were categorised into a smaller number of categories. After that, the basic statistical analysis was performed and the correlation matrix (Spearman's correlation coefficients (SCC)) was also calculated.

Although a number of respondents explicitly expressed no hesitation in giving their responses and comments in an identifiable manner, we decided to maximise our efforts to conduct this investigation in an anonymous manner in order to minimise the potential impact of the head of the laboratory being involved in the analysis and interpretation of the study. The members of the research team were explicitly told that their participation in this study is voluntary.

# 3. Results

The questionnaires were filled out by 12 males and 10 females (Q2), 35 years old (Q1) on average (min. 24, max. 62, st.dev. 8.9). The mean value of their working period in any of the laboratories (Q3) was 10 years (min. 1, max. 30, st.dev. 7.8).

## 3.1 Results of the Simple Statistics

The following set of results is based on open questions as follows in Tables 1 to 5:

*Table 1: Q5 - If your working day is on average longer than eight hours, indicate some underlying reasons (according to importance) which lead to the extension of the working day. (Each respondent had an opportunity to indicate various reasons.)*

| Categorised answer | Responses | |
|---|---|---|
| | N | Percent |
| deadline | 8 | 13.30% |
| nature of work | 7 | 11.70% |
| additional work | 6 | 10.00% |
| reading literature, analysing problems | 5 | 8.30% |
| wish for problem solving | 5 | 8.30% |
| publications preparations | 5 | 8.30% |
| curiosity | 4 | 6.70% |
| overly large volume of work | 3 | 5.00% |
| PhD work | 3 | 5.00% |
| perfectionism, systematic work | 3 | 5.00% |
| others (laboratory occupation, good relations with co-workers, unexpected additional urgent work, good working conditions, work with students, unequally distributed work, trying not to work more than 8 hours, wish to succeed, sense of responsibility | 11 | <5% |

Analysing the results, it may be established that most of the underlying reasons are somehow connected to the nature of scientific work itself. It should be emphasised this is not a routine work, in which all the activities could be well-planned and could always be equally distributed during a certain period of time.

*Table 2: Q6 - Which are the motivating reasons for your above-average efforts invested into R&D work? Indicate according to importance. (Each respondent could state various reasons.)*

| Categorised answer | Responses | |
|---|---|---|
| | N | Percent |
| wish for achieving new knowledge and results | 10 | 19.60% |
| joy of working, personal satisfaction | 9 | 17.60% |
| wish to succeed | 7 | 13.70% |
| good relations with co-worker | 4 | 7.80% |
| personal development, knowledge | 4 | 7.80% |

| Categorised answer | Responses | |
|---|---|---|
| | N | Percent |
| desire to retain employment | 3 | 5.90% |
| others (sense of responsibility, fear of non-finishing the work, good working conditions, PhD work, perfectionism, nature of work, possibility of freedom on work, trying not to work more than 8 hours, conference participation, work with young researchers) | 11 | <5% |

This question (as with some others) is based on our presumption that most of these researchers are willing to invest extra hours in their work. As evident in Q4 (see Table 6), it may be observed that the employees work 30% over the expected norm.

*Table 3: Q7 - Identify the main factors related to lab management and work organisation that influence your willingness/readiness to invest above-average efforts into R&D work. (Each respondent could indicate various reasons.)*

| Categorised answer | Responses | |
|---|---|---|
| | N | Percent |
| flexibility of work (time, place) | 14 | 24.10% |
| good relations with co-workers | 13 | 22.40% |
| organisation of work | 7 | 12.10% |
| respect, acknowledgment, appraisal | 5 | 8.60% |
| good technical conditions | 5 | 8.60% |
| good relations with management | 5 | 8.60% |
| team/project team vision | 3 | 5.20% |
| others (wish for achieving new cognitions and results, publications preparation, content of work) | 11 | <5% |

A detailed analysis shows that most of the answers are closely connected to the role of management via the organisation of work (e.g., flexibility of work, organisation of work), motivation instruments as an important factor (e.g., respect, acknowledgment, appraisal), common team vision as well as good technical conditions. As to the question (Q8) of how long they were prepared to work at such a pace, the mean value of the answers recorded was 12.3 years (min. 3.5 max. 40, st.dev. 12.3). Most of the respondents (N=14) did not provide a numeric value but filled in descriptive answers as follows: do not know, not overloaded, depending on the family (has one or not) and their needs, depending on work distribution, depending on motivation and needs.

It is expected that most of the respondents could not forecast their readiness to work in the future in the same way. However, we can find indications that they are not ready to work unconditionally. Moreover, the average age of the team members (35 years only) supports this thesis.

*Table 4: Q9 - Specify what else would contribute to your commitment and satisfaction at R&D work. (Each respondent could indicate various reasons.)*

| **Categorised answer** | **Responses** | |
|---|---|---|
| | **N** | **Percent** |
| higher salary | 11 | 26.80% |
| more interesting work | 5 | 12.20% |
| better relations with colleagues | 4 | 9.80% |
| more acknowledgment, respect | 4 | 9.80% |
| support, better relations with the boss | 3 | 7.30% |
| others (more secure employment, more freedom, better work organisation, more employees, less stress and obligations, he/she is satisfied, more time for private life, better technical conditions, possibility of promotion | 14 | <5% |

Interestingly, the preceding questions concerning reasons for extended working day/week (Q5) and above-average efforts invested into R&D work (Q6) reveal that no one mentioned money, which could mean that the salary is not especially important. However, in this question, the salary is the most important single factor that would additionally contribute to their commitment and satisfaction. It is worth mentioning that the researchers' salaries, especially those of young ones, are unenviably low.

*Table 5: Q10 - Do you have a feeling that you are burning out at work. If yes, indicate why. (Each respondent could indicate various reasons.)*

| **Answer (if burning out at work)** | **Frequency** | **Percent** |
|---|---|---|
| yes | 2 | 9.1 |
| periodically | 9 | 40.9 |
| seldom | 1 | 4.5 |
| not burning out | 10 | 45.5 |

| **Answer (reasons why)** | **N** | **Percent** |
|---|---|---|
| not burning out | 10 | 40.00% |
| simultaneous work on various unconnected projects | 4 | 16.00% |
| deadlines | 4 | 16.00% |
| teaching obligations | 2 | 8.00% |
| lack of organisation | 2 | 8.00% |
| no feedback after finishing work, monotonous work, others do not finish their obligations | 3 | <5% |

Even though the average age was only 35 years, stress seems to be present already. Such stress is associated mainly with overload (teaching, deadlines) and simultaneous work on various unrelated projects; it is also reflected in the length of the working day (Q4). It may be expected that the problem of burning out could become a somewhat more serious problem if the average age increases.

The following set of results is based on closed questions as follows in Table 6:

*Table 6: Set of results for closed questions.*

| **Question** | **N** | **Min.** | **Max.** | **Mean** | **Std. dev.** |
|---|---|---|---|---|---|
| Q4a - Estimate an average length of your working day regardless of the place of work (job, home, elsewhere) in hours, over the week | 22 | 6 | 13 | 9.07 | 1.47 |
| Q4b - Estimate an average length of your working day regardless of the place of work (job, home, elsewhere) in hours, over the weekend | 19 | 0 | 8 | 3.37 | 2.24 |
| Q11 - With R&D work, my objectives are clearly set and I follow these objectives (1-Extremely unclearly set objectives, 7-Extremely clearly set objectives) | 22 | 3 | 7 | 5.32 | 1.29 |
| Q12 - At my R&D work I'm (1-completely ardent and dedicated, 7-apathetic and I work due to obligation) | 22 | 1 | 5 | 2.59 | 1.05 |
| Q13 - Indicate how you address new challenges in your life (1-With courage and decisively, 7-Prudently with a great amount of caution) | 21 | 1 | 6 | 3.17 | 1.56 |

| Question | N | Min. | Max. | Mean | Std. dev. |
|---|---|---|---|---|---|
| Q16 - The results of my work as to my comparable colleagues (education, length of period of service, field of work and suchlike) are (1-Extremely poor, 7-Extremely good) | 22 | 1 | 6 | 4.32 | 1.32 |

It may be established that the working week lasts 52.1 hours/week, which is 12.1 hours or 30% more than the expected norm of 40 hours (Q4a, Q4b). The respondents have quite clear objectives as to their R&D work (Q11) and are to a similar degree ardent and dedicated to their work. As to the new challenges in life, the answers are more diverse: they addressed them both with courage and decisively as well as prudently with a great amount of caution. They also evaluated the results of their work to be better than that of their colleagues.

The respondents became involved in R&D work mainly due to a wish for self-development; significant factors are also hopes and aspiration for progress in science and self-affirmation. The earnings and the inevitability are by far the less important factors (more in Table 7).

*Table 7: Q14 - I've decided for R&D work due to (Each respondent could indicate none, one or more appropriate answers)*

| Answer | Responses | |
|---|---|---|
| | N | Percent |
| a) a wish for self-development | 20 | 37.00% |
| b) hopes and aspiration for progress in science | 10 | 18.50% |
| e) self-affirmation | 8 | 14.80% |
| g) other (not specified) | 7 | 13.00% |
| d) success in the society | 4 | 7.40% |
| f) earnings | 3 | 5.60% |
| c) inevitability | 2 | 3.70% |

It may be observed in Table 8 that factors concerning the work itself (content, nature, creativity) as well as the lab organisation (relations, organisation of work) are the most important reasons for satisfaction. Even though the salary and employment security are ranked last among factors of satisfaction (e.g., respondents are the least satisfied with), the researchers are only partially dissatisfied.

*Table 8: Q15 - Assess factors of satisfaction (1- Completely unsatisfied, 7- Entirely satisfied)*

| Question | N | Min. | Max. | Mean | Std. Dev. |
|---|---|---|---|---|---|
| b) relations | 22 | 3 | 7 | 5.73 | 1.03 |
| d) content of work | 22 | 3 | 7 | 5.55 | 1.01 |
| c) nature of work | 22 | 2 | 7 | 5.55 | 1.5 |
| f) a possibility of creative work | 22 | 2 | 7 | 5.45 | 1.5 |
| e) organisation of work | 21 | 2 | 7 | 5.24 | 1.37 |
| g) promotion in scientific field | 22 | 1 | 7 | 4.32 | 1.76 |
| a) money | 22 | 2 | 6 | 4.14 | 1.32 |
| h) employment security | 21 | 1 | 7 | 3.71 | 1.95 |

## 3.2 Correlation Matrix

In addition, the correlations were calculated for the numerical part of the answers according to the concept shown in Table 9.

*Table 9: This table indicates types of connections/correlations that were assessed. The symbol ✓✓ refers to correlations among variables concerning organisational aspects (variables: organisational 1, 2...n.) of the research unit and the personnel one. These correlations were in focus. The symbol ✓ refers to the connections between R&D results and other parameters which were not in the research focus.*

| **CORRELATIONS** <br> **variables – aspect (X,Y)** | personnel 1 | personnel 2... | organisational 1 | organisational 2... | R&D result 1 | R&D result 2... |
|---|---|---|---|---|---|---|
| personnel 1 | 1 | ✓✓ | ✓✓ | ✓✓ | ✓ | ✓ |
| personnel 2... | | 1 | ✓✓ | ✓✓ | ✓ | ✓ |
| organisational 1 | | | 1 | ✓✓ | ✓ | ✓ |
| organisational 2... | | | | 1 | ✓ | ✓ |
| R&D result 1 | | | | | 1 | ✓ |
| R&D result 2... | | | | | | 1 |

Even though the correlation coefficient itself cannot indicate which of two variables is the influencing one – but only the correlation factor – we tried to assign which of them is the influencing one. This interpretation was made according to the knowledge as to the content of the relation. The most interesting and significant correlations are presented in Table 10.

*Table 10: The correlation results – most important and significant correlations taken from the correlation matrix.*[1]

| Qx/Vx | Qy/Vy | SCC | Interpretation |
|---|---|---|---|
| Q1 | Q12 | -.476(*) | Senior researchers are more dedicated to their work |
| Q3 | Q12 | -.519(*) | Those who have been working in labs for a longer period are more dedicated they are to their work |
| Q3 | Q4a | .432(*) | Those who have been working in labs for a longer period have a longer working day |
| Q4a | Q12 | -.602(**) | Those, who are more dedicated to R&D spend more time working during the week |
| Q4a | Q10 | .440(*) | Those who have a longer working day during the week more often have the feeling of burning out. |
| Q4b | Q15c | .635(**) | Those, who are more satisfied with the content of work spend more time working during the weekend |
| Q4b | Q10 | -.477(*) | Those who have a longer working day during the weekend have more often the feeling of burning out. |
| Q8 | Q15b | .869(**) | Those who are more satisfied with relations at work are prepared to work at higher pace longer |
| Q8 | Q15d | .913(**) | Those who are more satisfied with content of work are prepared to work at higher pace longer |
| Q15g | Q10 | -.431(*) | Those who are more satisfied with promotion in scientific field are more often burn out |
| Q12 | Q11 | -.440(*) | Those who have clearly set objectives are more ardent and dedicated to R&D work |
| Q15g | Q15a | .509(*) | Those who are more satisfied with promotion in their scientific field are more often satisfied with the salary. |
| Q15b | Q15d | .553(**) | Relations are connected with the content of work. |
| Q15b | Q15e | .540(*) | Relations are connected with the organisation of work. |

1 *Legend: Q - question, V - variable, SCC – Spearman's correlation coefficients, **Correlation is significant at the 0.01 level (2-tailed), * Correlation is significant at the 0.05 level (2-tailed).*

| Qx/Vx | Qy/Vy | SCC | Interpretation |
|---|---|---|---|
| Q15f | Q15e | .500(*) | A possibility of creative work is connected with the organisation of work. |
| Q15f | Q15g | .489(*) | A possibility of creative work is connected with promotion in scientific field |
| Q15f | Q15h | .481(*) | A possibility of creative work is connected with employment security |

# 4. Discussion

Almost all of the presented correlations are medium to strong, and most of them could be expected except for the Spearman's correlation coefficient between Q15g and Q10: Those who are more satisfied with promotion in scientific fields are more prone to burning out. It is also interesting that there is no significant correlation between work results (Q16) and other variables.The study indicates that the extension of the working day is a part of life in the analysed successful research team. It is mainly related to the nature of the R&D work itself, with the researchers' personal characteristics and organisational aspects within the research team. As demonstrated, the burnout syndrome could be a problem; especially if the mode of working remains unchanged for years or even decades. The results could be compared with Chandler's (2008) findings showing that academic stress is associated with a variety of negative outcomes, such as physical illness and deteriorating mental health. However, if management wishes to maintain high R&D performance in the long run, conditions for satisfactory work and minimum-stress conditions should be assured. Despite the fact that the average age is only 35 years, stress seems already to be present (Q10). It is associated mainly with overload (teaching, deadlines) and simultaneous work on various unrelated projects. There are also significant correlations ($0.440<SCC<0.477$) indicating that those who have longer working days during the week and weekends more often have the feeling of burning out. Let us mention the average working week is 30% longer than the official 40 hours; while the maximum length of the working day is 13 hours. We could expect that the problem of burning out would become a more serious problem if the average age and the years working in research teams increased. The reasons for the extension of the working day (Q5) and the burnout syndrome (Q10) might be a part of the same pattern: the nature of scientific work itself has some properties which require extra work (at least occasionally). Moreover, the problem can be enhanced by additional pressure of research requirements, projects and pedagogical work.

Summarising the results, we can see that we have two typical influencing categories: the group of factors that positively influence the readiness/willingness to perform/take extra work (which seems to be obvious if the researcher/team would like to achieve remarkable results) and the other group of factors connected with decreasing the R&D performance causing dissatisfaction and stress (e.g., Hystad, S.W. et al., 2009; Sheard et al., 2007).

At this point, management and connected organisational and leadership aspects start to play an important role. These is probably one of most important instruments to set conditions for employees to achieve good results and to be simultaneously satisfied, motivated and not burning out.

We established the importance of the management's role via the organisation (e.g., flexibility of work, organisation of work), motivation instruments as an important factor (e.g., respect, acknowledgment, and appraisal), common team vision as well as good technical conditions (Q7). Even though the research results show that the lab management and work organisation is good, the results (Q9) show the urgent importance of this issue, which probably needs further improvements. Interesting work, relations with one's colleagues and supervisors, acknowledgment and respect are the factors that would additionally improve the research team's performance. Even though our research is not completely comparable with Vaill's (1982), certain findings are very similar, mainly those regarding the importance of clarity of purposes, commitment to purposes and teamwork.

As shown in Q14, salaries and inevitability are the least important factors as to the decision for the R&D work. The answers to Q15 show that, among factors of satisfaction, money and the employment security are ranked last. However, regarding the analysis of additional factors that would contribute to their commitment and satisfaction (Q9) the respondents emphasised higher salaries in the first place. As the average age of researchers was 35 years, and some of them do not have families yet, the earnings are probably not the most important factor. However, for senior researchers with families, the salary is obviously more important.

The correlations also indicate ($0.602<SCC<0.635$) that those who are more dedicated to R&D and more satisfied with the content of work spend more time working in the lab. However, other correlations ($0.440<SCC<0.477$) indicate that those who have longer working days during the week and weekend more often have the feeling of burning out. Even though these two facts seem to imply that they should be connected, they should not be simply put into a cause-consequence relation. It seems that successful work in top R&D teams requires an extension of the working week and/or working at higher pace. However, we believe it is important to enable researchers to work under circumstances diminishing stressful situations. If we want people to be working at higher pace, which is closely connected with effectivenes, satisfaction with work content and relations among researchers was shown to be extremely important (0.869<SCC<0. 913); similarly, Morgan et al. (1976) showed that in more effective teams, members experience more satisfaction of their professional needs and are more attached to their teams.

If we want satisfied researchers, systemic organisational activities should be focused on building common team vision, relations among co-workers and with management, flexibility of work (as to time and place), creative and engaging work resulting in success, personal development, acknowledgment and respect. In contrast, the negative effect of stress influenced by deadlines, uninteresting work, simultaneous work on various unconnected projects, bad relations and extra additional work should be avoided. We believe these are important directions for the management and effective organisation of work. It is important that all the activities are more optimally planned and ways for more equal distribution during a certain period of time are found; probably not at the level of the individual researcher but at the team level. On the other side, the employees/researchers themselves can also optimise their work following these findings.

The change in terms and conditions in the field of R&D national policies due to the lack of funds as a reflection of the harsh economic situation; researchers being considered and paid as public workers may inevitably bring more dissatisfaction, insecurity for jobs and, as such, an increase in stress levels. Motivation may deteriorate as one of the most appreciated 'values' of being researcher is choosing when and where one works may soon vanish; in some institutes, one's presence at work is already being recorded. Furthermore, as society and most politicians on behalf of society are expecting returns on investment in terms of more new knowledge incorporated into services and products resulting in higher added value, research and work as such may become even more diversified, and working on more unrelated small projects may become a necessity. These all can have negative consequences on performance and results.

It is interesting to note that, in spite of the fact that two thirds of the members of the research team investigated have no permanent job and for some of the members their contracts are soon to expire, the answer about job security Q15 – although ranging from 1 to 7 – is not as low as could be expected.

# 5. Limitations

Because the research experience, related R&D titles and lengths of employment were extremely different among researchers, due to a combination of senior researchers, young researcher and absolute newcomers, it is not very easy to compare the R&D results. For further study, we suggest placing researchers in categories and using more objective criteria (SCI articles, citations etc.) for R&D results evaluation.

We also believe the additional relations could be observed, which were of an indicative nature only in a moderately small sample.

Furthermore, if we want to generalise results obtained in our study, a study involving different research teams concerning the R&D content, result performance and various social environments would obviously be required. Furthermore, an industrial environment would represent an additional challenge.

## References

André, F., Gehl, J., Serša, G., Préat, V., Hojman, P., Eriksen, J., Golzio, M., Čemažar, M., Pavšelj, N., Rols, M.P., Miklavčič, D., Neumann, E., Teissié, J., Mir, L.M. (2008): Efficiency of high- and low-voltage pulse combinations for gene electrotransfer in muscle, liver, tumor, and skin. *Human Gene Ther.* 19, pp. 1261–1271.

Carayannis, E. G., Laget, P. (2004): Transatlantic innovation infrastructure networks: Public-private, EU-US R&D partnership, *R & D Management*, Vol. 34, No. 1, pp. 17–32.

Chandler, S. & Richardson, S. (2008): *100 Ways to Motivate Others: How Great Leaders Can Produce Insane Results Without Driving People Crazy* Revised., Career Press, pp.19–20, 178–179, 191–193.

European Commission (2010): Public consultation on the Europe 2020 strategy, Brussels, 24.11.2009–15.01.2010, http://ec.europa.eu/dgs/secretariat_general/eu2020/consultation_en.htm. Accessed on 15 August 2010.

Hystad, S.W. et al. ( 2009). Academic Stress and Health: Exploring the Moderating Role of Personality Hardiness. *Scandinavian Journal of Educational Research*, 53(5), 421–429.

Javna agencija za raziskovalno dejavnost RS (2009a): *Pravilnik o kazalcih in merilih znanstvene in strokovne uspešnosti (neuradno prečiščeno besedilo št.*

*1)* - v veljavi do 15.07.2010* (http://www.arrs.gov.si/sl/akti/prav-znan-strok-uspesn-okt09.asp) Accessed on 15 August 2010.

Javna agencija za raziskovalno dejavnost RS (2009b): *Metodologija ocenjevanja prijav za (so)financiranje raziskovalne dejavnosti v letu 2010 (razpisi v letu 2009)* (http://www.arrs.gov.si/sl/akti/metod-skupna-09.asp) Accessed on 15 August 2010.

Likar, B. (2009): *University - business dialogue: could that be a solution?* European innovating minds, European Parliament, 29.01.2009, J. Zverina (Editor), EPP-ED – Group of the European Peoples' Party and European Democrats, Brussels.

Marty, M., Serša, G., Garbay, J.R., Gehl, J., Collins, C.G., Snoj, M., Billard, V., Geertsen, P.F., Larkin, J.O., Miklavčič, D., Pavlović, I., Paulin-Košir, S.M., Čemažar, M., Morsli, N., Soden, D.M., Rudolf, Z., Robert, C., O'Sullivan, G.C., Mir, L.M.. (2006): Electrochemotherapy – An easy, highly effective and safe treatment of cutaneous and subcutaneous metastases: Results of ESOPE (European Standard Operating Procedures of Electrochemotherapy) study. *Eur. J. Cancer Suppl.* 4, pp 3–13.

Maslach, C., Goldberg, J. (1998): Prevention of burnout: A new perspective. *Applied Preventative Psychology*, Vol. 7, pp. 63–74.

Miklavčič D, Čorović S, Pucihar G, Pavšelj N. (2006): Importance of tumour coverage by sufficiently high local electric field for effective electrochemotherapy. *Eur. J. Cancer Suppl.* 4, pp 45–51.

Morgan, C. P., Dailey, R. C., Kulisch, W. A. (1976): The Composition of Effectiveness and Ineffectiveness in R & D Project Teams, *Academy of Management Proceedings*, pp. 500–505.

Pavšelj, N., Préat, V., Miklavčič, D.. (2007): A numerical model of skin electropermeabilization based on in vivo experiments. *Annals Biomed. Eng.* 35, pp 2138–2144.

Pavšelj, N., Préat, V.(2005): DNA electrotransfer into the skin using a combination of one high- and one low-voltage pulse. *J. Control. Release* 106, pp 407–415.

Ross, R. R., Altmaier, E. M. (1994): *Intervention in Occupational Stress*. London: Sage.

Schaufeli, W. B., Buunk, B. P. (2002): Burnout: An overview of 25 years of research and theorizing. *Handbook of Work and Health Psychology*. M. J. Schabracq, J. A. M. Winnubst, C. L. Cooper (Editors), Wiley, Chichester.

Sheard, M. and Golby, J. (2007) Hardiness and undergraduate academic study: The moderating role of commitment. *Personality and Individual Differences* 43, pp. 579–588.

Vaill, P.B. (1982): The Purposing of High-Performing Systems, *Organizational Dynmics,* Vol. 11, No. 2, pp. 23–40.

## About the Authors

**Borut Likar** is a professor at the University of Primorska, Faculty of Management and a head of the Department of Innovation and Technology Management. Furthermore, he is a successful innovator. Among numerous lectures he has given, the talks at the United Nations' headquarters in Geneva and at the European Parliament in Brussels were met with a particularly wide response.

**Damijan Miklavčič** is a professor at the University of Ljubljana, in the Faculty of Electrical Engineering. He has been the Chair of Department of Biomedical Engineering since 2007, and has been the Head of the Laboratory of Biocybernetics since 1998. He and his colleagues from the Laboratory of Biocybernetics are recipients of numerous domestic and international awards and prizes. Damijan Miklavčič is serving as editor, associate editor, member of the editorial in a number of scientific peer reviewed journals; he serves as reviewer in more than 30 journals and is a member of scientific and counselling boards at various institutions in Slovenia and abroad.

# Influence of Business Ethics and Morals on the Efficiency of Organizational Systems in Public Administration

***Bojan Vavtar***

*bojan.vavtar@fov.uni-mb.si*

## Abstract

The influence of business ethics and morals was addressed by a theoretical and empirical study performed in Slovene public administration organisations. The hypothesis that the environment in which ethical and moral values are respected contributes to a better efficiency and higher trust in public administration organisations was examined. A total of 618 subjects participated in a survey, which provided the data for an empirical analysis. In addition to Ward's linkage method for the hierarchical cluster analysis and Sheffe's post-hoc test, procedures of descriptive statistics were applied in the analysis. The performed analysis confirmed the hypothesis stating that the organisational and legal culture influences the organisational performance. Moreover, it was indicated that the main factor influencing the organisational performance is the organisational culture found in public administration organisations. Here, legal principles are of prime importance, interrelating with the ethical and moral principles, supporting one another.

**Keywords:** public administration, enterprises, morals, ethics, government administration

## 1. Introduction

The financial crisis that began in the year 2007 has brought focus on the ethics and morals in society and in the business world as the key causes for the crisis (Ferrell 2009). This chapter discusses the influence of ethics and morals on the efficiency of social and organisational systems. It is in the interest of global society to ensure better stability and to avoid this type of crisis or similar situations also having such extremely negative effects. The hypothesis that was put forward states that efficiency is influenced by both ethical behaviour and behaviour in accordance with the moral and legal principles of employees in general government organisations. We assume that important differences exist between the behaviour of managers and that of the employees. Management strengthens ethical business when encouraging it and when aware of its meaning.

Interest in business ethics has been well established in public administration and in business of all branches. Particular attention in the field of business ethics of organisations is focused on the investigation of influences in a wide set of organisation members, i.e., employees, buyers, social community, business partners, investors and competition. The organisational management devotes more attention to the progress and motivation of employees, the use of knowledge, the selection of trustworthy suppliers and loyal buyers, as well as its own reputation in the business environment. We understand that there are different structures of organisations in the field of general government and in the public sector. The findings presented by other researchers indicate that values are the basis of ethical knowledge in the organisational culture of an organisation (Verschoor, 2002).

In his recent research, Hofstede (2010) added the fifth dimension of organisational culture, i.e., dealing with an ethical attitude towards certain parts of a company. The research performed by Vitell and Hidalgo (2006) demonstrates that the perception of ethical behaviour affects the effectiveness of an organisation. Caroll (1979) determined that organisation fulfils its responsibility by achieving the economic goals, i.e., by selling its products and services to those buyers who are interested in buying them. An organisation satisfies its legal responsibility when it operates within the boundaries of law and in accordance with various regulations. We often mark professional ethics as deontology within the meaning of moral duties that has to be considered by the performers of an individual profession (Igličar, 2006: 20).

In previous research, some of the authors were engaged in theoretical and philosophical questions of business ethics: (Bennet, 1946), (Bennet, J.C. et al., 1954) (Dubbink, 2010, Marquis & Cater, 1954). In their dissertation, Newton et al. (2009) established an attitude between ethics and business. One could divide research in the field of business ethics into the following three fields:

1. **Theoretical concepts:** (Elm, D.R., & Weber, J., 1994; Reilly, 1994; Vitell, Nwachukwu & Barnes, 1993)

2. **Empirical research:** (White & Rhodeback, 1992; Nyaw & Ng, 1994; Small, 1992; Stevens, Harris & Williamson, 1994; Hansen, 1992)
3. **Empirical research, particularly in larger organisations:** (Ulrich & Thielemann, 1993; Pratt & James, 1994; Lincoln et al., 1982).

Studies within each category have their advantages and their deficiencies. They often resemble purely theoretical studies, as if they were completely set aside from reality, and thus indicate the lack of communication between academic researchers and business practitioners. The majority of researchers in the field of business ethics concentrate on the research of ethical knowledge within large organisations, although, in business, small organisations are prevailing.

Grindle and Hilderbrand (1995) established that successful organisation in the public sector involves a strong organisational culture with quality management practitioners being employed and efficient communication nets being developed. Similarly, Hennessey (1998) determined that direction strongly influenced the productivity of organisation in the nine federal offices examined. Hennessey further emphasises the influence of management culture on the organisational culture.

In the analysis published in the Atlantic Monthly, Drucker (1994) emphasises his doubt in the unilateralism of business. He claims that ' ...in the society of organisations every new organisation engages only in its own goals and missions. It is not interested in anything else. This also means that a certain organisation is not interested in being responsible for anything. Who at all is then interested in the common well-being?' He further attempted to emphasise that social awareness does not merely offer a chance for the successful activity of the private sector, but also of the public sector.

When discussing various opinions on business ethics and the ethical behaviour of managers and workers, it is important to understand the differences in the features of both groups. Ginsberg & Buchholz (1989) performed much research in this field. Cantillon (Hayek 1985) was the first to define the term 'enterprise manager'. He characterised the manager as a rational and strong-willed person who understands the risks and hazards, and knows how to lead a company. The owner, the entrepreneur and the manager have thus become roles managed by a single person.

Chandler (1962) distinguished the managerial role from that of an entrepreneur. Hierarchy and responsibility are distinctive features of the managerial role in a modern organisation. Managers supervise finances, people, organisation, research and information. Entrepreneurs know how to work on longer terms and how to strategically set aside resources, which allows for long-term organisation activity.

Being the owner of a company, a businessman can do that. The manager, however, merely manages the company. In the organisations of the public sector, similar subcultures exist between managers and other employees. The importance of the ethical component is also stressed in the field of commercial law. In the latter, legal principles, legal norms and legislative acts are all of significant importance. In many ways, the field deals with relations between the company and other legal subjects in the ethical as well as in the mutual relations sense (Mežnar, in 2006).

Deming (2000) was the first theorist to apply the system approach to quality, setting the rudiments of organisation theory and the systemic view, which is interwoven with mutually influenced processes. In such systems, quality is the measurement of its capacity. Deming (1986) did not attribute any particular meaning to personal factors in the process of development as he believed they do not contribute to the system as such. We can thus deduce that a certain ethical praxis is determined as an outcome of activities in an organisation as a whole within the meaning of systems theory (Kljajić, 1994, Škraba et al., 2003).

In a sociological sense, the outcome is described by interactions between moral principles of the environment and the ethical component of a certain group or organisation and, at the same time, also as an outcome of the activity of that group and of the organisation in business networks. Activities are being shown as ethical codes on the level of business networks. The European Group for General Government (EGPA), a special body of the International Institute for Administrative Sciences (MIAZ), organised a special conference on December 8 2003 with the intention of treating the consequences brought about by the introduction of a new method of administration in the general government, concerning the ethics and values of the public sector.

In the conference based on the articles of desk officers from numerous states, the following conclusions were made: the values of the employees within a general government as well as their ethical and moral knowledge have a significant influence on the quality of services, on their efficiency and consequently also on the trust and satisfaction of parties and citizens. Furthermore, analogous findings were presented by the participants of the previous conference organised by EGPA on September 2–5 2009 in Malta (European Group for Public Administration).

The present research should confirm the power of legal principles in the theory of law manifested by the following three features: a) guidance and direction of everyone's act, which is an important unifying principle from within the meaning of systems theory (Kljajić, 1994; Pavčnik, 2007); b) legal principles support the interpretation of legal norms; c) the legal 'gray areas' could be avoided by a strict application of the above-mentioned legal principles.

Legal principles therefore represent norms and values being the legal guidance that directs the contextual development of legal rules and their constitution. In the present research, significant emphasis is placed on the legal norms that are embedded in the legal practice in the domain of organisations and government, and are the object of scientific systematisation in the field of legal research.

## 2. Definition of the Starting Point and Methodology of Research

The theoretical concept that was introduced as the starting point of our research represents the basis for further empirical research and analysis. Here, we have studied the influence of ethical behaviour and legal culture, which is based on the respect of general ethical, moral and legal principles, on the efficiency of public administration performance. The empirical model was formed; its structure was studied in detail, as shown in Figure 1:

*Figure 1: Expanded empirical model of research*

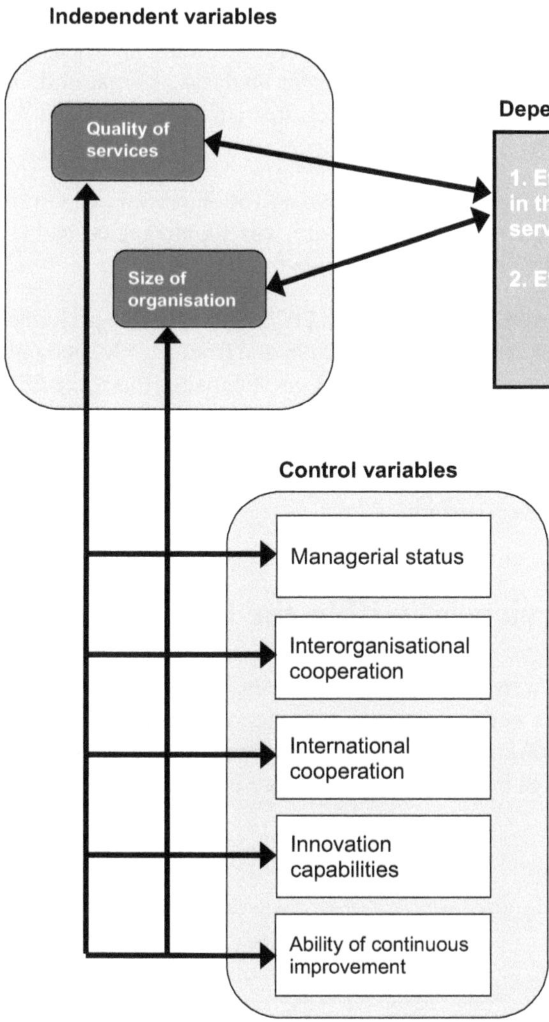


The following two categories of variables were introduced into the model as independent variables: the dimension of ethical organisational performance, and the ethical and legal culture of an organisation. We assumed that both the ethical way of doing business as well as the ethical and legal culture within an organisation influence the effectiveness of an organisation.

In order to prove the effects of ethical business and the effects of the ethical and legal culture on the efficiency of business, procedures of quantitative statistical analysis were applied. We formed a questionnaire and performed a survey within different structural types of organisations of the general government. Then, procedures of descriptive statistics, a hierarchical cluster analysis of organisational values (Ward's linkage method for hierarchical cluster analysis, and Scheffe's post-hoc test analysis) were performed.

In 2005, pilot research was carried out on a sample of 150 interviewees. On the basis of the outcome of the latter, the questionnaire was supplemented and the theoretical starting points of the research were adapted.

The research in the field of Slovenia was finished in 2006. Surveys were performed in two periods: from November 2005 to February 2006 and from March 2006 until the end of the year. The surveys were examined and questionnaires that were filled in incorrectly were eliminated from the sample. Data was then entered into the Statistica 7.1 Company Statsoft program for statistical data processing. The accuracy of data entry (double data, missing data, and partially met questionnaires) was checked and descriptive analysis of data was performed.

## 3. Sample of Interviewees within the Research

Slovenia-based organisations were engaged in the survey with cluster sampling. The number of questionnaires collected in each category is shown in Table 1. Interviewees were chosen according to the size of organisation, allowing a subsequent comparison of differences based on the knowledge of small, medium-sized and large organisations.

*Table 1: Organisations by size*

| Ref. Num. | Organisations by size | Total number of interviewees | Number of questionnaires used in the survey |
|---|---|---|---|
| 1 | Small organisations of up to 50 employees | 235 | 149 |
| 2 | Middle-sized organisations (between 51 and 300 employees) | 171 | 110 |
| 3 | Large organisations (more than 300 employees) | 212 | 164 |
| 4 | TOTAL | 618 | 425 |

Since we assumed that, along with the ethical and legal culture and in accordance with the general ethical standards, the work setting is another factor of influence, interviewees were chosen from organisations in different geographical environments as described in Table 2.

*Table 2: Organisations by geographical range*

| Ref. Num. | REGION | Total number of interviewees | Number of questionnaires used in the survey |
|---|---|---|---|
| 1 | Maribor | 180 | 129 |
| 2 | Ljubljana | 159 | 73 |
| 3 | Ptuj | 112 | 100 |
| 5 | Ajdovščina | 126 | 97 |
| 6 | Kočevje | 39 | 26 |
| 7 | TOTAL | 618 | 425 |

We assumed that ethical knowledge of managers and employees differs, since the management personnel in different levels create a certain ethical climate and organisational legal culture. In all, 144 managers of all levels and 281 employees of organisations taking part in the research were involved in the survey. The data summary is shown in Table 3.

*Table 3: Organisations by the status of interviewees*

| Ref. Num. | Organisational environment | Total number of interviewees | Number of questionnaires used in the survey |
|---|---|---|---|
| 1 | Managers | 219 | 144 |
| 2 | Employees | 401 | 281 |
| 4 | TOTAL | 618 | 425 |

# 4. Research Instruments

For the research of ethical and legal culture in relation to the activities of the studied organisations, a questionnaire with a metric chart determining the agreement of the Likert type (1967) was made and pre-tested in the pilot research. It was then updated on the basis of results of the pilot questionnaire; the following assemblies of claims were used in the later research: values of an organisation, ethical principles of operations, ethical behaviour of employees and managers in the organisation.

We measured the independent and control variables used in the questionnaire with measures shown in Table 4. Furthermore, the ethics of the business and organisational culture were measured on the level of perception of ethical behaviour with claims on the Likert-type scale ranging from 1 to 5, where 1 represents those who completely disagreed with the claim and 5 those who completely agreed with the claim.

*Table 4: Independent variables within model*

| **Independent variables** | | | |
|---|---|---|---|
| | YES | NO | |
| Management or manager position | YES | NO | |
| Size of an organisation | Up to 50 employees | Between 51 and 300 employees | More than 301 employees |
| Evaluation of the quality of services of an organisation | **Evaluation (%) from 0 to 100%** | | |

# 5. Explanation of the Results of the Empirical Analysis

## 5.1 Analysis of Values of the Employees within a Company

The ethical culture of an organisation is based upon the values that employees of an organisation believe in and value. In the first phase of the research, we analyzed the strength of certain values in the ethical model of an organisation. In this phase, we were interested in the hierarchical structure of values of all interviewees regardless of their status. The average level of agreement within the research was 3.76. The aggregated data is shown in Table 5.

*Table 5: Analysis of values in a company*

| | N | AVG | Minimum value | Maximum value | STD |
|---|---|---|---|---|---|
| affiliation | 425 | 3.92 | 1 | 5 | 0.89 |
| responsibility | **425** | **4.05** | **1** | **5** | **0.88** |
| cost of services | 424 | 3.93 | 1 | 5 | 0.81 |
| respect of the rules and agreements | **425** | **4.09** | **2** | **5** | **0.79** |
| business process ethics | **425** | **3.77** | **1** | **5** | **0.83** |
| equality | 425 | 3.44 | 1 | 5 | 1.03 |
| justice | 424 | 3.53 | 1 | 5 | 1.09 |
| progress of the employees | 424 | 3.58 | 1 | 5 | 1.01 |
| remuneration policy | 425 | 3.29 | 1 | 5 | 1.15 |
| reward according to achievement | 425 | 3.29 | 1 | 5 | 1.05 |
| attention to the values of employees | 425 | 3.43 | 1 | 5 | 1.09 |
| democracy | 424 | 3.45 | 1 | 5 | 1.05 |
| efficiency | 425 | 4.02 | 1 | 5 | 0.86 |
| effectiveness | **425** | **4.10** | **1** | **5** | **0.88** |
| economy | 424 | 3.92 | 1 | 5 | 0.95 |
| quality of services | **425** | **4.22** | **2** | **5** | **0.74** |
| managing the nature | 425 | 3.68 | 1 | 5 | 0.88 |
| environmental responsibility | **425** | **3.87** | **1** | **5** | **0.91** |
| responsibility to social justice | **425** | **3.88** | **1** | **5** | **0.83** |

Interviewees put the largest value on the quality of services; they assessed it with the highest rank, i.e., value (avg = 4.22; std: 0.74), effectiveness (avg = 4.10; std = 0.88), respect of rules and agreements (avg = 4.09; std: = 0.79) and responsibility (avg = 4.05; std = 0.88).

The hierarchy of values of the employees within our research indicates that interviewees place quality of services, successful business operations and respect of rules and agreements before all the other values. They value the ethics of business processes less (avg. = 3.77; std = 0.83), which indicates that, in the realistic environment, business ethics depend on the circumstances in which a certain organisation operates. From the hierarchy of values, it is possible to deduce that respect of rules and agreements represents an important element of ethical business and is strongly connected with the success and efficiency of business operations.

We then combined the values by means of analysis and by sorting units into groups (chandelier analysis). Our goal was to determine how the hierarchy of values supports the tree of values. In the diagram of the performed hierarchical cluster analysis of organisational values (Ward's linkage method for hierarchical cluster analysis), shown in Figure 2, we can see that values are clustered into two groups. The first and stronger cluster represents economic values. These values support the successful and efficient business operations of an organisation in a particular social environment.

The arrangement of values in this cluster supports our basic hypothesis, stating that successful business operations are connected with a responsible attitude towards social community and with ethical business. They are united into the second cluster achievement values, which are described by the equal status, justice integrity and rewarding. These values also support the idea of common good, which is based upon a fair and equal division and development, and which is a basis of ethical business in a public administration organisation.

*Figure 2: Hierarchical cluster analysis of organisational values, Ward's linkage method for hierarchical cluster analysis*

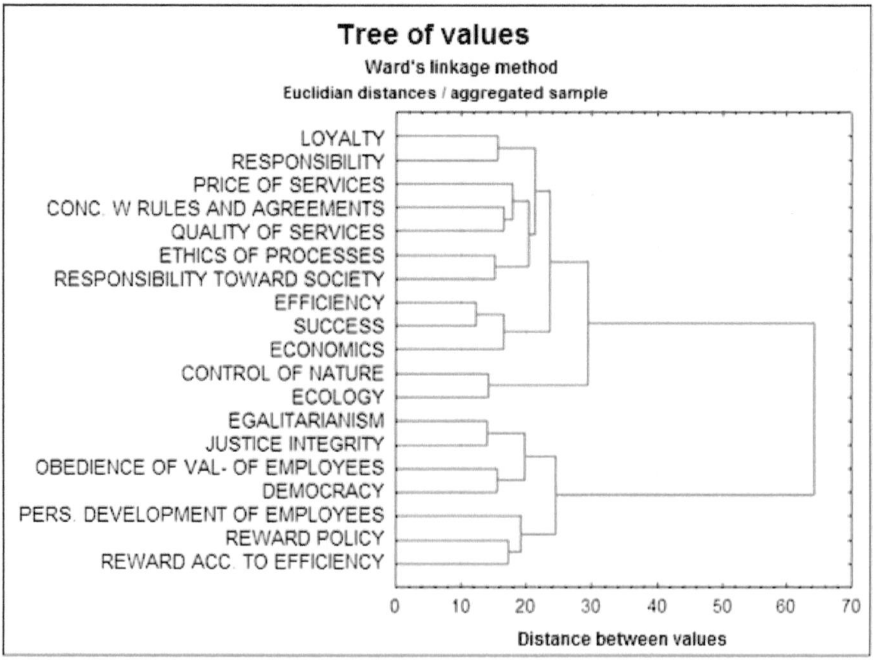

Due to its position and power in public administration, management plays a central role in the development of ethical citizen services. On account of its power, management co-creates the organisational culture and by that also the ethical culture of public administrative organisation. In order to confirm the role of management and observe the inner structure of the hierarchy of values in relation to the group status in an organisation, an ANOVA analysis of variance was performed. The difference between the value system of managers and that of the employees was analyzed in the studied companies.

*Table 6: Multivariate significance test*

| | Test | Value | F | Effect | Error | p |
|---|---|---|---|---|---|---|
| **Employees** | Wilks | 0.02 | 1074.35 | 19.00 | 400.00 | 0.00 |
| **Management** | Wilks | 0.86 | 3.50 | 19.00 | 400.00 | 0.00 |

The multivariate significance test in Table 6 indicates a statistically significant difference between the opinions of the manager group and those of the employee group in public administration.

It can be concluded that the values of managers and the values of employees differ significantly, with ANOVA $p=0.01$. Managers place the values lower than the employees. Preference is given to the economic effect; the latter is prioritised in comparison to business ethics. The result is in accordance with theoretical assumptions that the management enforces the ethical operation of business if such operation is rewarded and if the management is aware of the ethical component of business.

## 5.2 Regression Analysis of the Empirical Model

The test of regression model was performed in order to estimate the influence of innovation, ethical guidelines of business and ethical behaviour on the effectiveness of an organisation. As independent variables, the following parameters were included:

- Number of organisational improvements in the last three years in the organisation considered
- Number of procedural improvements in the last three years in the organisation considered
- Ethics of leadership (dimensions of ethical organisational culture)
- Interpersonal relationships among employees

- Customer relationships
- Public relations
- Cooperativeness bias
- Partnership bias
- Accordance with the ethics rules
- Ethical principles in an organisation
- Fulfilment of the expectations
- Realisation of the promised activities
- Fairness of procedures
- Self-criticism
- Common good

As a dependent variable, the growth of an organisation measured by the number of employees and the quality of services, products and organisational performance was considered in the model. As the categorical (mediation) variable, the organisational environment was included, in which the fact that an organisation operates in the international environment was considered. In the present study, EU institutional relations were the primary activity of the organisations, which were classified as those with intensive international activity.

*Figure 3: Structure of the regression model*

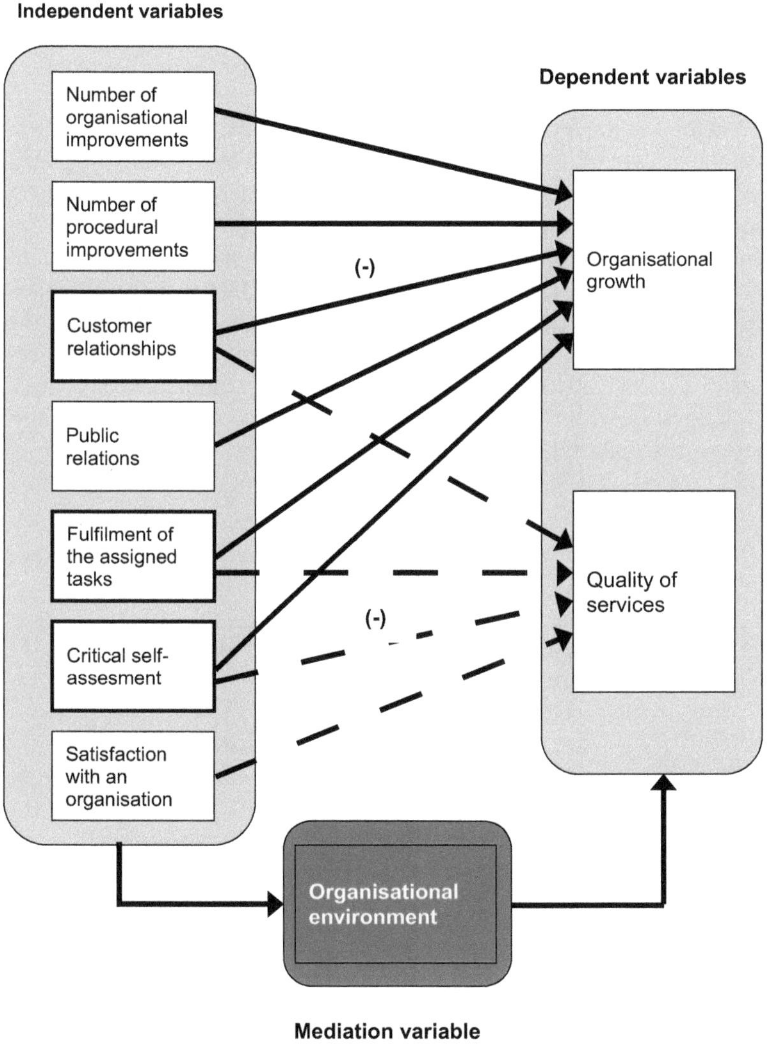


The analysis of the regression analysis showed that the number of employees and the quality of organisational performance are in a statistically significant relation with the independent variables ($R^2 = 0.20$; $F = 13.59$; $p = 0.00$) and ($R^2 = 0.19$; $F = 12.99$; $p = 0.00$).

*Table 7: Results of the regression analysis*

| Dependent variables | $R^2$ | F | p |
|---|---|---|---|
| Number of employees | 0.21 | 13.59 | 0.00 |
| Quality | 0.19 | 12.99 | 0.00 |

The growth potential of the organisation was measured by the number of employees. The potential growth of the organisation was described by the following variables: number of organisational improvements, number of procedural improvements, customer relationship, public relations, fulfilment of tasks, self-criticism of performance, and integration of the organisation into the international environment. The largest part of variance was explained by the fact that the organisation considered interacts with the international environment, public relations, the number of organisational improvements and the number of procedural improvements that are in a statistically significant relation with the number of employees. A negative relationship with the number of employees was indicated in the following variables: customer relationships, fulfilment of tasks and self-criticism of performance. These relations are also statistically significant (p=0.05).

*Table 8: Results of regression analysis of the ethics of organisational performance - partial coefficient of the size of organisation*

| Variable | Deviation | $R^2$ | β | Partial coefficient | Semi-partial coefficient | t | p |
|---|---|---|---|---|---|---|---|
| Number of organisational improvements | 0.98 | 0.02 | 0.10 | 0.11 | 0.09 | 2.62 | 0.01 |
| Number of procedural improvements | 0.98 | 0.02 | 0.12 | 0.13 | 0.12 | 3.31 | 0.00 |
| Customer relationship | 0.28 | 0.72 | -0.23 | -0.14 | -0.12 | -3.37 | 0.00 |
| Public relationship | 0.28 | 0.72 | 0.24 | 0.14 | 0.12 | 3.46 | 0.00 |
| Fulfilment of tasks | 0.36 | 0.64 | -0.14 | -0.09 | -0.08 | -2.31 | 0.02 |
| Self-criticism of performance | 0.28 | 0.72 | -0.14 | -0.09 | -0.08 | -2.12 | 0.03 |
| Integration of the organisation into the international environment | 0.94 | 0.06 | 0.27 | 0.29 | 0.27 | 7.37 | 0.00 |

A high level of ethics in the organisational performance in the international environment, an ethical attitude towards the public, obligation, innovation culture as well as continuous improvements of organisational procedures contribute to a successful organisational performance, which is, furthermore, expressed by the number of employees. An organisation is recognised as successful if the ethical attitude is expressed in the relation towards each particular public administration client, i.e., towards each citizen. The subtle recognition of clients' needs, expectations and wishes, sustainable assessment of relationship ethics and fulfilment of the assigned tasks ensure a timely and efficient support for the citizens.

On the individual level, a positive attitude towards organisational performance creates an organisational culture that both enables the personal growth of employees and the fulfilment of particular needs, expectations and wishes of an individual client, i.e., of a citizen. The performance of each organisation is embedded in particular societal group, which guarantees the common good and wealth of citizens. Unethical organisational behaviour indirectly threatens the common well-being, since it hinders the possibilities of consistent societal organisation; for example, the number of new, productive working places is lower in the case of unethical employment policies. Ethical organisations, therefore, establishes a system of control, and continuously and critically monitors its performance. Moreover, it involves a critical assessment of a wider societal group. All organisations work in a broader business environment. Therefore, ethical organisations' behaviour becomes a measure contributing to their efficiency in this environment and improving their ability of competitiveness.

*Table 9: Results of regression analysis of the ethics of organisational performance - partial coefficient of the quality of organisation*

| **Quality** | **Deviation** | **$R^2$** | **β** | **Partial coefficient** | **Semi-partial coefficient** | **t** | **p** |
|---|---|---|---|---|---|---|---|
| Customer relationship | 0.28 | 0.72 | 0.30 | 0.17 | 0.16 | 4.30 | 0.00 |
| Fulfilment of tasks | 0.36 | 0.64 | 0.11 | 0.07 | 0.07 | 1.81 | 0.07 |
| Self-criticism of performance | 0.28 | 0.72 | -0.12 | -0.07 | -0.06 | -1.71 | 0.09 |
| Satisfaction with the organisational structure | 0.40 | 0.60 | 0.17 | 0.12 | 0.10 | 2.88 | 0.00 |
| Organisational environment | 0.94 | 0.06 | 0.09 | 0.09 | 0.08 | 2.33 | 0.02 |

The success of an organisation measured by the quality of its services is statistically explained by the following variables: customer relationship, self-criticism of performance, satisfaction with the organisational structure, and organisational environment.

To a large extent, the variance can be explained with the following independent variables: customer relationship, satisfaction with the organisational structure, and the organisational environment. These are in statistically significant relation with the quality of the organisational performance.

Organisations function ethically by developing quality relations with clients, i.e., citizens. This is achieved by fairness, solid task fulfilment efficiency, and reliability of provided information about the state of procedures and services. The clients are well informed about what to expect from the organisation. A special emphasis should be placed on clients' (i.e., citizens') legal protection and consideration of their financial status.

Ethical attitudes towards clients, respect of a particular organisation and management, and ethical attitudes to partner organisations and international operations improve the quality of organisational performance as well as the reputation of an organisation. The ethics of relationships in public administration networks between government actors is the starting point for the successful performance that is expressed by the quality of organisational performance.

An organisation that is aware of its duties and obligations and operates in accordance with them strengthens the quality of its performance and successfully interacts with EU institutions.

A quality organisational performance targeted towards clients' (i.e., citizens') satisfaction can only be an ethical performance, which is characterised by an ethical relationship with clients, based on the fulfilment of tasks, critical assessment of organisational performance with regard to the societal environment and the reputation of the organisation in the eyes of employees and societal environment.

## 6. Conclusions

The research confirmed the hypothesis stating that the organisational and legal culture influences the organisational performance. The hypothesis that the ethical principles influence the organisational performance is not in a statistically significant relation with the positive organisational performance. One should take into consideration that the merely declared ethical code and law (which is not enforced) cannot influence organisational performance. The main factor that influences the organisational performance is the indicated organisational culture found in the public administration organisation. Here, legal principles are of prime importance, interrelating with the ethical principles, supporting one another.

An ethical organisational culture develops over a longer timeframe. On the short run, unethical acts and activities that are in conflict with the legal principles might contribute to the organisational performance. However, on the long run, such acts unavoidably lead to failure. The successful organisation is characterised by a stable performance, long-range planning and activities enhancing its capabilities and improving the organisational structure and quality of services. Further research should indicate how ethics influence the organisational performance regarding the respect of legal principles. The impact on the quality of organisational performance as a measure of effectiveness should also be considered via a set of key influencing factors.

The system of values of subcultures represents the main framework for the development of ethical principles and ethical behaviour in an organisation. The test of the influence of managerial and employee subcultures on ethical behaviour and principles indicates that the understanding of ethical principles of the above-mentioned subcultures differs. An ethical code is frequently the tool with which the organisations try to unify the operations. In certain operational circumstances, especially in critical circumstances, this difference becomes apparent and triggers ethical conflict between the common good and the expectations of citizens, which is of significant interest to political parties in public administration.

The value model of managers in the research significantly emphasises the respect of employees' values and democracy in the organisational processes. Both values form the base for transparent organisational processes and a fast flow of knowledge. They, furthermore, emphasise the equality of service performance, which is not constrained by cultural, regional, personal and other factors accompanying the performance of public administration organisations.

If the organisational performance was considered only on the short term and in the frame of instant success following performance of a particular task and neglecting the moral and ethical values, then such consideration would not be necessary. However, if one desires to maintain the stability of organisational performance and quality with the preserved development component, the optimal decision should necessarily consider the application of one of the legal options (having a greater support in morals and ethics). This also holds true for the aspirations to constant improvements of the organisational performance. In addition to its legal dimensions, each decision alternative also has its moral and ethical dimension.

An entirely legal decision with a smaller support in the morals and ethics will be harder to accept; this will be even harder in the case when they contradict. It is certain that a particular decision that has insufficient support in morals and ethics will be difficult to optimally realise in praxis. The decisions that have no support in morals and ethics, i.e., those contradicting ethical and moral principles, trigger questions of legitimacy of otherwise perfectly legal decisions. This raises the demand for their additional consideration and evaluation. As the final consequence, the demand for systemic changes is identified, i.e., termination, complaints and, finally, the enforcement of law, which all should significantly be improved.

The importance of the present methodological approach is further confirmed by its vision; it has to be considered that the research was started far before the global crisis has occurred (Vavtar 2009). The provided guidance was therefore available before the year 2007; however, due to the low interest of key players in the legal norms and principles research, the current situation is rather unavoidable. The present research should therefore be considered as a role research in the field of law, ethics and morale and should prepare the society for the next possible downturn.

## References

Bennet, J.C. (1946): *Christian Ethics and Social Policy,* New York: Scribner.

Bennet, J.C. et al. (1954): *Christian Values and Economic Life,* New York: Harper&Row.

Caroll, A. (1979): A Three-Dimensional Model of Corporate Performance, *Academy of Management Review* (4), 497–505.

Chandler, A. D. (1962): *Strategy and Structure: Chapters in the History of the Industrial Enterprise*, M.I.T. Press (Cambridge).

Deming, E.W. (2000): Out of the Crisis, The MIT Press.

Drucker, P. (1994): The Age of Social Transformation, *Atlantic Monthly*, November, p. 62.

Dubbink, W., Luijk H., Liederkerke, L. (2010*): European Business Ethics Cases in Context: The Morality of Corporate Decision Making (Issues in Business Ethics).* Springer.

Elm, D. R., Weber, J. (1994): Measuring Moral Judgment: The Moral Judgment Interview of the Defining Issues Test? *Journal of Business Ethics*, 13, 341–355.

European Group for Public Administration, www.iias-iisa.org/egpa/ (Accessed 17.4.2010).

Ferrell O.C., Ferrell J.F. (2009): *Business Ethics Update: Ethical Decision Making and Cases*. South-Western College Pub; 7th edition.

Ginsberg, A., Buchholz A. (1989). Are Entrepreneurs a Breed Apart? A Look at the Evidence. *Journal of General Management*. Winter 1989, pp.32–40

Grindle, M.S., Hilderbrand, M.E. (1995): Building Sustainable Capacity in the Public Sector: What Can Be Done, *Public Administration and Development* 15,441–63.

Hansen, R.S. (1992). A multidimensional scale for measuring business ethics: A purification and refinement. *Journal of Business Ethics*. Volume 11, Number 7, 523–534.

Hayek, F.A. (1985) "Richard Cantillon". *Journal of Libertarian Studies*, Fall 1985, 7(2), pp. 217–247.

Hofstede G., Hofstede, G.J., Minkov M. (2010): Cultures and Organizations: Software for the Mind, Third Edition

Igličar, A. (2004): *Sociologija prava*, Cankarjeva založba, Ljubljana.

Ivanjko, Š. (2006): Poslovna etika v gospodarstvu, *Podjetje in delo*, 32, 1154–1167.

Kljajić M., (1994): Teorija sistemov, *Moderna organizacija*, Kranj, Slovenia.

Lincoln D.J., Pressley, M.M., Little T. (1982) Ethical beliefs and personal values of top level executives. *Journal of Business Research*. Volume 10, Issue 4. pp 475–487.

Marquis, C.W., Cater, D. (1954): Ethics in a Business Society. New York: Harper & Brothers.

Mežnar, D. (2006): Podjetniško pravo: pravna ureditev organiziranja in opravljanja podjetništva, *Moderna organizacija*, Kranj: Slovenia.

Newton, L. Englehardt, E., Pritchard, M. (2009): *Taking Sides: Clashing Views in Business Ethics and Society*, McGraw-Hill/Dushkin

Nyaw, M.K, Ng I. (1994). A comparative analysis of ethical beliefs: A four country study. Journal of Business Ethics. Volume 13, Number 7, 543–555.

Pavčnik, M. (1997): Teorija prava, Cankarjeva založba, Ljubljana.

Pratt, C.B., James E.L. (1994). Advertising ethics: A contextual response based on classical ethical theory. *Journal of Business Ethics*. Volume 13, Number 6, 455–468.

Reilly, B. J. (1994): Meta-Ethical Reasoning: Applied to Economics and Business Principles, *American Journal of Economics and Sociology*, 53 (2), 147–162.

Škraba, A., Kljajić, M., Leskovar, R. (2003): Group exploration of system dynamics models – is there a place for a feedback loop in the decision process? *System Dynamics Review*, 19(3), pp. 243–263

Small, M.W. (1992) Attitudes towards business ethics held by Western Australian students: A comparative study. *Journal of Business Ethics*. Volume 11, Number 10, 745–752.

Stevens, R. E., Harris, 0. J. & Williamson, S. (1994): A Compariosn of Ethical Evaluations of Business School Faculty and Students: A Pilot Study. *Journal of Business Ethics*, 12, 611–619.

Stevens, R. E., Harris, O.J., Williamson, S. (1994): A Comparison of Ethical Evaluations of Business School Faculty and Students: A Pilot Study, *Journal of Business Ethics*, 12, 611–619.

Ulrich, P., Thielemann, U. (1993): How do Managers Think about Market Economies and Morality? Empirical Enquiries into Business-Ethical Thinking Patterns, *Journal of Business Ethics*, 12, 879–898.

Ulrich, P., Thielemann, U. (1993): How do Managers Think about Market Economies and Morality? Empirical Enquiries into Business-Ethical Thinking Patterns. *Journal of Business Ethics*, 12, 879-898.

Vavtar B. (2009): *Pravna načela in poslovna etika kot dejavnika uspešnosti poslovanja podjetja* : doktorska disertacija, Ljubljana.

Verschoor, C. (2002): It isn't enough to just have a code of ethics, *Strategic Finance*, 84 (6), 22.

Vitell, S.J., Hidalgo, E. R. (2006): The Impact of Corporate Ethical values and Enforcement of Ethical Codes on the Perceived Importance of Ethics in Business: A Comparison of US and Spanish Managers, *Journal of Business Ethics*, 64 (1), 31–43.

Vitell, S. J., Nwachukwu, S. L., Barnes, J. H. (1993): The Effects of Culture on Ethical Decision-Making: An Application of Hofstede's Typology. *Journal of Business Ethics* , 12, 753-760.

White, L.P, Rhodeback M.J. (1992): Ethical dilemmas in organization development: a cross-cultural analysis. *Journal of Business Ethics*, 11(9), 663–70.

## About the Author

**Bojan Vavtar** holds a PhD in Law from the University of Ljubljana. He has published several papers in the field of law, legislation and control in government administration of the Republic of Slovenia. He is a former Chief of the Slovene Security Intelligence Department at the Slovene Ministry of Defence.

# The Challenges of Human Resource Management in Reducing Youth Unemployment

***Mojca Bernik***

*mojca.bernik@fov.uni-mb.si*

***Katjuša Golmajer***

*katjusa.golmajer@rzisnik-perc.si*

## Abstract

Research on the challenges of human resource management in reducing youth unemployment is presented. The field research has been conducted by the means of online survey in Gorenjska region of Slovenia. The survey was carried out in 78 sole proprietor (SP) and limited liability companies (LLC). The results show that correlations between the competences of the young population and legal forms of organisation (SP, LLC) and between the legal form of organisations and staffing methods exist, but they do not exist between the number of first-time employees in a company and a view on student employment.

**Keywords:** youth unemployment, labour market, human resource management

## 1. Introduction

Due to the extension of employed persons' employment period and the ageing of the population in Slovenia, the unemployment of young people who have completed schooling is on the rise. School systems do not enable young people to acquire relevant experience during the course of their studies that they could use as references when seeking employment. For this reason, young people often have difficulties finding employment, which means there is a great deal of unused intellectual capital in Slovenia, with people going abroad or stagnating in their field, having no opportunities to apply and develop the knowledge acquired during their education.

Options for youth unemployment management by companies and ways of linking human resources functions and young job seekers in the labour market in the framework of research conducted in the Gorenjska region of Slovenia are described.

## 2. Labour Market and Unemployment

We encounter the supply and demand of labour in the labour market, where demand is represented by people seeking work and supply by employers. The perfect balance and so-called full employment occur only rarely. However, a view of the real market reveals that full unemployment also does not exist. This is why we will examine both sides of the labour market in theory.

- **Labour demand**

As stated by Samuelson and Nordhaus (2002), there is a link between the quantity of labour and the quantity of manufactured goods in a given time and with given technologies. However, with regard to this we must also be familiar with what a marginal value product is. If the persons responsible in a company wonder whether it is sensible to employ additional labour, they must take into consideration the criterion of marginal product of labour, in which it is considered that employment of such a unit is sensible if additional labour generates a profit that is higher than the costs of this unit (Prašnikar, 1999).

It is also considered that marginal productivity will increase if workers will have better goods at their disposal, with which they will work. Therefore, with better goods one additional worker may bring in more profit for the company than was the case before. Thus, educated workers with more knowledge should also bring more to the company. Without knowledge, today's technology would not exist. Recently, knowledge has been accumulating to a great extent and has had tremendous value as a marginal product. A good example of the cumulativeness and contribution of one additional product to the already acquired knowledge is information technology, which is developing very rapidly.

In contrast, the quality of labour is also increasing. Years of schooling, education and accumulating knowledge have fostered development almost everywhere. Over the years, literacy, education and qualifications have increased

In the Norway in 1998/99, 29,422 students completed their graduate study, but in the year 2008/09 the number of graduated students was higher: 34,119 (Statistics Norway, 2010). In Canada, the percentage of individuals with university degrees rose from 11% in 1990 to 19% in 2007(Human Resources and Skills Development Canada, 2010).

The share of those who enrol in tertiary education is also greatly increasing in Slovenia. Lukič (2008) states that while 38,151 students enrolled in tertiary education in 1991, the number grew to 115,944 students in 2006, which amounts to 48.2% of Slovene population between the ages of 19 and 23.

Labour supply depends on the number of working hours the population (labour force) wishes to carry out in gainful activities. There are three key elements of labour supply: hours per worker, labour force participation and immigration.

The concept of working hours includes the amount of effective working time with a break for lunch. Full-time working time must not be longer than 40 hours per week or shorter than 36 hours per week, on the assumption that the working day cannot be longer than 10 hours (Mežnar, 2004).

In Slovenia, we have noticed a trend of young people often choosing to continue their studies at university to obtain a higher level of education and thus better employment possibilities. In spite of their perception, this is not so; this is indicated by data on unemployment of people with higher education. In December 2008, the share of unemployed persons with higher education amounted to 9.3% (4,508), while in June 2009 it was already 10.5% (9,351), which means that the number of people with higher education doubled in six months (Miloševič, 2010). The majority of young people are not aware that this decreases the number of working hours in their lives; deciding for early retirement or merely partial employment has the same effect (Samuelson, Nordhaus, 2002). From a global standpoint, this could lead to so-called overeducation, which is increasing in Europe and has a sort of an opposite effect as young people with higher education who have never been exposed to the labour market have even more difficulties finding employment due to lack of experience (Lukič, 2008).

By increasing salaries, the quantity of labour usually increases, but only to a certain point; later, the situation reverses. People makes decisions about their time and organise it into time for work and free time. If they are offered a higher salary, they are tempted to work more as every hour of work is paid better; however, at the same time, every hour of free time becomes more expensive. This refers to the so-called opportunity costs or the costs of an alternative foregone. At a certain point, the income effect occurs. The income effect dictates that by increasing the salary, we also increase our income. With a higher income, the employee wants to buy more goods and free time. What will prevail depends on the individual: the motives for money or for free time; however, at a certain point, free time becomes priceless for everyone (Samuelson, Nordhaus, 2002).

Over the years, groups in the labour force change. The number of women actively seeking work has increased in recent decades (Samuelson, Nordhaus, 2002). In contrast, an increasing number of young people with higher education seeking first employment have been observed (Verša, 2004).

The third factor mentioned by Samuelson and Nordhaus (2002) is immigration. There is a great deal of immigration of citizens of the former Yugoslavia and some from the EU to Slovenia. Work permits for workers from countries that are not members of the EU are issued by the Employment Service of Slovenia, whereas the quota of these work permits is determined by the Government of the Republic of Slovenia.

- **Unemployment**

If perfect competition with many workers and many employers (where none of them could influence salaries) existed in the labour market, there would be full employment; which would mean that supply and demand would be equal. At such prices or salaries, employers are willing to employ everyone qualified for the work and prepared to work for such salary (Belčič, 2002). In such cases, everyone who wishes to work for such a salary is employed. In contrast, everyone who does not wish to work for the given market price (salary) and prefers to stay at home, in school, travel etc. is voluntarily unemployed. The so-called frictional unemployment and first-time job-seekers must also be added to this kind of unemployed persons.

Involuntary unemployment, which is the sort most commonly discussed, has also been observed as taking place in the market. Its occurrence can be logically explained. The labour market is slow, inflexible and reacts to changes in the environment slowly, which is why certain prices (salaries), which have been established, are in effect in the market. These are usually also influenced by trade union negotiations, which set the salaries during negotiations a little higher than they would in conditions of perfect competition, as well as for a period of several years. A logical consequence is that some who would be voluntarily unemployed in conditions of trade competition wish to work. However, at such prices (salaries), employers are willing to employ fewer people. Therefore, some who wish to work still gain employment and even receive a higher salary than in conditions of perfect competition; nevertheless, some who wish to work do not find employment. In such cases, we talk about the so-called involuntary unemployment (Belčič, 2002).

The labour market does not react to influences from the environment in the short term; consequently, salaries also do not change from one minute to the other, as is typical for auction markets, but operate in a more rigid manner. In the long term, the labour market must react to changes; for this reason, significant occurrences of unemployment disappear as salaries are adjusted to market conditions. Such adjustments can go on for several years and thus periods of significant unemployment can last for longer periods of time (Samuelson, Nordhaus, 2002).

A survey on the structure of young unemployed persons was carried out in Slovenia in 2006 (Trbanc, 2007); it shows that the level of education of young people who are employed is higher than the level of education of unemployed young people. It is also evident from the results of the survey that as many as 96% unemployed young people seek full-time employment, while a majority would also accept part-time employment (82.2% aged 15–19, 88.4% aged 20–24 and 70% aged 25–29).

# 3. Human resources Function and Employment of Young People

Companies, with their human resources function, are one of the important factors in the labour market and can increase or decrease unemployment. Companies increasingly depend on the people employed by them; organisations that do not have the right people on the right position and the right time quickly go bankrupt in today's market. The globalisation of markets and the free movement of people, goods and services inside the EU have forced organisations to adjust rapidly and consequently have caused a greater flexibility of the human resources function. Nonetheless, as it is bound by regulations, an organisation cannot completely freely employ or dismiss people.

It is important to be aware that people bring competitive advantage to the market. The causes for the failure of a company are often found in incompetent management, poor organisation, low levels of knowledge and a lack of work experience. Consequently, the task of human resources management is to motivate employees for training, to enable additional work experience for them and, most significantly, to include employees in the reorganisation of the company.

Before a company opens and makes public a position of employment, it is naturally necessary to do much more. A plan of employees, based on the general company management plan and also refers to other plans (e.g., sales plan, procurement plan, financial plan etc.), is drawn up in the company. It is important to make a plan of employees as it helps predict the number of employees for a certain time period, while at the same time informing management of the critical analysis of existing employee structure. In addition, an employee plan enables the human resources function to monitor and improve the structure of employees employed in the company. The plan is also a starting point for drawing up a plan of education and promotion of employees within the company (Florjančič et al., 1999).

There are quite a few regulations with regard to employee planning, which must be complied with by an organisation. Employee planning must be in accordance with the constitution and laws in force in the country. Workers also have the right to participate in organisation with regard to co-management as well as the right to organise themselves in trade unions (Florjančič et al., 1999). The Slovene constitution guarantees freedom of work and everyone can choose his employment freely. In particular, there should be no discrimination, which is stipulated by the constitution, as every position of employment is available to everyone under equal conditions (Mežnar, 2004). Notwithstanding, migrants seeking employment in the developed world are faced with numerous discriminatory actions in employment (Moraes, 2006).

A company that recruits employees in a planned and premeditated manner can decrease unemployment. Florjančič et al. (1999) define recruitment of employees as:

> "...formation of a group of candidates, in which we find the most appropriate person for a particular position of employment. Recruitment of employees is a process of seeking new staff, choosing and integration into the organisation."

We must be aware of the fact that companies employ people on the basis of their employment needs in the future as well as the existing employee structure (Florjančič et al., 1999). Companies may recruit employees from internal or external sources; both options have advantages and disadvantages.

The advantage of internal recruitment is the selection of a person whose competences for the position of employment are already well known. The employee is familiar with the company's operations, knows its advantages and shortcomings. Therefore, the time needed for training and integration is shorter. Apart from reducing costs of advertising the vacant position, internal recruitment also offers the chance of building a career in the company. It represents a tool for increasing the employee's commitment toward the company while simultaneously enabling the company to keep its key employees within the company.

However, this kind of recruitment also has shortcomings, which are demonstrated primarily in the small number of appropriate employees. The labour market offers candidates with different knowledge and skills, who can be more experienced and are not unilaterally tied to the company's problems, which means that they have a comprehensive view – from different standpoints – of tackling the problems. At the same time, they are not burdened with personal relationships and relations between employees in the company, which enables them to focus primarily on tackling the problems and developing their creativity (Agarwal, 2008).

This chapter examines the issue of young people aged 30 and less with the first and second stage of tertiary education, who generally still have no experience and are not employed, which means they are at the disposal of companies only when these recruit employees from external sources. Companies employ persons from external sources predominantly when they are faced with a shortage of employees within the company. External candidates represent a potential source of new ideas and richer experience for the company and, as candidates coming from the outside, they often know the company's competition well and the company can take advantage of this and increase its competitive advantage. Therefore, in most cases, companies make use of employee recruitment from external sources primarily for management positions, where it is necessary to determine the development strategy of the company's operations, and thus surpass their competition (Novak, 2008).

Prior to inviting the candidates to an interview, the descriptive characteristics a candidate should have for a particular position must be defined. We must be aware that some characteristics are absolutely necessary for the performance of particular work, whereas others are only desirable. On the basis of these characteristics and definitions, we can also draw up support for decision-making in expert systems such as Dexi (Bernik et al., 1999). A personal and professional profile, containing information on qualifications, work experience and personal data is defined. The latter include appearance, intelligence, interests, inclinations, social status, individual's natural talents, motivation, adaptability and individual's compliance. However, decisions should not be made solely based on these data, which could be the basis for discrimination and with which we would consequently breach regulations. In addition to all these data, employers are usually interested in the place of residence, prior employment, different references and other information (Florjančič et al., 1999).

Where, when and how the candidates will be invited to the vacant position of employment depends on the position of employment, costs, time frame available etc. It is important to be aware that a vacant employment position must be advertised in media if it refers to a management body (Mežnar, 2004). We must also pay attention to the definition and duration of the employment relationship. It is also desirable to indicate basic information that we wish to obtain from the candidates upon their application and in their professional curriculum vitae (education, qualifications, work experience etc.). This is an attempt to influence the candidate to start developing the following mental processes: attention (awareness), interest, desire, action – the AIDA model (Florjančič et al., 1999).

The labour market is demanding, as work supply and demand are never completely balanced. Consequently, various groups face unemployment. The Employment Service of Slovenia offers assistance to first-time job seekers at all regional units, while a national active employment policy programme also aims at helping young, difficult-to-employ and older persons to find employment.

Currently, many companies are dealing with a lack of orders and funds, and insolvency. Human resource functions in different companies tackle human resource planning and selection among those available on the labour market. Globalisation has resulted in seeking suitable staff across borders, thus bringing new methods and tools of human resource management to the fore (Kim et al., 2003). This requires a new approach to managing the classic human resource function, which no longer implements traditional staffing procedures (Florjančič et al., 2004) but also faces various international pressures (Farndale et al., 2010). As modern human resource functions are now concerned with global human resource management and seeking the most suitable candidates for vacancies on a daily basis, they face two crucial challenges: global competitiveness and new forms of international migration (Farndale et al., 2010). According to ILO data (ILO, 2008), migration of highly educated and professionally trained persons is most common in European and North American countries and less so in the rest of the world. Nevertheless, studies show (Syed, 2008) that the human resources function discriminates against foreigners in the employment process on the basis of their social and cultural habits. In the last 50 years, as a rule, more people immigrated to Slovenia per year than emigrated from it. In 2009, the share of foreign nationals in the total population of Slovenia was 3.9% (SURS, 2010).

The human resource function thus faces new ways of finding the most suitable candidates for vacancies as well as new methods and techniques of defining the competences required for specific posts. Generally, young people seeking first employment after graduation do not have suitable work experience, but do have various competences that may be advantageous in comparison with other candidates.

# 4. Research

Our study addressed unemployment among young graduates (up to 30 years of age with completed undergraduate or graduate education), the labour market and solving the unemployment issue with the help of the human resource function.

The human resource function involves tasks such as establishing contact with employees on the labour market and ensuring the appropriate staff required for a job vacancy at a company as quickly as possible and with minimal costs. Considering that in Slovenia companies embark on a search for prospective staff in their own particular ways, we have made use of thi“as research in order to determine which method of employment seeking seems to be optimal for the young population seeking first employment and what are the preferable competences of young candidates when deciding upon the most adequate applicant for a vacant post.

The research also enquired about the type of staff the employers most prefer, whether these are young and educated people, or whether their decision is based primarily on this individual employee. Seeing that there exist several staffing methods for a vacant post, we have tried to determine which is the most preferable to young graduates.

W“e have also examined companies’ views on student employment. The aim of the research was also to find out whether there is any correlation between the number of first-time employees and student employment.

## 4.1 Hypothesis

We have proposed the following hypotheses:

*H1: Claims about competences show the same average estimates irrespective of the two most frequent legal forms of organisation (SP and LLC).*

The 1st hypothesis (H1) postulates that irrespective of the two most frequent legal forms of organisation we focus on, the overall view on competence of the young population remains the same. Seeing that the target group represents a part of the labour market, there should not be statistically important deviations among the average estimates of individual claims regardless of whose statement is to be considered. The sole proprietor (SP) is not in fact to be taken as a business entity, but rather as a person; however, since this type of business often occurs at the market and recruits a considerable amount of staff on the labour market, it had to be included as a part of the issue on legal forms of organisation.

*H2: Legal form of organisation and staffing methods are dependent variables.*

The 2nd hypothesis (H2) tackles the research concerning the influence of the legal form of organisation on staffing methods. We expected to reject H2, realising that the particular legal forms of organisation usually entail the costs intended for staff recruitment. More importantly though, the larger the company, the more carefully conducted the human resource function tends to be. The human resource function in micro and small businesses is often handled by the director of a company.

*H3: Correlation between the number of first-time employees in a company and a view on student employment exists.*

The 3rd hypothesis (H3) shows the existence of correlation between the number of first-time employees in a company and a general opinion on student employment. The companies employing young people and offering them their first job often acknowledge experience gained through student employment brokerage services. This type of mediated work enables them to handle work assignments in the working environment and is often not very different from the work performed by regular employees.

## 4.2 Instrument

We tested the hypotheses through an e-questionnaire in an online survey. The questionnaire was of the closed type, comprised of 31 questions relating to:

- data on the company (community, number of employees, number of first employment employees, public or private sector, legal form of organisation)
- factors relating to the competences of young educational job seekers
- factors relating to different ways of searching new employees
- factors relating to the company's opinion on student employment

In connection with the competences of young educational job seekers, the following statements were offered:
S1 – Young people are adaptable
S2 – Young people are inventive

S3 – Young people are open to enter additional educational courses
S4 – Young people can transcend geographical limitations
S5 – Young people are prepared to move in pursuit of a job
S6 – Young people show considerable work potential
S7 – Young people have experienceS8 – Young people are independent
S9 – Young people are responsible
S10 – Young people are organised
S11 – Young people form a vast social network

In connection with the different ways of searching for new employees, the following factors were offered:
S1 – The ESS board
S2 – Daily newspapers
S3 – Company's website
S4 – Employment advertising websites
S5 – Recruitment agencies
S6 – Students employed in a company
S7 – Head hunting
S8 – Employee recommendations
S9 – Inclusion in APE
S10 – Recruitment from schools
S11 – Offering scholarships

With regard to companies' opinion on student employment, the following statements were offered:
S1 – All work is experience accumulation
S2 – Student employment is similar to a company's open position
S3 – Student employment is similar to courses studied
S4 – Student employment is not to be considered

## 4.3 Sample

The field research was conducted by the means of online survey in May 2009 in Gorenjska region of Slovenia. With the help of the two recruitment agencies, an email was sent to all of the Gorenjska companies in the initial random sample, irrespective of their size. Seventy-eight surveys proved to be useful (from 112). Verification of questionnaire reliability was made with a reliability test and item-total statistics.

We consider the criteria that define whether the scale is reliable when the variables have strong correlation (between 0.7 and 1.0), medium correlation (between 0.5 and 0.7) and weak correlation (between 0.3 and 0.5). In our case, the Cronbach alpha coefficient was estimated at 0.74, which indicates a strong reliability of measurement. According to the composition and characteristics of the sample, it is representative.

## 4.4 Methodology

In the research, we used a descriptive method to examine the facts and processes described in different references in the field of human resource management and youth unemployment.

With the compilation method, we summarised some thoughts, views and results of other authors' research papers.

The research data was analysed with different statistical methods:

- Independent T-test – we verified the average estimation of individual statements in one group with the same statement in another group
- Pearson's correlation coefficient – showing what kind of connection is between two parameters

We used the statistical tool SPSS[1] for to analyse the gathered data and to confirm or to reject defined hypothesis.

## 4.5 Result Analysis

The questionnaire survey data enabled us to confirm or reject the following hypotheses:

*H1: Claims about competences shows the same average estimates irrespective of the two most frequent legal forms of organisation (SP and LLC).*

Table 1 shows that all the views on the competences of young persons support the first hypothesis (H1); we can accept it as plausible. Thus, this points to the fact that the claims about competence show the same average estimates irrespective of the most frequent legal forms of organisation (SP and LLC).

1 www.spss.com; Statistical Package for Social Sciences

*Table 1: The average estimates of individual competence items according to legal form of organisation*

| | | Sig. | Sig. (2-tailed) | Mean Difference | Std. Error Difference |
|---|---|---|---|---|---|
| Young people are adaptable | Equal variances assumed | .315 | .876 | -.037 | .233 |
| | Equal variances not assumed | | .863 | -.037 | .211 |
| Young people are inventive | Equal variances assumed | .792 | .824 | -.036 | .160 |
| | Equal variances not assumed | | .832 | -.036 | .167 |
| Young people are open to enter additional educational courses | Equal variances assumed | .190 | .377 | -.157 | .177 |
| | Equal variances not assumed | | .411 | -.157 | .189 |
| Young people can transcend geographical limitations | Equal variances assumed | .232 | .355 | -.211 | .226 |
| | Equal variances not assumed | | .405 | -.211 | .250 |
| Young people are prepared to move in pursuit of a job | Equal variances assumed | .319 | .829 | .049 | .224 |
| | Equal variances not assumed | | .826 | .049 | .220 |
| Young people show a considerable work potential | Equal variances assumed | .512 | .481 | .175 | .246 |
| | Equal variances not assumed | | .456 | .175 | .232 |
| Young people have experience | Equal variances assumed | .403 | .803 | .057 | .228 |
| | Equal variances not assumed | | .810 | .057 | .236 |
| Young people are independent | Equal variances assumed | .009 | .544 | .110 | .179 |
| | Equal variances not assumed | | .461 | .110 | .148 |

| | | | | | |
|---|---|---|---|---|---|
| Young people are responsible | Equal variances assumed | .381 | .529 | -.133 | .211 |
| | Equal variances not assumed | | .538 | -.133 | .214 |
| Young people are organised | Equal variances assumed | .388 | .829 | -.050 | .230 |
| | Equal variances not assumed | | .819 | -.050 | .218 |
| Young people form a vast social network | Equal variances assumed | .747 | .679 | -.101 | .244 |
| | Equal variances not assumed | | .661 | -.101 | .230 |

*H2: Legal form of organisation and staffing methods are dependent variables.*

Table 2 indicates that all the staffing methods items and the legal form of organisation are dependent variables (except for two variables). According to these results, we can accept H2 as plausible.

*Table 2: The interdependence between the staffing methods and company's legal form of organisation*

| Staffing methods | | Value | Df | Asymp. Sig. (2-sided) |
|---|---|---|---|---|
| The ESS board | Pearson Chi-Square | 3.172(a) | 4 | .529 |
| | Likelihood Ratio | 3.509 | 4 | .476 |
| | Linear-by-Linear Association | .583 | 1 | .445 |
| | N of Valid Cases | 61 | | |
| Daily newspapers | Pearson Chi-Square | 1.943(a) | 4 | .746 |
| | Likelihood Ratio | 2.008 | 4 | .734 |
| | Linear-by-Linear Association | .443 | 1 | .506 |
| | N of Valid Cases | 62 | | |
| Company's website | Pearson Chi-Square | 1.519(a) | 4 | .823 |
| | Likelihood Ratio | 1.583 | 4 | .812 |
| | Linear-by-Linear Association | .991 | 1 | .320 |
| | N of Valid Cases | 60 | | |

| | | | | |
|---|---|---|---|---|
| Employment advertising websites | Pearson Chi-Square<br>Likelihood Ratio<br>Linear-by-Linear Association<br>N of Valid Cases | 3.787(a)<br>4.003<br>.161<br>61 | 4<br>4<br>1 | .436<br>.406<br>.689 |
| Recruitment agencies | Pearson Chi-Square<br>Likelihood Ratio<br>Linear-by-Linear Association<br>N of Valid Cases | 4.145(a)<br>6.298<br>.971<br>60 | 4<br>4<br>1 | .246<br>.098<br>.324 |
| Students employed in a company | Pearson Chi-Square<br>Likelihood Ratio<br>Linear-by-Linear Association<br>N of Valid Cases | 13.487(a)<br>15.129<br>1.690<br>68 | 16<br>16<br>1 | .637<br>.515<br>.194 |
| Head hunting | Pearson Chi-Square<br>Likelihood Ratio<br>Linear-by-Linear Association<br>N of Valid Cases | 2.146(a)<br>3.336<br>.833<br>57 | 2<br>2<br>1 | .342<br>.189<br>.361 |
| Employee recommendations | Pearson Chi-Square<br>Likelihood Ratio<br>Linear-by-Linear Association<br>N of Valid Cases | 5.317(a)<br>5.317<br>.029<br>61 | 4<br>4<br>1 | .256<br>.256<br>.865 |
| Inclusion in APE | Pearson Chi-Square<br>Likelihood Ratio<br>Linear-by-Linear Association<br>N of Valid Cases | 1.821(a)<br>2.403<br>.443<br>61 | 4<br>4<br>1 | .769<br>.662<br>.506 |
| Recruitment from schools | Pearson Chi-Square<br>Likelihood Ratio<br>Linear-by-Linear Association<br>N of Valid Cases | 1.016(a)<br>1.335<br>.015<br>61 | 3<br>3<br>1 | .797<br>.721<br>.901 |
| Offering scholarships | Pearson Chi-Square<br>Likelihood Ratio<br>Linear-by-Linear Association<br>N of Valid Cases | .973(a)<br>1.286<br>.805<br>61 | 4<br>4<br>1 | .914<br>.864<br>.369 |

*H3: Correlation between the number of first-time employees in a company and a view on student employment exists.*

Table 3 proves that H3 is not plausible, seeing that there is no correlation between the number of first-time employees in a company and the general view of student work. This is an unexpected result considering we have presumed that those who have more first-time employees are more likely to benefit from experience gained through the student employment brokerage service.

*Table 3: The correlation between first-time employees in a company and student employment*

| | | The number of first-time employees | Student employment |
|---|---|---|---|
| The number of first-time employees | Pearson Correlation | 1 | -.111 |
| | Sig.(2-tailed) | | .344 |
| | N | 75 | 75 |
| Student employment | Pearson Correlation | -.111 | 1 |
| | Sig.(2-tailed) | .344 | |
| | N | 75 | 78 |

# 5. Conclusion

There is much debate over uniting the school system with the economy, which consequently leads to uniting the academic sector with the private sector. However, in practice, most students become aware this is not in fact the case. Employers do not approach those students who stand out during their schooling. This has also been indicated by our research, which proves that the employers only rarely carry out recruitment directly from schools (e.g., monitoring the most prominent students). On account of the best students not having advantages at the labour market, they therefore see no point in struggling to obtain high marks in exams. Students enrolled in academic study programme, with few exceptions, are not required to do mandatory practical training. This makes it difficult for them to establish a connection between theory and the actual state of affairs or to relate to a concrete example, which often results in them experiencing an inability to grow in their knowledge; consequently, graduates can no longer cope with a given situation. The young generation should be better informed of current economic issues during the course of their formal education, something the current school system does not provide.

Young graduates have little knowledge about the possibility of self-employment. Only a small number of young entrepreneurs can be found in Slovenia. They come up with fresh ideas, but sometimes do not know how to or are not bold enough to put them into effect. The idea of setting up one's own private business or becoming self-employed does not appeal to young people on the grounds that it is too time-consuming and involves too much paperwork. This often prompts them to quit even before they have got started. As it is evident from the survey, they seek employment with employers who hold no particular positive or negative opinion of their generation. They are undoubtedly the prospective labour force; however, many employers see them as mere expense and a waste of time. Although gaining work experience through a student employment brokerage service is generally well-accepted, as the majority put much emphasis on this line of work. It seems that the students are quite oblivious as to really making use of their experience.

The European labour market represents a major opportunity for the young people, if they are prepared to move somewhere else in pursuit of a particular job. However, we have noticed that the vicinity of the university is an important criterion when enrolling at it. It is true that young people depend more on their parents; however, nothing seems to change even after a few years of schooling. Europe is witnessing a common practice of young people, who otherwise have a degree and a job, to continue living with their parents. Needless to say, buying a flat or paying rent poses a considerable financial pressure for the young generation: so much so that they are reluctant to show any real self-initiative and start their own business or move somewhere further away in search of better working conditions and a higher salary.

It would certainly be challenging if, sometime in the near future, we were to undertake research on the young population's view of their competences, work experience through the student employment brokerage services and whether they only strive to attain a particular level of education or are interested in the process of obtaining education as well (e.g., average assessment mark, the time needed to finish a study programme etc.). Due to time limitations and lack of funds, we have not decided to conduct such research. The latter would, however, be particularly efficient in explaining some labour market responses, but this is currently impossible due to the one-sided nature of the results obtained.

## References


Agarwal, A. (2008), *Internal Recruitment – Advantages and Disadvantages Explained*

http://ezinearticles.com/?Internal-Recruitment---Advantages-And-Disadvantages-Explained&id=1663907 (Accessed 12 January 2010)

Belčič, F. (2002) *Proces zaposlovanja kadrov*, Založba Moderna organizacija, Kranj

Bernik M., Rajkovič V., Florjančič M. (1999) *Teaching team-work organization by knowledge based decision aid*, Strategic management and its support byinformation systems, ed. Jindřich Kaluža, Technical University of Ostrava, Faculty of Economics,pp. 114–119

Farndale E., Paauwe J., Morris S. S., Stahl G. K., Stiles P., Trevor J. (2010) Context – bound configurations of corporate HR functions in multinational corporations around the globe, *Human Resource Management*, no.49 (1)

Farndale E., Scullion H., Sparrow (2010) The Role of the corporate HR function in global talent management, *Journal of World Business*, no. 45, pp. 161–168

Florjančič J., Bernik M., Novak V. (2004) *Kadrovski management*, Založba Moderna organizacija

Florjančič J., Ferjan, M., Bernik, M. (1999) *Planiranje in razvoj kadrov*, Založba Moderna organizacija v okviru FOV, Kranj

*Human Resources and Skills Development Canada* (2010), http://www4.hrsdc.gc.ca/.3ndic.1t.4r@-eng.jsp?iid=29#M_1 (Accessed 12 January 2010)

ILO (2008), *Youth Employment Programme,* http://www.ilocarib.org.tt/portal/index.php?option=com_content&task=view&id=1166&Itemid=1272 (Accessed 12 January 2010)

Kim K., Park J. H. & Prescott J. E. (2003) The global integration of business functions: A study of multinational businesses in integrated global industries, *Journal of International Business Studies* no. 34, pp. 327–344

Lukič, G. (2008) *Strategija zaposlovanja mladih v družbi znanja*, Analiza stanja, Študentska organizacija Slovenije, Ljubljana

Mežnar D. (2004) *Delovno pravo s temeljnimi pravnimi pojmi*, Založba Moderna organizacija s okviru FOV, Kranj

Miloševič V. (2010) Kako bo trg dela reševal prihod mladih s fakultet, *HRM strokovna revija za ravnanje z ljudmi pri delu*, št.33, str. 12–15

Moraes C. (2006) Challenges for anti-discrimination law and policy for the 2007 year of equal opportunities, *European Anti-Discrimination Law Review*, no.4, pp. 31–35

Novak V. (2008) *Kadrovanje*, Založba Moderna organizacija, Kranj

Prašnikar J. (1999) Poglavje o temi trga proizvodnih dejavnikov, Uvod v mikroekonomijo - izbrana poglavja, strani 233–249, *Gospodarski vestnik*, Ljubljana

Samuelson P., Nordhaus W. (2002) *Ekonomija*, GV založba, Ljubljana

*Statistics Norway* (2010), http://www.ssb.no/eksuvh_en/tab-2010-06-01-01-en.html (Accessed 14 January 2010)

*SURS* (2010), http://www.stat.si/novica_prikazi.aspx?id=2735 (Accessed 14 January 2010)

Syed J. (2010) Employment prospects for skilled migrants: A relational perpective, *Human Resource Management Review*, no. 18, pp. 28–45

Trbanc M. (2007) *Poti mladih v zaposlitev: primerjava Slovenije z drugimi državami EU*, Založba FDV, Ljubljana

Verša D. (2004) *Mladi diplomanti na trgu dela*, Zavod Republike Slovenije za zaposlovanje

## About the Authors

**Mojca Bernik** is an assistant professor for Human Resource Management at the Faculty of Organizational Sciences of the University of Maribor. She is Head of the Human Resource Management Department. Her research field is strategic human resource management within organizations. She has published research results in different publications in Slovenia and foreign countries.

**Katjuša Golmajer** finished her studies at the Faculty of Organizational Sciences at University of Maribor. She was on top of her class, for which she was given the dean's award (University of Maribor). For her thesis, she was acknowledged by the Youth Council of Slovenia, because it is considered research that contributed to solving youth problems. Presently, she is a post graduate student at the University of Maribor, Faculty of Organizational Sciences.

# Special Characteristics of Slovene Military Pilots: Improving Human Resource Selection of Military Pilots

***Iztok Podbregar***

*iztok.podbregar@fvv.uni-mb.si.*

***Maja Meško***

*maja.mesko@fm-kp.si*

## Abstract

The nature of work in military organisations involves a high level of responsibility as it so directly affects human lives. Therefore, the significance of appropriate candidate selection is vital. In air forces, one of the most important goals is to achieve and maintain a high level of the required qualifications. In order to achieve this goal, candidates for military pilots have to be highly qualified and should meet all requirements. Good psychological readiness and motor ability in military pilots are among the requirements necessary for qualification.

In our study, we aimed to determine which tests differentiate Slovene military pilots from the control groups (general population, sport pilots and soldiers), and produced a profile of a military pilot. We gathered data by means of the following tests: push-ups, crunches, motor coordination and speed tests, several psychomotor tests, a personality questionnaire and one on coping with stress. Data processing was carried out using SPSS Version 15.0. Basic statistical parameters for the selected variables were calculated separately. To evaluate the differences, discriminant analysis was used. The results shows that the special features or characteristics of military pilots include better emotional control, a higher level of emotional stability, extroversion, and higher impulse control. Military pilots use strategies focused on a problem, they cope with problem situations effectively and they have shorter reaction times in the test of spatial coordination. The research findings can be used to determine specific criteria for a high quality military pilot selection and to provide directions for the development in this field.

**Keywords:** human resource management, personnel selection, Slovene army, military pilots, motor abilities, psychomotor abilities, personality, stress-coping strategies.

# 1. Introduction

Since 2004, major changes have been introduced in the Slovene Armed Forces. Slovenia became a NATO member as well as the European Union member, which requires new solutions in the organisation and functioning of the Slovene Armed Forces. A new law on military duties was adopted, introducing a combination of a professional army and voluntary contract reserve formation in the Slovene military system. In Slovenia, changes in global security conditions have emerged, all of which require a higher level of professionalism as well as higher standards and better combat readiness. Slovenia's Military Air Force (Vojaško letalstvo) has a significant role in the state's defence system, be it in peace or in a period of crises, because manoeuvring aircraft can control the airspace and thus assure the sovereignty of a state, in particular one in a sensitive geostrategic position. The success of the military and its desired goals cannot be achieved without highly qualified staff. Selection models and instruments should be found to make an optimal selection of candidates possible. This is especially true for smaller states that lack qualified personnel. The nature of work in military organisations involves a high level of responsibility as it so directly affects human lives. Therefore, the significance of appropriate candidate selection is even more important. In air forces, one of the most important goals is to achieve and maintain a high level of required qualifications with regard to personnel. In order to achieve this goal, candidates for military pilots have to be highly qualified and should meet all requirements, including a good psychological readiness and motor ability (Podbregar, 1997).

In the Slovene Armed Forces, there is a tendency towards well-developed motor abilities among the majority of its members as the motor abilities of each individual soldier, as well as the whole army, are one of the key elements of combat readiness, which emphasises the significance of army training (Cambell & Catano, 2004; Karpljuk, Rožman, Suhadolnik & Karpljuk, 2000). Motor abilities are not equally developed in all people, which results in differences in motor efficiency among individuals. The psychological characteristics of each individual soldier are, beside motor abilities, the starting point of combat readiness (Novak 2003; Takada, Hisada, Kuwada, Sakai & Akamatsu, 2009) as well being useful predictors of job performance (Arendasy, Sommer & Hergovich, 2007; Borman, Penner, Allen, & Motowidlo, 2001; Salgado, 1998; Salgado, 2002; Vasilopoulos, Cucina

& Hunter, 2007). Therefore, we can conclude that the motor abilities and psychological characteristics of soldiers are of utmost importance for appropriate combat readiness of an army.

## 2. History of Military Pilot Selection

The nature of work in military organisations involves a high degree of responsibility as directly affects human lives. Therefore, the importance of an appropriate candidate selection is of utmost importance. The need for a professional approach to candidate selection was perceived as early as in World War I. Implementing the selection process, military institutions motivated psychology experts to cooperate with them in this process. 'Army Alpha' and 'Army Beta' tests were applied to almost two million soldiers; however, these activities had no direct impact on the selection process (Hunter, 1989; Siem, Carretta, & Mercatante, 1987; Zeidner & Drucker, 1989).

The Air Force also aims to achieve and maintain a high level of the required qualification of staff. To achieve this goal, qualified pilots have to meet the requirements of the position (Caretta & Ree, 2003). Since World War II, human resource experts have been devoting their time, efforts and financial resources to identifying the characteristics of a well-qualified pilot and the instruments to be used in measuring (assessing) these characteristics (Caretta, 1989). Pilot selection as an element of a recruitment process has begun by implementing self-selection, which is still an important factor in civil pilot as well as in military pilot selection. Only those who have a strong desire to fly a plane are able to try and may consequently obtain a flying licence (Pohlman & Fletcher, 1999). In aviation, motivation is one of the prerequisites for military pilot service; it is a fundamental factor of success in this profession. Motivation enables people to function effectively while possessing certain abilities and knowledge. With prospective pilots, perseverance is a characteristic that represents a basic kind of a natural selection. It is demonstrated in the completion of the course and pursuing the career of a pilot. Later on, the procedure of pilot selection began to develop in more depth, since pilot training represented a significant expense. Therefore, in addition to self-selection more systematic and formalised procedures were introduced, initially by implementing a general selection method for selecting military staff, i.e., by physical qualification (Pohlman & Fletcher, 1999). At first, physical requirements for military pilots differed only marginally from the requirements for other military staff (Brown, 1989; Hilton & Dolgin, 1991). Subsequently, they tried to upgrade the military pilot selection process by conducting various research projects, at first in Italy and

France (Dockeray & Isaacs, 1921). Pilot selection procedures have been rendered more effective due to their stringency. Researchers established that pilots should be emotionally stable, possess good psychomotor reactions and mental concentration, and should be able to make swift decisions. Italian researchers developed instruments for measuring reaction times, emotional states, balance, attentiveness and muscle strength, which were included in standard selection procedures. Shortly afterwards, research also began in other countries. In addition to the selection tests, they began to apply mental ability tests (pen and paper tests), which contributed to a stricter military pilot selection (Pohlman & Fletcher, 1999).

Military pilot selection is now a multi-stage process. It is a process in which the decisions are taken in stages, from reviewing references, the number of flight hours, the test, the interview, the evaluation of the flight on a simulator to the evaluation of flying an aircraft and final interview (Caretta & Ree, 2003).

# 3. Military Pilot Selection in the Slovene Armed Forces

According to the planned development of the military aviation, the Slovene Armed Forces plans the long-term needs for aviation staff. Therefore, the Government of the Republic of Slovenia, on the initiative of the Ministry of Defence, opens applications for study grants (for aviation staff) every year. By way of the selection method, the most appropriate applicants are recruited. The selection involves a practical testing of candidates and is performed at the military airport in Cerklje by the Krka River. To serve this purpose, the methodology of candidate selection is designed.

- The Flight Rules of Military Aircraft (Official Gazette 82/2009, 19.10.2010) determine that members of the military can manage or fly a military aircraft as a pilot, or they can fly as crew members if they meet the following requirements (provided for by the regulations):
- they have an appropriate aviation licence, i.e., a licence that is an upgraded civil licence with the prescribed military power;
- they have been passed as medically fit to perform aviation tasks on the same category of an aircraft on which they are trained;
- they are theoretically and practically competent in performing tasks on a certain aircraft;
- they are issued with a flight order, which is to be approved by a competent authority.

A candidate applying for a position of a military pilot in the Slovene Armed Forces who has been selected to be trained according to the existing needs and plans must fulfil the following requirements:

- higher professional or university education in the aviation field
- an A-level health certificate awarded by an organisation authorised for the medical checks of aviation staff
- 200 flight hours in a motor airplane
- examination for a sport pilot
- examination for a professional pilot

Aviation staff can be subdivided according to the levels of professional aviation qualifications in terms of skills or qualification and training for performing aviation tasks. The number of levels and the assessment procedure defining the level of professional aviation qualification are determined by regulations on military aviation professional staff. Checking the level of qualification is performed every two years in accordance with the regulations on military aviation staff.

The basic purpose of our research is to study some special characteristics of military pilots and to establish whether it is possible to design a model or a profile for Slovene military pilots. In our research, we attempted to define the special features of some motor abilities and psychological characteristics of Slovene military pilots, and to define those parameters that have lead to such a position. We also aimed to examine the relation between military pilot's age, the so-called Big-Five personality factors and strategies for coping with stress among Slovene military pilots.

# 4. Method

## 4.1 Participants

The sample consisted of 120 participants, 30 of whom were in an experimental group while the other 90 were in a control group. All participants in our research were male, aged between 31 and 45. The experimental group included military pilots and the control groups included the general population, sport pilots and soldiers with no relation to aviation. The members of the control group were selected with regard to the qualities of the experimental group members so that both groups were equivalent in terms of relevant factors (sex, age, health condition, level of education etc.), thus participating in the study of equivalent pairs. We chose three different control groups because of the small experimental sample size and in order to obtain a higher reliability in the differences between the groups. Members of experimental group included Slovene qualified military pilots; however, some were new members of the Slovene Air Forces while others had several years of military experiences in the military aviation field. Some of the pilots also had experience in civil aviation. All of the military pilots were male (presently there are no women in this occupation in Slovenia).

## 4.2 Materials and Procedure

The BFQ (Big Five Questionnaire) is a tool for measuring personality structures according to the model of the 'Big Five', i.e., the five major factors: energy, agreeability, conscientiousness, emotional stability and openness. The questionnaire design is based on considering the classical qualification of these five personality factors and their sub-dimensions, an additional scale of the social desirability of responses (L scale or Lie Scale), care in establishing sub-dimensions and in the number of items.

The BFQ questionnaire consists of 132 items and is designed for measuring the Big Five dimensions and ten sub-dimensions. For each sub-dimension, half of the statements have a positive meaning and half of the statements have a negative meaning with regard to each dimension. We used the L scale to measure one's tendency towards giving unjustified answers, whether 'positive' or 'negative'. The L scale consists of 12 items that refer to socially desired behaviour or answers. The items are set in such a manner that total agreement or total disagreement is very unlikely to happen. Therefore, a very high or a very low score might signify that one is trying to present himself in a more positive or in a more negative way.

To identify the strategies for coping with stressful life situations, we used the CRI-Adult inventory designed by Rudolf H. Moss (1992). The inventory consists of two parts. The introductory part (10 items) in which the testee is presented with a major problem from the last year of their life is followed by a longer second part (48 items) in which the coping style is assessed using eight CRI sub-scales: logical analysis (LA), positive appraisal (PA), seeking guidance or support (SS), problem-solving action (PS) (thus assessing problem-focused coping styles) on one side, followed by cognitive avoidance (CA), acceptance or resignation (A), seeking alternative rewards (AR) and emotional discharge or emptying (ED) (thus assessing coping styles focused away from the problem). The authors of the Slovene translation of the CRI are Masten, Tušak and Ziherl who were the first to apply this instrument to the Slovene population (frame norms exist). The reliability of the instrument was adequate. The established degree of constructive validity was also adequate (Moss, 1992).

The Complex Reactionmeter Drenovac (CRD) is an originally developed and rationally structured psycho-diagnostic laboratory composed of four electronic instruments (reaction meters), an IBM personal computer, professional printer, functional software for automatic measurement, generator of new tests and data base (Drenovac, 1994). In the CRD series, there are different instruments (CRD1, CRD2, CRD3 and CRD4), consisting of various tests. For the purpose of our research, we implemented CRD 2–1, CRD 4–31 AND CDR 4–32.

CRD2–1

CRD2–1 is a test of spatial coordination measures mental function, which involves complex analytical procedures in the process of definition and task solution, the task being represented by revealing or discovering the hidden objective of orientation, which is defined not only by physical features or properties but is also logically determined by a logical rule (i.e., determined by a rule and not by a physical property of the objective). On the signal-control board, there are two signal lights simultaneously and constantly turning on and off (physical feature); the tested person has to press the key located at the intersection of the coordinates of these two signals (the logical rule which should be adopted and taken into consideration by the tested person during the task-solving activity) (Molan & Arnerič, 2000).

Procedure: The test contains 35 tasks that are to be performed on a signal-control board. The signal elements are placed along the board's edges (five signal elements in the upper and lower edge and four on the left and right edge). In the lower part of the board, there are 20 signal lights in four lines and five columns. The lights and the keys are located on the same axes (imaginary straight lines) and are arranged in series (lines). For each test item or task (stimulus), two signal lights light up (physical background) simultaneously. Each signal is located on a certain light axis (in a certain line and column). The task is to find a latent signal, i.e., the point where the axes of the both light signals intersect. The tested person is to press the two keys at the edge, the keys forming the coordinate of the latent signal (the logically determined rule that should be mastered and considered by the tested person).

The test runs continuously, its speed being directed by the dynamics and accuracy of the tested person's reactions.

CRD 4-31

The CRD 4-31 test measures the function of the visual proprioceptive regulation and control of performing a motor activity done in various combinations by the four extremities. It involves operative thinking, which could be labelled as visual-motor coordination. The instrument includes four lights and two keys (left and right) on the control board and two pedals (left and right). The signal lights providing or giving the tasks to the tested person are located in the middle part of the board (part or field A). According to the signal lights, the testee is to press an appropriate combination of lights and pedals. The test is an example of simple stimuli (Molan & Arnerič, 2000).

Procedure: The instrument consists of a signal board. The signal elements are four signal lights on the signal board forming the angles of a trapezium, with the longer side facing the upper edge of the instrument. The two upper lights have the function of emitting signals to which the tested person responds with his hands (the left light for the left hand, the right light for the right hand), while the lower two lights emit signals to which the tested person responds by pressing his left (bottom-left light) or right (bottom-right light) foot. Due to the minimum level of the motor component, the length of the reaction is considered to be the reflection of the speed of the cognitive component (reaction time). The stimuli are of different difficulty levels and follow a random sequence. They include one, two or three light signals and are to be reacted to by pressing the relevant pedals as quickly as possible. The efficiency and inventiveness (ingenuity) in such a situation are shown in the speed, accuracy (the number of incorrect reactions) and stability of individual reactions.

CRD 4-32

The tasks in CRD 4-32 test measure the function of signal noticing. The test is classified as a standard or simple reaction meter, measuring simple reaction time (the speed of information processing). The signal element is one signal light. The participant's task is to press the key when a light signal appears. When the signal light is shut off, the participant has to quickly withdraw his hand from the key. The signal light appears discontinuously every 1–3 seconds after repeated pressing. In this case, the speed and stability are the indicators of the effect. The dispersion (diffusion) of reaction times also provides an indirect picture of attention stability (Molan & Arnerič, 2000).

The evaluation of CRD tests: the result (performance indicator) is thus the total (cumulative) time required for solving all the tasks and the total number of errors. The time spent signifies the level of actualisation of the measured cognitive function (shorter time presents a better result or achievement), while the number of mistakes is an indicator of the quality of problem-solving (fewer errors indicate a higher level of accuracy and consequently a higher level of the quality of problem-solving).

The testing of motor abilities includes four tests: push-ups, trunk lifting, coordination testing and speed testing.

## 4.3 Procedure

The data were collected during the spring and summer of 2007 at different locations in Slovenia. The participants in this research completed the BFQ and CRI in a classroom, following the instructions specified on the inventory. There was no time limit to complete the inventory. All motor tests and CRD tests were performed in a gym.

The data were processed using the following methods:

- calculation of basic statistical parameters (descriptives);
- discriminant analysis; and
- Pearson's correlation coefficients (for computing relationship between military pilots' age, personality factors and the strategies for coping with stress).

All hypotheses were verified at a 5% risk level ($p = 0.05$). The SPSS software was used for the data analysis.

# 5. Results

By using discriminant analysis, we attempted to determine a linear combination of the measured variables that would best discriminate between the groups (the experimental group of military pilots, and the control groups including the general population, sports pilots and soldiers); consequently, the error in classifying the units would be the lowest. We thus searched for those dimensions that best explain the differences between the groups. The discriminant analysis was applied to all the groups. The analysis was applied to all the obtained variables in the following tests: push-ups, trunk-lifting, coordination and speed, in some of the tests in the CRD series, in the questionnaire measuring personality structure using the model of the 'Big Five' questionnaire (BFQ), and then identifying the strategies for coping with stressful life circumstances (CRI, i.e., coping responses questionnaire).

*Table 1: Box's Test of Equality of Covariance Matrix for two groups (military pilots and control groups)*

| | | | | | |
|---|---|---|---|---|---|
| r-group | Rank | Log Det | Box's M | | 48.886 |
| 1 | 4 | 12.86 | F | Approx. | 4.624 |
| 2 | 4 | 9.96 | | df1 | 10.000 |
| Pooled within | 4 | 12.56 | | df2 | 13625.621 |
| | | | | Sig. | 0.000 |
| Log Dets | | | Test Results | | |
| r-group | Rank | Log Det | Box's M | | 4.032 |
| 1 | 1 | 4.39 | F | Approx. | 3.983 |
| 2 | 1 | 3.75 | | df1 | 1.000 |
| Pooled within | 1 | 4.27 | | df2 | 19464.709 |
| | | | | Sig. | 0.046 |
| Log Dets | | | Test Results | | |
| r-group | Rank | Log Det | Box's M | | 12.048 |
| 1 | 1 | -0.92 | F | Approx. | 11.907 |
| 2 | 1 | -2.10 | | df1 | 1.000 |
| Pooled within | 1 | -1.11 | | df2 | 19464.709 |
| | | | | Sig. | 0.001 |
| Log Dets | | | Test Results | | |
| r-group | Rank | Log Det | Box's M | | 3.242 |
| 1 | 3 | 11.99 | F | Approx. | 0.518 |
| 2 | 3 | 11.61 | | df1 | 6.000 |
| Pooled within | 3 | 11.92 | | df2 | 17996.323 |
| | | | | Sig. | 0.795 |
| Log Dets | | | Test Results | | |
| r-group | Rank | Log Det | Box's M | | 38.294 |
| 1 | 4 | 8.52 | F | Approx. | 3.622 |
| 2 | 4 | 8.10 | | df1 | 10.000 |
| Pooled within | 4 | 8.74 | | df2 | 13625.621 |
| | | | | Sig. | 0.000 |

*Legend: 1- group of military pilots; 2- control groups.*

Using Box's test, we test the zero hypothesis claiming that the covariance matrices are equal. The data above show that the variance-covariance matrices for particular groups are about equal; therefore, the assumption for applying discriminant analysis is met (variance in all groups should be approximately equal).

Using Box's test, we test the zero hypothesis claiming that the covariance matrices are equal. The above data show that the covariance matrices for particular groups are about equal; therefore, the assumption for applying discriminant analysis is met.

*Table 2: Summary of discriminant analysis for two groups (military pilots and control groups (altogether) after classification into separate variable clusters*

| ALL TESTS Function | Proper value | % variances | Cumulative % | Canonical correlation | Test of functions | Wilks' Lambda | Hi - square | df | p |
|---|---|---|---|---|---|---|---|---|---|
| All tests | 0.372 | 100.00 | 100.00 | 0.52 | 1 | 0.729 | 36.65 | 4 | 0.000 |
| Motor tests | 0.052 | 100.00 | 100.00 | 0.22 | 1 | 0.950 | 6.00 | 1 | 0.014 |
| CRD | 0.070 | 100.00 | 100.00 | 0.26 | 1 | 0.935 | 7.96 | 1 | 0.005 |
| BFQ | 0.301 | 100.00 | 100.00 | 0.48 | 1 | 0.768 | 30.69 | 3 | 0.000 |
| CRI | 0.231 | 100.00 | 100.00 | 0.43 | 1 | 0.812 | 24.13 | 4 | 0.000 |

*Legend: Motor tests: push-ups, crunches, motor coordination and speed tests; CRD tests: tests for assessing psychomotor abilities; the BFQ (Big Five Questionnaire): a self-completed instrument to assess the five factor model of personality; the CRI: Coping Responses Inventory for assessing respondents' stress coping styles.*

We were interested in calculating the discriminant functions for the two groups (the military pilot group and the group including all the three control groups) by separate variable clusters. A summary of the discriminant analysis is presented in Table 2. A canonical correlation between all the variables and the first discriminant function is 0.52. A canonical correlation between four motor variables, which are (considered separately) all statistically significant, and the discriminant function is 0.22. A higher canonical correlation is shown only with the variables in the personality questionnaire BFQ, and amounts to 0.48. This canonical correlation is calculated from 17 variables, among which 15 variables are established as being statistically significant, according to the variance analysis. The CRD test group has the canonical correlation of 0.26, the CRI tests 0.43. The size of the canonical correlation is also related to the number of variables in the group and to chi-square as well as to the statistical significance of the function.

Table 2 also shows which tests distinguish military pilots from the other groups. The military pilots are best distinguished from the other participants if a cluster of all tests applied in the research is used. They are also well distinguished from the other groups by applying BFQ and CRI tests. A lower level of discrimination is shown by applying CRD tests and motor tests.

The structural matrix of correlation coefficients between the variables and the discriminant function applied for classifying the participants into two groups (military pilots and control groups) was also calculated.

The function is a positive saturated function with the BFQ sub-dimension of emotion control (aspects related to tension control, concerning emotional experiences), with the emotional stability dimension (the ability of emotional self-control, the ability of keeping steady nerves, e.g., not losing one's temper and (mental) balance, absence of negative emotional states), the BFQ energy dimension (energetic and dynamic activity, communicativeness and enthusiasm, assertiveness, pushing oneself forward and influencing others; extroversion), the impulse control subdimension (the aspects relating to the ability of one's own behaviour, also in unpleasant, conflict and dangerous situations), there is a negative saturation with the subscale of CRI cognitive avoidance (cognitive efforts to avoid a realistic thinking about a problem), the sub-dimension of kindness (kindness, confidence in others and openness towards others) and maximal reaction time in seconds in the test of spatial coordination (CRD2) measuring the mental function including complex analytical processes. These are the variables that most strongly correlate with the function. All the other variables do not correlate so strongly with this function.

With the discriminant analysis and its results, we attempted to discover the characteristics of separate groups, i.e., the characteristics containing all the variables included in the research: in motor ability tests, the results in CRD tests, variables in personality test and the test of ascertaining or determining stress-coping strategies. Using discriminant analysis, we attempted to work out those functions that discriminate the groups to the highest extent. We were able to compare the groups according to various criteria at one time.

The discriminant analysis was done for both of the groups (the experimental group and the group including the three control groups) and for all separate clusters of variables. Therefore, we were able to establish which of the tests best differentiated military pilots from the other groups and designed a profile of a military pilot, i.e., we defined special characteristics (personal traits) typical for this profession. We established that military pilots are the best classified in comparison to the other participants of the research by all the tests used in the research, they are also well classified by the BFQ test and CRI test. A slightly lower discrimination is shown by CRD tests and motor tests.

The special features or characteristics of military pilots, discriminating them from the other groups, include a better control of emotions (aspects that relate to tension control and involve emotional experiences, a higher level of emotional stability), the ability of emotional self-control, the ability of keeping steady nerves (not losing one's temper) and (mental) balance, absence of negative emotional states, energetic and dynamic activity, communicativeness and enthusiasm, the ability of self-assertion, pushing oneself forward and influencing others and in turn a higher level of extroversion, a higher impulse control (aspects relating to the ability of one's own behaviour), also in unpleasant, conflict and dangerous situations. However, in comparison with other groups, the military pilots are less distinct in their strategy of coping with stress, cognitive avoidance representing cognitive efforts to avoid realistic thinking about the problem, kindness as a personal trait as well as shorter maximum time in completing the test of spatial coordination measuring a mental function, including complex analytical processes.

Table 3 shows Pearson's product-moment correlations among the measures of military pilot's age, personality factors and the stress coping strategies. Among the correlations several were statistically significant: between age and stress coping strategy problem-solving action (.63), between the personality factor of energy and stress coping strategies logical analysis (.53), problem-solving action (.58) and emotional discharge or emptying (.71); and between conscientiousness and logical analysis (-.62).

*Table 3: Pearson's correlation coefficients among selected measures (military pilots group)*

| | | | | Stress Coping Strategies | | | | | | | | |
|---|---|---|---|---|---|---|---|---|---|---|---|---|
| | Characteristic measure | | | A | LA | PA | SS | PS | CA | ACC | AR | ED |
| M | | | | 34.6 | 10.33 | 7.90 | 6.40 | 11.63 | 4.97 | 3.50 | 6.50 | 1.90 |
| SD | | | | 3.02 | 4.10 | 3.83 | 3.11 | 3.39 | 4.25 | 3.34 | 2.81 | 2.04 |
| | | M | SD | | | | | | | | | |
| A-Age | A1-31 to37 | | | | | | | | | | | |
| | A2-38 to 45 | 34.6 | 3.02 | | .12 | -.13 | .27 | .63* | .00 | -.06 | .08 | .44 |
| | E | 51.40 | 5.88 | .10 | .53* | .15 | -.02 | .58* | -.12 | -.16 | -.17 | .71** |
| | A | 46.50 | 8.02 | -.01 | -.24 | -.04 | .22 | .27 | -.13 | .40 | .11 | -.00 |
| Personality Characteristic | C | 52.17 | 6.77 | .00 | -.62* | -.38 | .01 | -.22 | -.08 | .17 | -.06 | -.45 |
| | ES | 54.07 | 6.71 | .38 | -.14 | -.04 | .04 | .21 | -.08 | .08 | .07 | .13 |
| | O | 48.57 | 9.65 | .24 | -.31 | -.14 | -.36 | -.10 | -.26 | -.00 | .07 | -.06 |
| | SINC | 51.93 | 6.01 | -.04 | -.11 | -.30 | -.29 | -.36 | .01 | .01 | .09 | -.28 |

*Note. LA: logical analysis; PA: positive appraisal; SS: seeking guidance or support; PS: problem-solving action; CA: cognitive avoidance; ACC: acceptance or resignation; AR: seeking alternative rewards; ED: emotional discharge or emptying; E: Energy; A: Agreeability; C: Conscientiousness; ES: Emotional stability; O: Openness; SINC: Sincerity scale.* $^{*}p < .05$. $^{**}p < .01$.

# 6. Discussion

People who are involved in any kind of cooperating or functioning inside a certain organisation are the most important elements of each organisation – in combination with other elements (such as forms of organisational connections or networks, resources) – and they are involved in the process of accomplishing common or individual goals (Bartone, Roland, Picano & Williams, 2008; Bertoncelj, Kovač & Bertoncel, 2009; Meško Štok, 2008; Ostroff, Kinicki, & Tamkins, 2003, Zysberg, 2009).

Human resources are an important success factor in performing some of the tasks of special troops of the Armed Forces; therefore, it is necessary to design the models and find the tools of selection that will enable an optimal selection of candidates, not only in the military environments but also in wider society (Bertoncelj & Kovač, 2009; Harrison, Neary, Albert, Veillette, McKenzie & Croll, 2007; Sava, Gutierrez, Lirn Duh & Jazmin, 2007; Steege & Fritscher, 1991). This is especially true for small countries, because they are limited in terms of human resources.

In the research, we focused on discovering the main motor abilities and psychological characteristics of the Slovene military pilots group, i.e., on determining the special characteristics of this group. We believed that the special characteristics of the Slovene military pilots can be defined in terms of the subspace of motor ability variables and in terms of the subspace of psychological characteristic variables. The results of previous studies of pilots' showed that military pilots tend to exclude emotions and that they cope with stress more effectively when they are facing a problem, or when their coping strategy is problem-focused and requires their immediate response or action (Ashman & Telfer, 1983; Picano, 1990; Retzlaff & Gibertini, 1987) and that specific personality characteristics, such as emotional stability, extraversion, sociability, conscientiousness, balance and orientation towards actions and activity, occur commonly in pilots (Ashman & Telfer, 1983; Bartram, 1995; Dillinger, Wiegmann, & Taneja, 2003; Fine & Hartman, 1968; Okaue, Nakamura, & Nira, 1977; Fitzgibbons, Davis & Schutte, 2004).

First in our study, we aimed to identify the personal characteristics of Slovene military pilots and compare them to appropriate control groups. If we revise the differences between groups, we can see that statistically significant differences occurred in the dimensions of energy, agreeability, conscientiousness, emotional stability and openness. In the dimensions of energy, conscientiousness and emotional stability, according to the results of the BFQ questionnaire, the military pilots scored significantly higher than the control groups. Thus, the military pilots seem to be more energetic and dynamic, more communicative and enthusiastic, as well as capable of asserting themselves leading and influencing other people.

Another main aim of the study was to establish how the stress-coping techniques of the Slovene military pilots differ from those of the control groups. In this study, the experimental group was comprised of military pilots, while the control groups were composed of members of the general population, sport pilots and soldiers. The results of this study suggest that military pilots have preferred ways of coping with stress that are different from those of the control groups. A closer look at the differences between military pilots and the control groups in terms of their stress-coping strategies shows that statistically significant differences emerged in the following dimensions: cognitive avoidance and emotional discharge or emptying. These CRI dimensions represent the stress-coping strategies not connected with a problem. In both of these dimensions, the pilots achieved lower results on average than the rest of the control groups.

We also identify some motor abilities that are characteristics for Slovene military pilots. In comparison to the control groups, the military pilots scored particularly high results in the tests of motor coordination and speed; moreover, their visual motor coordination and motor response also proved to be better.

Accordingly, via discriminant analysis we also aimed at discovering the characteristics of the Slovene military pilots group, i.e., the characteristics including all the applied variables in this research.

We made a discriminant analysis for the two groups (the military pilots and the control groups) in the area of separate test clusters. We attempted to establish which tests most accurately discriminated the military pilots from the other groups and best defined the characteristics of the military pilots group. In our study, we established that the military pilots were best distinguished from the other groups in the research by the cluster of all the tests used in our research, and they could also be quite equally distinguished by the BFQ test and CRI test. The CRD test series and the motor ability tests distinguished them to a somewhat lower extent. Through discriminant analysis, we established or determined the special characteristics of the military pilots that separate them from the other groups. These characteristics involved better emotion control (i.e. aspects that relate to tension control and involve emotional experiences), a higher level of emotional stability (i.e., emotional self-control, the ability of keeping steady nerves (not losing one's temper) and (mental) balance, absence of negative emotional states, energetic and dynamic functioning, communicativeness and enthusiasm, the ability of self-assertion, pushing oneself forward and influencing others, and in turn a high level of extroversion, a high impulse control (aspects relating to the ability to control one's own behaviour, in unpleasant, conflict and dangerous situations). Nevertheless, in comparison to other groups, the military pilots were less distinguished by stress-coping strategies, cognitive avoidance representing cognitive efforts to avoid realistic thinking about the problem, amiableness (as a personal trait) as well as shorter maximum time in completing the test of spatial coordination measuring a mental function involving complex analytical processes.

Some stress-coping strategies adopted by Slovene military pilots are significantly related to their age and various aspects of their personalities. The age of military pilots correlated with stress-coping strategies and problem-solving actions. Older Slovene military pilots use problem-solving actions as their stress-coping strategy more often than their younger colleges. The personality factor 'energy' correlated with stress-coping strategies, logical analysis, problem-solving action and emotional discharge or emptying. Personality factor conscientiousness was related negatively with stress-coping strategies and logical analysis (the cognitive effort to understand the stressor and the attempt to mentally prepare for the stressor and its consequences). Differences in coping strategies might affect more than performance. Coping style may affect self monitoring and the willingness to admit problems. Such insight could be valuable for teaching both aviation and stress-coping skills to military aviation students, as well as improving aviation safety programs in general.

Therefore, we can conclude that there is a correlation between the military pilots' motor abilities, psychomotor abilities, personality, stress-coping strategies and success in the profession of military pilot. This correlation explains a part of success variability in the profession of military pilots and cannot be neglected. In military pilot selection, increasing importance is given to motor abilities and the psychological characteristics of military pilots as they represent performance parameters in this profession.

The research findings can be used to determine specific criteria for a high-quality military pilot selection and to provide directions for the development in this field.

## References

Arendasy, M., Sommer, M., Hergovich, A. (2007): Statistical judgment formation in personnel selection: A study in military aviation psychology, *Military Psychology*, Vol. 19, No. 2, pp. 119–136.

Ashman, A., Telfer, R. (1983): Personality profiles of pilots, *Aviation Space and Environmental Medicine*, Vol. 54, No. 10, pp. 940–943.

Bartone, P. T., Roland, R. R., Picano, J. J., Williams, T. J. (2008): Psychological hardiness predicts success in US army special forces candidates, *International Journal of Selection and Assessment*, Vol.76, No. 1, pp. 78–81.

Bartram, D. (1995): *Personality factors in pilots selection: Validation of the Cathay Pacific Airways selection procedures*. Proceedings of the Eight International Symposium on Aviation Psychology, Columbus, Ohio, April 24th–27th 1995, R. S. Jensen (Editor), The Ohio State University, Columbus, OH.

Bertoncelj, A., Kovač, D. (2009): Gender difference in the conative of entrepreneurial orientation, *J. East Eur. manag. stud.,* Vol. 14, No. 4, pp. 357–368.

Bertoncelj, A., Kovač, D., Bertoncel, R. (2009): Success factors and competencies in organisational evolution, *Kybernetes*, Vol. 38, No. 9, pp. 1508–1517.

Brown, D. C. (1989): *Officer Aptitude Selection Measures. Military Personnel Measurement: Testing, Assignment, Evaluation*, M. F. Wiskoff, G. M. Rampton (Editors), Praeger, New York.

Borman, W. C., Penner, L. A., Allen, T. D., Motowidlo, S. J. (2001): Personality Predictors of Citizenship Performance, *International Journal of Selection and Assessment,* Vol. 9, pp. 52–69.

Cambell, S. H., Catano, V. M. (2004): Using Measures of Specific Abilities to Predict Training Performance in Canadian Forces Operator Occupations, *Military Psychology,* Vol. 16, No. 3, pp. 183–201.

Caretta, T. R. (1989): USAF pilot selection and classification system, *Aviation, Space, and Environmental Medicine,* Vol. 60, pp. 46–49.

Caretta, T. R., Ree, M. J. (2003): *Pilot Selection Methods. Principles and practice of aviation psychology,* P. S. Tsang, M. A. Vidulich (Editors), Lawrence Erlbaum Associates, Publishers, London.

Dillinger, T. G., Wiegmann D. A., Taneja, N. (2003): *Relating personality with stress coping strategies among student pilots in a collegiate flight training program.* Proceedings of the 12th International Symposium on Aviation Psychology, Dayton, Ohio, April 14th–17th 2003, R. S. Jensen (Editor), The Ohio State University, Dayton, OH.

Dockeray F. C., Isaacs, S. (1921): Psychological research in aviation in Italy, France, England, and the American Expeditionary Forces, *Comparative Psychology,* Vol. 1, No. 2, pp. 115–148.

Drenovac, M. (1994). *Serija psihodijagnostičkih instrumenata CRD: priručnik* [Series of psychodiagnostic instruments, CRD: manual], Zavod SR Slovenije zaproduktivnost dela, Center za psihodiagnostična sredstva, Ljubljana.

Fine, P. M., Hartman, B. O. (1986): P*sychiatric Strengths and Weaknesses of Typical Air Force Pilots* (SAM-TR-68-121), USAF School of Aerospace Medicine Brooks AFB, TX.

Fitzgibbons, A., Davis, D., Schutte, P. C. (2004): *Pilot Personality Profile Using the NEO-PI-R,* NASA Langley Research Center, Hampton Virginia.

Harrison, M., Neary, J. P., Albert, W. J., Veillette, D. W., McKenzie, N. P., Croll, J. C. (2007): Physiological effects of night vision goggle counterweights on neck musculature of military helicopter pilots, *Military Medicine,* Vol. 172, No. 8, pp. 864–870.

Hilton, T. F., Dolgin, D. L. (1991): Pilot Selection in the Military of the Free World. in *Handbook of Military Psychology*, R. Gal, A. D. Mangelsdorff (Editors), Wiley, New York.

Hunter, D. R. (1989): *Aviator Selection. Military Personnel Measurement,* M. F. Wiskoff , G. Rampton (Editors), Praeger, New York.

Karpljuk D., Žitko M., Rožman F., Suhadolnik M., Karpljuk K. (2000): *Teoretične osnove in praktična izhodišča športne vadbe, namenjene višjim častnikom Slovenske vojske* [The theoretical basics and practical principles of physical training aimed at senior officers], Ministrstvo za obrambo RS, Ljubljana.

Meško Štok, Z. (2008): Menadžeri i stres menadžment [Managers and stress management], *Svet rada,* Vol. 5, No. 3, pp. 323–334.

Milgram, N. A. (1991): *Personality Factors in Military Psychology. Handbook of Military Psychology,* R. Gal, D. Mangelsdorf (Editors), Wiley Chichester.

Molan, M., Arnerič, N. (2000): Struktura psihološkega pregleda za oceno delazmožnosti [The structure of psychological check-up in assessing work capacity], *Psihološka obzorja*, Vol. 9, No. 4, pp. 115–126.

Moss, R. H. (1992): *Coping Responses Inventory Manual. Assessment: A Mental Health Portfolio,* D. L. Milne (Editor). NFER Nelson, Windsor.

Novak, M. (2003): *Razvoj motoričnih sposobnosti pripadnikov SV po standardih ameriške vojske* [Development of motor skills in SAF members according to the standards of the US Army], Bachelor's thesis, Univerza v Ljubljani, Fakulteta za šport, Ljubljana.

Okaue, M., Nakamura, M., Nira, K. (1977): Personality characteristics of pilots on EPPS, MPI and DOSEFU, *Reports of Aeromedical Laboratory,* Vol. 18, pp. 83–93.

Ostroff C, Kinicki A. J., Tamkins M. M. (2003): *Organizational Culture and Climate. Handbook of Psychology,* W. C. Borman, D. R. Ilgen, R. J. Klimoski (Editors), Wiley, Hoboken, NJ.

Picano, J. J. (1990): An empirical assessment of stress-coping styles in military pilots, *Aviation Space and Environmental Medicine,* Vol. 61, No. 4, pp. 356–360.

Podbregar, I. (1997): Vojstvo [Army], Ministrstvo za obrambo, Ljubljana.

Pohlman, D. L., Fletcher J. D. (1999): Aviation Personnel Selection and *Training. Handbook of Aviation Human Factors*, D. J. Garland, J. A. Wise, V. D. Hopkin (Editors), Lawrence Erlbaum Associates, Mahwah, New Jersey.

*Pravilnik o letenju vojaških zrakoplovov* [Rules on flights of military aircraft], Ur.list RS (Official Gazette of the Republic of Slovenia), no. 46/2000.

Retzlaff, R. D., Gibertini, M. (1987): Air Force pilot personality: Hard data on the right stuff, *Multiple Behavior Research,*Vol. 22, pp. 383–389.

Salgado, J. F. (1998): Big Five personality dimensions and job performance in army and civil occupations: A European perspective, *Human Performance,* Vol. 11, pp. 271–288.

Salgado, J. T. (2002): The Big Five Personality Dimensions and Counterproductive Behaviors. *International Journal of Selection and Assessment*, Vol. 10, pp. 117–125.

Sava, R. R., Gutierrez, A. M. J. A., Lirn Duh, H. B., Jazmin, C. (2007): An evaluation of CRM Attitudes of Filipino pilots in four Philippine aviation companies, *International Journal of Aviation Psychology,* Vol. 17, No. 3, pp. 285–298.

Siem, F. M., Carretta, T. R., Mercatante, T. A. (1987): *Personality, attitudes, and pilot training performance: Preliminary analysis,* Air Force Human Resource Laboratory, Manpower and Personnel Division, Brooks Air Force Base, TX.

Steege, F. W., Fritscher,W. (1991): Psychological assessment and military personnel management. in *Handbook of Military Psychology,* R. A. Galand, A. D. Mangelsdorff (Editors), Wiley, Chichester, England.

Takada, Y., Hisada, T., Kuwada, N., Sakai M., Akamatsu, T. (2009): Survey of severe spatial disorientation episodes in Japan air self-defense force fighter pilots showing increased severity in night flight, *Military Medicine,* Vol. 174, No. 6, pp. 626–630.

Vasilopoulos, N. L., Cucina, J. M., Hunter, A. E. (2007): Personality and training proficiency: Issues of bandwidth-fidelity and curvilinearity, *Journal of Occupational and Organizational Psychology,* Vol. 80, pp. 109–131.

Zeidner, J., Drucker, A. J. (1989): *Behavioral science in the Army: A corporate history of the Army Research Institute,* Army Research Institute, Alexandria.

Zysberg, L. (2009): An emerging new component of cognitive abilities in human resource selection: preliminary evidence to the existence of "process-analytic" factor in selection batteries, *International Journal of Selection and Assessment,* Vol. 17, No. 1, pp. 69–75.

## About the Authors

**Iztok Podbregar** is a full professor at Faculty of Criminal Justice and Security, University of Maribor. He is chairman of the Institute for Security Strategy in Ljubljana, Slovenia. He also teaches courses on the intelligence and security activity and oversight of intelligence and security services at the University of Maribor, Slovenia.

**Maja Meško** is an assistant professor at the Faculty of Management, University of Primorska and is active in the field of civil and military aviation. Her main areas of research interest are human resources management, organisational culture, organisational social climate, aviation psychology and sports psychology. Her work has been published in professional and academic journals. She actively participates in local and international conferences.

# From Innovation Followers to Innovation Leaders – the Transitional Aspects

***Peter Fatur***

*peter.fatur@fm-kp.si*

***Borut Likar***

*borut.likar1@guest.arnes.si*

## Abstract

This chapter investigates the relationship between a company's innovation inputs and its innovation performance. The research was carried out on a sample of 2,500 companies from the manufacturing and selected service sectors.

The results indicate a correlation between (i) the revenues from innovations and (ii) the relative share of these revenues arising from 'breakthrough' innovations and the company's performance in terms of financial ratios, in particular ROE and growth of revenues from sales.

An interesting nonlinearity between the volume of financial assets invested in innovation and the volume of revenues arising from innovations was found, indicating that investments do not necessarily result in increased innovation performance. An increase in investments is related to the growth of productivity of invested assets in the case of companies that record relatively low innovation revenues. However, investing with the purpose of increasing a relative share of 'breakthrough' innovations reduces the productivity of these assets. On the basis of these findings, recommendations are provided as to which policies of innovation investments different types of innovation followers should adopt so as to catch up with the group of innovation leaders.

**Keywords**: innovation, R&D, productivity, performance, management, sustainability of growth

# 1. Introduction

The European Union's Lisbon goal of becoming the world's most competitive business environment by 2010 was not met. According to the recent statistical indicators (Eurostat 2008, 6), the European Union (EU) is still losing ground in business exploitation of knowledge and creativity to the United States and Japan. Although the innovation gap has been reduced in recent years (from 41 to 28% with regard to the USA, and from 42 to 38% with regard to Japan in the period from 2004 to 2008), it remains significant.

The national innovation performances of European countries vary substantially. The European Innovation Scoreboard (EIS) classifies the countries into the following groups (Eurostat 2008, 7): (i) the innovation leaders, consisting of Denmark, Finland, Germany, Israel, Japan, Sweden, Switzerland, the UK and the USA. Sweden is the most innovative country, largely due to its strong innovation inputs although it remains less efficient in transforming these into innovation outputs than some other countries; (ii) the innovation followers include Austria, Belgium, Canada, France, Iceland, Ireland, Luxembourg and the Netherlands; (iii) the moderate innovators group includes Australia, Cyprus, Czech Republic, Estonia, Italy, Norway, Slovenia and Spain; (iv) the catching-up group consists of Bulgaria, Croatia, Greece, Hungary, Latvia, Lithuania, Malta, Poland, Portugal, Romania and Slovakia. These groupings appear to have been relatively stable over the last years.

An indicator of innovation capability is the turnover of new or significantly improved products to the market as a percentage of the total turnover. For 2004, it amounted to 3.5% for the medium-sized and 8.5% for the large companies of the EU-27. The relative turnover of new or significantly improved products to a company amounts to 5.1% for the medium-sized and 9.3% for the large companies.

A positive correlation between the ability to successfully launch new products and sustained economic performance has been confirmed in a number of studies (Geroski and Machin, 1992; Neely and Hii, 1998; Sharma and Thomas, 2008; Altman, 2008; Roper, Du, and Love, 2008)). Pursuant to the national statistical data (SURS 2008), only 35.1% of Slovene companies prove to be innovative, 41.2% of these in the manufacturing sector. Furthermore, an in-depth analysis evidently shows that the situation regarding innovation in Slovene small and medium-sized enterprises is even worse, with large companies recording approximately 50% more innovativeness than the medium-sized ones, while small companies even threefold less than the large ones (SURS 2008) (Here it needs to be taken into consideration that an enterprise – regardless of its size – is classified in the statistical group of innovative enterprises by introducing at least one new product. The latter thus represents the 'statistical benefit' for the large companies). Apparently, Slovene industry needs an innovation push to outrun the group of innovation followers and catch up with the group of innovation leaders.

Various hampering factors have an impact on innovation. It seems that, in the below-average innovating countries, the barriers are more common and more difficult to overcome. For instance, the Spanish study has revealed that the most important barriers are associated with innovation costs (Madrid-Guijarro, Garcia, and Auken 2009). However, as for the case of Croatia, companies that report facing obstacles are not less likely to innovate less, which suggests that innovators are able to work around obstacles without causing damaging effects to innovation (Radas and Bozic 2009).

The relevant literature tackles different approaches in pursuing innovation, yet one of the fundamental ones proves to be an analysis of innovation processes based on input, process and output groups of indicators (Likar 2008, 116; Fatur and Likar 2010, 490), either individual or composite.

Individual indicators (Coombs, Narandren, and Richards, 1996; Freel, 2005; Hollenstein, 1996) measure single influential factors (e.g., the amount of resources invested into research and development (R&D), the annual number of days dedicated to training of management/employees). The problem of individual indicators remains their incapacity to deal with the complexity of the innovation management field. Consequently, the composite indicators prove to be more appropriate since they regard the invention-innovation process with due complexity, as an intertwinement of related and correlated factors (Hagedoorn and Cloodt, 2003).

The input indicators (also referred to as 'investment' indicators) include expenditure on R&D or employees training (Iansiti, 1997; Carayannis, Gonzales, and Wetter, 2003). The process indicators take into account the organisation or management of innovation processes, the use of appropriate management techniques (market research, problem analysis and idea creation techniques, forecasting techniques, and suchlike), and innovation environment within a company. The output indicators identify results, e.g., the number of patents and new products, market shares, revenues from the sales of innovations, etc. Several studies have shown the correlations among the input, process and output variables. Hollenstein shows the correlations between the input (e.g., research input, development input) and the output-oriented indicators (e.g., number of patents, number of innovation projects) and the market-oriented measures (sales share of new products), thus indicating the innovativeness of a firm (Hollenstein 1996). Iansiti shows correlations among input (e.g., technology from suppliers, technology from other groups) and process indicators (e.g., research groups, project management, communication) and technological potential and yield (Iansiti 1997).

Parthasarthy and Hammond show that both the innovation input and the innovation process have implications for innovation frequency, i.e., the number of new products introduced (Parthasarthy and Hammond 2002). They realised that R&D intensity, by itself, positively influences the invented technologies; developing them into new products and marketing them frequently requires a corresponding level of functional integration.

# 2. Methodology

The purpose of this research is to indicate a relationship between the innovation inputs (financial as well as organisational factors) and the companies' performance in achieving innovation results. The following research questions were set:

1. How does the organisational structure of innovation activities influence the revenues arising from innovation activities?
2. Are the revenues arising from innovation related to the companies' financial results?
3. Is there a relation between the amount of financial investments into innovation and the volume of revenues arising from innovation (productivity of investments)?

Pursuant to the official classification, the sample included companies having their registered office in Slovenia, active either in the manufacturing industries or in selected service industries. The sample size is 2,503 companies, 65% of which are classified as small (less than 50 employees), 27% as medium-sized (50–249) and the remaining 8% as large companies (>249).

The manufacturing sectors account for 56% and the service sectors 44% of the sample (Table 1). A relatively small subsample of innovating companies within the observed sample (companies having any revenues from innovation introduced in the 2004–2006; n=713) limited detailed research at the sectoral level. However, recent major research based on the CIS data confirmed that little difference exists between the patterns of manufacturing and services, once the complexity and variety of technological activities is considered, and no difference in the innovation-related determinants of profits (Bogliacino and Pianta 2009, 35).

*Table 1: The structure of the sample*

| Code* | Industry | N | % |
|---|---|---|---|
| G | Wholesale & retail, repair motor vehicles, personal & household goods | 432 | 17% |
| DJ | Manufacture of basic metals and fabricated metal products | 305 | 12% |
| I | Transport, storage and communication | 259 | 10% |
| K | Real estate, renting and business activities | 249 | 10% |
| DI | Manufacture of other non-metallic mineral products | 217 | 9% |
| DD | Manufacture of wood and wood products | 199 | 8% |
| DA | Manufacture of food products, beverages and tobacco | 181 | 7% |
| - | Other manufacturing | 170 | 7% |
| DK | Manufacture of machinery and equipment not elsewhere classified | 144 | 6% |
| DE | Manufacture of pulp, paper and paper products, publishing and printing | 98 | 4% |
| J | Financial intermediation | 86 | 3% |
| E | Electricity, gas and water supply | 69 | 3% |
| DB | Manufacture of textiles and textile products | 68 | 3% |
| - | Other services | 26 | 1% |
| | | 2503 | 100% |

* *SKD - Standard Classification of Activities, 2002, http://www.stat.si/klasje/tabela.aspx?cvn=1891*

Pursuing the standardised methodology (Eurostat 2007; European Commission 2008), the Statistical Office of the Republic of Slovenia regularly collects data on the target industries. The statistical survey providing the core data for our research is the most recent Community Innovation Survey (CIS 2006), which was carried out throughout Europe in 2007. The Slovene contribution to the CIS 2006 survey includes data for the period from 2004 to 2006 on the enterprises' product (goods or service), organisational and process innovations, innovation activities and expenditures, co-operation in innovation and the effects of innovation. In addition, companies' financial data (balance sheet, profit and loss account and some key financial ratios) was collected from the official statistical database on companies (the Agency of the Republic of Slovenia for Public Legal Records and Related Services (AJPES), while the third statistical database (Statistical Register of Employment (SRDAP)) provided data on the educational structure of employees. The employment data refer to the fiscal year 2006 while the financial data encompass the period between 2003 (a year before the CIS survey) and 2007 (the following year).

The two key variables that represent a measurable (financial) output from the innovation process were defined as: RII ('Index of revenues from innovation'), i.e., a relative share of turnover resulting from innovations, and RMI ('Index of revenues from market innovation'), i.e., a ratio of turnover from innovations new to the market to total innovation turnover. A definition of indices is shown in Table 2; both refer to the innovations introduced in the 2004–2006 period.

As suggested by literature, innovations are positively influencing the business performance of companies. Therefore, it is favourable to increase the relative share of turnover from innovations (RII). However, from the market perspective, a company's innovation can either be entirely new to the market or just new to the company, having merely followed the market development (the relative share of turnover from the former is measured by RMI). To increase the turnover from innovations, a company can increase either the portion of innovative products in its portfolio or the market value of its products. The higher is the rate of innovation of a product, the higher its market value (cream-skimming effect). Thus, it is also favourable to increase the relative share of turnover from innovations new to the market (RMI).

Obviously, RII and RMI are partly interrelated: increase in RII is affected by the increase of RMI and both indicate the company innovation performance. The aim of this chapter to discuss some measures available to the management in order to raise either of the two indices.

*Table 2: The output variables from the innovation process*

| Variable | Definition | Measurement scale | Value range |
|---|---|---|---|
| RII – Revenues from innovation | $\frac{\text{Turnover from innovations introduced *}}{\text{Total turnover}} \times 100$ | Metric | 0, 100 |
| RMI – Revenues from market innovation | $\frac{\text{Turnover from innovations new to the market}}{\text{Turnover from innovations introduced *}} \times 100$ | Metric | 0, 100 |

**either new to the market or new to the company only*

The companies recording any revenues arising from innovations (RII>0) were divided into four groups. In order to ensure an equal representation of companies across all four groups, the medians of RII and RMI were chosen as a limit of division. After having excluded the companies with no innovation revenues (RII=0), both medians were calculated for the remaining subsample (median values are indicated in Table 3; row 'Innovators in total'). Dividing the RII/RMI matrix in points predefined with both medians, four quadrants are obtained, assuring that the companies are distributed evenly in all of the four groups. The group of companies that failed to record any revenues arising from innovation in the period observed (RII=0) was defined as the fifth group (group 0).

Next, the innovation groups were in pairs compared using nonparametric tests (Mann-Whitney and Kruskal Wallis Tests) and the Pearson Chi-Square Test so as to establish in which variables the groups significantly differ among themselves. We compared as follows: (i) the relations between the groups' innovation and business results (Section 4), (ii) the volume and productivity of their investments into innovation (Section 5), and (iii) the organisational structure of innovation activities (Section 6). In Section 6, the nonparametric tests were supplemented with Spearman's correlation analysis between the RII and RMI and other organisational variables in order to obtain a clearer picture of factors influencing the innovation capabilities.

# 3. Definition of Innovation Groups

As demonstrated in Section 2, the values of the two primary output indices of the invention-innovation process (RII and RMI) served as criteria for grouping the companies. These values are indicated separately for non-innovative (0) and innovative (1 & 2) companies (these are further divided into 4 subgroups 1a, 1b, 1c and 2) in Table 3.

*Table 3: Basic statistics for indices RII and RMI as per innovation groups*

| Group | N | Variable | Median | Mean |
|---|---|---|---|---|
| Non-innovators (0) | 1790 | RII | 0.00 | 0.00 |
| | | RMI | - | - |
| Innovators in total (1 & 2) | 713 | RII | 20.00 | 29.31 |
| | | RMI | 40.00 | 41.89 |
| Innovation followers (1c) | 206 | RII | 10.00 | 9.39 |
| | | RMI | 0.00 | 6.60 |

| | | | | |
|---|---|---|---|---|
| Innovation followers (1b) | 195 | RII | 10.00 | 10.59 |
| | | RMI | 100.00 | 79.39 |
| Innovation followers (1a) | 163 | RII | 48.00 | 52.42 |
| | | RMI | 1.01 | 11.83 |
| Innovation leaders (2) | 149 | RII | 50.00 | 56.05 |
| | | RMI | 71.43 | 74.48 |

We aimed at identifying a relationship between RII and RMI. After having eliminated the *non-innovators* group (Group 0), Spearman correlation analysis was applied to the sample. However, no correlation has been found between RII and RMI (Spearman's correlation coefficient *SCC*=0.01; *sig*=0.94). Representing our sample in the RII/RMI scattered plot has shown a fairly uniform distribution, biased towards the low RII/low RMI quadrant. Therefore, there are a number of companies with both a high relative share of turnover from innovations and a high relative share of turnover from 'radical' innovation in total innovation turnover (high RII and high RMI). These companies are evidently *innovation leaders* in the industry (Group 2 in Figure 1).

The remaining part of the sample consists of the *innovation followers*.

On the 'low RII/low RMI' side of the matrix, there are companies (Group 1c) with poor revenues from innovations and these innovations are of minor impact (presumably of the incremental type, e.g., incremental improvements to the companies' existing products to follow the technology or market trends).

The third group (Group 1a) of companies (high RII and low RMI) generates a notable part of its revenues out of recently introduced products. However, these products again act as substitutes to the companies' existing products with no radical improvements incorporated.

Companies from the fourth group (Group 1b) produce some market inventions, resulting in new products being introduced onto the market before competitors (low RII and high RMI). Such products normally incorporate a much higher degree of creativity. However, these companies somehow fail to make substantial revenues out of such products.

*Figure 1: RII/RMI matrix*

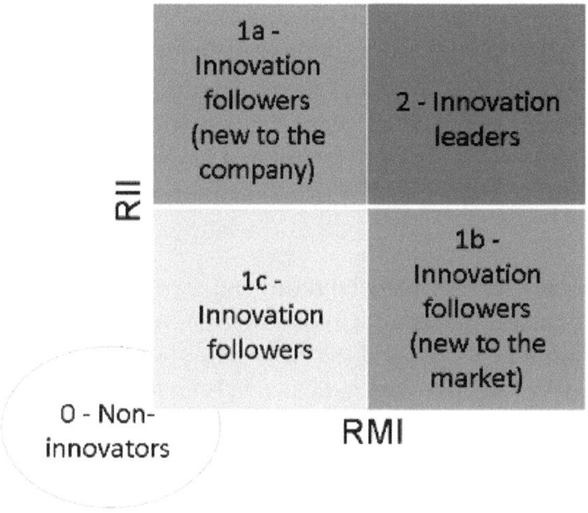


# 4. Relationship between the Innovation and Business Performance

In Section 3, the method of dividing the companies active in the field of innovation into four groups on the basis of RII and RMI indicators was demonstrated. Companies classified in different groups differ at least pursuant to the volume and structure of their innovation revenues, i.e., direct results of innovation recorded on the market. However, differences in the revenues from innovation do not necessarily also indicate differences in the companies' business performance. Furthermore, revenues arising from innovation do not provide any conclusions with regards the organisation of innovation systems in the companies.

Let us therefore examine whether there are any differences among the groups regarding their business performance. The Mann-Whitney rank sum test is applied to compare the financial ratios for the groups 0, 1 (a, b, c) and 2. The Mann-Whitney test is one of the non-parametric significance tests for assessing whether two independent samples of observations come from two populations with the same mean value (Kanji, 2006, 101). This test is used in the same situations as the independent samples Student's t-test. However, as it compares medians, which are insensitive to outliers compared to means, the Mann-Whitney test is less likely to spuriously indicate significance than the t-test because of the presence of outliers, i.e., Mann-Whitney is more robust.

A detailed testing revealed that there are not any significant differences as to demographic characteristics and business performance among the groups of followers (1a, 1b and 1c). Therefore, for the purposes of simplification, all three groups of followers are regarded as a homogenous Group 1. A group of innovation leaders (2) is thus compared with the group of non-innovators (0) and the group of followers as a whole (1).

Table 4 shows the values of medians for the financial ratios and significant differences in medians between the innovation leaders (2) and the non-innovators (0) as well as between the innovation leaders (2) and the followers (1). Statistically significant differences among pairs of medians are indicated in bold in the last two columns (where the value is lower than 0.05, the medians significantly differ).

*Table 4: Comparison of mean values of the financial ratios as per groups*

| Variable description | Median | | | Mann-Whitney test; Sig. (2-tailed) | |
|---|---|---|---|---|---|
| | Group 0 | Group 1 | Group 2 | 0 vs. 2 | 1 vs. 2 |
| Operating efficiency ratio | 1.02 | 1.02 | 1.02 | 0.67 | 0.90 |
| Return on sales – ROS | 0.02 | 0.03 | 0.04 | **0.02** | 0.28 |
| Pre-tax return on sales | 0.03 | 0.03 | 0.04 | **0.04** | 0.29 |
| Total revenues per employee (€) | 82183 | 85601 | 81794 | 0.90 | 0.41 |
| Net profit per employee (€) | 1906 | 2439 | 3079 | 0.17 | 0.53 |
| Gross profit per employee (€) | 2332 | 2905 | 3490 | 0.25 | 0.55 |
| Operating profit per employee (€) | 2963 | 3168 | 3976 | 0.37 | 0.57 |
| Labour costs per employee (€) | 17690 | 18396 | 18884 | **0.01** | 0.20 |
| Average salary per employee (€) | 12613 | 12962 | 13345 | **0.02** | 0.19 |
| Return on equity – ROE | 0.10 | 0.10 | 0.14 | **0.01** | **0.00** |
| Return on assets – ROA | 0.03 | 0.04 | 0.05 | **0.04** | 0.17 |
| Sales-to-Assets | 1.33 | 1.27 | 1.26 | 0.21 | 0.66 |
| Return on equity before taxes – ROEBT | 0.13 | 0.12 | 0.17 | **0.02** | **0.00** |
| Growth of net revenues 07/06 (%) | 3.63 | 3.60 | 3.84 | 0.06 | 0.01 |
| Average growth of net revenues (%) | 9.62 | 9.06 | 12.81 | **0.01** | 0.00 |
| Number of employees | 22 | 70 | 25 | **0.03** | 0.00 |

As evident in Table 4, Groups 1 and 2 significantly differ with regard to the return on equity ROE (invested capital creates to the owners in Group 2 by 1.4 higher gross profit and 1.4 higher net profit). At the same time, the revenues appertaining to the Group 2 recorded between 2006 and 2007 increased by a factor of 1.07, while the average revenues from 2003 to 2007 increased by a factor of 1.41.

Similar relations may be observed between Groups 0 and 2; additionally, statistically significant differences in return on sales (ROS) and return on assets (ROA) may be observed. Companies appertaining to Group 2 pay 6% higher salaries than the companies in Group 0.

On the basis of the aforementioned findings, it may be concluded that the companies appertaining to the Group 2, which in comparison with Groups 0 and 1 innovate more successfully (achieve higher values of RII and/or RMI), also record better company performance (assessed with financial ratios). Such companies' performance in terms of ROE proves to be 40% higher in the group of innovation leaders that among followers and non-innovators.

Observing the differences between Groups 0 and 2, we may observe that these are statistically insignificant for the variables measuring profits as per employee, while they are significant for the variables measuring profits as per equity (ROE), assets (ROA) and sales (ROS). Investigating this in detail revealed that (i) the companies in Group 2 are on average larger than in those in Group 0 in terms of numbers of employees, and that (ii) the number of employees tends to negatively affect financial ratios. Therefore, we may expect lower profits per employee in Group 2 due to the higher average employee count.

# 5. Extent and Productivity of Innovation Investments

What portions of financial assets do companies in a particular group invest into innovation, and how efficiently do these companies turn such investments into revenues arising from innovations? To answer these two questions, the group of followers (1) shall again be examined divided into three subgroups as indicated in Figure 1, i.e., 1a, 1b and 1c.

A company of type 1a may enter into the category of innovation leaders (2) by increasing its RMI; a company of type 1b by increasing its RII, and a company of type 1c by increasing both RII and RMI. In order to make the examination simpler, let us suppose that simultaneously only one of both coefficients may be increased, i.e., a path from the subgroup 1c into Group 2 leads either through 1b or through 1a.

Using Mann-Whitney's test, it shall be established in which variables the groups 1b and 1a significantly differ from Group 2 and between each other. A comparison with the group of non-innovators (0) is not possible, since this group fails to record any costs of innovation. The efficiency of turning the invested assets into revenues arising from innovations, i.e., productivity of investments, shall be expressed with a CRIT variable (share of innovation expenditure to total revenues arising from innovations), representing a reciprocal value of the productivity of investments, which also enables its calculation for the companies that recorded revenues arising from innovation in the period in question (as in the case of Groups 1 and 2), yet did not record any innovation costs.

Table 5 shows variable medians of innovation expenditure and productivity of investments (CRIT) for Groups 1a, 1b and 2. Statistically significant correlations are indicated in bold.

*Table 5: Comparison of medians of innovation expenditure and productivity of investments as per groups*

| Variable description | Median | | | Mann-Whitney test; Sig. (2-tailed) | | |
|---|---|---|---|---|---|---|
| | Group 1a | Group 1b | Group 2 | 1a vs. 2 | 1b vs. 2 | 1a vs. 1b |
| Total innovation expenditure / Net revenues from sales | 0.023 | 0.017 | 0.033 | **0.048** | **0.001** | 0.205 |
| Total innovation expenditure / Number of employees (€) | 1920 | 1391 | 2623 | 0.059 | **0.001** | 0.269 |
| CRIT (Relative share of innovation expenditure to total revenues from innovations) | 0.051 | 0.178 | 0.072 | 0.112 | **0.000** | **0.000** |

A comparison of Groups 1a and 2 in Table 5 indicates that the companies appertaining to the Group 2 invest significantly more than the companies in Group 1a (innovation costs as a relative share of revenues from sales in Group 2 are higher by 1.4 times).

Regarding Groups 1b and 2, companies in Group 2 invest more than Group 1b (innovation expenditures in Group 2 are 1.9 times higher). The productivity of innovation investments is significantly higher in Group 2 than in Group 1b. The companies in Group 2 succeed in making an average of €14 from every euro invested in innovation (or almost 2.5 times more than the companies in Group 1b).

Groups 1a and 1b do not differ regarding the costs, but do so with regards the productivity of innovation investments. The productivity of innovation investment is 3.5 times higher in Group 1a than in Group 1b. This result may be explained by the fact that by investing similar amount of financial assets Group 1a on average generates higher revenues from innovation (RII).

Which type of innovation investment policies do companies in the groups of innovation followers (1a or 1b) need to adopt in order to reach the group of innovation leaders (2)? Companies in Group 1a need to increase investments in innovation in order to increase RMI and thus enter Group 2 (by a factor of 1.4 on average at unchanged exploitation of these assets).

So as to increase RII and enter Group 2, companies in Group 1b need to ensure simultaneous increases in investments and in the efficiency of their exploitation. Therefore, a transition through the intermediate level (1a) is in this case reasonable. Transition from Group 1b to 1a shall not demand an increase in the invested financial assets, yet it shall require a substantial increase in the efficiency of exploiting the existing assets (by a factor of 3.5 on average). The next step, transition from the Group 1a into the Group 2 shall (in contrast) demand more intensive investments into innovation, at unchanged efficiency of their exploitation.

# 6. Impact of Organisational Factors onto the Revenues from Innovation

Section 5 revealed that an improvement in innovation capabilities may be achieved by increased investing into innovation and/or by increasing the efficiency of turning these investments into innovation revenues. The efficiency of investments is influenced by an appropriate organisation of innovation processes. How does the organisation of an innovation system in a company influence its innovation abilities?

As demonstrated in Sections 4 and 5, the groups of innovation followers and innovation leaders are significantly different with regards to their business performance, the volume of innovation investments and the productivity of these investments. Moreover, these two groups also differ regarding the values of variables RII and RMI, which represent the basic criteria for dividing the companies into groups. Consequently, the characteristics of the innovation system of a group may be concluded on the basis of comparing RII and RMI with the other examined organisational variables. Let us thus examine which organisational variables record statistically significant relations with the variables RII and RMI. Spearman's correlation was carried out for this purpose.

A correlation with the share of turnover from innovations (RII) has been established for the following organisational variables:

1. A high correlation with the introduction of 'techn(olog)ical' innovations (new products, either goods or services, and new processes) *(SCC=0.87; sig=0.00)*. A moderate correlation with the introduction of organisational innovations *(SCC=0.48; sig=0.00)*.
2. A moderate correlation with the extent of cooperation in innovation activities with other organisations. Companies with a high RII collaborate particularly with their customers *(SCC=0.27; sig=0.00)*, less with other potential partners (other companies, universities, research institutions or consultants). These cooperation partners are more likely found abroad *(SCC=0.31; sig=0.00)* than within the country *(SCC=0.21; sig=0.00)*.
3. A high correlation with the total innovation expenditures *(SCC=0.75; sig=0.00)* and intramural innovation expenditures *(SCC=0.69; sig=0.00)*. Less correlation with the expenditures for the acquisition of innovation (extramural innovation) *(SCC=0.41; sig=0.00)*. To cover these expenditures, companies with a high RII have received financial support from the national *(SCC=0.37; sig=0.00)* and EU sources *(SCC=0.26; sig=0.00)*, rather than from local governments *(SCC=0.15; sig=0.00)*. There is a correlation of RII with the innovation efficiency (productivity of innovation expenditures in their transformation into the innovation revenues) *(SCC=0.32; sig=0.00)*.
4. A moderate correlation with the level of education of the employees (share of employees with a masters or doctoral degree) *(SCC=0.25; sig=0.00)*.
5. Low correlation with the average number of employees *(SCC=0.21; sig=0.00)*; thus the number of employees as a proxy to the company size (data on balance sheet total required to classify companies according to size was unavailable) has little affect on the innovation performance in terms of innovation revenues. RII shows no correlation with the companies' financial result.

Further, the correlation of RMI with the surveyed organisational variables was investigated. Surprisingly, no correlations were found. A detailed examination of this fact at the industry level revealed that these correlations vary significantly among industries. Consequently, investigating them at the level of the entire sample shows no results. Obviously, increasing RMI requires different organisational approaches in different circumstances.

# 7. Discussion

Some questions regarding the innovation capabilities of companies were researched in this chapter. The main findings are summarised hereunder.

i) On the basis of revenues arising from innovation, expressed with coefficients RII and RMI, five groups of companies were formed: a group of non-innovators (0), three groups of innovation followers (1a, 1b, 1c) and a group of innovation leaders (2). The groups of followers were in part examined as a uniform group (1). We were interested as to whether there is a relationship between the revenues from innovation and the companies' financial results. The group of innovation leaders (2) significantly differs from the group of innovation followers (1) as to the return on equity (ROE), i.e., regarding the net income divided by the shareholder's equity. ROE indicates the amount of profit the company records as to the sources provided by its owners/shareholders or how many units of profit shareholders may expect to be generated per unit of invested capital. It proves evident that this is definitely an indicator that is fundamental from the investor's point of view (also/particularly for an investor who is making a decision as to whether it is reasonable to invest into the R&D and innovation or whether it proves more rational to invest into the traditional production factors would definitely provide physical growth of the companies' operations, e.g., via mergers and acquisitions).

   Beside ROE, significant differences between Groups 1 and 2 may be observed regarding the growth of revenues from sales in the period in question. If profit is an economic category on which it is possible to influence by way of accountancy, e.g., with an objective of lowering taxes, then the growth of revenues from sales proves to be a more 'factual' category. Growth of revenues from sales indicates entering new markets, increasing market shares on existing markets or, last but not least, achieving higher selling prices. The company recording an increase in sales may be perceived as successful. The relationships between Groups 1 and 2 are similar to the relationships between

Groups 0 and 2, also revealing statistically significant differences in the return on sales (ROS) and the return on assets (ROA).

We thus demonstrated that there is a correlation between the revenues arising from innovation and the financial results of a company. The companies belong to Group 2, which in comparison with Groups 0 and 1 innovate more successfully (record higher values of RII and/or RMI), also achieve better business performance assessed with the financial ratios. Companies' performance in terms of ROE is 40% higher in the group of innovation leaders than in the groups of followers and non-innovators.

ii) The relationship between the financial investments into innovation and the revenues arising from innovation (productivity of investments) is only partially confirmed. Significant differences may be observed between Groups 1b and 2, yet not between Groups 1a and 2. The impact of innovation investments is thus not linear; increased investments do not (necessarily) result in an improved innovation performance.

How, therefore, does an increase in innovation investments influence the productivity of these investments? An increase in investments boosts the productivity of invested assets in companies recording relatively low revenues from innovations (RII), i.e., in Group 1b. In contrast, investing with the purpose of increasing the share of 'breakthrough' innovations (share of RMI), i.e., in Group 1a, reduces the productivity of these assets. As demonstrated in Section 5, substantial financial inputs are required so as to increase RMI. However, these inputs fail to return with the same rapid growth in revenues (at least in the short-term). In the event we wish to increase RMI, the investments prove to be less efficient from the invested assets point of view yet prove to be essential for achieving a larger relative share of breakthrough innovations.

Which policies of innovation investments are thus to be selected by the companies in the group of innovation followers (1a or 1b) so as to enter the group of innovation leaders (2)? A company in Group 1a needs to increase investments into innovation in order to increase RMI and thus enter Group 2 (at unchanged efficiency of exploiting these assets). So as to increase RII and enter Group 2, a company in Group 1b needs to ensure a simultaneous increase in investments and increase in the efficiency of their exploitation. Therefore, a transition through the intermediate level (1a) is reasonable in this case. Transition from the Group 1b into 1a shall not demand an increase in the invested financial assets, but it shall require a substantial increase in the efficiency of exploiting the existing assets (by a factor of 3.5 on average). The next step, transition from Group 1a into Group 2 shall in contrast require more intensive investments into innovation, at an unchanged efficiency of exploitation.

iii) In the concluding parts of this research, we explore the correlations between the organisational structure of innovation activities and the revenues arising from innovation. Using Spearman's correlation analysis, it was confirmed that statistically significant correlations may be observed between the variable RII and individual organisational variables. The latter indicates that the method of organisation of innovation process is related to the market results from innovations. Introducing primarily technological innovations, innovation co-operation with external partners (buyers in particular), investing financial assets into innovation activities and an efficient use of assets prove to be the main factors influencing the growth of revenues arising from innovation (RII). In-depth research into these impacts was hindered by the limited set of secondary data available.

Our research was based on secondary data obtained pursuant to the standardised methodology of Eurostat; however, the CIS research is primarily intended for innovation policy makers and not for managers. It is thus possible that some questions important for the organisation of innovation within companies were not examined. Our research shall in the future be supplemented with a survey questionnaire intended for companies' managers, which shall thus evaluate the contents not encompassed in the CIS research.

Another issue to be considered is a time lag with which the results of innovation activities are reflected on the market. The new technologies, ideas and knowledge that resulted from R&D investments will be diffused, used and thus depreciated only after the completion of the R&D project (rather than immediately) (Kafouros and Wang 2008, 234). It is shown by Ernst (2001, 153) that national patent applications lead to sales increases with a lag of two to three years after the priority year. European patent applications, which are of higher quality than national patent applications, have an even higher impact on sales increases, with a lag of three years after the priority year. The RII and RMI indices used in our research are based on the market revenues arising from innovations. Since these revenues refer to the period from 2004 to 2006, a substantial part of innovations had only just been introduced onto the market in the time of our survey (spring 2007). Since such innovations are mostly still in the launching phase or the phase of growth; they have not yet reached their target market share, and their revenues are consequently lower. Therefore, it proves reasonable to compare market data for the period after 2007 in the subsequent research.

Our research was carried out on a sample of companies from Slovenia. Medians of variables RII and RMI (and thus examined innovation groups) may well prove to be different in other environments. However, as regards the relations in innovation activities, it may be expected that the results can be generalised to a large extent. Recent research based on the same CIS data for seven major EU countries has shown that as regards the variables associated with R&D and new products, the sectoral specificities appear much stronger than country specificities (Bogliacino and Pianta 2009, 15). Furthermore, the most recent issue of the European Innovation Scoreboard shows that Slovenia is performing almost exactly at the EU average regarding the Summary Innovation Index (Eurostat 2010, 6), thus being a good representative of the population.

Finally, there is a clear indication as to the measures required to boost RII. Regarding RMI, the requirements are not as evident. As shown above, reaching a high RMI involves different approaches in different circumstances. Investigating this fact in detail would have exceeded the scope of this study, but is worth considering in our further research.

## 8. Conclusion

Despite some encouraging indicators and at times somewhat misleading statistical data, it is obvious that only a moderate relative share of the innovative potential of enterprises in the Slovene economy is exploited. The incontestable fact remains that the influence of innovation on the companies' revenues and profit remains too low. A clear strategy of innovation and appropriate further activities are the crucial factors leading to an increase of this influence (Collins 2001). The strategy should consistently support the innovation process and strongly focus on the most important activities leading to the best innovation performance. Since the innovation introduced onto the market is only the last of the links in the invention-innovation chain, a comprehensive and systematic approach is required. In order to ensure such an approach, the 'innovation of management' (Mulej and Ženko 2004) in such a way that it would be able to manage the innovation process effectively remains a prerequisite.

## References

Altman, W. (2008): Are you leading the way in innovation? *Engineering & Technology* 3, no. 19: 72–75.

Bogliacino, F., and M. Pianta (2009): *Innovation performances in Europe: a long term perspective*. EIS Thematic Paper, European Commission, DG Enterprises, Brussels.

Carayannis, E., E Gonzales, and J Wetter (2003): The Nature and Dynamics of Discontinuous and Disruptive Innovations from a Learning and Knowledge Management Perspective. In *The International Handbook on Innovation*, ed. Larisa V. Shavinina, 115–138. Amsterdam [etc.]: Pergamon; Elsevier.

Collins, J.C. (2001): *Good to Great: Why Some Companies Make the leap... and Others Don't*. London: Random House Business Books.

Coombs, R., P. Narandren, and A. Richards (1996): A literature-based innovation output indicator. *Research Policy* 25, no. 3: 403–413. doi:10.1016/0048-7333(95)00842-X.

Ernst, H. (2001): Patent applications and subsequent changes of performance: evidence from time-series cross-section analyses on the firm level. *Research Policy* 30, no. 1 (1): 143-157. doi:10.1016/S0048-7333(99)00098-0.

European Commission (2008): *Science, technology and innovation in Europe*. 2008. ed. Luxembourg: Office for official publications of the European Communities. http://epp.eurostat.ec.europa.eu/cache/ITY_OFFPUB/KS-EM-08-001/EN/KS-EM-08-001-EN.PDF.

Eurostat (2007): Fourth Community Innovation Survey. More than 40% of EU-27 enterprises are active in innovation Co-operation with customers. Eurostat. http://europa.eu/rapid/pressReleasesAction.do?reference=STAT/07/27&type=HTML.

(2008): *European Innovation Scoreboard 2007. Comparative Analysis of Innovation Performance*. Luxembourg: Office for Official Publications of the European Communities, February. http://www.proinno-europe.eu/admin/uploaded_documents/European_Innovation_Scoreboard_2007.pdf.

(2010) *European Innovation Scoreboard 2009. Comparative Analysis of Innovation Performance*. European Union. http://www.proinno-europe.eu/page/european-innovation-scoreboard-2009.

Fatur, P., and B. Likar (2010): Statistical Analysis for Strategic Innovation Decisions in Slovene Mechanical Industry. *Journal of Mechanical Engineering* 56, no. 7-8: 489–496.

Freel, M. S. (2005): Patterns of innovation and skills in small firms. *Technovation* 25, no. 2: 123–134.

Geroski, P., and S. Machin (1992) Do Innovating Firms Outperform Non-Innovators? *Business Strategy Review* 3, no. 2: 79-90. doi:10.1111/j.1467-8616.1992.tb00030.x.

Hagedoorn, J, and M Cloodt (2003): Measuring innovative performance: is there an advantage in using multiple indicators? *Research Policy* 32, no. 8: 1365–1379. doi:10.1016/S0048-7333(02)00137-3.

Hollenstein, H. (1996): A composite indicator of a firm's innovativeness. An empirical analysis based on survey data for Swiss manufacturing. *Research Policy* 25, no. 4: 633-645. doi:10.1016/0048-7333(95)00874-8.

Iansiti, M. (1997): From technological potential to product performance: an empirical analysis. *Research Policy* 26, no. 3 (October): 345–365. doi:10.1016/S0048-7333(97)00021-8.

Kafouros, M., and C. Wang (2008): The Role of Time in Assessing the Economic Effects of R&D. *Industry & Innovation* 15, no. 3 (6): 233–251. doi:10.1080/13662710802041638.

Kanji, G. K. (2006): *100 Statistical Tests*. 3. ed. London; Thousand Oaks; New Delhi: Sage Publications.

Likar, B. (2008): The influence of innovation, technological and research processes on the performance of Slovenia's woodworking industry. *Wood Research* 53, no. 4: 115–120.

Madrid-Guijarro, A., D. Garcia, and H. Van Auken (2009): Barriers to Innovation among Spanish Manufacturing SMEs. *Journal of Small Business Management* 47, no. 4: 465-488. doi:10.1111/j.1540-627X.2009.00279.x.

Mulej, M., and Z. Ženko (2004): *Introduction to systems thinking with application to invention and innovation management*. Maribor: Management Forum.

Neely, A., and J. Hii (1998): *Innovation and business performance: a literature review*. The Judge Institute of Management Studies, University of Cambridge. http://89.249.21.76/data/696/521/1221/litreview_innov1.pdf. (Accessed September 1, 2010)

Parthasarthy, R, and J. Hammond (2002): Product innovation input and outcome: moderating effects of the innovation process. *Journal of Engineering and Technology Management* 19, no. 1 (March): 75–91. doi:10.1016/S0923-4748(01)00047-9.

Radas, S., and L. Bozic (2009): The antecedents of SME innovativeness in an emerging transition economy. *Technovation* 29, no. 6: 438–450. doi:10.1016/j.technovation.2008.12.002.

Roper, S., J. Du, and J. H Love (2008): Modelling the innovation value chain. *Research Policy* 37, no. 6: 961–977.

Sharma, S., and V. J. Thomas (2008): Inter-country R&D efficiency analysis: An application of data envelopment analysis. *Scientometrics* 76, no. 3 (7): 483-501. doi:10.1007/s11192-007-1896-4.

SURS (2008): Inovacijska dejavnost v predelovalnih in izbranih storitvenih dejavnostih, Slovenija, 2004–2006, začasni podatki. Statistični urad RS. http://www.stat.si/novica_prikazi.aspx?ID=1592. (Accessed September 1, 2010)

## About the Authors

**Peter Fatur**'s professional career consists of several positions in the technology and management spheres within two multinational companies. Currently, he holds an academic position at the University of Primorska. He is an author or a co-author of several scientific and professional publications on innovation management and mass customisation.

**Borut Likar** is a professor at the University of Primorska, Faculty of Management and the head of the Department of Innovation and Technology Management. Furthermore, he is a successful innovator. Among the numerous lectures he has given, his talks at the United Nations' headquarters in Geneva and the European Parliament in Brussels were met with a particularly wide response.

# The Importance of Structural Indicators in Assessing the Efficiency of Business Process Performance

***Benjamin Urh***

*benjamin.urh@fov.uni-mb.si*

***Špela Kokalj***

*spela.kokalj@fov.uni-mb.si*

***Maja Zajec***

*maja.zajec@fov.uni-mb.si*

## Abstract

This chapter presents an assessment of the efficiency of business process performance. Primarily, we focused on the structural indicators of efficiency, since we believe that the structural complexity of business processes is one of the key points in process performance management. In doing so, we were interested in which structural indicators of business process efficiency are interconnected, which are independent from the others and which illustrate the situation the most relevantly or, as the case may be, have the greatest influence on the efficiency of an individual business process performance. The connectedness and influence of individual structural indicators on the efficiency of business process performance was researched using the concrete example of three business systems.

**Key words:** business processes repository, analysis of business processes, indicators of efficiency, key performance indicators

# 1. Introduction

In recent decades, changes in the business environment have been accompanied by continuous changes in the organisation of business systems and the related orientation of organising business operations. We can distinguish four key periods:

- Orientation into departments
- Orientation within the business system
- Orientation into business systems
- Orientation outside of business systems (Davis, 2001).

Change has become a constant; the existing situation can be termed 'a continuous evolution of changes'. These are not just occasional changes in product design or the implementation of a new information system; everything changes these days, including recently developed products, newly established business systems organisation models and newly acquired knowledge.

From the 1990s onward, many business systems have been trying to adapt to the changed conditions of business operations by renewing their business processes (Davenport, 1992) (the most frequently used expression in literature is Business Process Reengineering, i.e., BPR), which requires that a business system applies profound changes in its work performance and establishes processes.

In addition to BPR, numerous other approaches to renewing business operations have been developed in the business world during this period (over 50 according to Vila, 2006); these include Continuous Process Improvement (Harkness et al. 1996), Total Quality Management (Deming, 1982), Business Process Regeneration (Kettinger & Teng, 2000), Business Process Redesign (Davenport, & Short, 1990), Kaizen and others, all of which are supported by specific methodologies. However, these diverse approaches all have more or less the same goal: to achieve more efficient business process operations. The differences between the approaches lies in the method they propose for achieving this goal, from fast and profound (revolutionary) changes on the one hand to slow and gradual (evolutionary) changes on the other.

Managers of business systems, who have realised that their future can only be successfully planned with adaptation to ever-new requirements and conditions, follow guidelines that have recently been created. The guidelines that present a continuation of business process reengineering and, simultaneously, a reply to the ever-changing business environment include BPM – Business Process Management (Holt, 2000; Hung, 2006), PPM – Process Performance Management (Smith, 2005; Scanlon, & Watts, 2009) and BPE – Business Process Excellence (London

2002; Kennedy, 2006). All of these emphasise that the need for process management is the key to success.

# 2. Process Performance Management

Having successfully adapted to changes or carried out business process reengineering, top managers in business systems often ask themselves important questions, such as: 'Have we met our objectives?', 'Is this what we needed?' and 'Where do we go from here and how?' However, once a business system has established a reengineered state, it is soon realised that it does not suffice: the environment and, consequently, the demands, change ever-faster, leading to ever-new needs for adaptation and changing the processes. At this point, top managers come face to face with very important and difficult questions for any business system, for example:

- What is the level of efficiency of business process performance?
- Is business process performance still acceptable for the business system in terms of demands?
- Is it necessary or reasonable to adapt or change the process?
- What changes or adjustments must be made to the business process performance?
- How will the envisaged changes influence the efficiency of the business process performance?

Many business systems have their operations (business processes) supported by expensive software, which they will be able to use and upgrade for a number of years (Prijatelj et al. 2010; Roblek et al. 2010; Dibrell et al. 2008). These software packages often include efficient tools that can be used to create a detailed report of the existing ('AS-IS') business processes in a business system.

However, despite the implemented software solutions, top managers on different levels of business systems often lack reliable feedback on the efficiency of 'AS-IS' business process performance. To ease the work of many managers when searching for a solution to these questions, software tools have been developed and launched that enable business systems to measure and assess the efficiency of their business process performance, insofar as their performance is supported by standard computer software (Ranjan, 2008).

Using these software tools, managers have been given the opportunity to provide answers to questions on the efficiency of business process performance at any given moment. However, the managers are now faced with new questions. For example:

- Which of the 'operational' indicators (business process performance indicators) (Valiris, & Glykas, 2004; Sharma, 2009) and which of the 'structural' indicators (business process design or process flow indicators) (Poniatowski, & Wichser, 2006; Bassi, & McMurrer, 2007; Frederiksen, & Mathiassen, 2008; Fitz-enz, 2009) show the situation in the most relevant way or, as the case may be, have the greatest influence on the efficiency of performing an individual business process, and
- How are these efficiency indicators interconnected or interdependent?

## 2.1 Assessment of the Efficiency of Business Processes

The efficiency of business process performance is an important indicator of the success of business operations, though this success is not only influenced by the efficiency of business operations, but by many other factors. Similarly, the efficiency of business process performance is influenced by numerous factors (Kaplan, & Norton, 2008). Each business system is subject to the influences of different factors originating from the widest environment of a business system.

The efficiency of business process performance is influenced by various factors from the wider external environment, from the narrower external environment and form internal factors. Consequently, the business process performance in business systems (company, institution etc.) is adapted to the 'needs' of these factors. In practice, this is reflected in the changing value of key business process performance indicators.

The assessment of the current state of the efficiency of business process performance can be imagined in practice as an on-line collection of data (key performance indicators[1]) on operational indicators, as well as an overview and calculation of the structural indicators of the efficiency of business process performance. There is also the analysis of the latter (in the case of operational indicators establishing deviations from the expected results due to inconsistent performance)

1 Key Performance Indicators are quantifiable measurements that help an organisation measure progress toward meeting its planned goals and objectives within a business system (Bauer, 2004). They can express strategically important indicators for the business system or express the efficiency of performing irrelevant processes or activities. They can be adapted to all the levels of the business system, from an individual performer to a business unit. The success in establishing business process management in a business system largely depends on the selection of key performance indicators. Furthermore, it is important that the key performance indicators are used to 'measure' at least the most essential activities, processes and indicators that show how "healthy" a business system is.

and adopting decisions on further business process performance. Processes may remain unchanged, or they may be adapted to the changeable demands of the environment (market, clients etc.) (Urh et al., 2008).

When reading relevant literature on research in this field, we find numerous proposals for assessing the efficiency of business process performance (Aguilar et al., 2006; Kaplan, & Norton, 2008; Dibrell et al., 2008; Frederiksen & Mathiassen, 2008). The majority of proposals refer to assessing the results that were achieved by business process performance following the operational indicators, which (as such) include spending time and/or the costs incurred. Few proposals are connected with assessments of the structural complexity of business processes following structural indicators.

Primarily, we focused on structural indicators of efficiency, since we believe that the structural complexity of business processes presents one of the key points in process performance management. The evolution of the complexity of business processes according to the structural indicators presents a suitable starting point for managing problems with the efficiency of business process performance. We were interested in the following:

- **Which structural indicators of business process performance are interconnected or, as the case may be, independent from the others?**
- **Which structural indicators show the situation in the most relevant manner or, as the case may be, have the greatest influence on the efficiency of an individual business process performance?**

# 3. Research

When choosing business systems to include in our research, we were limited by the research methodology. Research into the influence of the structural complexity of business processes on the efficiency of their performance can only be achieved when the business processes are known in detail within a given business system. Therefore, process mapping should have already been performed within a business system and its records stored in a corresponding repository.

When carrying out process mapping (modelling the existing situation), various methodologies can be used, for example: REAL, BPMN, ARIS, ARMA and others (according to an independent analysis by Gartner Group assessors, the ARIS methodology by IDS Scheer has been the most advanced methodology for a number of years, and is most effectively supported by software) (Erickson & Siau, 2007).

For the purposes of evaluating the efficiency of business process performance, we therefore chose the ARIS methodology and Event-driven Process Chain type of model (eEPC).[2]

We included three business systems in our research, all located in Slovenia; we had already cooperated with them in applicative projects recording their business processes. In this way, these business systems ensured a comparable level of recording (the same convention or rules for recording the business processes). Had this not been so, it would have been impossible to carry out a joint research.

## 3.1 The Interconnectedness or Dependence of Structural Indicators of Efficiency

The research was carried out in several stages. Firstly, we prepared an assessment of the efficiency of an individual business process performance by following selected structural indicators and based on the recorded business processes in the repository of the individual business system. The assessment included 386 business process models from three business systems, whose records were based on an object approach to modelling (eEPC models).

By analysing the business process models, we collected the basic data (key performance indicators) for assessing the efficiency of the business process performance per individual indicators. In our analysis, we collected the following data (KPIs):

- The number of events in a process
- The number of initial events in a process
- The number of completed and/or terminated events in a process
- The number of activities in a process (functions and process interfaces)
- The number of activities with connections to other processes (process interfaces)
- The number of decisions during process performance
- The number of possible transitions between activities in a process
- The number of loopbacks in a process
- The number of activities in a process where added value is created
- The number of connections between work positions and process activities

2 In Slovene, the abbreviation eEPC (Event-driven Process Chain) is usually translated as 'model of the event-driven process chain'. This model is based on the logic that an event triggers an activity (task) or several activities; consequently, the activity ends with a new event or with several events. Hereinafter, we will use the abbreviation eEPC whenever we want to emphasise the type of model used.

- The number of performers (work positions) participating in a process
- The number of hierarchical levels of performers participating in the process
- The number of work positions participating in performing all the business processes in a given business system
- The number of performers (work positions) in a business system
- The number of documents used in a process
- The number of documents that are to be created within a process
- The number of documents entering the process
- The number of software solutions used in the process
- The number of process activities whose performance is supported by software solutions.

According to the objects or symbols mapped in business process models (386 process models from three business systems), basic data or key performance indicators were chosen.

With regard to the objects or symbols forming the eEPC business process models, we can classify the structural indicators of efficiency into four basic groups, i.e., indicators, expressed on the basis of:

- Key process flow indicators (slim eEPC model)
- Key connection indicators
- Key process performance indicators or organisational structure elements
- Key product indicators or support objects (documents, software solutions etc.) (Aguilar et al., 2006)

Based on the selected key business process performance indicators, we assessed the efficiency of an individual business process performance, wherein we used the following 18 structural indicators of efficiency.

**Process Flow Indicators**

**1. Initial Process Event Indicator (SK01)**

The indicator is expressed as a relationship between the basic key performance indicator that shows the number of initial or, as the case may be, trigger events and the basic key indicator showing the number of events in a given business process. The more initial events and/or additional entry events there are during the process, the greater the likelihood for the process flow to be complicated or for delays in the process flow to occur due to the harmonisation of the events. Therefore, the greater the number of initial and/or entry events, the greater the likelihood that the business process performance efficiency will be poor.

$$K_{SE} = \frac{n_{SE}}{n_E} \cdot 100$$

**2. The Number of Completed and/or Terminated Events in a Process (SK02)**

The basic key performance indicator for calculating this indicator is the number of completed and/or terminated events, correlated to the number of events in the given business process. The more terminated events there are, the greater the likelihood for the process to be left incomplete; the more completed events there are, the greater the number of different completion results (products, documents etc.) there are in a given process. All this indicates the complexity of a process flow and, consequently, the possibility of reduced efficiency in the business process performance.

$$K_{FE} = \frac{n_{FE}}{n_E} \cdot 100$$

**3. Process Activity Indicator (SK03)**

This indicator is expressed as the differential quotient between the basic key indicator of the number of activities in a given business process and the number of activities connected to other processes. This indicator shows the scope of an individual process. The greater the scope (i.e., more activities) of the process, the more time and sources it requires. The scope of time taken and resources used can be connected to the performance of individual activities and/or transitions or, as the case may be, the progress of the process during individual activities. The use of time and resources is directly connected to business process performance efficiency.

$$K_A = \frac{1}{(n_{PA} - n_{PI})} \cdot 100$$

**4. Indicator of Process Decisions (SK04)**

This indicator is expressed as the key indicator of the number of decisions in a given business process, correlated with the difference between the basic key indicator of the number of activities in a given process and the number of activities connected to other processes. This indicator shows the diversification or, as the case may be, multi-variability of the process performance and the related complexity of the process. With each decision made, there exist at least two possibilities for how to continue the process (the most frequent are a loopback or the continuation of the process). Each decision of this kind or, as the case may be, between a greater number of possibilities, is connected to the use of time, which is (as we have already written) directly connected to business process performance efficiency.

$$K_D = \frac{n_{DP}}{(n_{PA} - n_{PI})} \cdot 100$$

**5. Indicator of Process Added Value (SK05)**

The indicator of business process added value is determined by the relationship between the basic key performance indicator and the number of activities within a given business process that creates added value, and the difference between the basic key indicator of the number of activities in the business process and the number of activities connected to other processes. This indicator focuses on determining the processes or, as the case may be, activities that represent a value to the customer and the business system as a whole (Harington, 1993).

$$K_{VAP} = \frac{n_{VAA}}{(n_{PA} - n_{PI})} \cdot 100$$

**Indicators of Connections**

**6. Indicator of Process Connection (SK06)**

This indicator shows how connected the process is to other processes within a business system or, as the case may be, its inclusion in the previous and/or consequent processes. It is the relationship between the basic key indicator, the number of activities with connections to other processes and the number of activities within the process. For these business processes, it is also true that the chain is only as efficient as its weakest link. Therefore, the more the processes are connected, the higher the probability that there is a less efficient process among them.

$$K_{PI} = \frac{n_{PI}}{n_{PA}} \cdot 100$$

**7. Indicator of the Number of Transitions between Activities (SK07)**

This indicator is expressed using the key performance indicators, i.e., as a relationship between the key indicator of the number of possible transitions between activities within the process (all the available routes) and the difference between the basic key indicator of the number of activities in the process and the number of activities with connections to other processes. The indicator demonstrates the complexity of the process by taking the possible loopbacks into consideration, since they can significantly delay the completion of the process. The level of connectedness between the activities in a business process is largely connected to the number of levels in the organisational (management) structure and to leaving decision making to the lower levels. A higher number of levels within an organisational structure of performers in a business process mean higher costs for the transitions between individual activities (Valiris & Glykas, 2004).

$$K_{PAT} = \frac{n_{AT}}{(n_{PA} - n_{PI})} \cdot 100$$

**8. Loopback Indicator (SK08)**

This indicator is expressed as the key indicator of the number of decisions in a given business process, correlated with the difference between the basic key indicator of the number of activities in a given process and the number of activities connected to other processes. This indicator presents the scope of control included in the performance of an individual process. For each control activity that checks compliance of work performed, in the event of non-compliance, the work is returned one or more activities backwards in the process flow. By means of control or, as the case may be, the number of loopbacks in the process, the amount of time spent increases, which negatively affects the efficiency of the performance.

$$K_{LB} = \frac{n_{LB}}{(n_{PA} - n_{PI})} \cdot 100$$

**Indicators of Process Performers**

**9. Indicator of the Level of Inclusion of the Performers (SK09)**

This indicator is expressed using the key performance indicators, i.e., as a relationship between the key indicator of the number of connections between the performers (work positions) in the process and the activities in the process, and the difference between the basic key indicator of the number of activities in the process and the number of activities with connections to other processes, multiplied by the number of performers (work positions), which are included in performing business process activities (Meglič et al. 2009). The indicator shows the level of work difficulty in individual activities in the process or, as the case may be, the level of established teamwork in an individual process.

$$K_{CLP} = \frac{n_{CPA}}{(n_{PA} - n_{PI}) \cdot n_{PP}} \cdot 100$$

**10. Indicator of Process Performers (SK10)**

This is expressed by the quotient of the key indicator of the number of performers (work positions) that participate in process performance. The indicator indicates the type of work positions (specialist or general) that are included in the process performance or, as the case may be, the type of systematisation that is applicable in the business system. Performing processes that include general work positions can be organised much more efficiently than performing processes that include specialist work positions.

$$K_{PP} = \frac{1}{n_{PP}} \cdot 100$$

**11. Indicator of Included Performers (SK11)**

This indicator shows the relationship between the number of performers participating in the process and the number of performers that participate in business processes throughout the business system. It is expressed using the key basic performance indicators, i.e., as the relationship between the key indicator of the number of performers (work positions) included in the business process performance and the key indicator of the number of work positions that participate in performing all the business processes in the business system. The greater the share of performers included, the greater the level of work fragmentation; consequently, the process requires more time, as each change of performer causes non-productive work transfer time and waiting for the work to continue.

$$K_{PPA} = \frac{n_{PP}}{n_{PAP}} \cdot 100$$

### 12. Indicator of the Hierarchy of Process Performers (SK12)

The indicator of the fragmentation of the organisational structure evaluates the efficiency of the business process from the perspective of the suitability of the organisational structure or, as the case may be, the appropriateness of the hierarchy of resource management. It is expressed as the quotient of the basic key indicator of the number of hierarchical levels of management that are included in the process (the transfer of messages and decision-making from manager to manager at a higher level as well s– the amount of reporting and decision-making within the process). A higher number of levels can only be justified by means of control, but not at all for increasing the speed of exchange of information, as this can be solved more efficiently using information technology (Bassi, & McMurrer, 2007).

$$K_{HP} = \frac{1}{n_{HLP}} \cdot 100$$

### 13. The Indicator of Scope of Process Performance (SK13)

This indicator shows the level of workload on the employees due to process performance with regard to the availability of the entire business system. It is expressed using key performance indicators, i.e., as the relationship between the number of employees participating in the process and the total number of employees in the business system. The higher the ratio is, the greater the level of work fragmentation in the process. The indicator of fragmentation is considered extremely important due to its direct connection with the business system strategy. The more a process important for achieving business goals is, the lower the fragmentation or, as the case may be, the inclusion of employees in the process and vice versa.

$$K_{EP} = \frac{n_{PP}}{n_{PBS}} \cdot 100$$

### Indicators of Process Support Objects

### 14. Indicator of the Relationships of Outgoing Documents (SK14)

This indicator shows the share of outgoing documents, i.e., documents that are created in the process or created while performing activities. It is expressed as a relationship between the basic key indicator of the number of documents that are created in the process and the basic key indicator of the number of documents that are used in the process. The greater the share of outgoing documents, the greater the use of time for preparing the documents in paper form and, consequently, reduced efficiency.

$$K_{POD} = \frac{n_{POD}}{n_{DP}} \cdot 100$$

**15. Indicator of the Relationships of Incoming Documents (SK15)**

This indicator is expressed by means of key performance indicators, i.e., as a relationship between the number of documents that enter into the process or, as the case may be, that are required for performing activities, and the number of documents that are used in the process. It shows the scope of the documentation that the process performers need to be acquainted with for uninterrupted process performance. The greater the number of incoming documents in the process, the more time performers need to dedicate to "reading" or checking documents, which negatively influences process performance efficiency.

$$K_{PID} = \frac{n_{PID}}{n_{DP}} \cdot 100$$

**16. Indicators of the Relationships of Outgoing Documents and Process Activities (SK16)**

This indicator shows the relationship between the outgoing documents and documents that are created in the process with regard to the number of activities that have to be created in the process. It is expressed using key performance indicators, i.e., as a relationship between the number of documents that are created in the process and the difference between the number of activities in the process and the number of activities with connections to other processes. The greater the ratio is, the greater the workload on the performers of an individual activity due to the preparation of paper documents. Increasing this kind of workload decreases the process performance efficiency.

$$K_{PODA} = \frac{n_{POD}}{(n_{PA} - n_{PI})} \cdot 100$$

**17. Indicators of Software Solutions for the Process (SK17)**

This indicator is expressed as a quotient of the basic key indicator of the number of different software solutions that are used in the process. This indicator shows the process load with different kinds of information technology support or software solutions, including the preparation time or data transfer time required for each software solution. The greater the number of different software solutions in the process, the more preparation time needed, which decreases the process performance efficiency.

$$K_{SWP} = \frac{1}{n_{SWP}} \cdot 100$$

**18. Indicator of Information Technology Support for Process Activities (SK18)**

This indicator shows the share of activities in the process whose performance is supported by one or several software solutions. It is expressed using key performance indicators, i.e., as the relationship between the number of activities in the process whose performance is supported by software solutions and the difference between the number of activities in the process and the number of activities with connections to other processes. Work on activities whose performance is supported by a software solution takes place faster or, as the case may be, in a more automated fashion (Roblek et al. 2005). The greater the share of software-supported activities, the more efficiently work takes place in the process.

$$K_{PSWA} = \frac{n_{SWA}}{(n_{PA} - n_{PI})} \cdot 100$$

## 3.2 Independent Structural Indicators of Efficiency

Due to the greater number of structural indicators of the efficiency of business process performance that we used to assess the efficiency of business process performance, we performed a factor analysis using the obtained assessments. By means of the factor analysis, we attempted to simplify the complexity of the connections between the set of structural indicators, i.e., by designing common dimensions or factors that enable an insight into the basic data structure.

While performing the factor analysis, the indicators of efficiency SK11 'Indicator of Included Performers' and SK13 'Indicator of Scope of Process Performance' were seen to be very interconnected, as their mutual correlation coefficient was no less than 0.990. Since the correlation coefficient was greater than 0.900, we excluded one of the indicators from further analysis. We decided to exclude indicator SK13, as this enabled us to obtain more favourable results in the analysis that followed.

During the factor analysis, we encountered some problems with indicators SK02 'Indicator of Completed and/or Terminated Events' and SK15 'Indicator of the Relationships of Incoming Documents'. The true reasons for these difficulties were only revealed by in-depth analysis of the calculation for an individual indicator. The indicators were awkwardly expressed and, as such, did not show a real picture of what was going on in the process.

- **The Indicator of Completed and/or Terminated Events** takes into consideration all the completed and terminated events of the business process; in practice, with a single process performance, only one segment or, as the case may be, one 'branch' of the process can be performed. Thus, only some completed and terminated events are fully expressed. All other completed or terminated events in this case distort the actual state (unacceptably large deviations may occur); therefore, we decided to exclude indicator SK02 from further analysis.
- **The Indicator of the Relationships of Incoming Documents** in the calculation takes into account the different documents that occur as incoming documents in connection to an individual process activity. The problem occurs because certain incoming documents occur as incoming while, in some other earlier activity in the same business process, they occur as outgoing documents. Should that occur in the process, it would distort the actual picture; therefore, we decided to exclude indicator SK15 from further analysis.

With the newly obtained variables (latent variables that are independent due to their nature), we calculated seven factors that we can use to explain 77.068% of the variability of the basic variables or structural indicators. The structure of the factors was cleared using rotation, whose essence is to provide theoretically important factors and the simplest possible factor structure. We used the rectangular 'varimax' rotation, which maximises the variance of the square weight in each factor, thus simplifying the structure per columns. In this manner, we came to a reasonable interpretation of the factors obtained with regard to the individual indicators of efficiency that an individual factor includes. The shares of explained variance per individual factor are explained in the table below.

*Table 1: Variance values per factors*

| Factor | Own values | | |
|---|---|---|---|
| | Value | % variance | Total variance % |
| 1 | 3.635 | 24.237 | 24.237 |
| 2 | 1.885 | 12.565 | 36.802 |
| 3 | 1.549 | 10.328 | 47.130 |
| 4 | 1.395 | 9.303 | 56.432 |
| 5 | 1.296 | 8.643 | 65.075 |
| 6 | 0.943 | 6.286 | 71.361 |
| 7 | 0.856 | 5.706 | 77.068 |

We decided to select seven factors, because we only obtained results with reasonable content in this way. The following table (Table 2) shows the calculation of the factors and the level of saturation of an individual indicator, particularly within an individual factor. The table only shows the level of saturation of those indicators of efficiency within an individual factor that also constitute the factor.

*Table 2: The creation of factors*

| **Indicators of efficiency** | **Factors** | | | | | | |
|---|---|---|---|---|---|---|---|
| | Factor 1 | Factor 2 | Factor 3 | Factor 4 | Factor 5 | Factor 6 | Factor 7 |
| SK10 | 0.905 | | | | | | |
| SK12 | 0.846 | | | | | | |
| SK09 | 0.785 | | | | | | |
| SK11 | 0.744 | | | | | | |
| SK04 | | 0.871 | | | | | |
| SK08 | | 0.870 | | | | | |
| SK16 | | | 0.868 | | | | |
| SK14 | | | 0.859 | | | | |
| SK03 | | | | 0.847 | | | |
| SK07 | | | | 0.677 | | | |
| SK01 | | | | | 0.793 | | |
| SK06 | | | | | 0.775 | | |
| SK17 | | | | | | 0.814 | |
| SK18 | | | | | | 0.784 | |
| SK05 | | | | | | | 0.927 |

As usually happens with factor analysis, the first factor immediately explains the biggest share of variance. The jointly explained variance, which can be explained using seven factors, is relatively high and is correspondingly amended (content-wise) by classifying the indicators of efficiency into an individual factor. To obtain a better overview of which indicators of efficiency create which factor, we have prepared tables and classified them according to the individual indicator of efficiency in the selected factor.

Indicators of efficiency that are combined by the first factor (Table 3) show us the organisation of a business system from different perspectives.

*Table 3: Indicators of efficiency in the first factor*

| Factor 1 | The organisation of the business system |
|---|---|
| SK10 | Indicator of process performers |
| SK12 | Indicator of the hierarchy of process performers |
| SK09 | Indicator of the level of inclusion of performers |
| SK11 | Indicator of included performers |

The second factor (shown in Table 4) combines the indicators of efficiency, thus illustrating the business processes from the perspective of their performance complexity.

*Table 4: Indicators of efficiency in the second factor*

| Factor 2 | The complexity of the business processes |
|---|---|
| SK04 | Indicator of process decisions |
| SK08 | Loopback indicator |

The documentation of the work performed, as shown by the indicators combined in the third factor (Table 5), is shown the level of work formalisation.

*Table 5: Indicators of efficiency in the third factor*

| Factor 3 | Documented performed work |
|---|---|
| SK16 | Indicators of the relationships of outgoing documents and process activities |
| SK14 | Indicator of the relationships of outgoing documents |

The fourth factor (Table 6) combines the indicators of efficiency that show the scope of the business process.

*Table 6: Indicators of efficiency in the fourth factor*

| **Factor 4** | **The scope of the business processes** |
|---|---|
| SK03 | Indicator of process activity |
| SK07 | Indicator of the number of transitions between activities |

The fifth factor (Table 7) includes indicators that assess the efficiency of the processes from the perspective of their interconnectedness or connectedness.

*Table 7: Indicators of efficiency in the fifth factor*

| **Factor 5** | **The interconnectedness of the processes** |
|---|---|
| SK01 | Initial process event indicator |
| SK06 | Indicator of process connection |

The sixth factor (Table 8) combines the indicators of efficiency that show the support for activities in a business process provided by information technology.

*Table 8: Indicators of efficiency in the sixth factor*

| **Factor 6** | **The support of information technology** |
|---|---|
| SK17 | Indicators of software solutions for the process |
| SK18 | Indicator of information technology support for process activities |

The seventh factor (Table 9) includes only one indicator of efficiency, i.e., the indicator of process added value.

*Table 9: Indicators of efficiency in the seventh factor*

| **Factor 7** | **Creating added value** |
|---|---|
| SK05 | Indicator of process added value |

## 3.3 The Influence of Independent (Latent) Structural Indicators

By performing the factor analysis, we obtained seven independent variables or, as the case may be, factors that can be considered independent structural indicators.

The share of explained variance (Table 10) in an individually created factor or, as the case may be, independent structural indicator, shows the intensity of the connection between the change of an individual independent structural indicator and the actual state of business process performance efficiency.

*Table 10: The influence of independent factors*

| Factor | Independent indicator label | Name of the independent factor, i.e., indicator | % variance |
|---|---|---|---|
| 1 | NSK01 | The organisation of the business system | 24.237 |
| 2 | NSK02 | The complexity of the business processes | 12.565 |
| 3 | NSK03 | Documented performed work | 10.328 |
| 4 | NSK04 | The scope of the business processes | 9.303 |
| 5 | NSK05 | The interconnectedness of the processes | 8.643 |
| 6 | NSK06 | The support of information technology | 6.286 |
| 7 | NSK07 | Created added value | 5.706 |

Results in the upper table shows us that the current structural business process performance efficiency (in the three selected business systems) is the most connected with 'the organisation of the business system'. The second factor 'the complexity of the business processes' shows the high level of business processes complexity at their performance. At the third place, we can find the factor 'the documentation of the work performed' which results in creation and usage of printed documents in large scale during business process performance.

From the results shown, we can understand that the factor 'support of information technology' has a relatively small impact on total variance of the business process performance efficiency. That means that the business process performance is poorly supported with information technology or it is supported with partial programme solutions that do not have interfaces or have poor ones. The factor 'creating added value' explains the relatively small percentage of business process efficiency variance, which indicates on disproportionate activity distribution where the added value is created.

# 4. Conclusion

This research on the connectedness of the structural indicators of business process performance efficiency has shown that a large number of starting point indicators can be replaced with only seven independent indicators (factors). In doing so, there remains a high percentage (77%) of explained variability in the basic variables or, as the case may be, the basic structural indicators of efficiency.

Based on the data obtained and using factor analysis (the combination of basic indicators into factors), we can define the equation for calculating independent indicators using the statistical method, i.e., linear regression. The equation for calculating the indicators can be designed on the basis of key structural indicators, or it can be created by inserting key business process performance indicators.

The classification of the factors or independent (latent) structural indicators acquired through the factor analysis can vary between business systems. Likewise, the explained variance of individual independent indicator can vary between business systems. The share of the explained variance in an individual independent structural indicator of business process performance efficiency shows the influence that changes within the latter have on the joint or relevant state of business process performance efficiency.

When the request for business process performance efficiency improvement is defined, the business systems management decides on the basis of this analysis' results (changing the organisation of business system, transformation of the authorisations and responsibilities from upper to lower organisational levels, put in order the connectedness of business processes, upgrading the business process performance information technology support, reduction of non-value added activities or implementation of the e-commerce) that the business process performance efficiency is improved to the highest level.

## References

Aguilar, E. R.; Ruiz, F.; García, F., Piattini, M. (2006): Applying Software Metrics to evaluate Business Process Models, *CLEI Electronic Journal*, Vol. 9, No. 1, Paper 5.

Bassi, L., McMurrer, D. (2007): Maximizing Your Return on People, *Harvard Business Review*, Vol. 85, No. 3, pp. 15– 123.

Bauer, K. (2004): KPIs: Not All Metrics Are Created Equal, *DM Review,* 14(12), 42. Retrieved February 19, 2009, from ProQuest Computing database. (Document ID: 750265451).

Davenport, T. H., Short, J. E. (1990): The new industrial engineering: information technology and business process redesign, *Sloan Management Review,* page 11–27

Davenport, T. H. (1992): *Process Innovation: Reengineering Work through Information Technology,* Harvard Business School Press

Davis, R. (2001): *Business Process Modelling with ARIS–A Practical Guide,* Springer-Verlag, London

Deming, W. E. (1982): *Out of the Crisis,* Cambridge, Mass, Massachusetts Institute of Technology

Dibrell, C., Davis, P., Craig, J. (2008): Fuelling Innovation through Information Technology in SMEs*, *Journal of Small Business Management,* Vol. 46, No. 2, pp. 203–218.

Erickson, J., Siau, K. (2007): Theoretical and practical complexity of modeling methods, Association for Computing Machinery, *Communications of the ACM,* Vol. 50, No. 8, pp. 46–51.

Fitz-enz, J. (2009): Predicting People: From Metrics to Analytics, *Employment Relations Today,* Vol. 36, No. 3, pg. 1.

Frederiksen, H., & Mathiassen, L. (2008): A Contextual Approach to Improving Software Metrics Practices, *IEEE Transactions on Engineering Management,* Vol. 55, No. 4, pp. 602–616.

Harkness, W. L., Kettinger, W. J., Sagars, A. H. (1996): Sustaining Process Improvement and Innovation in the Information Services Function: Lessons Learned at the Bose Corporation, *MIS Quarterly*

Holt, P. A. (2000): *Business Process Management: Models, Techniques and Empirical Studies, Management-oriented Models of Business Processes,* pp. 99–109, Springer-Verlag, Berlin

Hung, R. Y. (2006): *Business process management as competitive advantage: a review and empirical study,* Total Quality Management & Business Excellence, Vol. 17, No. 1, pp. 21–40, Routledge Taylor & Francis Group, Abingdon

Kaplan, R. S., Norton, D. P. (2008): Mastering the Management System; *Harvard Business Review: Special HBS Centennial Issue*, Vol. 86, No. 1, pp. 62–77.

Kennedy, C. (2006): Business excellence in practising firms, *Accountancy Ireland,* Vol. 38, No. 4, pp. 67–69, Dublin

Kettinger, J. W., Teng, C. J. (2000): *Process Think: Winning Perspectives for Business Change in the Information Age,* Conducting Business Process Change: Recommendations from a Study of 25 Leading Approaches, pp. 2–22, Idea Group Publishing, London

London, C. (2002): Strategic planning for business excellence, *Quality Progress,* Vol. 35, No. 8, pp. 26–33.

Meglič, J., Kern, T., Urh, B., Balkovec, J., Roblek, M. (2009): Influence of polyvalence professionals on product development process efficiency, *Strojarstvo,* Vol. 51, No. 2, pp. 105–121.

Poniatowski, S., Wichser, J. D. (2006): A Better Metric For IT Efficiency, *Optimize,* Vol. 5, No. 5, pp. 43–46.

Prijatelj, V., Rajkovič, U., Šušteršič, O., Rajkovič, V. (2010): *Reengineering of nursing process: e-documentation case,* In: Weaver, C. A. (ed.), White, D. C. (ed.), Weber, P. (ed.), Carr, R. L. (ed.), Nursing and informatics for the 21st century: an international look at practice, Education and EHR trends, 2nd ed. Chicago: HIMSS, cop., pp. 447-454

Ranjan, J. (2008): Business justification with business intelligence, VINE, Vol. 38, No. 4, pp. 461–475.

Roblek, M., Urh, B., Zajec, M., Kern, T. (2010): *Uskladitev metod razvoja programskih rešitev z metodo vodenja projektov,* Človek in organizacija: zbornik 29. mednarodne konference o razvoju organizacijskih znanosti, pp. 1279–1285, Moderna organizacija v okviru FOV, Slovenija, Portorož

Roblek, M., Kern, T., Urh, B. (2005): *Business objects repository approach for managing changes in employee IT support,* In M. Khosrowpour (ed.), Managing modern organizations with information technology (pp. 1039–1041), San Diego, CA: Idea Group.

Scanlon, R., Watts, J. (2009): A New Route to Performance Management, *Baseline,* No. 92, pp. 38–40.

Sharma, A. (2009): Implementing Balance Scorecard for Performance Measurement, Institute of Chartered Financial Analysts of India (Hyderabad), *The ICFAI Journal of Business Strategy,* Vol. 6, No. 1, pp. 7–16.

Smith, M. (2005): Performance Management Methodology, *Business Credit,* Vol. 107, No. 10, pp. 54–55.

Urh, B., Kern, T., Roblek, M. (2008): *Business process modification management,* In G. Putnik (Ed.), Encyclopedia of networked and virtual organizations, Hershey, Information Science Reference, pp. 112–120.

Valiris, G., Glykas, M. (2004): Business analysis metrics for business process redesign, *Business Process Management Journal,* Vol. 10, No. 4, pp. 445–480.

Vila, A. (2006): *Sintetizirana organizacija,* Management sprememb: zbornik 25. mednarodne konference o razvoju organizacijskih znanosti, pp. 1–12, Moderna organizacija v okviru FOV, Slovenija, Portorož

## About the Authors

**Benjamin Urh** holds an MSc in organisational sciences and a BSc in mechanical engineering. He is a lecturer at the Faculty of Organisational Organizational Sciences of the University of Maribor, and lectures on project management and business processes. During his research work, he has actively participated in a number of scientific and professional conferences.

**Špela Kokalj** studied Business Processes at the Faculty of Organizational Sciences, completing her Bachelor''s degree in 2006. In 2006, she enrolled in the Business Process Management postgraduate studies programme, at the same time becoming a young researcher at the University of Maribor, Faculty of Organizational Sciences. Her field of research involves Business Process Management and Reengineering, Project Management and Manufacturing Management.

**Maja Zajec** holds the position of the assistant for Integral Production Organization and Information Systems at the Faculty of Organizational Sciences in Kranj, University of Maribor, Slovenia. Her professional work includes researching the management of small family companies. In addition, she works as an analyst for the Employment Agency of the Republic of Slovenia and, consequently, learns about the problematic of employees in this kind of companiescompany.

# Enhancing Core Technological, Marketing and Complementary Competencies in Promoting Innovative Performance

***Tanja Rajkovič***

*tanja.rajkovic@inovema.si*

***Janez Prašnikar***

*janez.prasnikar@ef.uni-lj.si*

## Abstract

A model of technological, marketing and complementary competencies in relation to firms' innovative performance is presented as a tool for managing competitive positioning in new product development. It is applied to a set of 53 established Slovene manufacturing firms that participated in a cross-industry survey. Segmentation indicates differences among companies acting as technology leaders and those that are technology followers, the main differences being attributed to the level of the development of technological competencies. Further, key competencies are established for different strategies that companies can pursue in new product development, among which are incremental innovations, radical innovations and trend setting. For this purpose, partial least square structural modelling is used. These implications are valuable to firms aligning their competencies with their competitive strategy, and to policy makers in technology follower countries.

**Keywords**: technological competencies, marketing competencies, complementary competencies, technology leaders, technology followers, innovation, new product development

# 1. Introduction

In a dynamic environment, companies strive for ways to differentiate themselves from their competitors, and thus aim to benefit from the created competitive advantage. Innovation activity is recognised for creating such opportunities (Teece et al., 1997). The strategic management literature and the theories of competitive advantage present a perspective on the means of competition, in which the source of a firm's competitive advantage rests on its capabilities and competencies (Song et al., 2005; Lynskey, 1999; Prahalad and Hamel, 1990).

In recent decades, a competence-based view of competitive advantage has gained considerable attention (Prahalad and Hamel, 1990; Hamel and Heene, 1994). Figure 1 shows the architecture of core competencies as proposed by Hafeez et al. (2002).

*Figure 1: The architecture of core competencies*

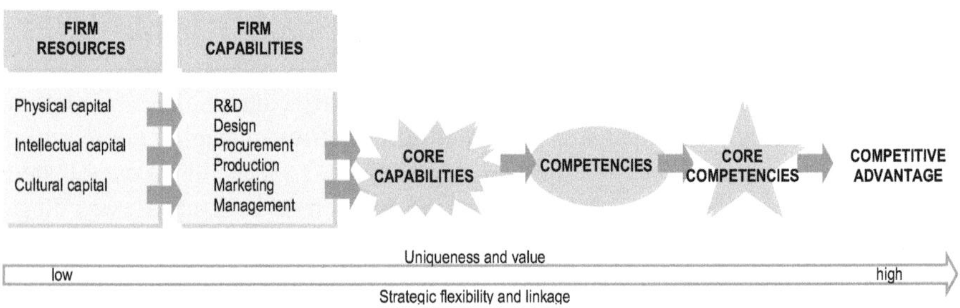


*Source: Hafeez et al., 2002, p. 31.*

The resources are inputs to capabilities. Those capabilities that are relatively more important for realising a firm's business objectives are its key capabilities. Only those key capabilities that are relatively unique and common to various business functions, products and business units are likely to form the competencies of a company. The hierarchy between competencies and capabilities is distinguished in their work. Usually, competencies are not based on a single activity but represent a network of capabilities (Sanchez et al., 1996). The critical task is to assess capabilities relative to those of the competitors'. Core competencies are those competencies that help a company achieve a sustainable competitive advantage. These are competencies that are by nature strategically flexible and dynamic.

The question that remains is how a technology follower country should approach its growth strategy, narrow the gap with technology leaders and increase its competitiveness. The Lisbon Strategy as an action and development plan for the European Union proposes to increase public and private investments in R&D as well as to develop an innovative climate for entrepreneurship (Commission of the EC, 2005). By focusing on quantitative goals, such as the share of R&D expenditure in GDP, there exists a danger that investments will not effectively translate into concrete actions.

## 1.1 Model and Theoretical Background

The strategic model to be presented is based on theories of competitive advantage and innovation, in which technological, marketing and complementary competencies are first linked to innovative performance and then further to business performance (Figure 2). From the theoretical point of view, this is the first attempt to link all three concepts in the same model. As such, it not only supports the positive linkage between innovation and business performance, which is the objective of innovative activity, but also sheds light on the underlying competencies or, in other words, specific competitive strengths of innovation within a firm. Technological, marketing and complementary competencies best account for the key knowledge, skills and capabilities that are central to new product development (Rajkovič, 2009).

*Figure 2: Operational model of the influence of technological, marketing and complementary competencies on innovative performance and business performance*

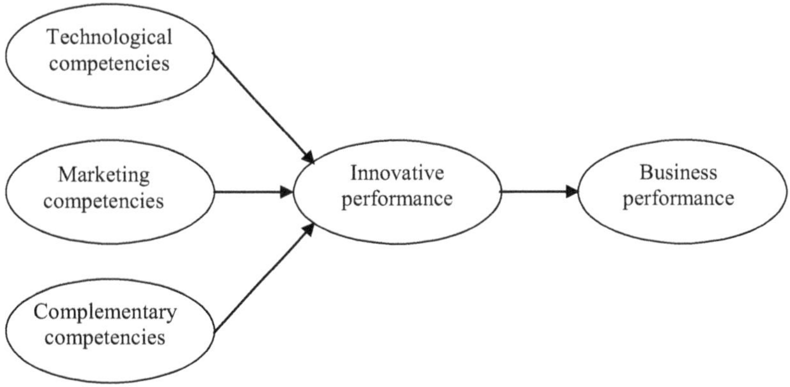

Technological competencies incorporate practical and theoretical know-how, as well as the methods, experience and equipment necessary for developing new products (Wang et al., 2004). According to Swink and Song (2007), technological competencies influence all four stages of the new product development process. At the first stage (business/market analysis), technological competencies help address the technical feasibility of the products in question. The next stage (technical development) incorporates product and process engineering studies, and continues with establishing product designs and specifications, prototyping the product and approving final designs. In all of these tasks, technological competencies have a central position. During the third stage (product testing), technological competencies are of secondary importance; still, they influence the design of consumer tests and the interpretation of the results. At the last stage (product commercialisation), they are key for production plans and production ramp-up.

Companies with well-developed marketing competencies are well aware of customer needs and are capable of value creation on all elements of a product or service that are relevant to the customers (Day, 1994). At the business/market analysis stage, marketing competencies provide an evaluation of market impacts of product feature options, as the aim is to understand the competitive positioning of the future product. During the technical development stage, marketing competencies facilitate product feature decisions. Marketing usually takes a leading role in product testing, which involves the selection of key customers and sites, the testing of markets, and the analysis of results. Marketing plans, product promotion and distribution are tasks that require marketing competencies for product launch at the product commercialisation stage (Swink and Song, 2007; Paul and Peter, 1994).

According to Wang et al. (2004), the role of complementary competencies is to 1) integrate different technological specialties; 2) combine different functional specialties; 3) exploit synergies across business units; 4) combine in-house resources with the external capabilities required and 5) integrate the dynamic competence building process for superior performance. Aligning the new product features (technological aspect) with potential customers' needs (marketing aspect) is the role of complementary competencies at the first stage of new product development. They are also employed in the assessment of the needed investment and accompanying risks (Swink and Song, 2007). Similar complementarity of technological and marketing knowledge is also of key importance during the second stage of technical development. At the same time, it proves to be positively related to translating testing results into product and process design modifications (Song et al., 1998) during the product testing. Integration of both streams of competencies contributes to better coordination of production planning and demand management activities during product commercialisation.

Innovative performance in the broader sense refers to new product development. Unlike innovation performance, it is not directly a measure of the economic success of an innovation (Hagedoorn and Cloodt, 2007; Lanjouw and Schankerman, 1999). A separate measure is also innovativeness, which is defined as the capacity to introduce some new process, product or idea into an organisation (Hult et al., 2004). Firms' new product portfolios are balanced between new products based on incremental innovation and those based on fundamental innovation (Schewe, 1996). In the case of incremental modifications of products, 'market pull' provides the information on customers' preferences, while 'technology push' prevails with completely new technologies that address customers' latent needs (Tidd and Bodley, 2002). Since consumers buy products for the benefits they gain from them, 'technology push' still has to observe customer needs.

A successful new product development process contributes to the financial success of the product, and consequently to the overall business success of a firm via lower costs and shorter lead times (Brown and Eisenhardt, 1995). Empirical studies provide evidence that both radical and incremental innovations contribute to a firm's survival, growth and profitability (Varadarajan, 2008).

To overcome shortcomings of the most widely used quantitative measures of innovative performance, the model is built on selected qualitative measures. Indicators of innovative performance that can be found in the literature are R&D inputs, usually R&D expenditure, including past R&D expenditure, patent count, new product announcements and aggregated constructs of these indicators. Different sectors are characterised by different levels of innovation inputs as well as innovation outputs (Tidd et al., 1996), which makes comparisons across industries difficult.

R&D intensity alone does not necessarily reflect innovative intensity for several reasons. Firms tend to broaden their base of R&D expenditure with the purpose of taking advantage of possible tax cuts when such innovation policies are in place. At the same time, R&D stands for only a fraction of innovation, which especially holds for companies with a less formalised R&D function. Consequently, total R&D expenditure is difficult to define (Bougrain and Haudeville, 2002). For example, companies reported on the practice of outsourcing their R&D to their suppliers, covering the incurred R&D expenditure via purchasing costs of the parts and materials specifically developed for them once supplied and sold.

Patent counts and new product announcements are also biased measures, as differences in the propensity of firms to patent or publish will affect such measurements (Frumau, 1992), depending on the dynamics in the industry, firm size, secrecy of details to be disclosed and protection offered.

## 1.2 Definition of Variables

Variables to simulate the proposed theoretical concepts in the model were initially selected on the basis of economic, organisation and management literature (listed with their operational abbreviations in Figure 3). Research shows that technological competencies usually encompass three categories: 1) how advanced research and development is; 2) the number of available technological capabilities inside the firm or through strategic partnerships, and 3) how good the company is at predicting technological trends (Eisenhardt and Martin, 2000; Wang et al., 2004).

Marketing competencies capture marketing research as well as other marketing activities (Paul and Peter, 1994). To include marketing research and forecast competencies, the indicator 'obtaining information about changes of customer preferences and needs' was applied. The competitors' patterns of activities are illustrated with 'acquisition of real-time information about competitors', customer relationship management with 'establishing and managing long-term customer relations' and supplier relations using an indicator 'establishing and managing long-term relations with suppliers'. Selected indicators reflect Porter's competitive forces to some degree.

Complementary competencies represent the congruence between technological and marketing competencies. The internal environment is thus measured with 'good transfer of technological and marketing knowledge among business units'. The indicator 'intensity, quality and extent of research and development knowledge transfer in co-operation with strategic partners' evaluate the dynamic perspective and competence acquisition through strategic partnerships. The efficiency of economic utilisation of technological and marketing resources engaged in the product development is evaluated with 'product development is cost efficient'. The organisational focus is measured with the indicator 'activities of the business units in the corporate strategy of our firm are clearly defined'.

The general extent of innovative performance was measured by 'number of modified, improved and new products' representing new product variety or level of innovation. Technical performance was added and included by the variable 'quality of products'. A number of studies in the operations management literature confirm the relations between product development and product innovation and quality, whereby high levels of innovation are associated with high levels of product quality (Clark and Fujimoto, 1991; Koufteros and Marcoulides, 2006). While product innovation as such refers to the competence responsible for introducing new products and features, product quality or technical performance stands for the respective competence of a firm to produce products that would satisfy customer needs for quality and performance (Kim et al, 2005).

The indicator 'time needed to develop an improved product' was applied to determine the effectiveness of improving existing products (incremental innovation). 'Time' refers to the development project lead time and not to the array of products developed, as with the baseline general indicator. Similarly, the effectiveness of new product development referring to radical innovation was measured by 'time needed to develop a completely new product' (Chang, 1996). The role of innovativeness of the firm in the industry was represented by the indicator 'firm's substantial contribution to global trends in the industry'. With this last indicator, it is assumed for the market pioneers with innovations that their competitors find worth imitating.

Measures ROA and ROE were included as indicators of profitability and thus integrated business performance. Actual financial statements data were used. Business performance is measured in our model by average ROA and ROE during the three-year period between the years 2004 and 2006, which is the same period for which the firms were asked to evaluate their innovative performance. ROA measures management's ability and efficiency in issuing firm's assets to generate profits (White et al., 2003). ROE, in contrast, reports on return on total stockholders' equity.

## 2. Application of the Model to a Slovene Sample

The nature of competencies makes it possible to compare companies from different industries (multi-industry analysis), since they are not industry-specific and are not bounded to particular products and companies (Sanchez, 2004). Furthermore, as firms try to take advantage of synergies and economies of scale and scope, many diversify into different businesses (Gollop and Monahan, 1991), drawing from mutual synergies. Products becoming increasingly multi-technological also require companies to develop competence in an increasing range of technological fields to maintain their competitiveness (Tidd, 2006; Markides and Williamson, 1994).

Resources, knowledge and technologies belonging to a specific product line can still be very specific. In addition to this, the various products can be present in very diverse and specific markets. This makes generalisations across product lines less reliable. A literature review of cross-industry studies has shown that none have analyzed either companies' capabilities or competencies for specific product lines.

Due to the novelty and specifics of the developed model, as explained above, it could not be tested using existing datasets. Therefore, a survey questionnaire was designed to be used for multi-industry studies of firm competencies. In order to control for the industry characteristics, environmental effects were also considered as moderating variables in the analysis.

A cross-industry survey was carried out among medium-sized and large manufacturing firms in Slovenia. Included were 382 firms that were not registered later than 2002 and were operating throughout the 2002-2006 period. In total, 53 companies returned valid questionnaires yielding a 13.8% response rate. Respondents were management-level employees in charge of company R&D. The questionnaire was initially tested in 12 firms. The main segments of the questionnaire referred to firm competencies, innovative performance and business performance.

The intention was to further account for the product diversification that has also proven to be an important facilitating factor during the new product development stage. Thus, firms were asked to provide data for individual product lines where applicable. Nine companies gave responses for more than one product line, thus providing a sample of 70 observations. In further analysis, three companies with five product lines in total were excluded as statistical outliers, due to their continuous negative business performance.

The interviewees evaluated their competencies on a five-point scale relative to their main competitors, and thus estimated the competitiveness of their individual competencies within the industry. The time frame for data gathering (data for competencies, innovations and R&D activities) was a three-year period from 2004 to 2006, inclusive, as proposed by the OECD methodology for measuring innovation (1997).

The companies included in the survey were medium and large sized. These companies are more likely to have a systematically organised R&D function and are continuously forced to innovate in order to sustain or improve their competitive position and withstand dynamics in industries, unlike small firms that often provide for small niche markets, with their innovative products.

The initial descriptive analysis for aggregate data implied that Slovene firms are operating in dynamic environments and are (on average) taking an active part in their environments. To be precise, firms generally witnessed short product lifecycles and intense competition through R&D as well as design. On average, firms generate a vast majority of their sales with products branded as their own. Not only is this encouraging, since it is important for the companies to enhance their brand recognition, but also because own brands enable higher price mark-ups. The motivation behind innovation is more defensive than offensive, making use of incremental innovations. Better company image and improved appearance rank as top motivations, which points to the role of design.

## 2.1 Aligning Competencies with the Market Position in the Industry

Segmentation based on competencies revealed that the most innovative companies, so-called technology leaders, were shown to have all competencies highly developed (above the average value of 3; see Table 1).[1] Identified were also two segments of followers that predominantly rely on imitation in their innovation strategy: technology followers with weak competencies and technology followers with strong competencies (relatively poor performance in terms of new product development measures).[2]

1 Segmentation was performed using a two-step clustering methodology. This technique proposes improving segmentation that was initially obtained through hierarchical clustering methods by additionally applying non-hierarchical methods in order to optimise classification of observations.

2 In Table 1, for each variable a segment is described by a mean value (except numbers of product lines and firms counted from the sample). The ANOVA, 'post-hoc Duncan test', $P<0.05$ was applied. Statistically significant differences among the three segments are depicted with different number of plus symbols [+] next to the average value of the measure. An equal number of plus symbols in different segments denotes that no statistically significant differences were found among the segments. A different number of plus symbols confirms differences. A higher number of plus symbols implies that it is a statistically different segment with a higher average value of the measure. For example, there are no statistically significant differences among the technology follower segments with respect to the variable 'advancement of R&D'. It is only the segment of technology leaders that proves to perform better with regards to this variable.

*Table 1: Product lines' segments described by innovative performance, competencies and new product development characteristics*

| Variables | Segments: Technology followers – weak | | Technology followers - strong | | Technology leaders | |
|---|---|---|---|---|---|---|
| No. of product lines | 25 | | 19 | | 21 | |
| No. of different companies | 21 | | 16 | | 20 | |
| **Innovative performance (IP)** | | | | | | |
| Number of modified, improved and completely new products in period 2004-2006, inclusive | 2.84 | + | 2.89 | + | 4.24 | ++ |
| Quality of products | 2.96 | + | 4.21 | ++ | 4.24 | ++ |
| **Technological competencies (TC)** | | | | | | |
| Advancement of R&D | 2.84 | + | 3.16 | + | 3.86 | ++ |
| Number of quality technological capabilities inside the firm or through strategic partnerships | 2.72 | + | 3.32 | ++ | 4.10 | +++ |
| Prediction of technological trends | 2.68 | + | 3.00 | + | 3.95 | ++ |
| **Marketing competencies (MC)** | | | | | | |
| Obtaining information about changes of customer preferences and needs | 2.92 | + | 3.26 | + | 3.95 | ++ |
| Acquisition of real time information about competitors | 3.00 | + | 3.16 | + | 3.29 | + |
| Establishing and managing long-term customer relations | 3.32 | + | 3.79 | ++ | 4.10 | ++ |
| Establishing and managing long-term relations with suppliers | 2.92 | + | 3.58 | ++ | 3.67 | ++ |
| **Complementary competencies (CC)** | | | | | | |
| Good transfer of technological and marketing knowledge among business units | 2.80 | + | 3.32 | ++ | 3.52 | ++ |
| The intensity, quality and extent of R&D knowledge transfer in co-operation with strategic partners | 2.48 | + | 3.00 | + | 3.57 | ++ |

| | | | | | | |
|---|---|---|---|---|---|---|
| Cost efficiency of product development | 2.84 | + | 3.37 | ++ | 3.52 | ++ |
| Clearly defined activities of business units in the corporate strategy of our firm | 2.88 | + | 3.58 | ++ | 3.62 | ++ |
| **New product development** | | | | | | |
| Time needed to develop an improved product | 2.76 | + | 3.21 | ++ | 3.76 | +++ |
| Time needed to develop a new generation product | 2.48 | + | 2.63 | + | 3.71 | ++ |
| Contribution of the firm to industry trends | 2.44 | + | 2.47 | + | 3.24 | ++ |
| Imitation VS innovation strategy | 2.32 | + | 2.74 | + | 3.33 | ++ |

The distinctive core competencies of technology leaders are, notably, technological competencies. Strong technology followers build their competitiveness on marketing and complementary competencies. Cooperating in strategic technological partnerships and thus broadening the scope of technological capabilities at hand is an important distinctive complementary competence for technology leaders. They are innovators and perform very favourably regarding new product development lead times, and contribute to industry trends.

One marketing competence that exhibits no differences among the three segments is 'acquisition of real-time information about competitors' (denoted by one plus symbol in each segment). It implies that regardless of the innovative performance, companies understand the importance of being aware of the dynamics in the industry. Furthermore, this variable no longer appears to be a potential source of competitive advantage in current times or, in other words, this kind of information is widely available within the industry, regardless of the company's position.[3]

3 A comparison of data for Slovenia and Croatia showed main differences between the two countries for the marketing competencies of firms in the segment of technology followers with weak competencies. Croatian firms within this segment are comparably more competitive at establishing and managing long-term relations with suppliers and in co-operation through strategic technological partnerships, which can both be important sources of external knowledge (Prašnikar, Rajkovič, Vehovec, 2008).

## 2.2 Aligning Competencies with the Innovation Strategy Pursued

It is possible to establish what competencies firms develop and employ when pursuing different innovation strategies. The baseline model measures innovative performance by two general indicators: 'number of modified, improved and completely new products in 2004–2006 period, inclusive' and 'quality of products'.

The indicator 'time needed to develop an improved product' was applied to determine the effectiveness of improving existing products, replacing the first indicator in the baseline model, thereby constructing the innovative performance measure of the incremental innovation model, i.e., firms pursuing the incremental innovation strategy. Time refers to the development project lead time and not to the array of products developed as with the baseline general indicator.

Similarly, the effectiveness of new product development referring to radical innovation strategy was measured by 'time needed to develop a completely new product'. Again the second indicator, 'quality of products', was kept the same.

In the model accounting for trend-setting, the first indicator of innovative performance measure was substituted by the indicator 'firm's substantial contribution to global trends in the industry'. In this way, it is assumed for the innovation strategy of market pioneers with innovations that their competitors find worth imitating.

The Partial Least Square structural equation modelling was used, more specifically SmartPLS software (Ringle et al., 2005). All four models were tested for consistency reliability, convergent validity and discriminant validity (Anderson and Gebring, 1988).

By comparing the path coefficients of the four models (see Table 2), it can be observed that the incremental innovation model yields results most similar to those of the baseline model. The highest path coefficients in both models are attributed to the technological competencies (0.409, $P<0.001$ and 0.341 $P<0.01$, respectively). These are followed by marketing competencies in the baseline model (0.250, $P<0.01$) and complementary competencies in the incremental innovation model (0.301, $P<0.01$). This result shows that the efficiency of new-product development processes relies to a greater extent on competencies of a technological nature than on those of the marketing type.

The above result is in line with the finding of Swink and Song (2007) that integration of technological and marketing knowledge can prolong the technological development stage of a new-product development process. This is even more evident in development endeavours that are technologically more demanding. These are represented by the last two models. In these two cases, the path coefficients for marketing competencies are not statistically significant. However, this is not to suggest that market knowledge plays no role whatsoever in technologically more complex projects. It can be clearly seen that complementary competencies (as an integrators of both technological and marketing knowledge) are statistically significant both of the models (0.352, P<0.01; 0.381, P<0.01, respectively).

This result is partially aligned with the findings of Lynn et al. (1996), which suggest that the use of commonly known market tools – including concept testing, customer surveys, conjoint analysis, focus groups, and demographics segmentation – is limited when developing innovative products, as they rely on users being able to articulate their needs. Furthermore, in the model accounting for trend-setting, complementary competencies outperform technological competencies.

*Table 2: Comparison of path coefficients of the constructs for the four models*

| Path | Baseline model[4] | Incremental innovation model | Radical innovation model | Model accounting for trend-setting |
|---|---|---|---|---|
| TC→IP | 0.409 (4.075) * | 0.341 (2.843) ** | 0.363 (2.787) ** | 0.307 (2.537) ** |
| MC→IP | 0.250 (2.346) ** | 0.211 (1.537) **** | 0.137 (1.192) | 0.115 (0.813) |
| CC→IP | 0.235 (2.280) *** | 0.301 (2.423) ** | 0.352 (2.769) ** | 0.381 (2.582) ** |
| $R^2$ | 0.63 | 0.57 | 0.58 | 0.52 |

*T-values are stated in parentheses.*
** / ** / *** / **** P<0.001, P<0.01, P<0.05 and P<0.1, respectively.*

Table 3 lists, for each of the four models, the weights of specific indicators with respect to their corresponding latent variables, thus making it possible to take a more detailed look at the competencies. These weights explain the link between the manifest variables and their latent counterparts in the structural model. For example, technological competence measures or manifest variables in the struc-

4 The baseline model was additionally extended for indicators of environmental effects – technological and market turbulence – as proxies of industries (Wang et al., 2004; Calantone et al., 2003). Both effects have little impact on how innovative performance affects firm performance. This can signify that firms have a very good awareness and understanding of their environments. Further, it could also imply that the general perception of the conditions among competitors in their respective industries is unanimous and transcending local markets.

tural model could be written as a weighted sum of the corresponding indicators/ constituent variables.

*Table 3: Weights of manifest variables for the four models*

| *Indicators* | *Baseline model* | *Incremental innovation model* | *Radical innovation model* | *Model accounting for trend-setting* |
|---|---|---|---|---|
| **Technological competencies** | | | | |
| Advancement of R&D | 0.3257 | 0.3371 | 0.3551 | 0.3237 |
| Number of quality technological capabilities inside the firm or through strategic partnerships | 0.4074 | 0.4234 | 0.3984 | 0.4181 |
| Prediction of technological trends | 0.3874 | 0.3608 | 0.3688 | 0.3786 |
| **Marketing competencies** | | | | |
| Obtaining information about changes in customer preferences and needs | 0.4289 | 0.4007 | 0.4020 | 0.4012 |
| Acquisition of real-time information about competitors | 0.2203 | 0.2752 | 0.2960 | 0.2662 |
| Establishing and managing long-term customer relations | 0.3490 | 0.3368 | 0.3262 | 0.3396 |
| Establishing and managing long-term relations with suppliers | 0.2897 | 0.2893 | 0.2808 | 0.2936 |
| **Complementary competencies** | | | | |
| Good transfer of technological and marketing knowledge among business units | 0.3390 | 0.3507 | 0.3306 | 0.3334 |
| The intensity, quality and extent of R&D knowledge transfer in co-operation with strategic partners | 0.3524 | 0.3405 | 0.3772 | 0.3284 |
| Cost-efficiency of product development | 0.2852 | 0.3067 | 0.2962 | 0.2728 |
| Clearly defined activities of business units in the corporate strategy of our firm | 0.3571 | 0.3391 | 0.3323 | 0.3948 |

In the baseline model, 'number of quality technological capabilities inside the firm or through strategic partnerships' (0.4074) has a beneficial effect on innovative performance and thus also new-product variety. It is interesting to note that among technological competencies 'advancement of R&D' (0.3257) comes last, even after 'prediction of technological trends' (0.3874).

Firms wishing to accelerate new-product development should combine both radical and incremental innovation capabilities (Zahra and Ellor, 1993), which makes advanced R&D capabilities an indispensable element of the process. However, the performance of a higher novelty development process is, in turn, both more uncertain and more risky, although such projects tend to yield high returns if successfully commercialised. The causes of this uncertainty are technically unfeasible project goals and insufficient market demand. Therefore, R&D activities may not necessarily be as effective when measured in terms of innovative performance.

While the weight of the variable 'number of quality technological capabilities inside the firm or through strategic partnerships' remains the highest of the technological competencies indicators in all four models, it has the lowest value within the radical innovation model (0.3984; baseline model: 0.4074; incremental innovation model: 0.4234; model accounting for trend-setting: 0.4181). The indicator that simultaneously, and conversely, appears to gain the most weight in this same model is 'advancement of R&D' (0.3551 compared to 0.3984 of the 'number of quality technological capabilities...' variable; respectively for other three models: 0.3257 compared to 0.4074, 0.3371 compared to 0.4234, 0.3237 compared to 0.4181). Technological novelty and superiority appear to be prerequisites for the development of completely new products.

The importance of customer orientation is confirmed through marketing competencies. In the model of incremental innovation, some of the weight of 'obtaining information about changes in customer preferences and needs' is lost relative to information on competitors ('acquisition of real-time information about competitors') (0.3490 compared to 0.2203 in the baseline model; 0.3368 compared to 0.2752 in the incremental innovation model.

As incremental innovations tend to be closely connected to imitation (Schewe, 1996), information regarding the activities of competitors' can be an important guideline aiding in the formulation of R&D strategy and the generation of new products. The relative importance of information on competitors also increases in the last two models; however, they allow only limited conclusions to be drawn, since the relation between marketing competencies and innovative performance is not statistically significant, as discussed before.

In the group of complementary competencies for the baseline model, it is the indicators regarding strategy (variable 'clearly defined activities of business units in the corporate strategy of our firm' with a weight of 0.3751) and strategic partnerships in R&D (variable 'the intensity, quality and extent of R&D knowledge transfer in co-operation with strategic partners' with a weight of 0.3524) that stand out. It can be concluded that innovation strategy not only has to be a clearly stated strategy of a firm, but also well defined. Strategic partnerships in R&D can be viewed as an extension of the technological competencies indicator regarding their extent and quality by including the external environment of the firm.

While developing new technological capabilities in-house can prove to be very costly both financially and timewise, cooperation in R&D with external partners offers a viable alternative, especially to those companies that could otherwise not afford R&D at all (Hagedoorn, 2002). Involving suppliers in product design both early and extensively can serve to reduce the complexity of the design project, resulting in faster and more productive R&D processes (Gupta and Wilemon, 1990). Customer involvement also notably improves the effectiveness of the product concept (Zirger and Maidique, 1990).

The 'cost efficiency of product development' contributes the least of all complementary competencies (0.2852). Although integration of technological and marketing knowledge can positively influence the efficiency of the development processes, it is also possible that the processes become lengthier and more costly due to the complexity arising from such coordination.

The model of incremental innovation differentiates itself decisively from the baseline model by virtue of the variable 'good transfer of technological and marketing knowledge among business units' being of primary importance (0.3507). This finding very much represents what the essence of incremental innovations is: addressing different market needs by producing a variety of products within the same product family. Since incremental innovations are less costly and technologically demanding, it is also to be expected that the cost efficiency of product development will gain some importance relative to other indicators.

Strategic partnerships in R&D (variable 'the intensity, quality and extent of R&D knowledge transfer in co-operation with strategic partners') are the indicator with the highest weight (0.3772) among complementary competencies within the third model, i.e., the radical innovation model. As the knowledge base grows, the application of which a firm has to be proficient in so as to develop the most advanced products, strategic partnerships appear to be of increasing importance in facilitating the R&D activities. Access to technological capabilities may prove to be particularly problematic in a small economy, such as Slovenia. The companies are relatively small compared to their international counterparts, and have fewer funds available for the financing of their R&D. Strategic partnerships are a way to gain access to additional capabilities through much smaller investments. The result is in line with the finding of Tidd and Bodley (2002) who confirmed, in the cases of both customer and user, that partnerships are more effective for highly innovative projects than for less-innovative ones.

It is interesting to note that variable 'clearly defined activities of business units in the corporate strategy of our firm' is the main driver of complementary competencies for the model accounting for trend setting (0.3948). It implies that clear strategic orientation is of key importance when pursuing this position in the industry. The next most important variable in this model is 'good transfer of technological and marketing knowledge among business units' (0.3334), again emphasising the importance of the integration of both technological and marketing capabilities. Understanding the market nevertheless appears to be of vital importance. The strategy of being an industry leader, however, proves to be incompatible with building a competency based on cost efficiency in R&D (the value of its weight 0.2728 is the lowest among the four models).

# 3. Lessons for the Companies and Industrial Policy Makers

From the practical point of view, the presented approach of measuring firm competencies can be useful because of the many opportunities it provides for interpreting data. Enabling cross-industry comparisons of country level data can be analyzed. In this way, an insight into the dynamics of the economy is obtained. National policies often focus on select industries that are thought to have the greatest potential. The competencies and innovative performance approach clearly shows that companies with potential are not necessarily contingent on industry but more likely on the competencies they are able to develop.

On the firm level, an aggregate analysis of competencies can provide firms with guidelines for their innovative strategy. Firms can use these findings to elaborate and define their own innovation strategy. At that stage, they can refer to the findings presented and look for competencies they need to further develop. In order to understand what concrete actions are behind these competencies, they can make use of the approaches presented for breaking down competencies into industry- and firm-specific capabilities.[5] That will help them to identify concrete steps that

5 For a comprehensive methodology for identifying technological and market capabilities and their complementarities related to the R&D function at a firm level, see Prašnikar et al. (2008). The methodology starts with the identification of all significant technological and marketing capabilities, first at the individual strategic unit level and then at the firm level.

need to be taken. The measures of competencies proposed are, of course, not only limited to aggregate analysis on the country level, and that is why firms can use them also independently for positioning themselves within a more limited context. Moreover, they can be used as a tool in constructing scenarios in planning and dealing with lower levels of predictability (Wright and Goodwin, 2009).

The manufacturing sector was chosen, since its innovation activities as well as value chains are more standardised relative to services, and thus make inter-firm analysis with a corresponding comparison easier and more straightforward. Relying on the nature and scope of competencies and in accordance with the assimilation approach of the service industry, the conclusions of the present research can also be relevant for firms in the service sectors (Coombs and Miles, 2000).

The findings suggest that companies trying to improve their innovative performance should foremost focus on technological competencies. The availability of various quality technological capabilities was recognised as the most decisive dimension contributing to the new-product variety. However, marketing and complementary competencies should by no means be overlooked. From the viewpoint of the marketing competencies, most of the attention should be given to customer-related competencies that guide the new product development process towards best addressing customer needs. Among complementary competencies, companies should especially make sure that they have a clear strategic direction. Strategic technological partnerships are another key factor that facilitates firms in expanding access to different technological capabilities. It is also worth noting that a clear and well-defined strategy can help firms recognise their core competencies to make well-informed strategic management decisions in outsourcing non-core competencies (Hafeez et al., 2007).

Furthermore, innovative technologies require advanced R&D. Entering strategic technological partnerships proves to be almost an imperative in achieving this, by enabling access to additional technological and marketing capabilities. Moreover, firms directing trends in their industries and acting as market leaders build their competitive advantage foremost on complementary competencies, followed by technological competencies. Market leaders complement and support their technological competencies with a solid strategy, by integrating technological and

These capabilities are further evaluated, both internally and externally, in terms of the following dimensions: capability relevance, probability of technological success (for technological capabilities) or probability of attaining customer loyalty (for marketing capabilities), and competitive position.

marketing knowledge, and by expanding their access to capabilities through strategic technological partnerships.

Competencies no doubt offer an insight into a firm's strategy for creating competitive advantage. However, it is important to keep in mind that sustainable competitive advantage is not a final destination a company should reach, but more of a dynamic journey (Chaharbaghi and Lynch, 1999). Therefore, companies need to constantly possess an understanding of how their competencies are positioned compared to their competitors, and to commit themselves to constantly enhancing them, especially the select core competencies. The core of the strategy of creating competitive advantage has to be twofold: both striving to be better in order to remain competitive, and being different so as to get ahead of the competition (Porter, 1999). This line of thinking is inherent in the concept of core competencies.

Existing studies on the state of R&D in Slovene firms show that the economy falls into the category of a technology follower country (European Innovation Scoreboard, 2008). As part of the European Union, Slovenia is actively involved within the Lisbon Strategy. On the basis of the research, several conclusions that support strategies proposed by the Agenda can be made. Namely, for technology follower countries, technological competencies may be costly and time consuming to acquire. Yet marketing and complementary competencies can successfully facilitate the process of catching up via incremental innovation. Firms can thus choose imitation as a strategy for developing technological capabilities and bridging the gap to a certain extent.

Especially in the context of the current economic downturn, innovation, competencies and competitive advantage may appear to be less relevant or not very high on the agenda of firms' management. However, these concepts comprise the core of the firms. Therefore, innovation and competence building should constantly remain high among the priorities, yet an understanding of these concepts is needed in order to be able to reap the most benefits.

## Acknowledgement

This research was supported by a grant from the CERGE-EI Foundation under a program of the Global Development Network. All opinions expressed are those of the authors and have not been endorsed by CERGE-EI or the GDN.

## References

Anderson, J. C. & Gerbing, D. W. (1988). Structural equation modeling in practice: A review and recommended two-step approach. *Psychological Bulletin*, 103, 411–423.

Bougrain, F. & Haudeville, B. (2002). Innovation, collaboration and SME's internal research capacities. *Research Policy*, 31 (5), 735–747.

Brown, S. L. & Eisenhardt, K. M. (1995). Product development: Past research, present findings, and future directions. *Academy of Management Review*, 20 (2), 343–378.

Calantone, R., Garcia, R. & Dröge, C. (2003). The effects of environmental turbulence on new product development strategy planning, *The Journal of Product Innovation Management*, 20 (2), 90–103.

Chaharbaghi, K. & Lynch, R. (1999). Sustainable competitive advantage: towards a dynamic resource-based strategy. *Management Decision*, 37, 45–50.

Chang, T. (1996). Cultivating global experience curve advantage on technology and marketing capabilities. *International Marketing Review*, 13, 22–42.

Clark, K. B. & Fujimoto, T. (1991). *Product Development Performance*. Boston: Harvard Business School Press.

Commission of the EC (2005). *Working together for growth and jobs: A new start for the Lisbon strategy*. Luxembourg: Office for Official Publications of the European Communities. http://eur-lex.europa.eu/LexUriServ/LexUriServ.do?uri=COM:2005:0024:FIN:EN:PDF (Accessed 25 September 2008)

Coombs, R. & Miles, I. (2000). *Innovation, Measurement and Services: The New Problematique*. In Metcalfe, J.S. & Miles, I. (eds.), Innovation Systems in the Service Economy: Measurement and Case Study Analysis (85–103). Boston: Kluwer Academic Publishers.

Day, G. S. (1994). The capabilities of market-driven organizations. *Journal of Marketing*, 58 (4), 37–52.

Eisenhardt, K. M. & Martin, J. A. (2000). Dynamic capabilities: What are they? *Strategic Management Journal*, 21, 1105–1121.

European Innovation Scoreboard (2008). PRO INNO Europe paper N° 6, Luxembourg: Office for Official Publications of the European Communities. from http://www.proinno-europe.eu/admin/uploaded_documents/European_Innovation_Scoreboard_2007.pdf (Accessed 3 November, 2008)

Frumau, C. C. F. (1992). Choices in R&D and business portfolio in the electronics industry. *Research Policy*, 21 (2), 97–124.

Gollop, F. M. & Monahan, J. L. (1991). A Generalized Index of Diversification: Trends in US Manufacturing. *Review of Economics and Statistics*, 73, 318–330.

Gupta, A. K. & Wilemon, D. L. (1996). Changing patterns in industrial R&D management. *Journal of Product Innovation Management*, 13 (6), 497–511.

Hafeez, K., Malak N. & Zhang, Y. B. (2007). Outsourcing non-core assets and competences of a firm using analytic hierarchy process. *Computers & Operations Research*, 34 (12), 3592–3608.

Hafeez, K., Zhang, Y. B. & Malak, N. (2002). Core competence for sustainable competitive advantage: a structured methodology for identifying core competence. *IEEE Transactions on Engineering Management*, 49, 28–35.

Hagedoorn, J. (2002). Inter-firm R&D partnerships: An overview of major trends and patterns since 1960. *Research Policy*, 31, 477–492.

Hagedoorn, J. & Cloodt, M. (2007). Measuring innovative performance: is there an advantage in using multiple indicators? *Research Policy*, 32, 1365–1379.

Hamel, G. & Heene, A. (eds.) (1994). *Competence-Based Competition*. Chichester: John Wiley.

Hult, G.T.M., Hurley, R.F. & Knight, G.A. (2004). Innovativeness: Its antecedents and impact on business performance. *Industrial Marketing Management*, 33, 429–438.

Kim, J.Y., Wong, V. & Eng, T.Y. (2005). Product variety strategy for improving new product development proficiencies. *Technovation*, 25, 1001–1015.

Koufteros, X. & Marcoulides, G.A. (2006). Product development practices and performance: A structural equation modeling-based multi-group analysis. *International Journal of Production Economics*, 103, 286–307.

Lanjouw, J. O. & Schankerman, M. A. (1999). *The Quality of Ideas: Measuring Innovation with Multiple Indicators*. NBER Working Paper Series, w7345. from http://ssrn.com/abstract=194848 (Accessed 7 November, 2008).

Lynn, G. S., Morone, J. G. & Paulson, A. S. (1996), Marketing and discontinuous innovation. *California Management Review*, 38 (3), 8–37.

Lynskey, M. J. (1999). The Transfer of Resources and Competencies for Developing Technological Capabilities - The Case of Fujitsu-ICL. *Technology Analysis and Strategic Management*, 11, 317–336.

OECD. (1997). *Revision of High Technology Sector and Product Classification*. STI Working Papers 1997/2. Paris: OECD.

Paul, J. V. & Peter, J. W. (1994). *Core competencies, competitive advantage and market analysis: forging the links*. In Hamel, G. & Heene, A. (eds.), Competence-based Competition (77–110). New York: Wiley.

Porter, M. E. (1999) Creating Advantage. *Executive Excellence*, 16, 11, 13–14.

Prahalad, C. K. & Hamel, G. (1990). The core competence of the corporation. *Harvard Business Review*, 68, 79–91.

Prašnikar, J., Lisjak, M., Rejc Buhovac, A. & Štembergar, M. (2008). A methodology for analyzing inter-relationships between technological and marketing capabilities. *Long Range Planning*, In Press, Corrected Proof.

Prašnikar, J., Rajkovič, T. & Vehovec, M. (2008). *Competencies driving innovative performance of Slovenian and Croatian manufacturing firms*. Zagreb: Ekonomski institute, from http://www.eizg.hr/AdminLite/FCKeditor/UserFiles/File/WP-0802-December%202008.pdf (Accessed 15 February 2010).

Rajkovič, T. (2009). *Core technological, marketing and complementary competencies as determinants of innovative performance*. Doctoral dissertation, Faculty of Economics, Ljubljana.

Ringle, C.M., Wende, S. & Will, A. (2005). *SmartPLS 2.0* (beta). Hamburg: SmartPLS., from http://www.smartpls.de (Accessed 30August 2008).

Sanchez, R. (2004). Understanding competence-based management: Identifying and managing five modes of competence. *Journal of Business Research*, 57, 518–532.

Sanchez, R., Heene, A. & Thomas, H. (1996). *Towards the theory and practice of competence-based competition*. In Sanchez, R., Heene, A. & Thomas, H. (eds.), Dynamics of competence-based competition: Theory and practice in the new strategic management. London: Elsevier, 1–35.

Schewe, G. (1996). Imitation as a strategic option for external acquisition of technology. *Journal of Engineering and Technology Management*, 13, 55–82.

Song M., Droge C., Hanvanich S. & Catalone R. (2005). Marketing and Technology Resource Complementarity: An Analysis of Their Interaction Effect in Two Environmental Contexts. *Strategic Management Journal*, 26, 259–276.

Song, X. M., Thieme, R. J. & Xie, J. (1998). The impact of cross-functional integration across product development stages: An exploratory study. *Journal of Product Innovation Management*, 15 (4), 289–303.

Swink, M. & Song, M. (2007). Effects of marketing-manufacturing integration on new product development time and competitive advantage. *Journal of Operations Management*, 25, 203–217.

Teece, D. J., Pisano, G., & Shuen, A. (1997). Dynamic capabilities and strategic management. *Strategic Management Journal*, 18, 509–533.

Tidd, J. & Bodley, K. (2002). The influence of project novelty on the new product development process. *R&D Management*, 32 (2), 127–138.

Tidd, J. (2006). *The competence cycle: Translating knowledge into new processes, products and services*. In Tidd, J. (ed.), From Knowledge Management to Strategic Competence. Singapore: Imperial College Press.

Tidd, J., Driver, C. & Saunders, P. (1996). Linking technological, market and financial indicators of innovation. *Economics of Innovation and New Technology*, 4 (3), 155–172.

Varadarajan, R. (2008). Fortune at the bottom of the innovation pyramid: the strategic logic of incremental innovations. *Business Horizons*, In Press, Corrected Proof.

Wang, Y., Lo, H. P. & Yang, Y. (2004). The Constituents of Core Competencies and Firm Performance: Evidence from High-technology Firms in China. *Journal of Engineering and Technology Management*, 21, 249–280.

White, G.I., Sondhi, A.C. & Fried, D. (2003). *The Analysis and Use of Financial Statements*. Hoboken: John Wiley & Sons, Inc.

Wright, G. & Goodwin, P. (2009). Decision making and planning under low levels of predictability: Enhancing the scenario method. *International Journal of Forecasting*, 25(4), 813–825.

Zahra, S.A. & Ellor, D. (1993). Accelerating new product development and successful market introduction. *SAM Academy of Management Journal*, 58 (1), 9–15.

Zirger, B. J. & Maidique, M. A. (1990). A Model of New Product Development: An Empirical Test. *Management Science*, 36, 867–883.

## About the Authors

**Tanja Rajkovič** acquired her PhD from the Faculty of Economics, University of Ljubljana in 2009 while employed as a teaching and research assistant. Her main research fields include technological management and the management of innovation with an emphasis on competencies. She is the founder and the director of the Inovema consulting firm dealing with modern business consulting and research.

**Janez Prašnikar** is a full professor of Economics at the Faculty of Economics of the University of Ljubljana (FELU). He is also the Director of the Institute of South-east Europe at the Department of Economics, University of Ljubljana, a William Davidson Institute Research Fellow, a Visiting Professor at the Michigan University Business School, a Research Fellow at the Centre for Economic Policy Research in London, and a Director of the International Full Time Master's Program in Business Administration at the FELU.

# Stochastic Modelling of Spare Components Inventory

***Alenka Brezavšček***

*alenka.brezavscek@fov.uni-mb.si*

***Alenka Hudoklin***

*alenka.hudoklin-bozic@fov.uni-mb.si*

## Abstract

A simple stochastic model for planning the inventory level of spare components needed for industrial system maintenance is presented. The expected system downtime due to the shortage of spare components in a given time interval is chosen as the decision criterion for planning the spare inventory level. The model is based on the renewal function from the renewal theory. The calculation of the renewal function depends on the form of the probability density function of times to component failures. As a model of this function, we used the Weibull distribution, which is appropriate for the entire operating period of the component, consisting of the region of random failures and the region of wear-out failures. In the region of random failures, the renewal function can be obtained easily, while for components subject to wear-out failures, the calculation of the renewal function is generally difficult. To simplify the calculation, we propose a discrete approximation. It has been shown that the calculation of the renewal function can be further simplified for relatively short planning intervals. To illustrate the applicability of the model, two numerical examples are given. The results obtained indicate that even a small reduction of the number of spares in the inventory can result in a significant amount of expected system downtime, leading to increases of the total production cost.

**Keywords**: maintenance, spare components inventory, stochastic modelling, renewal function, Weibull distribution

# 1. Introduction

During operation time, many failures of production system components occur. In order to reduce system downtime due to component failures, various maintenance activities are performed. Maintenance costs represent a major part of the total system operating cost. A survey by Robertson and Jones (2004) indicates that the maintenance budget ranges from 2 to 90% of the total plant operating budget, with the average being 20.8%. Significant savings can be achieved by introducing an efficient maintenance policy. In defining a maintenance policy, great attention should be paid to provide the availability of spare components needed for component corrective replacements. A shortage of spare components causes additional system downtime, and consequently leads to loss of income.

Many models for spare component provisioning policy have been proposed in the literature. A comprehensive overview of published models is given by Kennedy et al. (2002). The optimal spare component provisioning strategy is obtained by minimising the total system maintenance cost that comprises component replacement costs (corrective and preventive) and inventory costs, including ordering, holding and shortage cost. Such mathematical models are usually quite complex, containing a great number of parameters, especially when preventive replacements of the components are performed (see Brezavšček and Hudoklin, 2003; Diallo et al., 2008; Hu et al., 2008; Huang et al., 2008; de Smidt-Destombes et al., 2009; Wang et al., 2009). Therefore, such optimisation models are often difficult to implement. From a practical point of view, simpler methods for defining an efficient spare component provisioning policy would be desirable.

We will study a situation, existing in many industrial plants, in which a failure of a given system component causes a failure of the system as a whole, and the cost of system downtime due to the shortage of spare components considerably exceeds all the others elements of the maintenance cost function. In such a case, there is no need to optimise the total maintenance cost function. In our opinion, it is enough to determine the sufficient number of spare components to prevent shortages in a given time. Such an approach represents the simplification of rather complicated optimisation models, widely used in the literature. In this chapter, we propose a simple stochastic model for determination of the minimal number of spare components of a given type needed to fulfil the expected demand due to component failures during a chosen time interval. The model is based upon the renewal theory. The expected system downtime due to shortages of spare components is used as the decision criterion. The model can be used when the maintenance policy includes corrective replacements or block replacements of system components.

# 2. Preliminaries

Demand for spare components depends on the number of component replacements. The process of successive corrective replacements of a particular component can be described by an ordinary renewal process. Renewal processes belong to the family of point processes. A realisation of the renewal process consists of a series of point events (renewals) occurring singly in time and completely randomly. The renewal process is ordinary when all inter-renewal times are independent identically distributed random variables, all with probability density function $f(t)$ (e.g., Cox, 1970, p. 25).

The essential characteristic of an ordinary renewal process, used in our model, is the renewal function $H(t)$ defined as the expected number of renewals of a single component in the interval $(0,t)$:

$$H(t) = E[N(t)]$$

where $N(t)$ represents the number of renewals in the interval $(0,t)$.

The renewal function $H(t)$ can be calculated according to the equation:

$$H(t) = \sum_{r=1}^{\infty} F_r(t) \tag{1}$$

with $F_0(t) = 1$. The symbol $F_r(t)$ in equation (1) denotes the $r$-fold convolution of the cumulative distribution function $F(t) = \int_0^t f(x)dx$ with itself. For an arbitrary time, $t$ a simple solution of (1) is obtainable for some specific types of $f(t)$ only.

Theoretically, the calculation of the renewal function $H(t)$ according to (1) can be simplified using Laplace transformations because there is a simple relation between the Laplace transform of a function and the Laplace transform of its integral. The Laplace transform $H^*(s)$ of the renewal function $H(t)$ is given by the expression:

$$H^*(s) = \frac{1}{s}\,\frac{f^*(s)}{1-f^*(s)} \tag{2}$$

where $f^*(s)$ denotes the Laplace transform of the function $f(t)$. The renewal function $H(t)$ is than obtained by the inversion of equation (2).

Another presentation of the renewal function is provided by the so-called renewal equation (e.g., Tijms, 2003, p. 4):

$$H(t) = F(t) + \int_0^t H(t-x) f(x)\, dx \tag{3}$$

It is evident that the calculation of $H(t)$ depends on the probability density function $f(t)$ of inter-renewal times. In our case, $f(t)$ is equal to the probability density function of component failure times. During the component lifetime, the function $f(t)$ exhibits different behaviour. From the reliability theory, it is known that the lifetime of a component can be roughly divided into three regions: the region of early failures, the region of random failures (also called the region of the normal operation) and the region of wear-out failures, shown in Fig. 1. Early failures are usually eliminated by screening or burn-in tests before the components are put into operation. The operating period of the component thus comprises only the region of random failures and the region of wear-out failures. Random failures are mainly due to inherently slow-acting defects in the component, or to sudden excessive loading. The main failure mechanism in the wear-out region is deterioration of the component materials. The region of the random failures is characterised by monotonically decreasing function $f(t)$. In the region of wear-out failures, the distribution of component failure times follows a peak shaped curve. In Fig. 1, general form of the function $f(t)$ during the component lifetime is presented. The instantaneous failure rate $\lambda(t)$ is also shown. It can be seen from Fig. 1 that during the region of random failures $\lambda(t)$ has an approximately constant value $\lambda$, called simply the failure rate. During the wear-out region, instantaneous failure rate $\lambda(t)$ increases with time. The behaviour of $\lambda(t)$ indicates that during the random failures region only component replacements on failure are reasonable, while in the wear-out region preventive replacements also make sense.

*Figure 1: General form of component failure functions: probability density function f (t) of failure times, and instantaneous failure rate λ (t)*

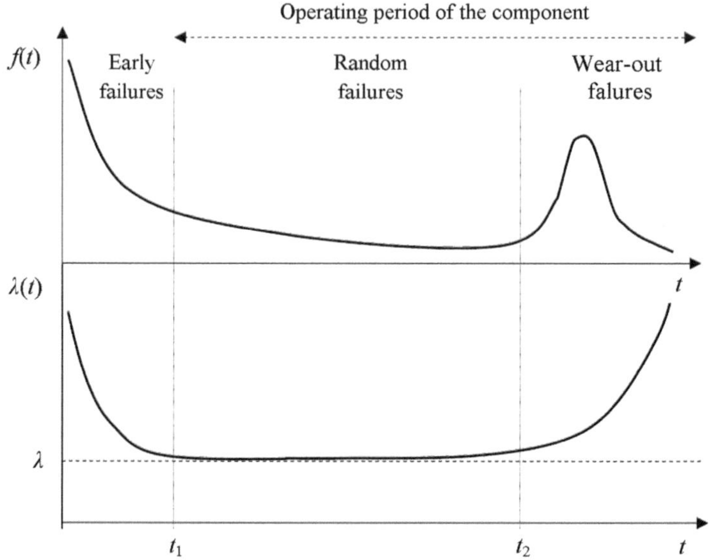


An appropriate mathematical model for $f(t)$ in the region of the constant failure rate is an exponential probability density function with parameter $\lambda$:

$$f(t) = \lambda \, e^{-\lambda t}$$

In the region of increasing instantaneous failure rate, times to failure of a component are distributed around a peak value, which is specific for a given deterioration mechanism due to material aging. A well-known peak-shaped probability density function that can be used to describe $f(t)$ in this region is the normal[1] (Gaussian) distribution:

1 The normal distribution, being defined in the interval $(-\infty, \infty)$, is an appropriate mathematical model for $f(t)$ only if the ratio between mean $\mu$ and standard deviation $\sigma$ is significantly higher than 1. In practice, we can assume that this condition is fulfilled when $\mu / \sigma \geq 3$. The area under the normal curve for negative values of time is then at most 0.0013. If the ratio $\mu / \sigma$ is less than 3, a truncated normal distribution should be used.

$$f(t)=\frac{1}{\sigma\sqrt{2\pi}}e^{-\frac{1}{2}\left(\frac{t-\mu}{\sigma}\right)^2}$$

with the parameters mean, denoted by $\mu$, and standard deviation, denoted by $\sigma$.

A very useful model for the function $f(t)$ is the Weibull probability density function, because it can describe $f(t)$ in both regions of the component operating time. The two-parameter Weibull[2] distribution is:

$$f(t)=\frac{\beta}{\eta}\left(\frac{t}{\eta}\right)^{\beta-1}e^{-\left(\frac{t}{\eta}\right)^{\beta}}$$

with shape parameter $\beta$ and scale parameter $\eta$. If the shape parameter $\beta$ is equal to 1, the Weibull distribution becomes exponential distribution with parameter $\lambda = 1/\eta$. The Weibull distribution with $\beta = 1$ can be therefore used for description of the function $f(t)$ in the region of random failures. If the value of $\beta$ is greater than 1, the Weibull probability density function exhibits a peak-shaped form. When $\beta = 3.3$ the Weibull probability density function approximates a normal distribution with mean $0.897\eta$ and standard deviation $0.299\eta$. The Weibull distribution with $\beta > 1$ can be therefore used for the description of the function $f(t)$ in the region of wear-out failures.

A useful tool for estimating the values of the parameters of the cited probability density functions from empirical data on component failures is an appropriate probability plotting paper.[3]

# 3. Model Development

The model is based on the following assumptions:

- The system contains $n$ independent components of a given type, operating in similar conditions.

2 In reliability theory, the three parameter Weibull distribution is also used. The third parameter $\gamma$, $-\infty < \gamma < \infty$, is the location parameter. When $\gamma = 0$ the distribution starts at time $t = 0$.

3 The exponential, normal and Weibull probability plotting papers are available on the web site http://www.weibull.com.

- A failure of any component under consideration results in a failure of the system as a whole.
- An inventory of spare components is planned for a given interval $T$.
- At the beginning of the planning interval, all components are new.
- A failed component is immediately replaced by a new one if a spare is available. The replacement time is negligible, there is no system downtime.
- The cost of system downtime due to a shortage of spare components considerably exceeds all the other elements of the maintenance cost function.

The model addresses components operating in the region of random failures and in the region of wear-out failures:

- In the region of random failures, components are replaced on failures only. The inventory of spares is planned for an arbitrary time interval.
- In the region of wear-out failures, periodical preventive replacements of components are performed according to the block replacement policy. To fulfil demand for spares in the interval between two successive preventive replacements, the inventory of spares is replenished in such a way that an order is received just before a planned preventive replacement. Each order includes spares for preventive replacements, and spares for corrective replacements.

The expected system downtime due to shortages of spares is used as a decision variable in planning the number of spare components in the inventory. Under the cited assumptions, the expected system downtime is zero if the existing inventory level of spares is at least equal to the expected number of component failures during $T$. Since the expected number of failures of $n$ components in the interval $(0, T)$ is equal to $nH(T)$, the required number of spares in the inventory is the minimal integer $Q$ satisfying the relation

$$Q \geq nH(T) \tag{4}$$

If we assume that the available inventory level is $Q_A$ where $Q_A < Q$, the expected system downtime due to shortage of spares in $T$ is equal to

$$D_S(T) = T - t_S \tag{5}$$

where $t_s$ denotes the expected time when the available inventory of spares is exhausted. The time $t_s$ can be determined as the minimal value of time satisfying the relation

$$Q_A < nH(t_S) \tag{6}$$

We have seen in Section 2 that the renewal function depends on the probability density function of component failure times. In calculating the renewal function $H(t)$ in equations (4), (5) and (6), the probability density function of component failure times will be modelled with the Weibull distribution. The values of parameters $\beta$ and $\eta$ can be obtained from reliability analysis of components observed. In the following, we will treat separately the calculation of $H(t)$ for components in the region of random failures ($\beta=1$), and for components in the region of wear-out failures ($\beta>1$).

## 3.1 Calculation of *H*(*T*) when *β*=1

When $\beta=1$, the calculation of $H(T)$ using equation (2) is straightforward. The Weibull probability density function is equal to:

$$f(T)=\frac{1}{\eta}e^{-\frac{T}{\eta}}$$

The renewal function $H(t)$ is obtained by the inversion of (2) using $f^*(s)=\frac{1}{1+s\eta}$.

We obtain $H^*(s)=\frac{1}{s^2\eta}$, and finally:

$$H(T)=\frac{T}{\eta} \tag{7}$$

## 3.2 Calculation of *H*(*T*) when *β*>1

When $\beta>1$, the Weibull probability density function follows a peak-shaped curve. For such Weibull distributions, the analytical solution of (1) or the exact inversion of (2) is not available. The numerical evaluation of the renewal function when the underlying distribution is the Weibull distribution has attracted the attention of several authors (Cui and Xie, 2003; Jiang, 2008; Jin and Gonigunta, 2009). Unfortunately, the calculations involved are quite demanding. A comprehensive overview of different approaches of calculating the Weibull renewal function is given in a recent book by Rinne (2009).

In this paper, we derived a simple discrete formula for $H(t)$ on the basis of the recursive integral equation (3). We assume that component renewals can occur only in the time points $i$, $i$=1,2, …, with the probability $p_i$. Our discrete approximation of (3) reads as follows:

$$H(T)=\sum_{i=1}^{T}p_i+\sum_{i=1}^{T}H(T-i)p_i \qquad T=1, 2, \ldots \qquad (8)$$
$$H(0)=0$$

The probability $p_i$ in (8) is approximated by the expression:

$$p_i=\int_{i-1}^{i}f(t)dt=F(i)-F(i-1), \qquad i=1,2, \ldots, \qquad \sum_{i=1}^{\infty}p_i=1$$

This approximation implies that discrete and continuous cumulative distribution functions are equal since:

$$\sum_{i=1}^{T}p_i=\sum_{i=1}^{T}\left[F(i)-F(i-1)\right]=F(T)$$

where $F(T)=1-e^{-\left(\frac{T}{\eta}\right)^{\beta}}$.

Equation (8) can be then rewritten in the following way:

$$H(T)=F(T)+\sum_{i=1}^{T}H(T-i)\left[F(i)-F(i-1)\right] \qquad T=1, 2, \ldots. \qquad (9)$$
$$H(0)=0$$

Because mathematical operations in (9) are rather simple, the renewal function can be calculated easily, regardless of the value of the shape parameter $\beta$. The approximation (9) can also be used for the calculation of the renewal function for other types of probability density functions. Similar approximations for calculating the renewal function have been proposed by Jardine (1973), Jardine and Tsang (2006), and van Noortwijk and van der Weide (2008).

The first term of (9) is associated with the first renewal in the interval $(0,T)$, while the second term is associated with the further renewals in the same interval. If the interval $(0,T)$ is relatively short, the probability of the occurrence of more than one renewal in $(0,T)$ is consequently very small. In this case, the second term in (9) can be neglected, and the renewal function $H(T)$ is approximated by the cumulative distribution function $F(T)$. In Fig. 2, the curves for the renewal function $H(T)$ and the cumulative distribution function $F(T)$ in the time interval $(0,2\eta)$ for $\beta$ between 1 and 6 are shown. The mean $\mu$ for each failure time distribution[4] is also marked.

4 $\mu=\eta\Gamma\left(\frac{1}{\beta}+1\right)$ where the symbol $\Gamma$ (.) denotes the Gamma function.

*Figure 2: The curves for H (T) and F (T) in time interval $(0,2\eta)$ for $\beta$ between 1 and 6*

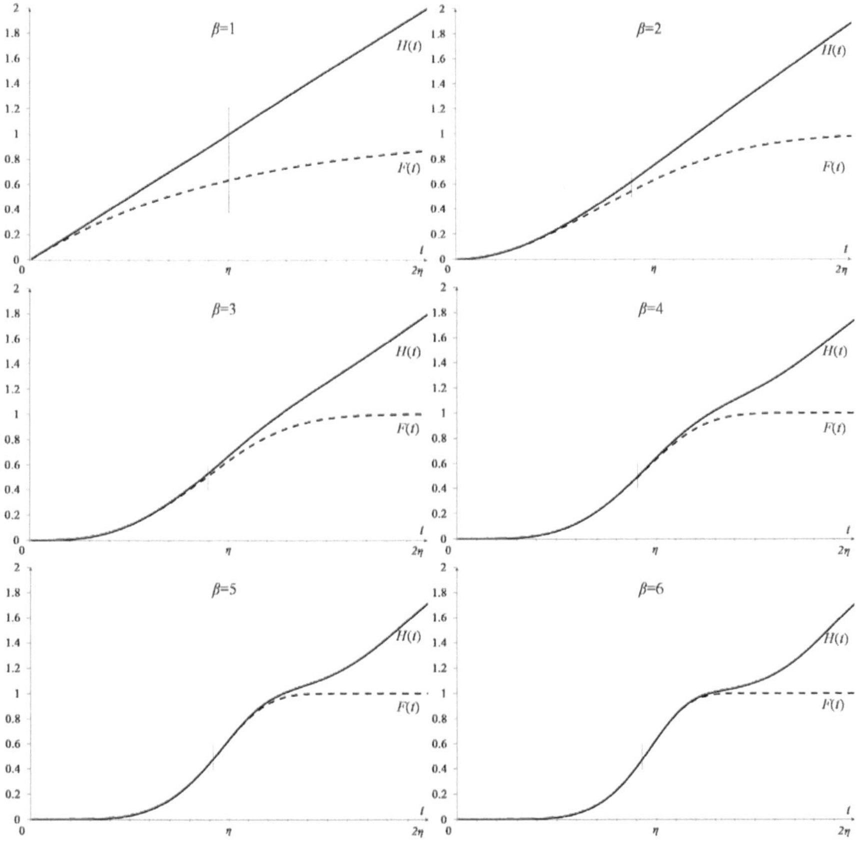


It is evident from Fig. 2 that the renewal function $H(T)$ is linear only when $\beta=1$ (see also equation (7)). The curves $H(T)$ and $F(T)$ overlap for small values of time $T$. The larger the value of $\beta$ is, longer is the region of overlap. When $\beta>3$ the region of overlap is longer than the interval $(0, \mu)$. These findings prove that for relatively short planning intervals the calculation of the renewal function is extremely simplified since the relation $H(T) \approx F(T)$ can be used

# 4. Numerical Example

We will illustrate the application of the model with two numerical examples. In both examples, we assumed that component times to failure are distributed according to the Weibull distribution. On the basis of a sample of component failure times, the values of parameters $\beta$ and $\eta$ are determined. These parameters are used to calculate the required inventory level of spare components needed to minimise the expected system downtime due to shortage of spare components. Additionally, the expected system downtime due to spare shortage is calculated in the case of insufficient inventory level of spare components.

*Example 1:*

There are $n = 98$ components under observation. No preventive replacements of components are performed. The inventory of spares is planned for the interval of $T = 9000\ h$.

On the probability plotting paper, shown in Fig. 3, twelve points defined by pairs $(t_i, F(t_i))$, where $t_i$ is the time to $i$-th failure, are plotted. The corresponding values of $\beta$ and $\eta$ are marked.

*Figure 3: Weibull probability plot for component failure times from the first numerical example*

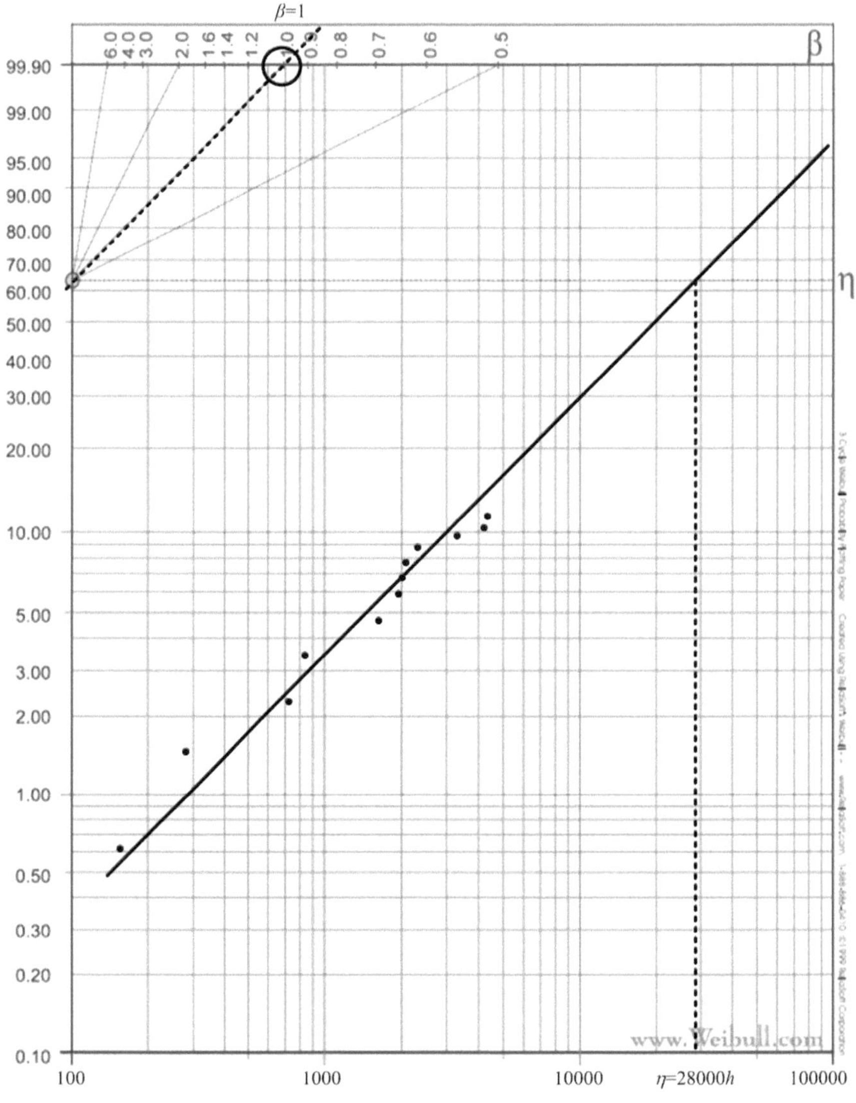

It can be seen from Fig. 3 that $\beta = 1$ and $\eta = \mu = 28000$ *h*. The value of $\beta$ implies that components under consideration are in the period of random failures. The minimal number of spares in the inventory is calculated using (4) and (7):

$$Q \geq n\frac{T}{\eta} = 31.5$$

The expected system downtime during $T = 9000$ *h* is zero if there is at least 32 spares in the inventory.

We assume that there are only 30 spares available. The expected system downtime due to shortage of spares can be calculated according to equation (5). The expected time $t_s$ when the available inventory of spares is exhausted is determined using (6):

$$30 < nH(t_s)$$

The value of $t_s$ is calculated to be 8571 *h*. The expected downtime due to shortage of spares in $T$ is finally obtained to be 429 *h* or 4.7% of $T$. Such an amount of expected system downtime can result in a substantial increase of the total production cost and a subsequent loss of income.

*Example 2:*

There are $\eta = 55$ components under observation. Preventive replacements of components are performed according to the block replacement policy every 2800 *h*. This time represents the planning interval $T$. Just before the planned preventive replacement, $Q$+55 spare components are received.

On the probability plotting paper, shown in Fig. 4, eight points defined by pairs ($t_i$, $F(t_i)$), where $t_i$ is the time to *i*-th failure, are plotted. The corresponding values of $\beta$ and $\eta$ are marked.

*Figure 4: Weibull probability plot for component failure times from the second numerical example*

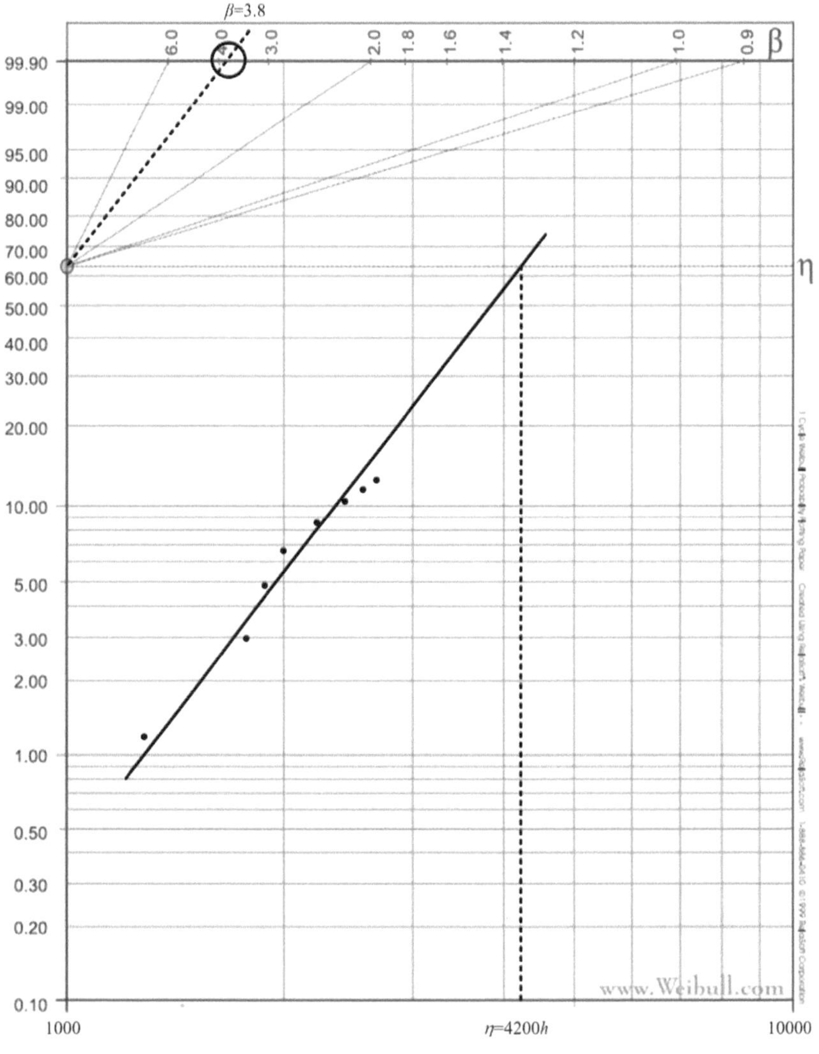


It can be seen from Fig. 4 that $\beta = 3.8$ and $\eta = 4200\ h$. The value of $\beta$ implies that the components under consideration are in the period of wear-out failures. Preventive replacements are therefore reasonable. Using values of $\beta$ and $\eta$ the mean $\mu$ is determined to be 3795.91 $h$.

The minimal number of spares in the inventory to minimise the expected system downtime due to shortage of spares is calculated using equation (4). The value $H(T)$ is calculated according to (9) to be 0.1936. Thus the minimal number of spares in the inventory is calculated to be:

$$Q \geq nH(T) = 10.65 \Rightarrow Q = 11$$

Since $T < \mu$ the calculation of the renewal function $H(T)$ can be simplified using the approximation $H(T) \approx F(T)$. We obtain $F(T) = 0.1928$, and $Q \geq nF(T) = 10.60$. We can conclude that the agreement between both calculated values of $Q$ is reasonably good.

If there are 11 spare components in the inventory, the expected system downtime is zero. If we assume that there are only nine spare components available, the expected system downtime due to shortage of spares can be calculated according to (5). The expected time $t_s$ when the available inventory of spares is exhausted is determined using (6):

$$9 < nH(t_s)$$

The value of $t_s$ is calculated by iteration to be 2670 $h$. The expected downtime due to shortage of spares in $T$ is finally obtained to be 130 $h$ or 4.6% of $T$. As in the first numerical example, we see that a small decrease of spare component inventory level results in considerable system downtime.

# 5. Conclusion

In this chapter, we present a simple stochastic model for planning the inventory of spare components needed to support the maintenance of an industrial system. The expected system downtime due to the shortage of spare components is chosen as the decision criterion. The model can be used to determine the minimal number of spare components in the inventory needed to minimise the expected system downtime due to spare component shortages in the planning time interval. Additionally, the model enables the calculation of the expected system downtime due to the spare component inventory level being insufficient.

The main idea of our model is the following: when the cost of system downtime due to shortages of spare components considerably exceeds all the other elements of the maintenance cost function, the spare provisioning policy can be reduced to preventing shortage of spare components instead of determining the optimal number of spare components in the inventory. This assumption is corroborated by the results of our previous work (Brezavšček and Hudoklin, 2003). The results of a numerical example that deals with the determination of the optimal spare inventory level (under very high costs of spare component shortages) show that the number of spare components in the inventory is optimal when the shortage probability is negligible.

In the development of the model, we have used the renewal theory approach. The characteristic of the renewal theory used in the model is the renewal function. It depends on the behaviour of the component failure time distribution during the operating period of the component. We modelled this distribution with the Weibull probability density function, which is useful in the region of component random failures as well as in the region of wear-out failures. In the period of random failures, the Weibull distribution becomes exponential, and the renewal function can be easily derived. In general, calculation of the renewal function for components subject to wear-out failures is difficult. To simplify the calculation, we have proposed a discrete approximation that can be used irrespective of the component operating period, and of the type of the underlying failure time distribution. We have proved that calculation of the renewal function can be further simplified if the planning interval is shorter than the component mean time to failure. In such a case, the renewal function can be approximated by the cumulative distribution function of component failure times.

Due to the small number of model parameters and the simplicity of the mathematical operations involved, the model presented is suitable for implementation in a variety of industrial plants. The applicability of the model has been illustrated through two numerical examples.

## References


Brezavšček, A. and Hudoklin, A. (2003): Joint optimization of block-replacement and periodic-review spare-provisioning policy, *IEEE Transactions on Reliability*, Vol. 52, pp. 112–117.

Cox, D.R. (1970): *Renewal Theory*, Methuen.

Cui, L.R. and Xie, M. (2003): Some normal approximations for renewal function of large Weibull shape parameter, *Communications in Statistics - Simulation and Computation*, Vol. 32, No. 1, pp. 1–16.

de Smidt-Destombes, K.S., van der Heijden, M.C. and van Harten, A.(2009): Joint optimisation of spare part inventory, maintenance frequency and repair capacity for k-out-of-N systems, *International Journal of Production Economics*, Vol. 118, pp. 260–268.

Diallo, C., Ait-Kadi, D. and Chelbi, A. (2008): (s,Q) Spare Parts Provisioning Strategy for Periodically Replaced Systems, *IEEE Transactions on Reliability*, Vol. 57, No. 1, pp. 134–139.

Hu, R., Yue, C. and Xie, J. (2008): *Joint Optimization of Age Replacement and Spare Ordering Policy Based on Genetic Algorithm*, Proceedings of the 2008 International Conference on Computational Intelligence and Security, Vol. 01, pp. 156–161.

Huang, R. et al. (2008): Modeling and Analyzing a Joint Optimization Policy of Block-Replacement and Spare Inventory with Random-Leadtime, *IEEE Transactions on Reliability*, Vol. 57, No. 1, pp. 113–124.

Jardine, A.K.S. (1973): *Maintenance, Replacement, and Reliability*, Pitman, London.

Jardine, A.K.S. and Tsang, A.H. C. (2006): *Maintenance, Replacement, and Reliability: Theory and Applications*, CRC/Taylor & Francis, Boca Raton.

Jiang, R. (2008): A Gamma-normal series truncation approximation for computing the Weibull renewal function, *Reliability Engineering & System Safety*, Vol. 93, No. 4, pp. 616–626.

Jin. T. and Gonigunta, L. (2009): Weibull and Gamma Renewal Approximation Using Generalized Exponential Functions, *Communications in Statistics - Simulation and Computation*, Vol. 38, No. 1, pp. 154–171.

Kennedy, W. J., Patterson, J. W. and Fredendall, L. D. (2002): An overview of recent literature on spare parts inventories, *International Journal of Production Economics*, Vol. 76, No. 2, pp. 201–215.

Rinne, H. (2009): *The Weibull Distribution: A Handbook*, CRC Press, Taylor & Francis Group.

Robertson, R. and Jones, A. (2004): *Pay day, Plant Engineering & Maintenance*, Vol. 28, No. 9, pp. 18–25.

Tijms, H.C. (2003): *A First Course in Stochastic Models*, John Wiley & Sons, Chichester.

van Noortwijk, J.M. and van der Weide, J.A.M. (2008): Applications to continuous-time processes of computational techniques for discrete-time renewal processes, *Reliability Engineering & System Safety*, Vol. 93, No. 12, pp. 1853–1860.

Wang, L., Chu, J. and Mao, W. (2009): A condition-based replacement and spare provisioning policy for deteriorating systems with uncertain deterioration to failure, *European Journal of Operational Research*, Vol. 194, No. 1, pp. 184–205.

## About the Authors

**Alenka Brezavšček** is an assistant professor at the Faculty of Organizational Sciences, University of Maribor. Her research fields are stochastic processes, system reliability and availability, and information system security.

**Alenka Hudoklin** is an emeritus professor at the Faculty of Organizational Sciences, University of Maribor. Her research fields are stochastic processes, system reliability and availability, and information system security.

# Assessing the Importance of Sustainable Development Factors in Dental Tourism

***Gabrijel Devetak***

*mandrija@siol.net*

***Elena Marulc***

*elena.marulc@siol.net*

## Abstract

Medical tourism is among the rare market segments registering growth in spite of the global economic situation. Therefore, many countries are actively trying to develop and strengthen their reputations as medical tourism destinations. Slovenia is at the beginning of its development as such a destination. In accordance with the ownership structure and healthcare system in Slovenia, it would be most appropriate to develop dental tourism.

In this chapter, the authors have analyzed the existing state of medical and dental tourism in Slovenia based on the existing literature, from the points of view of marketing and sustainable development. They researched the possibilities of marketing dental tourism in Slovenia among Slovene dentists and foreign prospective clients from 17 European and other countries. They researched the preparedness of Slovene dentists for cooperation in this field, what the prices should be in order to interest foreign prospective clients in dental tourism in Slovenia, what the necessity of sustainable development in this field of tourism is, what the influence of different positive effects on the environment is on foreign prospective clients' decisions for dental tourism services (from the point of view of customers as well as dentists), and a mutual comparison of these points of view. The results confirm the interest of dentists and customers in dental tourism in Slovenia when considering sustainable development. They show that the most important factor is the environmental protection, both according to dentists and the customers. It was also seen the evaluations are statistically different by 30% in the evaluation of all factors.

The results therefore show the inadequate knowledge of the dentists, who will need to have a clearer image of the actual state of affairs. For the successful development of dental tourism in Slovenia, more research needs to be implemented. In this way, the conditions would be shown from different points of view, thus enabling a better understanding of current circumstances and the problems of introducing and developing dental tourism in Slovenia. The research should also focus on the marketing of dental tourism and set itself a model in Slovenia.

**Keywords:** marketing, sustainable development, dental tourism, Slovenia

# 1. Medical and Dental Tourism

## 1.1 Background

Tourism has become an important sector of the global economy. The WTO (Tourism Highlights 2009, 3) reported that 2008 saw a total of 922 million international tourist arrivals, with international tourism receipts reaching 642 billion euros. Moreover, the organisation forecasts that international tourist arrivals would grow to one billion in 2010. Due to the global economic crisis, which has also strongly affected the tourism sector, negative economic growth has occurred. The regions most severely affected are the Middle East (-18%) and central and eastern Europe (-13%) (UNWTO World Tourism Barometer, 2009, 3).

The global crisis has had different effects on tourism; while most tourism sub-sectors have experienced negative growth, a few have shown expansion. One of the sub-sectors undergoing positive growth is medical tourism (Morgan, 2010), which is defined by the Medical Tourism Association (What is Medical Tourism, 2010) as travel to a foreign country to receive medical care which is of equal or better quality than available locally as well as being more affordable or/and accessible.

In the past, foreign medical care was typically sought across the border, in the neighbouring countries. Crossing the border, to neighbouring countries to improve living standards and life perspectives (Paape and Kiereta, 2008, 47) has always been part of near-border residents' lives, especially in rural areas. But foreign medical services are not only sought by near-border residents; people who live far away from the state borders also travel abroad for medical care. During the recession, health insurance and treatment costs have become too high for many citizens, thus forcing them to consider and seek medical care in foreign countries with lower medical service costs. Upon studying marketing materials, Lunt and Carrera (2010,

31) established that medical services from the field of cosmetic surgery, dentistry, cardiology, orthopaedics, gastrointestinal procedures, reproduction, tissue and organ transplant, and eye surgery are being offered to medical travellers. Cardiac surgery is currently the procedure most frequently sought through medical tourism at the global level; based on the medical tourism growth trend, however, cosmetic surgery and dentistry are predicted to take the lead in the future (Cornell, 2006, 1099).

The services provided in the context of medical tourism vary in percentage from country to country, depending on the state of their health care (quality and cost of certain medical procedures, ownership structure and the organisation of health care). In Slovenia, medical tourism is still in its infancy, and the country's health care system makes dental tourism the best choice to concentrate on initially. (Marulc, 2010, 167). Later, the provision of other medical services in the context of tourism would also have to be considered. Next to this, we need to be aware of the limitations and advantages of Slovenia in the field of medical tourism. Nevertheless, the development and advancement of medical tourism is both reasonable and necessary for its positive contribution to Slovene tourism, health care, employment and economic growth. Slovene health care and tourism are up against strong competition from numerous European countries.

According to the Medical Tourist Association (MTA Members in Europe, 2010), the leading European medical tourism providers are in Croatia, Latvia, Hungary, Germany, Romania, Spain, Sweden, Switzerland and the United Kingdom. These countries are leaders in the field because they present the most attractive opportunities for medical tourists and foreign investors alike. The biggest obstacle for Slovenia in the development of medical tourism is the number of health workers who can cooperate in the field of medical tourism. According to latest available information from WHO (Human Resources for Health – Physicians, Dentists, 2010), the stated countries have, on average, approximately 1,700% more physicians than Slovenia. The problem could be moderated by 'importing' foreign health workers. However, according to Slovene health legislation, due to constant complications and the resistance towards foreign physicians in granting concessions, limited possibilities for the 'import' of foreign physicians and the limited salaries of physicians, we cannot expect to substantially ease the problems due to the lack of staff.

Due to its small size and consequential limitations, it would be wrong to set an objective of making Slovenia one of the leading destinations for medical tourism. It is necessary to develop medical tourism within the given possibilities and try to exploit the competitive advantages that Slovenia has. It has a competitive advantage (Medical Tourism in Slovenia, 2010) over Croatia in being a member of the EU, which means greater safety for patients and the possibility of medical cost reimbursement. Slovenia's competitive advantages over developed countries such as Germany, Spain, Sweden and the United Kingdom are in savings, as the cost of the entire medical travel package is up to 70% lower than the cost of the medical procedure alone in the developed countries. The competitive advantage of Slovenia over Latvia and Sweden is its milder climate, while the country's advantages over Romania and other less developed countries are in medical practitioners with quality, EU certified university education, in their mandatory annual training courses on the latest health care trends, treatment methods and materials as well as in the use of top-quality materials and instruments. Delicious cuisine, great wines, beautiful surroundings, a safe environment, numerous tourist sites and many cultural events are some of the additional attractions that Slovenia has to offer to foreign patients.

Next to the positive effects in the introduction and development of dental tourism in Slovenia and in accordance with sustainable development, we can also expect problems that will require solutions. One major problem is hazardous waste, which would increase with the growth of dental tourism. In carrying out their work, dentists also pollute water they need for rinsing and cleaning. That is why business processes should be developed in dentistry clinics and outpatient clinics that would lead to reducing the adverse effects on the environment and would thus approach sustainable development.

According to Kern (2008, 29–30), one of the major problems is that outdated organisational structures still exist in today's companies, thus hampering development. In the case of Slovenia, we encounter the problem of small dental firms; 93.6% of Slovene business entities with dental activity (Poslovni register Slovenije, 2009) employ two or fewer persons (normally a dentist and a nurse) without any organisational and managerial skills needed to be able to carry out business processes in accordance with new knowledge and sustainable development. That is why it would make sense to consider establishing an association for dental services in medical tourism, within the framework of which the interested dentists would integrate and jointly solve common problems, including the problem of the sustainable development in the field of dental services in medical tourism.

## 1.2 Segmentation

The market for Slovene medical tourism services is global. This is why we need a segmentation of the market, which will make marketing easier (Devetak, 2007, 74). According to Pires and Stanton (2008, 46), segmentation in health care is typically based on nationality, age and income.

In terms of nationality, Slovenia should primarily address patients from developed European countries and North America. According to research, the number of Americans seeking medical care abroad will grow to 23 million by 2017, their annual expenditure for such services reaching $80 billion in total (Edelheit, 2008, 23). Research shows that 43 million people currently living in the USA have no health insurance and 120 million have no dental coverage (Albert, 2008, 16). In addition, research revealed that in 2008 11% of American employers decided to provide their employees with medical care abroad rather than health insurance due to the considerable financial savings (Stephano and Edelheit, 2009, 13). On account of the planned structural changes in medical cost reimbursement in the United Kingdom, Canada and some other developed countries, growing numbers of citizens from these countries are expected to seek treatment abroad. Other than that, long waiting lists for major surgeries is what often drives Canadian and British citizens to seek medical care abroad (Jones and McCullough, 2007, 1077).

Age-based segmentation may show considerable variation among medical specialities, which may be attributed to different age groups requiring different medical procedures. Dentists' experience suggests that persons aged from 51 to 70 are their main target group, as they most frequently suffer from serious dental conditions. Another interesting segment is persons between 29 and 40 years of age, who primarily seek cosmetic dentistry to meet the expectations of their workplace and social environments.

The role of income-based segmentation is to identify the prospective clients with incomes too low to afford health care services at home. Nevertheless, they must still earn enough to afford medical travel. Due to the economic crisis, the number of people unable to receive medical care in their local environment continues to grow. Research carried out in the USA shows that 61% of citizens, the highest percentage in the decade, believe that their income is insufficient to cover the cost of potential medical treatment (Newport, 2010). Income-based segmentation depends on the medical speciality, as the costs of medical procedures vary considerably; for example, the cost of cardiology services is a few hundred thousand euros, while dental care services are only a few thousand euros. (Patient Pricing Page, 2010).

## 1.3 Market Variables

Apart from market segmentation, target market identification and positioning, medical tourism also requires constant control over market variables. Other than the quality of medical and tourist services, one of the extremely important factors is the cost of medical services. A survey carried out by the Deloitte Center for Health Solutions Research (2009 Deloitte Survey of Health Care Consumers, 2009, 8) showed that 43% of Americans will travel abroad for testing, surgery or treatment if the cost of the required medical services was at least 50% lower than the cost of such services locally. Precise information (detailed classification by destination, types of medical and tourist services used, length of stay by destination, expenditure by medical tourism service, loyalty to destination, loyalty to doctor etc.) on the patients having undergone medical treatment abroad is not freely accessible and is carefully protected by medical tourism providers as a trade secret. The easiest to obtain is the cost data, which is at least partly public and thus accessible to potential medical travellers. The exact amount of money saved if comparing the price of the entire medical tourism package in Slovenia to the cost of medical services in the developed countries depends on the patient's homeland and the procedure required. Taking into account the considerably lower cost of medical treatment in comparison to developed European countries and the affordability of tourist services (accommodation, food, local transport, and additional tourist services), the savings may reach 70%. The exact amount, however, varies from case to case. On the basis of their previous year's business results, one of the few existing medical tourism providers operating in the field of dentistry in Slovenia, established that the savings of an average UK tourist having received their services (comparing the cost of the complete dental tourism package in Slovenia to the cost of local dental services alone) amounted to 4,600 euros (Affordable and Professional Dental Treatment Abroad, 2010).

As Slovenia is largely unknown, both direct and indirect marketing channels must be used in order for perspective medical tourism clients to notice and choose Slovene service providers. The internet and e-mail as well as adequate e-mail documentation make a particularly valuable contribution to efficient marketing and the provision of medical tourism services. Such marketing should, according to Rajkovič et al. (2008, 2261), allow traceability, transparency, selectiveness, monitoring and analysis, thus leading to the improvement of processes and systems and increasing the safety of patients and health care workers. With foreign patients, e-documentation has an even greater significance, as it allows foreign doctors to easily update a patient who has already returned home on the treatment given or surgery performed, to give the patient further treatment in his country if so desired, or to help the patient quickly and easily in case of post-operative complications.

As a largely unrecognised tourism market and an emerging medical tourism destination, Slovenia needs to intensify health travel promotional activities, with the support of the Slovene Tourism Organisation, the Ministry of Health and all other stakeholders. Satisfied patients will bring in their share by word-of-mouth promotion.

The satisfaction of market customers is likely to increase if they are faced with positive confirmation incurred as the result of customers getting more than they expect, not only in the event of dental and tourist services, but also in all other details and significant items/events affecting the achievement of increased profits. Image and reputation are two of those important details that tend to be overlooked in health care. And it is often the image and reputation that decisively affect a potential patient's decision. Prospective clients usually lack the knowledge to evaluate the expertise of the doctors they are considering. Therefore, they decide on the basis of what they can evaluate; image and reputation certainly fall into this category. The survey conducted by Ferjan (2008, 644) revealed that leader image makes a greater contribution to one's leader's reputation than the actual success of the department one runs. It was also established that shoes and clothes play a major role in one's reputation. Slovene doctors often pay no attention to image; in contrast, the authors' experience gained on visits to foreign facilities show that foreign doctors and other health care workers were extremely attentive to their appearance, which was often harmonised or even uniform (same uniforms and footwear) in numerous cases.

Abroad, special emphasis is dedicated to the education and awareness of physicians in the medical and non-medical field. Recently, much attention has been devoted to sustainable development, which has been included in development programmes by most European countries.

## 2. Sustainable Development and Dental Tourism

For a long time, the economy paid no attention to the environment; thus irreversible damage was done. Only when the environment was so damaged that it started to present a threat to the whole planet and its people, did a new model of development start to form. The so-called sustainable development satisfies today's needs without threatening the possibilities of future generations (Agenda 21 for the Travel & Tourism Industry, 1996). Sustainable development is based on three pillars (Mihalič, 2006, 95). The economic pillar refers to the economic efficiency of companies and their activities as well as to the long duration of operations. The social and cultural pillar refers to respect for human rights, equal opportunities, elimination of poverty, taking into account local community interests, promotion of development and progress, as well as recognition and respect for different cultures. The ecological pillar refers to the protection and management of resources, and requiring reduced pollution and environment protection. When we discuss the connection between sustainable development and dental services in medical tourism, we mean the positive and negative effects of dental services in medical tourism, which are triggered in economical, social and cultural, and ecological environments.

The group of adverse effects includes the outflow of a part of earnings to foreign countries, high infrastructure costs, inflationary effects, loss of cultural authenticity, local inhabitants feeling inferior in comparison to foreigners, criminal prostitution and drugs, negative impact on the water and air, noise and physical pollution. One of the priority tasks in the field of tourism from the sustainable development point of view is the improvement of the ecological footprint as well as reducing the carbon dioxide emissions. In this connection, considerations arise that travelling due to dental services in medical tourism additionally increase carbon dioxide emissions and thus fails to contribute to sustainable development. It should be noted that the majority of patients travel abroad because they are unable to financially afford dental services or because the patient waiting time is too long, and will travel abroad notwithstanding the promotion of the sustainable development and reductions of carbon dioxide emissions. The majority of people are still not sufficiently aware to give priority the issue of sustainable development before solving their own health-related problems. In addition, the majority of patients with financial problems have no other means of solving their medical problems. This is why the current situation will be carefully analyzed in order to determine how to develop dental services in medical tourism in Slovenia in the most sustainable way possible. The most environmentally sustainable are those dental services that will leave the lowest possible global ecological footprint. Dolnicar et al. (2010, 505) note that recent studies of the comprehensive environmental footprint indicated that transport has the largest share, representing from 59 to 97% of the environmental footprint of a tourist. That is why the greatest care shall be devoted to transport.

The majority of airlines are aware of the problem of greenhouse gas emissions and possible reductions in the number of flights due to the awareness of passengers, which is why in the last year the majority of Western airlines committed to the objective of reducing greenhouse gas emissions in aviation to zero in the near future. The calculations made by researchers indicated that in the event passengers cannot or do not want to travel other than by aeroplanes, the least environmentally burdening routes are short-haul flights. That is why targeting marketing efforts towards markets closer to the destination is suggested (Peeters and Schouten, 2006, 169). For the case of dental tourism in Slovenia, this means focusing on European customers. Furthermore, it is also necessary to consider travelling with low-emission modes of transport. Dental patients usually have no problems with physical mobility; therefore, they can come to Slovenia via train, bus or (in the worst case scenario) by their own car. It is important that everyone from the patients to the service provider is aware and that all negative effects are continuously reduced.

Next to reducing the negative effects due to the introduction and development of dental tourism (with regard to sustainable development), we also need to increase the positive. It is very important to know how to affect the decision of a market's prospect so that a customer will decide on the offered product from the field of dental tourism precisely due to the fact that this product has a certain positive effect on the environment. Knowing this significantly contributes to understanding the prospective clients' behaviour as a consumer and provides for more successful marketing. We did not come across any research that would explain how various positive economic impacts (earnings made from dental tourism for the national economy, an increase in budget funds, additional employment due to the development of dental tourism, infrastructure development, earnings made from dental tourism for the local economy, multiplicative function of dental tourism) and socio-cultural impacts (promoting the protection of the destination's cultural characteristics, preserving local culture, providing financial means for preserving the local craft industry, events and similar, recovery of almost forgotten cultural traditions, forming and enhancing cultural awareness, enhancing world peace due to new acquaintances, setting in motion favourable social effects, increasing the security in the local environment due to the development of dental tourism, affecting the promotion and image of the destination) and environmental impacts (dental tourism is a means of the environment protection, dental tourism is a source of funding for the protection of natural environment, dental tourism represents grounds for the improvement of the quality of the natural environment , dental tourism is a reason for enhancing ecological awareness, environment ethics and ecological responsibility, improvements in ecological management and planning are made) when selecting which products from dental tourism affect the clients.

Next to knowing how individual factors influence the choice of customers, it is also necessary to know how to market the factors of sustainable development and what is important for this. Apton (2010, 86) realises that in dentistry we still encounter the idea that the introduction of sustainable developments brings raised costs and that it is inconvenient. The reality is different, as it brings savings and presents a greater health security for the patients. The awareness of patients is constantly rising. The factors of sustainable development will soon present an inseparable part of dental tourism for all the patients, as well as food, transport, accommodation etc.; they will ask for it when they are considering the offer for dental tourism. Until then, it is necessary to make detailed research of all the factors of sustainable development, include them in the Slovene offer and visibly market them with the help of a promotional mix.

# 3. Survey

This section presents a part of the results of an extensive international survey conducted to examine the possibilities of marketing dental tourism in the light of sustainable development. The research was implemented for Slovenia. Slovene dentists and prospective clients from seventeen European, American and Asian countries took part in the survey.

More specifically, the survey that was done to determine whether Slovene dentists and foreign prospective clients are at all interested in taking part in dental services in medical tourism and, according to the prospective clients' opinions, what the prices of dental services in Slovenia should be in order for them to be willing to come for these services. Further on, it was necessary to determine whether Slovene dentists and foreign prospective clients have any attitude towards the sustainable development in dental services in medical tourism or what their opinion is on the urgent need to introduce sustainable development in this field of tourism. Furthermore, we also needed to check which of the positive economic, social and cultural, and ecological effects has the greatest impact on a prospective clients' decision to choose the offered service, particularly because it has a certain impact on the environment. A comparison of the prospective clients' assessment of themselves and assessments of dentists on prospective clients was made with the purpose of determining how well dentists are aware of the opinions or the decisions of their prospective clients. This chapter presents the part of the survey whose first six objectives were:

- establish the interest of Slovene dentists in providing services in the context of dental tourism in Slovenia,
- establish what (dental) prices would motivate foreign prospective clients to consider travelling to Slovenia for dental care,
- establish whether foreign prospective clients believe that dental tourism needs to incorporate sustainability,
- establish whether Slovene dentists believe that dental tourism needs to incorporate sustainability,

- establish which of the positive economic, environmental and socio-cultural impacts foreign prospective clients believe to decisively influence their choice of a dental tourism product for its environmental impact,
- establish which of the positive economic, environmental and socio-cultural impacts Slovene dentists believe decisively influence a foreign prospective clients' choice of a dental tourism product for its environmental impact.

The Slovene Tourist Organisation (Zeleni turizem, 2010) only started with a planned introduction of sustainable development in Slovene tourism in 2010. In the next two years, they are planning to implement basic research on the introduction and the instructions for marketing sustainable tourism. Since everything planned is directed towards general tourism, in the next five years we cannot expect the STO to implement any activities concerning niche tourism, such as medical tourism or its sub-type dental tourism. Slovene dentists will therefore have to acquire the information for successful marketing of dental tourism by themselves. For this, it is very important to know the demands, wishes and points of view of foreign prospective clients, as only these can enable the dentists to be successful. It is important to establish the differences in evaluations of various important factors between the dentists and the foreign prospective clients. In order to assess the situation in this field, the seventh objective was set:

- Discover the differences between the expectations of Slovene dentists and foreign prospects in the evaluation of important positive effects when making decisions about foreign prospects, particularly when selecting an offered service in the field of dental tourism precisely for the reason that this offered service has a positive effect on the environment.

The authors of the research are the collaborators at the only specialised centre for research and development in the field of medical tourism in Slovenia. In the centre, they have thus far participated in numerous research projects on medical tourism in Slovenia and abroad, in educating Slovene health and tourism workers about medical tourism and organising professional visits of Slovene health and tourism workers in many European and other destinations for medical tourism. On the basis of their experience, acquired through work in the centre, and the above-mentioned surveys, the following seven hypotheses were formed:

- H1: *Slovene dentists are generally willing to provide their services in the context of dental tourism in Slovenia.*
- H2: *Foreign prospective clients would generally be interested in dental travel to Slovenia if the cost of dental services was up to one-half of what they would pay in their place of residence.*

- H3: *Foreign prospective clients generally believe that dental tourism needs to incorporate sustainability.*
- H4: *Slovene dentists generally believe that dental tourism needs to incorporate sustainability.*
- H5: *Foreign prospective clients generally believe their choice of dental tourism product to be decisively influenced by its positive environmental impact.*
- H6: *Slovene dentists generally believe foreign prospective clients' choice of dental tourism product to be decisively influenced by its positive environmental impact (environmental protection reasons).*
- H7: *Among Slovene dentists and foreign prospective clients, there are differences in the evaluation of the importance of individual positive effects when making decisions about foreign prospective clients, particularly when selecting an offered service in the field of dental tourism precisely for the reason that this offered service has a positive effect on the environment.*

## 3.1 Methodology

The gathering and processing of secondary and primary data provided a basis for the survey. The scientific methods used in the survey were the study of literature, the descriptive method, the compilation method, the comparative method, the deductive method, analysis and synthesis, the survey method and the inductive method. Triangulation was also used to provide a more comprehensive insight into the issue studied by combining different methods. PASW STATISTICS 17.0 software was used for data processing. The statistical methods used were the calculation of basic procedures for descriptive statistics for individual variables, the t-test for establishing the differences between Slovene dentists and foreign prospective clients. Statistic significance was verified on level of 5% risk ($p=0.05$).

Two questionnaires were prepared. The questionnaire distributed to foreign prospective clients was in English and contained, in addition to the socio-demographic section, questions on:

- the subject's estimate of the prices of Slovene dental tourism services in comparison to the prices set by their current local dentist that would motivate them to consider dental travel to Slovenia,
- the subject's opinion as to the need for incorporating sustainability into dental tourism,
- the subject's opinion on which of the economic, environmental and sociocultural impacts decisively influences their choice of a dental tourism product for its positive environmental impact.

The questionnaire for Slovene dentists was in Slovene and included, in addition to the socio-demographic part, questions on:

- the subject's willingness to provide services in the context of dental tourism in Slovenia,
- the subject's opinion as to the need for incorporating sustainability into dental tourism,
- the subject's opinion on which of the positive economic, environmental and socio-cultural impacts decisively influences a foreign prospective clients' choice of dental tourism product for its positive environmental impact.

The evaluation was possible with the help of a regular five-point scale, in which 1 means that the effect has absolutely no influence on choice, 2 means that the effect has no influence, 3 means that the effect has no influence nor does it have any influence, 4 means that the effect has influence and 5 means that the effect has a major influence on choice.

In addition to the above-listed items, the questionnaire for Slovene dentists included other questions, such as the dentists' knowledge of foreign languages and language obstacles, about their ability as well as willingness to treat foreign patients with regard to their supposedly overbooked schedules, about the costs to foreign patients, etc. These questions had already been studied in the context of another research project, yielding similar results (for more details see Marulc, 2010).

Both questionnaires were tested prior to the research by 10 dentists and 51 prospective clients from abroad. The persons testing the questionnaires were not included in the research. Complete anonymity of all respondents was ensured.

The survey was conducted between 3rd August 2009 and 3rd February 2010 in the European Union, Croatia, Bosnia and Herzegovina, Serbia, Switzerland, the Russian Federation, Turkey, Canada, the USA, Australia, China, Korea and Japan. The questionnaires for Slovene dentists were sent to the addresses (928) of all business entities engaged in dentistry that were included in the AJPES database (Poslovni register Slovenije, 2009). The customer questionnaires were sent to prospective clients by e-mail (to 4,640 business partners included in the research authors' e-mail address database) or randomly distributed to prospective clients (81 questionnaires were distributed in person to randomly selected foreigners at the Ljubljana airport on 10th, 17th and 24th January 2010). The questionnaires (Arrivals and overnight stays by countries from which tourists come, Slovenia, June 2009) were sent or handed out exclusively to prospective clients from the countries from which Slovenia is most frequently visited and in countries with most medical tourists.

## 3.2 Results and Interpretation

### 3.2.1 The Socio-Demographic Data Provided by the Prospective Clients

A total of 1,496 of questionnaires that were returned by clients (and are valid) represent 31.7% of all questionnaires that were distributed; 1,415 (94.6%) of questionnaires were returned electronically and 81 in sealed envelopes. All personally distributed questionnaires were correctly completed and returned. Clients who returned valid and correctly completed questionnaires were from the following countries: 173 from Germany, 161 from France, 153 from Austria, 150 from Italy, 148 from Spain, 141 from the United Kingdom, 92 from the USA, 82 from the Russian Federation, 78 from the Netherlands, 75 from Belgium, 47 from Switzerland, 42 from Canada, 39 from Serbia, 38 from Sweden, 31 from Japan, 22 from Hungary and 14 from Croatia.

The socio-demographic data provided by the prospective clients show a prevalence of women (63.7%). The reason for the high percentage of female respondents could be interpreted with an explanation that opinions and decisions regarding travelling are often left to women. Barber (2009, 253) and Kozak (2010, 493) note that the decision-making process is divided between so-called female and male areas of decision making and that in most cases the policy applies in which men leave decisions on so-called female areas to women. In addition, the authors' experiences also confirm that tourism is classified as an area in which women dominate in decision making. The fact that the majority of respondents were women most probably affects the results of the study, because women have different needs and look at life differently from men. However, the intensive informing on the importance of sustainable development and the consequences for the entire humanity in the case of non-involvement of sustainable development into everyday life in recent years has changed and balanced views of both genders on the environment and life. Therefore, we assume that the predominant number of women among the interviewed clients did not significantly affect the results of the survey. In order to argue this with certainty, it would be necessary to do further research on the impact of gender in the light of the results of our study.

The prospective clients interviewed ranged from 18 to 75 years of age, with a mean age of 49.9 years and a standard deviation of 11.7 years. Most had vocational or secondary education (31.2%), while the smallest percentage had completed specialisation or held a master's or PhD degree (5.5%); 7.1% of persons had primary education, 26.3% higher education and 29.9% short-term higher education. Among the prospective clients enrolled, 78.1% were employed, 16.7% were retired and 5.2% were unemployed. The annual income of the interviewed clients per person in their common household shows that most interviewed clients (41.7% people) have annual incomes between €12,000 and 30,000, while 31.6% of clients have annual incomes between €30,000 and 48,000, and 20.4% have incomes below €12,000 per year. The lowest number of interviewed clients, (6.3%) has annual incomes of over €48,000.

The data suggests that 729 people or 48.7% of those interviewed had dental problems that would cost them more than €200 at their dentist. Most of them (49.8% of people) needed crowns, bridges and implants; most of these people (75.4%) are more than 51 years old. The smallest number, (15.0%) needed cosmetic dentistry; 81.2% of whom are less than 35 years old. This is not surprising since older people mentioned more complex interventions, while younger people needed cosmetic corrections. The remaining 24.0% needed restorative treatment and 11.2% required conservative treatment. In the latter two categories, no age-group stands out strongly, which is consistent with the fact that these treatments were needed in all age groups.

Insufficiently valid questionnaires from particular countries were returned in order to establish dental comparisons between different countries. In the future, extensive research should be carried out in each country, and the results should then be compared. This would require a detailed study for each country and an examination of possible constraints with which potential customers from abroad might be faced, assuming that the prices of foreign dentists meet their demands and that they want to travel in order to benefit from dental tourism. The major obstacles that clients of dental tourism may encounter include an unfavourable visa regime between their country of residence and the country where they wish to have dental services done, physical difficulties in travelling, and difficulties with individual dentists if the patient wants to go to a specific one.

### 3.2.2 The Socio-Demographic Data Provided by Dentists

A total of 327 valid questionnaires were returned to us by Slovene dentists. The socio-demographic data provided by the dentists' shows that 84.1% of the respondents were female and 15.9% were male. Women prevail among the interviewed since in Slovenia most dentists are women (62.5%) (Zobozdravniki po starosti in spolu, 2008, 596). In this particular case (as in the event of prospective clients), it is also very likely that women also preferred filling in the questionnaire compared to men. The dentists interviewed were aged between 32 and 70 years, the mean age being 49.9 years with a standard deviation of 7.5 years.

### 3.2.3 The Results of the Research among Slovene Dentists and Foreign Prospective Clients (Hypotheses 1 - 7)

Among all the dentists interviewed, 308 (94.2%) said that they would be willing to participate in dental tourism, which indicates a very high interest in providing their services to foreign clients. Based on this result, we can confirm the first hypothesis (H1) which says that Slovene dentists are generally willing to participate in dental tourism in Slovenia.

Our research has established that among all participants of the poll as many as 80.8% would not refuse (and would therefore accept) the possibility of taking advantage of dental tourism. Those persons (the aforementioned 80.8%) have assessed that the prices of dental services in Slovenia should be at least 54.26% lower compared to the price of their current dentist in order to gain the interest of possible clients for an organized appointment with a dentist in Slovenia.

The research has also showed that 78.3% of the participants of the poll have assessed that the prices of dentist services abroad should be at least 50% lower compared to the price of their current dentist in order to gain the interest of possible clients for an organized appointment with a dentist in Slovenia.

We researched/calculated the percentage of the participants of the poll (in our case 78.3%) who assess that the prices would have to be 50% lower compared to the prices abroad because in one of the hypotheses we presupposed (based on practice) that the aforementioned number of people would be the majority. It was of utmost importance to establish with the research if it really is the majority (i.e. at last 51%). It turned out it was the majority, since the number is 78.3%. Therefore the second hypothesis (H2) can be confirmed.

Among all the interviewed prospective clients from abroad, 1,479 (98.9%) felt that it is necessary to include sustainable development in dental tourism. Only two prospective clients (0.1%) considered this not strictly necessary; 15 prospective clients (1.0%) did not want to or could not decide. The result shows that almost 99% of all respondents recognised the importance of sustainable development and the need for its inclusion in the field of dental tourism. Based on this result, we can confirm the third hypothesis (H3) that potential customers from abroad generally believe that it is necessary to include sustainable development in dental tourism.

All (100.0%) questioned Slovene dentists believe that it is necessary to include sustainable development in dental tourism. The result shows that dentists are aware of the importance of sustainable development and the need for its inclusion in the field of dental tourism. Dentists are more aware of the risk and consequences of non-involvement of sustainable development in dentistry than clients (this may be the reason why the percentage of dentists who believe that it is necessary to integrate sustainable development in dental tourism is higher. Based on this result, we can confirm the fourth hypothesis (H4) that Slovene dentists generally consider it is essential to include sustainable development in dental tourism.

The results show (see Table 1) that all interviewed clients estimate that their decision on the selection of the offered product of dental tourism is highly influenced by only five of the effects that have an influence or a major influence on their choice: environmental protection (4.870), improving the quality of natural environment (4.411), promoting the protection of the cultural characteristics of the destination (4.352), reviving nearly forgotten cultural traditions (4.270) and preserving local cultures (4.263). Among them, environmental protection is most influential; therefore, we can confirm the fifth hypothesis (H5) that potential clients from foreign markets generally believe that the greatest impact that the product offered in the field of dental tourism will be selected because of the fact that the product has a positive (i.e., protective) impact on the environment.

Slovene dentists assessed (see Table 1) that decisions made by foreign prospective clients to choose the offered service precisely due to the fact that a particular service has a specific impact on the environment is highly influenced by only six of the effects that have significant influence on the choice of foreign prospective clients: environmental protection (4.090), improving the quality of natural environment (4.002), promoting the protection of the destination's cultural characteristics (4.001), preserving the local culture (3.972), recovery of almost forgotten cultural traditions (3.813) and infrastructure development (3.752). These results indicate that Slovene dentists believe that the interviewed prospective clients assess that among all the listed impacts on the environment, they (the prospective clients) are mostly influenced towards choosing the offered product of dental tourism precisely due to the fact that this product has a positive impact on the environment in the form of environmental protection. Thus, we are able to confirm the sixth hypothesis (H6) that Slovene dentists generally believe that prospective clients from abroad assess that what most influences their (the prospective clients') decision to choose the offered product from the field of dental tourism is precisely the fact that this offered product has a positive effect on the environment in the form of environmental protection.

With the help of the t-test, we also established potential differences between Slovene dentists and foreign prospective clients for their evaluations on the importance of individual positive effects on their decision-making. The calculated values of significance (Sig. two-tailed) between both groups are smaller than 0.05 (see Table 1, see **) at six effects. At all six significantly different differences, the average values were greater for Slovene dentists. This means that while comparing the dentists' and the prospective clients' opinions for these six factors, the dentists give greater importance to the foreign prospective clients' decisions to select a certain service from the field of dental tourism exactly for the reason that the offered service has the mentioned positive effect on the environment. The biggest differences between the mean values appear in the estimation of the effect 'provide funding for local cultural events, products etc.' (2.091) and 'employment generation' (1.719). This shows that the dentists overestimate the influence of funding for local cultural events, products etc., and of providing new employment. The results of the research show that the foreign prospective clients (as opposed to the dentists) do not give them any credit for their decision-making (see Table 1; mean values are 1.212 and 1.182). The dentists also overestimate the influence of 'financially contribute to the protection of nature' (the difference of mean values between dentists and prospective clients is 1.349) and 'increase safety levels in the destination' (difference 1.261). Those two effects also, according to foreign prospective clients' evaluations, do not have any influence on their decisions. The smallest differences between the mean values at statistically importance differences were calculated for 'contribution to local economics' (difference 0.830) and 'infrastructure development' (difference 0.611). According to foreign prospective clients, neither the first factor nor the second factor had any influence on them. We can see that statistically important differences between Slovene dentists and foreign prospective clients appeared at 30% of all factors, thus we can confirm the seventh hypothesis (H7) that between Slovene dentists and foreign prospective clients there are differences in the evaluation of the importance of individual positive effects for foreign prospective clients.

*Table 1: The comparison of results for individual positive economic, social, cultural or ecological effects on the environment affects the choice of the client in making a decision for a specific product in the field of dental tourism between Slovene dentists and foreign prospective clients. Source: Own survey.*

| The effects | PROSPECTS Mean | PROSPECTS std. deviation | DENTISTS mean | DENTISTS std. deviation | t | Sig. two-tailed |
|---|---|---|---|---|---|---|
| Reason for protecting and preserving the natural environment | 4.870 | 0.6443 | 4.090 | 0.9941 | 0.980 | .330 |
| Improvement of natural quality | 4.411 | 0.7920 | 4.002 | 1.0531 | 1.431 | .152 |
| Protecting the cultural authenticity | 4.352 | 0.8711 | 4.001 | 1.1043 | 1.522 | .123 |
| Help renew old, almost lost cultural events etc. | 4.270 | 1.1928 | 3.813 | 1.3945 | 0.450 | .650 |
| Help cultural authenticity not to disappear | 4.263 | 0.6424 | 3.972 | 0.9927 | 1.163 | .251 |
| **Infrastructure development** | **3.141** | **1.1814** | **3.752** | **0.9553** | **-2.520** | **.011**** |
| Increasing environmental awareness | 3.091 | 1.2431 | 2.201 | 0.9127 | 0.620 | .540 |
| Improve environmental management | 3.001 | 0.8573 | 2.362 | 0.9124 | 1.301 | .203 |
| Foster understanding between cultures and force for peace | 2.762 | 1.0112 | 2.650 | 1.3046 | 0.761 | .449 |
| Increase cultural awareness | 2.241 | 0.9824 | 2.351 | 1.1321 | -0.3022 | .773 |
| **Increase safety levels in the destination** | **1.451** | **1.3272** | **2.712** | **1.6624** | **-2.321** | **.020**** |
| **Financially contribute to the protection of nature** | **1.371** | **0.9825** | **3.322** | **1.2564** | **-2.581** | **.015**** |
| **Provide funding for local cultural events, products** | **1.212** | **0.8017** | **3.303** | **1.3524** | **-2.732** | **.009**** |
| Impact on promotion and destination image | 1.193 | 0.7442 | 1.031 | 0.9624 | 1.311 | .192 |

| | | | | | | |
|---|---|---|---|---|---|---|
| **Employment generation** | **1.182** | **1.5043** | **2.901** | **1.3429** | **-2.613** | **.010**** |
| Positive social impacts | 1.162 | 1.2612 | 1.051 | 0.8213 | 0.881 | .382 |
| **Contribution to local economics** | **1.152** | **0.3543** | **1.982** | **0.7442** | **-2.280** | **.031**** |
| Foreign exchange earnings | 1.151 | 1.1067 | 1.041 | 0.9824 | 0.477 | .632 |
| Multiplication function | 1.140 | 1.0823 | 1.002 | 1.1121 | 0.358 | .725 |
| Contribution to government revenues | 1.040 | 0.8839 | 1.000 | 0.9372 | 0.5214 | .607 |

The results show that the dentists do not have a correct image about their prospective clients when judging the influence of different sustainable positive effects on the environment in decision-making. This means that the dentists should acquire additional information that would enable them to correct this incorrect image and consequentially improve their performance in the field of dental tourism.

## 4. Conclusions and Directions for Further Research

The costs of medical treatment and health insurance have become too high for many people in many developed countries. In such cases, the solution is to seek treatment abroad, in countries providing quality yet more affordable medical care. Therefore, medical tourism, despite the recession, has been recording high growth. Virtually all countries realise the importance of medical tourism and therefore seek to gain and consolidate their status as a destination for medical tourism. With regard to quality and affordable medical care, Slovenia should be one of the countries that actively consider marketing medical tourism at the international level; considering health care organisation and ownership structure, dental tourism would be the best starting point.

This chapter is devoted to the analysis of the existing situation in medical and dental tourism in Slovenia in terms of marketing and the problem of dental tourism in Slovenia in accordance with the negative and positive effects on the environment, depending on the foundation of sustainable development.

The survey was conducted between 3rd August 2009 and 3rd February 2010 in Croatia, Bosnia and Herzegovina, Serbia, the territory of the European Union, Switzerland, the Russian Federation, Turkey, Canada, the USA, Australia, China,

Korea and Japan; 327 questionnaires distributed to Slovene dentists and 1,496 questionnaires distributed to potential clients were returned.

Based on the results of the research, the empirical part of the article adopts all the hypotheses that were set prior to the research:

The research shows that 94.2% of respondent dentists would participate in dental tourism, confirming the first hypothesis which says that Slovene dentists are generally willing to participate in the field of dental.

The research also shows that 80.8% respondent clients do not reject the possibility that they would participate in dental tourism. Such respondents estimated that Slovene dental services would have to be at least 54.26% cheaper than the services provided locally in order for them to be interested in organised dental tourism, with a tourist agency providing transport, accommodation and a quality dentist in Slovenia. Based on this result, we can confirm the second hypothesis that potential clients from abroad are generally interested in dental tourism in Slovenia if dental services cost up to one-half of what they would have in their place of residence.

The survey showed that almost 99% of all respondents and 100% of all dentists recognised the importance of sustainable development and the need for its inclusion in the field of dental tourism. Based on this result, we can confirm the third and the fourth hypothesis that potential customers from abroad and Slovene dentists generally believe that it is necessary to include sustainable development in dental tourism.

The survey showed that all interviewed clients estimated that their decision on the selection of the offered product of dental tourism is highly influenced by only five of the effects (environmental protection, improving the quality of natural environment, promoting the protection of the cultural characteristics of the destination, reviving nearly forgotten cultural traditions and preserving local cultures). Among them, environmental protection is the most influential; therefore, we can confirm the fifth hypothesis that potential clients from abroad generally believe that the greatest impact that the product offered in the field of dental tourism will be selected because of the fact that the product has a positive (i.e., protective) impact on the environment.

Slovene dentists assessed that decisions made by foreign prospective clients to choose the offered service from the area of dental tourism precisely due to the fact that such particular service has a specific impact on the environment, which is highly influenced by only six of the effects (the above five effects plus infrastructure development). Among them environmental protection is again the most influential. Thus we are able to confirm the sixth hypothesis that Slovene dentists generally believe that prospective clients from abroad assess that what most influences their (the prospective clients') decision to choose the offered product from the field of dental tourism is precisely the fact that this offered product has a positive effect on the environment in the form of environmental protection.

With the t-test, we established the differences relating to six effects (provide funding for local cultural events, products etc, employment generation, financially contribute to the protection of nature, increase safety levels in the destination, contribution to local economics and infrastructure development) between Slovene dentists and foreign prospective clients in their evaluation of the importance of individual positive effects on the decision making of foreign prospective clients. At all statistically important differences, the mean values were higher for Slovene dentists. This means that the mentioned effects are recognised as more important by the dentists than by the prospective clients. This shows a lack of knowledge about foreign prospective clients. As statistically important differences between Slovene dentists and foreign prospective clients appeared in 30% of all effects, we confirmed the seventh hypothesis, that among Slovene dentists and foreign prospective clients there are differences in the evaluation of the importance of the individual positive effects when deciding about foreign prospective clients, in the case when selecting an offered service in the field of dental tourism exactly for the reason that this offered service has a positive effect on the environment.

Considering the fact that the Slovene Tourist Organisation does not plan to implement any activities for dental tourism, it would be necessary to implement other research in Slovenia for its successful development. Due to different plans of the STO, the research will need to be implemented in the next short-term period outside of the STO framework. Firstly, we would need research that would clarify all points of view on the situation and the problems of the introduction and development of dental tourism in Slovenia. The research should focus on the marketing of dental tourism and set a model for dental tourism in Slovenia.

## References

*Affordable and Professional Dental Treatment Abroad* (2010): Dent-iq. Available from: http://www.dent-iq.co.uk/ . (Accessed June 20, 2010).

Agenda 21 for the Travel & Tourism Industry: *Towards Environmentally Sustainable Development* (1996): World Tourism Organization, Madrid.

Albert, D. (2008): Medical Tourism- Progress and Prospects, *Medical Tourism Magazine*, Vol.2, No.7, pp.15–17.

Apton, J. (2010): Whiter Teeth and a Green Environment – Dentistry Does its Part. *Medical Tourism Magazine*, Vol. 4, No.15, pp. 85–86.

Barber, N. (2009): Wine consumers information search: Gender differences and implications for the hospitality industry, *Tourism and Hospitality Research*, Vol.9, No.3, pp. 250–269.

Caruana, A. and Fenech, N. (2005): The effect of perceived value and overall satisfaction on loyalty: A study among dental patients, *Journal of Medical Marketing,* Vol.5, No.3, pp. 245–255.

Cornnell, J. (2006): Medical tourism: Sea, sun, sand and ... surgery, *Journal of Tourism Management*, Vol. 27, No.6, pp. 1093–1100. 2009 Deloitte Survey of Health Care Consumers: Key findings, Strategic *Implications*, *March 2009* (2009): V: Deloitte Center for Health Solutions

Research., Washington, D.C.. Available from: http:// www.deloitte.com/dtt/article /0,1002,sid%253D80772%2526cid%253D25239 6,00. html. (Accessed April 15, 2009).

Devetak, G. (2007): *Marketing Management*, Fakulteta za management, Koper.

Dolnicar, S. et al. (2010): Short-haul city travel is truly environmentally sustainable, *Tourism Management*, Vol. 31, No.4, pp.505–512.

Edelheit, J. (2009): The Effects of the World Economic Recession on Medical Tourism, *Medical Tourism Magazine*, Vol.3, No. 9, pp.22–24.

Ferjan, M. (2008): *Analiza dimenzij ugleda*. Book of Abstracts of the 27th International Conference on Organizational Science Development, Slovenia, Portorož, March, 19th–21st 2008, (eds.) Rajkovič, V., Jereb, E., Kern, T., Kljajić, M., Paape, B., Pagon, M. and Vukovič, G., Moderna organizacija, Kranj.

Human Resources for Health – Physicians, Dentists (2010): World Health Organisation. Available from: http://apps.who.int/globalatlas/dataQuery. (Accessed August 23, 2010).

Jones, J.W. and McCullough, L.B. (2007): What to do when a patient's international medical care goes south, *Journal of Vascular Surgery*, Vol. 46, No.5, pp.1077–1079.

Kern, T. (2008): *Business Repository as a Universal Organizational Concept*. Book of Abstracts of the 27th International Conference on Organizational Science Development, Slovenia, Portorož, March, 19th–21st 2008, (eds.) Rajkovič,

V., Jereb, E., Kern, T., Kljajić, M., Paape, B., Pagon, M. and Vukovič, G., Moderna organizacija, Kranj.

Kozak, M. (2010): Holiday taking decisions - The role of spouses, *Tourism Management*, Vol.31, No.4, pp. 489–494.

Lunt, N. and Carrera, P. (2010): Medical Tourism: Assessing the evidence on treatment abroad, *Journal Maturitas*, Journal is now in press, Corrected Proof, available online 24 Feb 2010 at www. sciencedirect.com.

Marulc, E. (2010): *Trženje stomatoloških storitev v zdravstvu*, Institut za turizem in marketing, Celje.

Medical tourism in Slovenia (2010): Dentiq. Available from: http://www.dent iq.co.uk/ . (Accessed June 18, 2010).

Mihalič, T. (2006): Trajnostni turizem, Ekonomska fakulteta, Ljubljana.

*MTA Members in Europe* (2010): Medical Tourism Association. Available from: http:// wwww.medicaltourismassociation.com/en/mta-members-in-europe. html.(Accessed June 17, 2010).

Newport, F. (2010): *Americans No Less Worried About Healthcare Costs*. Gallup, Inc. Available from: http://www.gallup.com/poll/127727/Americans-No-Less-Worried-Healthcare-Costs.aspx?version=print. (Accessed June 18, 2010).

Paape, B. and Kiereta, I. (2008): *Education and Migration in Poland: The Development of Rural Areas as a Push Factor for Future Migration from Poland (Part III)*. Book of Abstracts of the 27th International Conference on Organizational Science Development, Slovenia, Portorož, March, 19th–21st 2008, (eds.) Rajkovič, V., Jereb, E., Kern, T., Kljajić, M., Paape, B., Pagon, M. and Vukovič, G., Moderna organizacija, Kranj.

*Patient Pricing Page* (2010): Medical Tourism Association. Available from: http:// wwww.medicaltourismassociation.com/en/medical-tourism-faq-s.html.(Accessed June 17, 2010).

Peeters, P. and Schouten, F. (2006): Reducing the ecological footprint of inbound and transport to Amsterdam, *Journal of Sustainable Tourism*, Vol.14, No. 4, pp. 157–171.

Pires, G.D. and Stanton, J. (2008): Marketing issues in healthcare research, *International Journal of Behavioural and Healthcare Research*, Vol. 1, No. 1, pp. 38–60.

*Poslovni register Slovenije* (2009): V: AJPES. Available from: http://www.ajpes. si/prs/. (Accessed August 1, 2009).

*Prihodi in prenočitve turistov po državah, od koder turisti prihajajo*, Slovenija, junij 2009 (2009): V: Statistični urad RS. Available from: http:// www.stat.si/ novica_prikazi.aspx?id=2517 (Accessed August 1, 2009).

Rajkovič, U., Šušteršič, O., Zupančič, J. and Rajkovič, V. (2008): *Dokumentiranje v bolnišnični zdravstveni negi z uporabo novega organizacijsko-informacijskega pristopa*. Book of Abstracts of the 27th International Conference on Organizational Science Development, Slovenia, Portorož, March, 19th-21st 2008, (eds.) Rajkovič, V., Jereb, E., Kern, T., Kljajić, M., Paape, B. , Pagon, M. and Vukovič, G., *Moderna organizacija*, Kranj.

Stephano, R. M. and Edelheit, J. (2009): The Future of Medical Tourism, Medical Tourism Magazine, Vol.3, No.8, pp.10–15. *Tourism Highlights 2008* (2008): World Tourism Organization. Available from: http://unwto.org/facts /menu. html. (accessed April 2, 2009).

*UNWTO World Tourism Barometer* (2009): World Tourism Organization, Madrid. *What is Medical Tourism* (2010): Medical Tourism Association. Available from: http:// wwww.medicaltourismassociation.com/en/medical-tourism-faq-s.html. (Accessed June 17, 2010).

Zeleni turizem (2010): Slovenska turistična organizacija. Available from: http:// www.slovenia.info/si/Zeleni-turizem.htm?ps_eko_turizem=0&lng=1 (accessed August 23, 2010).

Zobozdravniki po starosti in spolu (2008): Zdravstveni statistični letopis 2008, Inštitit za varovanje zdravja, Ljubljana.

## About the Authors

**Gabrijel Devetak** is an associate professor of marketing. He engages in innovation and marketing and holds marketing lectures at various Slovene faculties. He has published nine specialist books and textbooks dealing with invention-innovation processes and marketing. He is also an expert witness in the field of innovation and marketing.

**Elena Marulc** has an MSc in business science and boasts 20-years experience in the field of tourism. She is the manager of a tourist agency specialised in professional travel and congresses. In addition, she continues to pursue non-formal education. Her field of research is medical marketing.

The authors are also the collaborators in the only specialised centre for research and development in the field of medical tourism in Slovenia.

# Development of a Simulation Model and Application of an Optimisation Algorithm for Determination of Control Strategy in a Hierarchical Human Resources System

***Andrej Škraba***

*andrej.skraba@fov.uni-mb.si*

***Miroljub Kljajić***

*miroljub.kljajic@fov.uni-mb.si*

***Davorin Kofjač***

*davorin.kofjac@fov.uni-mb.si*

## Abstract

This chapter describes the development of a human resources planning system for the Slovene armed forces in which a novel approach to the determination of recruitment and transition strategies was developed and applied. The reference mode of the system response was determined as the exponential approach to the desired trajectory. System dynamics as well as a discrete event simulation model of human resources transitions were developed and realised in MATLAB. The exponential function producing a wide spectrum of exponential curves that differ by the steepness of the goal attainment was developed and applied in the process of optimisation. The pattern search algorithm was applied at the optimisation process. The development of the user interface is described as the important part of the developed system. The results presented are applicable in the general field of supply chains and dynamical control of similar hierarchical discrete systems.

**Keywords**: human resources, manpower, system dynamics, simulation, control, strategy, army, discrete dynamics

# 1. Introduction

Hierarchical human resource systems can be found in many organisational systems, including army, police, consultancy etc. In this chapter, the problem of Slovene armed forces restructuring will be considered. Human resource planning in an army is a strategic governmental task (Vavtar et al., 2010) involving considerable resources; in our case, the research presented addressed the strategic human resource planning in the army. Since the addressed problem is rather complex, it should be supported by the development of a model that will enable a simulation of personnel dynamics, considering transitions amongst different ranks and their fluctuations, i.e., wastage. Simulation methodology at the control of mentioned complex systems has been substantially covered in previous research (Kljajić et al., 2000; Bajracharya in Ogunlana, 2001; Mayo, 2001; Wang, 1997). The main methodological approaches apply statistics and stochastics (Bartholomew et al., 1991; Grinold in Marshall, 1977; Vajda, 1978). In general, previous research did not address adequately the problem of oscillations in optimal strategies. Another insufficiently covered important topic is the understanding of model structure, which is often difficult due to the mathematical methodology involved (Mehlman, 1980). In the framework of previous research (Kljajić et al., 2007, Škraba et al. 2007a), the model was initially developed on the principles of system dynamics (Forrester, 1973, Sterman, 2000). In this chapter, the system dynamics model will be considered as the canonical form of exponential delays with wastages. The top eight ranks in Slovene army will be considered (second lieutenant, lieutenant, captain, major, lieutenant colonel, colonel, brigadier, major general). In order to enable restructuring, one should develop a validated model of the system structure, determine criteria function and subsequently apply optimisation algorithms that provide proper control strategies.

The developed system should allow:

a) Analysis of consequences of different policies applied to the system (e.g., change in transitions, fluctuations and recruiting)
b) Test of rationale for past recruitment policies
c) Understanding of basic dynamical processes
d) Design of a system that balances human resources requirements by determining proper transition and fluctuation levels
e) Design of a human resources information system that is in a proper form for analysis and human resources planning

The fact that the present chapter addresses only the eight top-most ranks characterises the developed model and methodology. In the addressed system, only the transitions between subsequent ranks are possible. The solutions gained by the present study are applicable to similar situations in which hierarchical human resources systems occur. The developed system should provide the support of strategic decision processes that address human resources in order to provide the proper management strategy. The research purpose in the present study is a) simulation model development and b) an application of the model for system control. Both would be considered as design (simulation model) and control (development of optimisation procedure on the model).

# 2. Simulation Model Development

Simulation methodology has been widely implemented in the field of workforce management (Bajracharya and Ogunlana 2001; Trust, 2003; Mayo et al., 2001). It is convenient for modelling hierarchical human resources system, since the stock and flow elements could be applied to represent the number of rank members and flows of men between ranks as well as fluctuations (wastages). At the determination of the reference mode, the exponential approach to the new goal values is anticipated as the response of the system. Figure 1 shows the reference mode of the hierarchical human resources system; ① represents the desired decrease in the number of men in particular rank while ② represents the desired increase in the number of men in a particular rank. The main characteristic of the anticipated response is that the desired goal (indicated by the dashed line) is exponentially approached. This is the most likely response since the desired values could not be instantly achieved; here one should consider the time needed to approach the desired values, which are determined by the time constants of the system. The values on the y-axis are not shown since only the response of the system is observed at the determination of reference mode.

*Figure 1: Reference mode;①: decrease of rank numbers and ②: increase of rank numbers*

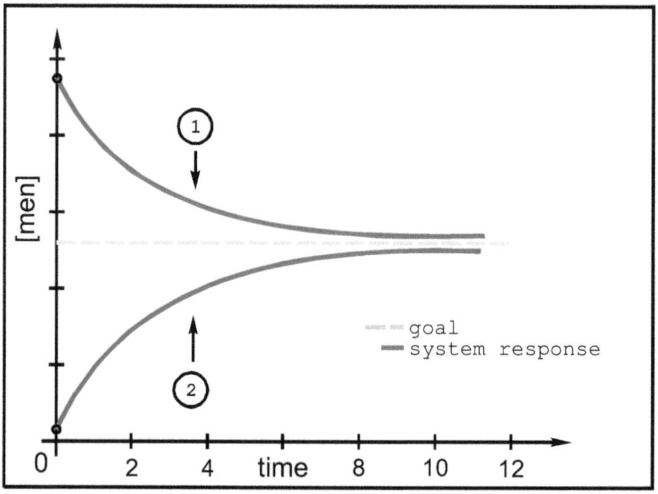


The structure of the systems incorporates eight ranks, transitions and fluctuations. Figure 2 shows the Causal Loop Diagram of the system. A, B, C…N represent the number of men in ranks A, B, …N. In our case, the eight topmost ranks are considered. Rv represents the recruitment to the system. An increase of recruitment causes an increase in the number of men in rank A. $R_A$, $R_B$, … $R_N$ represent the transitions between ranks. For example, $R_A$ represents promotions from rank A to rank B. $F_A$, $F_B$, … $F_N$ represent the fluctuations of men out of the system. Each particular rank is governed by two negative feedback loops; in the case of rank A: i) if the number of men in rank A increases, the fluctuations will increase above the level that it otherwise would have been. If fluctuations increase, the number of men would be below the level that there would otherwise have been; ii) if the number of men in rank A increases, the promotions from rank A to rank B would be above the level that otherwise would have been.

In contrast, if the promotion increases, the numbers of men in rank A decreases below the level that otherwise would have been. The described negative feedback loops are governed by the recruitment $R_v$, which provides the input to the system. By the determination of the extent of promotions and fluctuations, the desired levels in ranks could be achieved. One important observation is that each rank is dependent on the levels in the subordinate rank except for first, which is dependent on recruitment. The presented CLD is general and it could consider N ranks. In our case, the structure is strictly hierarchical; one cannot skip particular rank, since it is not possible in topmost ranks.

*Figure 2: Causal Loop Diagram of Hierarchical Human resources System*

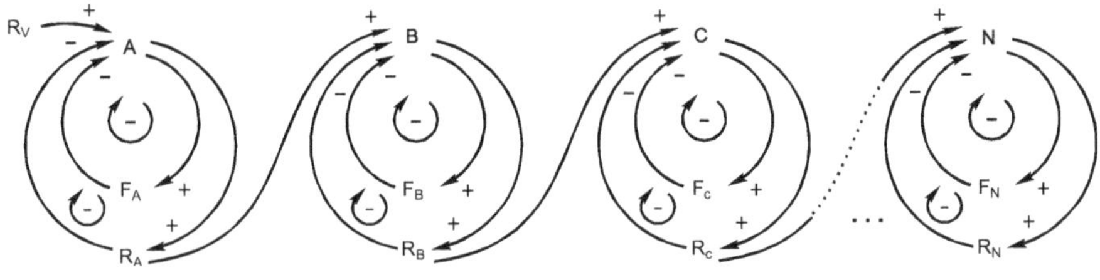


Since only negative feedback loops exist in the system, the dynamical hypothesis would consider the goal values attainment, which is dependent on the proper value of the recruitment (Rv), transitions and the fluctuations. Here, one should consider the rank dependence; for example, if we change transition between two ranks, the change influences all subsequent ranks.

States of the developed system, in our case ranks, could be observed in discrete time points; however, the whole system is considered to be continuous since causal interconnections are permanently present and determined by the structure of the system. The general equation of the SD model that represents the applied methodological concept is in continuous time, determined as (Sterman, 2000):

$$L(t) = \int_{t_0}^{t} [R_{in}(t) - R_{out}(t)]dt + L(t_0)$$

$$\frac{dL}{dt} = R_{in}(t) - R_{out}(t)$$

In our case, $L$ represents particular rank, while $R_{in}$ and $R_{out}$ represent input to particular rank and output, respectively. In our case, $R_{out}$ considers transition to a higher rank as well as the fluctuation. Figure 3 represents the developed SD model, which incorporates recruitment, transitions of human resources between individual ranks and fluctuations. The structure shows that the system is hierarchical, i.e., a higher rank depends on the state values of lower ranks. The model represents an exponential delay chain in which each rank is dependent on its preceding rank and corresponding flows. Coefficients $a$, $b$, ..., $n$ represent the ratios of promotions between ranks, $c$, $d$, ...; $v$ represents ratios of fluctuations, and $r$ represents the recruitment. All other elements have the same meaning as described by CLD. The central part of the model is a canonical form, which is determined by the number of ranks considered. One could apply the structure for the larger system; however, in top-most ranks the input in particular rank is not possible. If we consider a larger system, i.e., more ranks, one could be recruited in particular a rank from outside of the system.

*Figure 3: Structure of the system dynamics model of rank transitions in the canonical form. The structure shown represents a delay chain of first-order delay elements.*

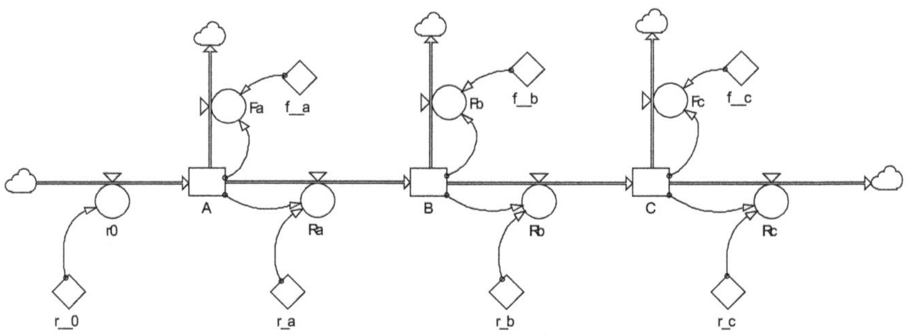


By using the model, the user is able to vary different parameters that impact the dynamics of the system, thus providing the user a chance to recognise potential undesirable states and determine the consequences of the selected strategy. Furthermore, possible corrective actions and rationalisations can be determined by the means of the simulation model. Transitions in the system are dependent on the demand for particular ranks and training capacity. The number of rank members also depends on the demand and training capacity, as well as on the transitions. Hence, the considered model could be represented as a cascading structure of negative feedback loops (Kljajić, 2006; Kljajić et al., 2007; Škraba et al. 2007a, 2007b) representing an exponential delay chain, which is also in the scope of complex supply chain system control (Kofjač et al. 2008). An important concept that should also be considered at the development of the described system is anticipation (Kljajić, 1998, Kljajić, 2001), which provides an efficient control mechanism enhancing the classical feedback loop concept and is inevitable in the control of complex systems.

The exponential delay chain SD model has been presented to the end users of the developed system. The SD model provided important insight into a system that should be controlled in order to achieve target values in particular ranks. An applied delay chain represents a conceptual framework for the development of the methods that should provide the proper strategies to achieve target values. The sensitivity of the model parameters is an important aspect of the system development. In our case, the sensibility of the model parameters is determined by the parameter boundaries. The most influential parameter is parameter $r$, which represents the recruitment to the system. If the extent of the recruitment is not sufficient (or it is too high), the goal values are not attainable in prescribed time. The transition coefficients have larger boundaries than fluctuations; furthermore, the transitions are more controllable than the fluctuations.

The model of transitions, developed by principles of continuous simulation using MATLAB/Simulink, is presented in Figure 4. Step and discrete time delay function $Z^{-1}$ are realised as inputs to the *Rank A*. The parameter values and simulation results are rendered through MATLAB *Workspace*. The level of the element *Rank A* depends on an initialisation value *init A* and the difference of $\frac{1}{s}$ integrator inputs, presented by parameters *fluctuation A ratio* and *transition A ratio*.

*Figure 4: Rank transition model developed by the principles of continuous simulation realised in MATLAB/Simulink*

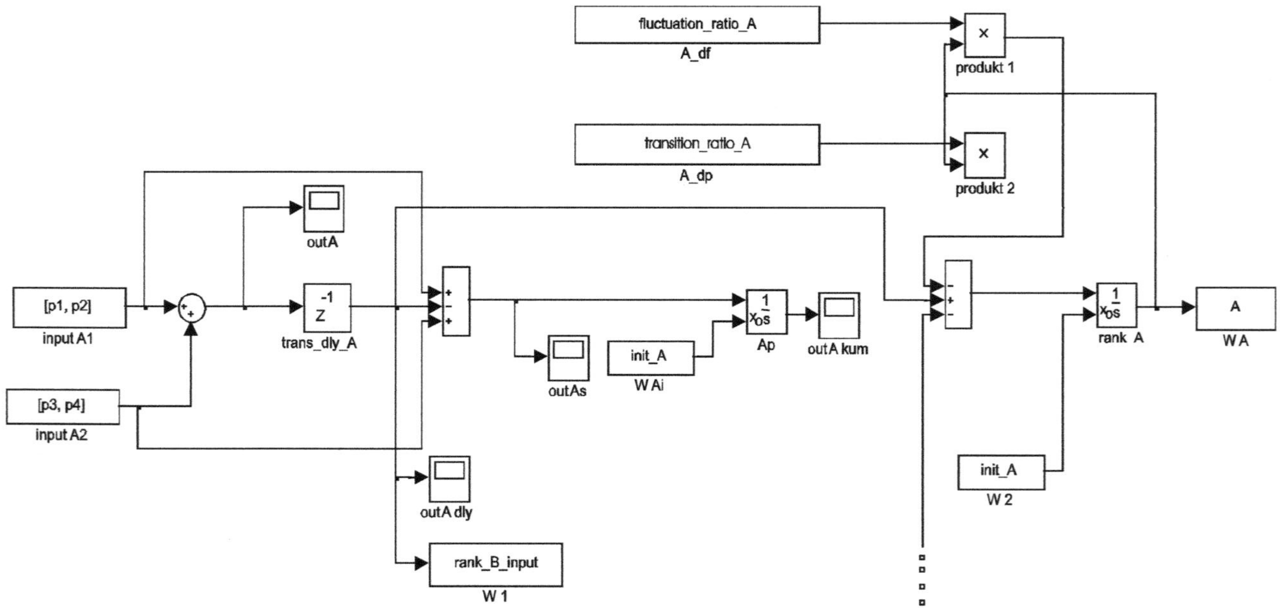

In contrast, the discrete event model (Kljajić et al., 2007, Škraba et al. 2007a, 2007b) was developed in the validation phase incorporating time distributions, thus providing more information about the dynamic response of the system. Here, the time of the training in a particular rank is considered before transition to the higher rank. The discrete event model was developed in the MATLAB/SimEvents shown in Figure 5.

*Figure 5: Model developed by the Discrete Event Simulation methodology (DES) in MATLAB/SimEvents*

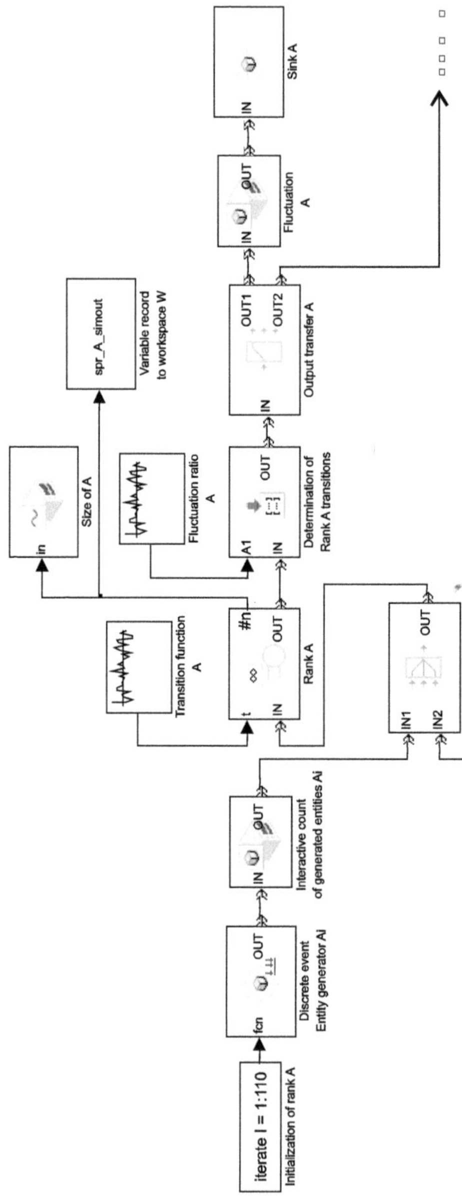

To perform a simulation as well as to determine different scenarios, a user interface was developed. Development in this phase dealt with concepts of transparency, ease of use and understanding. The developed system enabled the analysis of different simulation scenarios (Škraba et al, 2003, 2007), especially in the context of what-if analysis.

# 3. Model and Control Strategy Determination

Determination of the strategy was addressed as an optimisation problem considering the states of the system and parameter boundaries. The issue addressed at the development of the decision support system for controlling the human resources system is to find a strategy that is adequate to bring the system to a desired rank structure. The desired rank structure is defined by the new numbers of officers in particular ranks and the time at which the desired new numbers should be reached. Furthermore, there is a question of how the system should reach the final structure. By the application of the optimisation algorithm, proper parameter values (fluctuations, transitions between ranks) that would steer the system to the desired state by a predetermined trajectory were determined. The trajectory was determined as the target function. Several trajectories are possible: from the linear to steep convex exponential. The target function is defined by the following equation:

$$f(t) = x_k + \frac{(x_0 - x_k)(k - t)}{k} e^{-pt}, \quad (1)$$

where $x_0$, $x_k$ represent initial and end states, $k$ is the simulation time and $p \in [0, \infty]$ the importance factor. The equation describes a wide spectrum of exponential curves that differ by the steepness of the goal attainment. With the predetermined response of the system in the form of the exponential curve, an important reduction of the problem dimensionality was achieved.

At the determination of the strategy, one searches for the set of parameters in which the response of the system is as close to the target function as possible. This will be achieved if, for each particular set of parameters, the minimum sum of squared errors is determined. The optimisation algorithm is determined by the parameter boundaries determining the search space. The value of the criteria function is determined by the iteration of the numerical optimisation algorithm. 'Iteration' here refers to the performance of simulation run and calculation of the criteria function for which the minimum is searched.

Describing the system dynamics discretely, we take $x_n(i)$ the value of rank $n$ at time step $i$. Writing $\underline{x} = (x_1, ..., x_r)$, the feedback loops of the system are given by:

$$\underline{x}(i+1) - \underline{x}(i) = \underline{f}(\underline{x}(i), \underline{u}(i)), \quad (1)$$

where $u = (u_1, ..., u_m)$ is a time-dependent control variable vector and $f$ is a vector function. The goal is to minimise the distance to the target function:

$$J = \sum_{n=1}^{r}\sum_{i=0}^{t_k}\left(c_n(i) - x_n(i)\right)^2 = \sum_{i=0}^{t_k}\left(\underline{c}(i) - \underline{x}(i)\right)^2, \quad (2)$$

where $c_n(i)$ is the target function value for the rank $n$ at step $i$ determined by (1). The issue is to compute $\min_{U} J$ where $U$ is a set of input parameters with predefined value limitations.

To minimise the criteria function expressed by Equation (2), numerical optimisation methods were used. In the search for the optimal strategy according to target functions, an application of pattern search algorithm and genetic algorithms were performed. The analytical solution to the problem does exist for particular cases; however, the way one would derive analytical solution is far more time consuming than using the numerical approach. To show the basic idea, we are searching the solution within the parameter boundaries $a_{i1} \leq u_i \leq a_{i2}$. We could do that by applying every possible combination of constraints $u_i = a_{ij}$, $j = 1, 2$ and comparing the bounded minima. That is, we find the minimum within a cuboid in an $m$-dimensional space, where $m$ is the number of parameters included, and thus obtain a feasible solution. We can use the method of Lagrange multipliers. However, having a mere five control variables, we must deal with more than 200 nontrivial computations and the complexity of the problem rises exponentially. In our case, we are confronted with 90 variables.

The goal structure should be reached in prescribed time not exceeding the parameter boundaries determining recruitment, promotions and fluctuations. The general goal is to put the majority of the ranks to lower number than present. The cause of the tendency to lower the numbers in particular ranks is in the general reduction of the army as well as in new ratios between officers and soldiers. However, numbers in some ranks should be increased. Here, the costs of achieving the target value for particular ranks are of secondary importance. The main goal is to reach the desired number in ranks in a prescribed time and trajectory regarding the parameter boundaries. The promotions between ranks could be arbitrary as long as the parameter boundaries are satisfied. However, this is not the only criteria. The recruitment, promotions and fluctuations, which represent system derivatives, should obey the principle of moderate policy in which rates change in steady manner. Since this rule is important in order to provide acceptable strategy, the following explanation will clarify the objective. Figure 6 represents examples of four acceptable strategies for reaching the goal values according to target functions. There are many more possible strategies similar to the presented four, which will be defined by Finite Automata (FA) principle in the next section. Figure 6 (b) shows a variable increase in human resources flow. Here, the value increases from 2 to 8 [man/year]. In this case, one could observe variable acceleration in human resources flow; in first year, the acceleration is 4 [man/year^2], in second year 2 [man/year^2] and 0 [man/year^2] onwards. The acceleration in the first year is most likely limited with the capacity of the system.

In general, it would be desirable to achieve the target value in 0 time; however, this is bound to the infinite value of acceleration, which is not possible. Figure 6 (left) shows a variable increase in flow with three plateaus, where the values are held constant. The presented examples correspond to the fact that the strategy of achieving target values should be moderate, constantly increasing or decreasing and stabilising in the long run. The best case would be constant value of the flow and the worst case would be an example with one extreme point. Examples in which the strategy would oscillate should be avoided. This would mean, for example, that the recruiting centre should be changing its capacity from year to year, i.e., in one year large, in the next small etc. which is bound to the undesirable recruiting system changes and costs. If we consider the attainment of the target trajectory within the prescribed parameter boundaries, the problem of oscillating values in rate elements might occur. In a normal case, one would search for the strategy that would be moderately performed, meaning that there are no jumps in recruitment, promotions and fluctuations between successive years.

*Figure 6: Acceptable strategies*

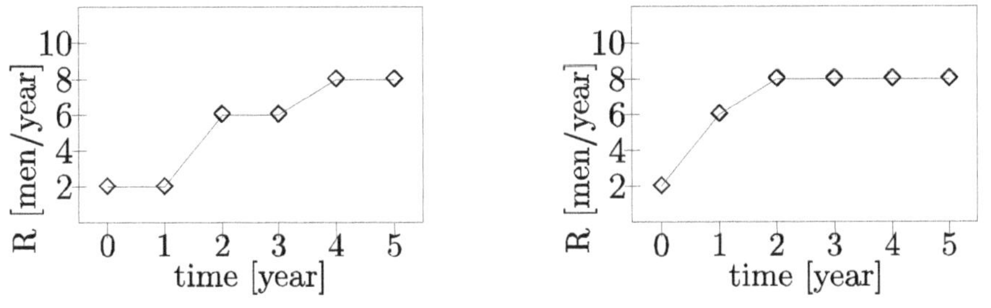

# 4. Application of Finite Automata

In order to perform the classification of different strategies that satisfy the conditions of moderate policy, which do not exercise oscillations, the principles of finite automata (FA) were applied. Each strategy could be represented as the sequence of symbols e, g and l, in which e denotes states where two neighbouring values are equal, g is inserted when the (i+ 1)-th term is greater than i-th, and l is inserted when the opposite applies. Automaton $A_1$ considers increasing or decreasing strategies where:

- The set of states is $S = \{S_0, S_1, S_2, S_3\}$
- The comparison alphabet is $A = \{l, e, g\}$
- The initial state is $i = S_0$
- The set of terminal states is $T = \{S_0, S_1, S_2\}$

The transition function of $A_1$, $\delta : S \times A \rightarrow S$ is defined by the following transition table:

| | $l$ | $e$ | $g$ |
|---|---|---|---|
| $\leftrightarrow S_0$ | $S_2$ | $S_0$ | $S_1$ |
| $\leftarrow S_1$ | $S_3$ | $S_1$ | $S_1$ |
| $\leftarrow S_2$ | $S_2$ | $S_2$ | $S_3$ |
| $\leftarrow S_3$ | $S_3$ | $S_3$ | $S_3$ |

FA is composed of a set of states S, and transition function δ.FA could be defined to recognise only particular sequences. The sequence is identified if it appears at the end in one of the terminal (acceptable) states.

Figure 7 represents FA, which will identify only increasing or decreasing strategies. Here $S = S_0, \ldots, S_3$. The starting state is $S_0$ and all states except $S_3$ are terminal. If letter e is encountered, the transition to the same state is made. When state g is encountered for the first time, the transition to $s_1$ is made, meaning that state g has already been encountered. Since only the increasing sequences will be accepted, a jump to $s_3$ will be made at the first occurrence of state l. State $s_3$, however, is not terminal. Once the sequence ends in this state, it remains there, i.e., it is not identified. The same is true for the right side, where the sequence decreases.

Example: Let us consider the following strategy: 1 1 5 4 7 8 1 8 8 2. The following sequence is set correspondingly: e g l g g l g e l.

*Figure 7: Four state FA for selection of proper strategies*

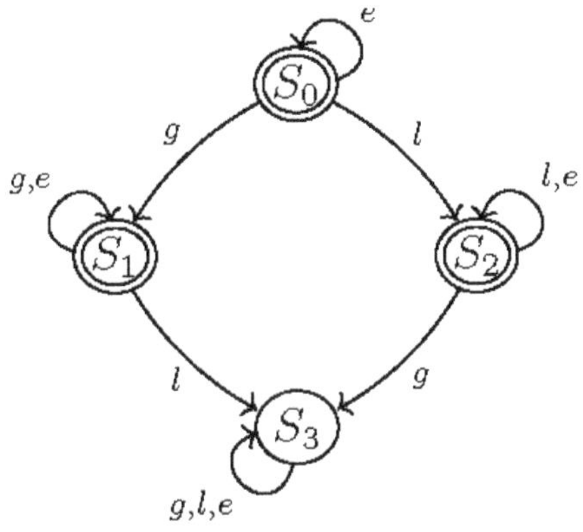


## 4.1 Parameter Boundaries and Goal Attainment

Parameter boundaries are determined according to the historical data for the past eight years. For example, if we consider the recruitment for the past eight years, the minimum value was 10 [men/year] and maximum value 25 [men/year]. Parameter boundaries, therefore, determine whether the target values could be reached at the prescribed time. The addressed optimisation problem is quite complex if we consider that the boundaries are time variant and that the goal is stated by the user-defined trajectory, which is also time variant. In order to illustrate the boundary problem, let us consider only one rank and influence of the changing boundaries on the reachability. Let us consider the system of first order with single input and single output:

$x(0) = 0$ (initial value of state element),

$e_i = (c - x(i)^2$ (squared error between goal and state value),

$x(i) = x(i-1) - r(i-1) + a$ (state equation),

$e = \sum_{i=1}^{n} e_i$ (sum of squared errors),

where $c$ is the goal value, $i$ discrete time step, $r$ control parameter, ~ in our case this determines transition to a higher rank (parameter $r$ represents a ratio of system fluctuations, i.e., the output of the system), *a* constant value of input to the considered rank and $e_i$ deviation between goal value and *i*-th value on the state element. The system of equations is set in which *r* is not explicitly stated; *r* is defined as a variable *r*(0), *r*(1), ...; for each time step the new value of parameter *c* is determined; here *r* is considered as the control vector. Optimisation of the stated problem is performed with regard to declared boundaries for parameter *r*. The solution of the system and its dependence on lower and upper boundaries set by minimisation problem is of special interest since this determines the reachability of the system.

Figure 8 shows the region in parameter space where the target strategy is reachable, marked with A. The X-axis represents the lower boundary, the Y-axis represents the upper boundary and the Z-axis represents the sum of squared errors at determined minimum. If the lower and upper boundaries fall outside the 'A' area, the target value is not reachable. In the case of a particular rank, this has the following two possible consequences: a) the target value is achieved after longer time than desired, and b) target value is not reached. The reachability of target values is dependent on the parameter limitations that determine the transitions between particular ranks and fluctuations. Parameter limitations have been determined according to the analysis of the past eight years. Minimum and maximum values in the mentioned period determine the range of the parameters.

*Figure 8: Reachability region of control problem.*

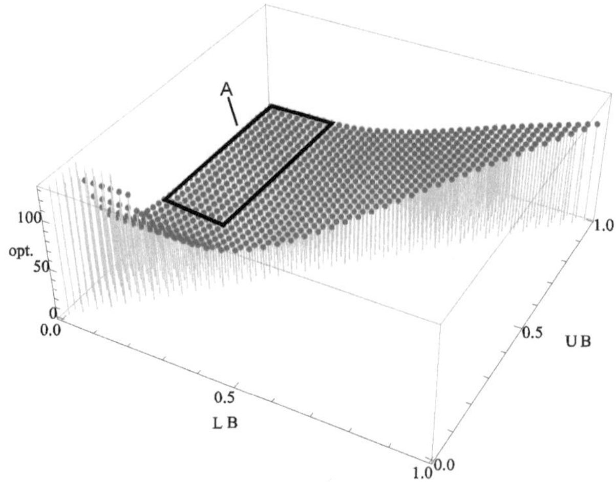

Since the boundaries are time variable, the analytical solution is hard to obtain or even not possible to obtain; it has not been known in the literature of such general solution. In such cases, only the numerical-heuristic approach could be considered.

# 5. User Interface and Input Data

In order to easily control the described model, the user interface was developed. The model developed with MATLAB is applied for the automatic search for adequate input and output parameters, i.e., for best fit to target functions in particular rank. It is important to note that the transparency of user interface plays an important role in proper methodology application. The problem is extremely complex for the human-resource officers due to the size of the problem considered and the relatively rare situation of large restructuring problem.

User interface includes the following functionality:

- setup of initial values for particular rank
- setup of goal values
- setup of input and output parameters for particular rank
- graphical preview of changes in input and output parameter for a particular rank
- simulation run control
- graphical and table output
- scenario description
- setup of transition function (trajectory from initial value to goal value)
- setup of the number of simulation iterations
- setup of lower and upper boundaries of input and output parameters (setup of numerical optimisation procedure)

The developed user interface enables conducting an automated procedure for parameter determination and strategy development. The model enables the user to perform specific what-if analyses. Figure 9 represents the user interface where the input data are defined. In our case, let us suppose that rank 'Major' is considered. The part of the user interface marked with (A) represents the initial and target values input, part (B) represents yearly data of Inputs Fluctuations and Promotions and part (C) represents yearly estimates for trends. Here the initial values of rank members are determined (198), initial year for simulation run (2008), goal value (109, i.e., in our case one would like to decrease the number of rank A members from 198 to 109). The year of goal attainment (2010) represents the year in which the goal state should be reached. The target function has four possible shapes: exponential, linear, constant or user defined. The user specifies the goal number by the determination of the shape of target function. In the part 'input', the user declares the estimate of inputs to rank by particular year. 'Lower Boundary' (LB) is the lower boundary of the inputs to the rank that is determined by user which is determined from the historical data. 'Upper Boundary' (UB) is determined in the similar way. In the part of the input called 'fluctuation', the user estimates the value of the expected fluctuations, lower boundary and upper boundary. In the part 'promotions to higher r.' (to higher rank), the user estimates the regular number of promotions, lower boundary and upper boundary.

In order to determine the trends, i.e., the dynamic response of the system, the user has to estimate the yearly transitions. In this part, the user determines the number of inputs, fluctuations and promotions to higher rank. The system automatically determines the coefficient that is applied at the determination of the dynamic response of the system for next period. The initial values are predefined and are determined according to the analysis of the historical data for the past eight years. The described determination of estimates and parameter boundaries contributes to better user perception of the problem definition and the regular values of parameters that determined the dynamics of the particular rank in past period.

*Figure 9: Data input ~ user interface*

**Rank: Major** Input data

(A)

| | | | |
|---|---|---|---|
| Initial number : | 198 | Goal number: | 109 |
| Initial year: | 2008 | Goal year: | 2010 |
| Transition function: | | Exponential | |

(B)

| | | Input | | | Fluctuations | | | Promotions | | |
|---|---|---|---|---|---|---|---|---|---|---|
| Y | Goal | Est. | LB | UB | Est. | LB | UB | Est. | LB | UB |
| 08 | 198 | 90 | 14 | 91 | 90 | 4 | 39 | 27 | 5 | 65 |
| 09 | 133 | 46 | 14 | 91 | 37 | 4 | 39 | 15 | 5 | 65 |
| 10 | 109 | 26 | 14 | 91 | 12 | 4 | 39 | 15 | 5 | 65 |
| 11 | 109 | 19 | 14 | 91 | 4 | 4 | 39 | 15 | 5 | 65 |
| 12 | 109 | 22 | 14 | 91 | 7 | 4 | 39 | 15 | 5 | 65 |
| 13 | 109 | 29 | 14 | 91 | 14 | 4 | 39 | 15 | 5 | 65 |
| 14 | 109 | × | × | × | × | × | × | × | × | × |

(C)

Yearly estimates for trends

| | Input | Fluctuation | Promotions |
|---|---|---|---|
| Number: | 112 | 9 | 33 |
| Ratio: | 25.0% | 4.5% | 16.7% |

The data described in the user interface should be considered as the input to the system. Here, the meaning of the particular input is presented, which different is for each particular case. The results of the numerical procedure defined by the user are a defined strategy that enables the attainment of target functions. Input parameters are bounded with the set of possible values determined from historical data and feasible values of considered systems. By considering the parameter boundaries, the strategy can be chosen and applied on the real system.

# 6. Results

Figure 10 shows an example of the strategy for determination of goal values for three ranks: 'A', 'B' and 'C'. The x-axis on the graphs represents time in years, while the y-axis represents yearly transitions with units [man/year]. 'P' represents input to particular rank, 'F' fluctuations and 'N' promotion to the higher rank. The intensity of changes in control actions that should be moderated is of particular interest here. Here monotone changes are desired, meaning that, for example, promotions should be monotonically increased or decreased in the following period. Such a condition provides moderated policies, which do not oscillate and are more convenient to carry out. The developed system considers the above-mentioned aspects and provides a moderate solution to stated goal.

*Figure 10: Example of strategies for achieving the goal trajectories for three ranks A, B and C*

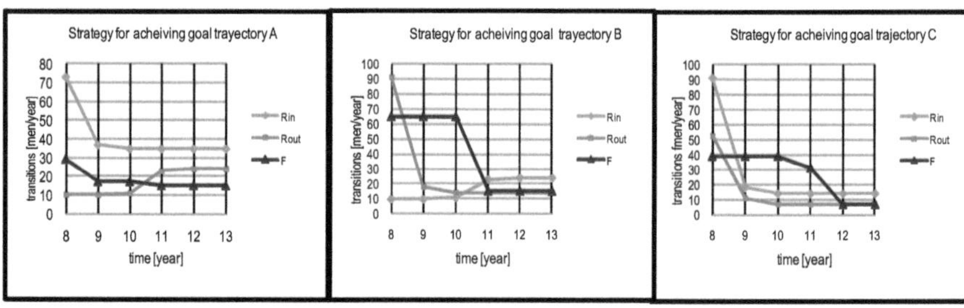


By the consideration of the strategies shown in Figure 10, the state of the system approaches the target values. The boundaries of parameters determine whether the target values will be attained in the given time period or not.

Figure 11 (left) shows the attainment of the target values for rank A when strategies shown in Figure 10 are carried out. On the x-axis, the time in years is represented, while number of men in each rank are shown on the y-axis the. Target values are defined by the exponential function. In this case, parameter boundaries did not significantly influence the target values attainment; the deviations of the system response from the target values are small. Figure 11 (Right) shows an example of unreachability of target function at time '9' and '10' and '11' in the case of rank 'B'. The cause for unreachability could be the following: a) the input is set too high to rank B, b) the fluctuations are too small or c) the number of promotions to the higher rank is too small. In this case, the target values are reached in four years for rank B.

*Figure 11: left) Reachability of the target values for rank A at the consideration of proposed strategy*
*right) Unreachability of target value at times 9, 10 and 11 due to the parameter boundaries*

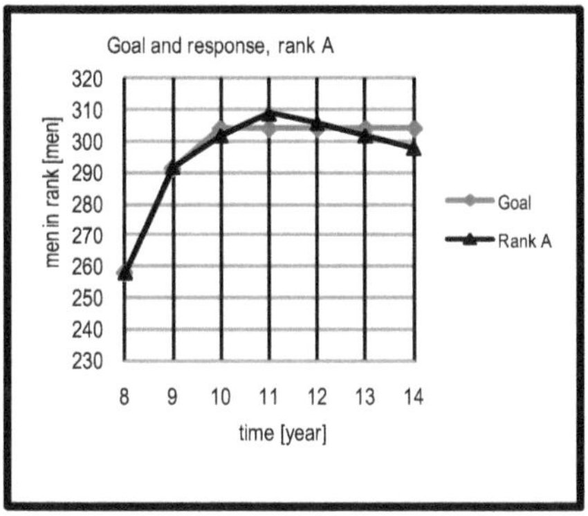


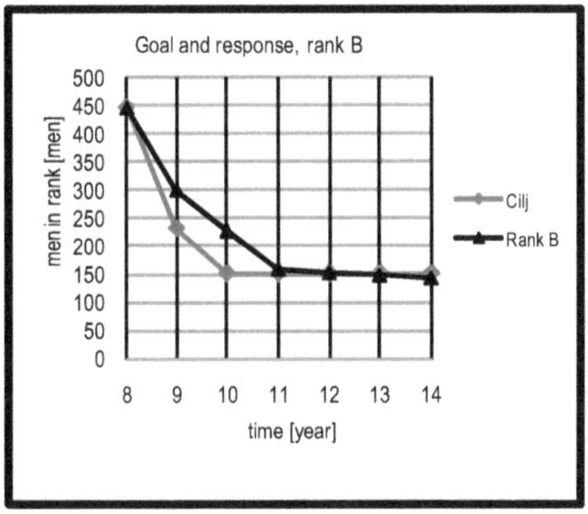


Figure 11 shows two distinct cases of system response that are dependent on the limitations of control actions. In our case, the boundary vectors with key parameters of simulation model are in question.

# 7. Conclusion

An important part of the addressed problem is the process of modelling of the hierarchical human resources system. Although there are many approaches possible, such as stochastic modelling or statistics, the system dynamics approach would be most easily understood. This is important for the end users, which should fully understand the applied model of the real system. In our experience, the developed system was easily adapted by the end users and was identified as clear and easy to understand. One important fact that should be understood by the end users is that the change in preceding ranks influences the whole chain of ranks upwards.

When designing the reference mode of the system response, the exponential approach to the new target values was considered. This was due to the fact that, on the account of the system inertia, only an exponential approach would be exercised.

The main contributions of present work could be abstracted as:

a) Determination of control strategies in hierarchical human resources system is a complex task
b) The classic approach by dynamical programming is not suitable for the task
c) Parameter boundaries increase the complexity of the optimisation problems
d) Parameter boundaries determine the reachability of the system
e) Oscillations in optimisation results should be avoided
f) Application of Finite Automata provides the means of selecting non-oscillating strategies
g) Application of predefined exponential function for target trajectory significantly reduces the dimension of optimisation problem
h) Application of Pattern Search algorithm is suitable for the determination of proper strategies

The major advantages of proposed approach, therefore, are in addressing the oscillation of the complex dynamic chain, which represent the transitions and the transparency of the modelling process. It is important for the end user and policy implementation that the structure of the system is well understood and that the oscillations in the variables should rather be avoided.

However, due to the application of numerical optimisation algorithms, the optimal strategy in the strictly mathematical sense could hardly be proven.

For only the eight ranks that were considered in our study, the user should define more than 300 variables, which indicates the complexity of the task. MATLAB has been identified as the proper tool for addressing such complex modelling tasks. Even more, the integrated optimisation algorithms prove to be extremely easy to use and suitable for rapid development. The discrete event model and continuous models were successfully applied at the validation process, when the previous, historical data was compared to the model outputs.

The developed user interface, in our case, enables transparent work at the determination of strategies. Automatic determination of key parameter values is important due to the scale of the addressed problem. The user has to experiment with the model in order to understand the structure of the system, its dynamics and limitations. When the user understands the system, proper strategies can be formed. The approach applied in the present research showed that, with the analysis of historical data, the parameters' boundaries could be determined, thus reducing the search space of the optimisation problem.

The problem stated as 'How can the target number of men in a particular rank be reached?' could actually be transformed to the question 'Is it possible to reach the target number of men in a particular rank by considering the limitations of the system?' In technical terms, one encounters the problem of the system reachability.

The SD methodology proved to be an excellent tool to present the users with solid methodological concepts. The cascading exponential delay structure represents an abstract form of the considered system whose main characteristics could be easily presented to the users with experimentation on the SD model. If the user does not fully understand the concepts applied in the developed system, the acceptance of the developed strategies cannot be reached.

The proposed strategies, which are automatically computed by the developed system, have a large impact on the national scale. Therefore, the decision whether to implement any particular strategy should be thoroughly considered by the expert group before putting it into action. Here, informed group decision making supported by the simulation model (Škraba et al., 2003, Kljajić, 2006, Škraba et al., 2007, Škraba et al., 2009, Rodič, 2008) is inevitable. In the end, one should be aware that the results and numbers represent people and, therefore, the results provided by the system should be applied with great care and in consensus of all involved.

## Acknowledgements

This research is financed by ARRS –the Slovene Research Agency – (Target research programmes – 'Science for Peace and Security 2006–2010', project code: M5-0175).

## References

Bajracharya, A., Ogunlana S. O., Bach N. L. (2001). Effective organizational infrastructure for training activities: a case study of the Nepalese construction sector. *System Dynamics Review*, volume 16(2):91–112.

Bartholomew, D., Forbes, A., McClean, S. (1991), *Statistical Techniques for Manpower Planning*, John Wiley & Sons, Chichester.

Dubois, D. and Resconi, G. (1992). *Hyperincursivity: a new mathematical theory*. Presses Universitaires de Liège, Liège.

Forrester, J. (1973). *Industrial Dynamics*. MIT Press, Cambridge, MA.

Grinold, R. and Marshall, K. (1977). *Manpower Planning Models*. Elsevier North-Holland, New York, NY.

Kljajić, M. (1998). *Modeling and understanding the complex system within cybernetics*. In Ramaekers, M., editor, 15th International Congress on Cybernetics, pages 864–869. Association International de Cybernetique, Namur.

Kljajić, M. (2001). *Contribution to the meaning and understanding of anticipatory systems*. In Dubois, D., editor, Computing anticipatory systems, pages 400–411. American Institute of Physics, Melville, NY.

Kljajić, M., Farr, J. V. (2008) *The Role of Systems Engineering in the Development of Information Systems, Information Technologies and Systems Approach*, IGI.

Kljajić, M., Bernik, I., Škraba, A. (2000). Simulation Approach to Decision Assessment in Enterprises. Simulation, 75 (4), *Simulation Councils Inc.*, pg:199–210.

Kljajić, M., Škraba, A., Knaflič, A., Kofjač, D., (2007): Razvoj simulacijskega modela prehodnosti človeških virov v Slovenski vojski. (Development of simulation model of human resources transitions in Slovenian Army) Str. 787–795. Ustvarjalna organizacija: zbornik 26. mednarodne konference o razvoju organizacijskih znanosti, Slovenija, Portorož, 28.-30. marec 2007, (eds.) Rajkovič, V., Kern, T., Kljajić, M., Leskovar, R., Mayer, J., Vukovič, G.., Moderna organizacija, Kranj.

Kljajić, B.M. (2006). *Relevance of Group Feedback Information to Learning in Decision-Making Process Supported by a Simulation Model*. Doctoral Dissertation. Kranj.

Kofjač, D., Kljajić, M., Rejec, V. (2008). The anticipative concept in warehouse optimization using simulation in an uncertain environment. *European Journal of Operational Research*, In Press, Corrected Proof, accessed 22 Oct. 2007.

Mayo D. D., Callaghan, M. J. and Dalton W. J. (2001). Aiming for restructuring success at London Underground. *System Dynamics Review,* volume 17(3):261–289.

Rosen, R. (1985). *Anticipatory Systems: Philosophical, Mathematical and Methodological Foundations*. Pergamon Press, Oxford, UK.

Mehlman, A., An approach to optimal recruitment and transition strategies for manpower systems using dynamic programming, *Journal of Operational Research Society* 31 (1980) 1009–1015.

Rodič, B. (2008). *Distributed Systems for Decision Support and Program Agents*. Nova Gorica: FUDŠ.

Sterman, J. D. (2000). *Business Dynamics: Systems Thinking and Modeling for a Complex World.* Boston, MA: Irwin/McGraw-Hill.

Škraba, A., Kljajić, M., Kofjač, D., Bren, M., and Mrkaić, M. (2005). Periodic cycles in discrete cobweb model. *WSEAS Transactions on Mathematics*, volume 3(4):196–203.

Škraba, A., Kljajić, M., Kofjač, D., Bren, M., and Mrkaić, M. (2006). Anticipative cobweb oscillatory agents and determination of stability regions by lyapunov exponents. *WSEAS Transactions on Mathematics*, volume 12(5):1282–1289.

Škraba, A., Kljajić, M., Borštnar, M. K., (2007). The role of information feedback in the management group decision-making process applying system dynamics models, *Group Decision and Negotiation* 16(1) 77–95.

Škraba, A., Kljajić, M., Knaflič, A., Kofjač, D., Podbregar, I., (2007a): *Development of a human resources transition simulation model in Slovenian Armed Forces*. Proceedings of the 25th International Conference [of the] System Dynamics Society and 50th Anniversary Celebration, Boston, Massachusetts, USA, July 29–August 2, 2007. Sterman, J., D. (ed.). The System Dynamics Society, cop. Albany (New York).

Škraba, A., Kljajić, M., Leskovar, R. (2003). Group exploration of system dynamics models – Is there a place for a feedback loop in the decision process? *System Dynamics Review*, 19, John Wiley & Sons, Chichester. pg. 243–263.

Škraba A., Kljajić M., Kofjač, D. (2009). A systems approach to the determination of control strategy in a hierarchical manpower system. *International Journal of Decision Support System Technology* vol. 1, no. 3, pg. 58–74.

Trust C. S. (2002). A dynamic model of work quality in a government oversight organization. *System Dynamics Review*, volume 18(4):473–495.

Wiener, N. (1948). *Cybernetics or Control and Communication in the Animal and the Machine*. Wiley, New York, NY.

Vajda, S. (1978). *Mathematics of Manpower Planning*, John Wiley & Sons, Chichester.

Vavtar B., Boh T., Demšar F. (2010). The reach of control in government administration of the republic of Slovenia. *Int. J. Management and Enterprise Development*, Vol. 8, No. 2. pp. 198–208.

Wang, J. (1997). *A review of Operations Research Applications in Workforce Planning and Potential Modelling of Military Training*, DSTO Systems Sciences Laboratory / report.

## About the Authors

**Andrej Škraba** obtained his Ph.D. in the field of organisational sciences from the University of Maribor. He works as a researcher and assistant professor at the Faculty of Organizational Sciences in Cybernetics and DSS Laboratory. His research interest covers modelling and simulation, system dynamics, decision processes and multiple criteria decision-making. His recent interests are focused on analysis of nonlinear chaotic systems.

**Miroljub Kljajić** completed his Ph.D. at the Faculty of Electronics in Ljubljana in 1974. He is a professor at the Faculty of Organizational Sciences in Kranj in the area of Systems Theory, Cybernetics and Computer Simulation. His main fields of research include decision support systems in global e-commerce and methods of modelling and simulation of organisational systems. He has been the principal investigator of many national and international modelling and simulation projects. He is the head of Cybernetics and Decision Support Systems at University of Maribor, Faculty of Organizational Sciences. As author and co-author he has published more than 20 scientific articles recognised in SCI.

**Davorin Kofjač** gained his Ph.D. from the Faculty of Organizational Sciences in Kranj. Currently, he is working as a researcher at that faculty. His research interests include modelling and simulation, artificial intelligence and operational research.

# A New Approach to Lease Accounting

*Aleš Novak*

*ales.novak@fov.uni-mb.si*

## Abstract

Lease contracts are very important sources of financing for entities and the existing accounting standards on lease accounting have been criticised. The U.S. Securities and Exchange Commission (SEC) also recognised the inadequacies of the existing lease accounting standards in its June 2005 report and recommended that the U.S. Financial Accounting Standards Board (FASB) undertake a project to reconsider leasing standards, preferably as a joint project with the London-based International Accounting Standards Board (IASB). In March 2009, the FASB and IASB (the Boards) issued a discussion paper (DP) *Leases: Preliminary Views*, in which a new approach for the recognition of assets and liabilities arising under lease contracts was developed. The proposed new approach, usually referred to as a 'right-of-use' approach, would treat all lease contracts as the acquisition of a right to use the leased item for the lease term, thus requiring capitalisation, i.e., the recognition of lease assets and liabilities for all the lease contracts. It should be noted that despite the fact that standards setters prioritise financial recognition over disclosure, empirical academic research does not provide a clear answer about the superiority of recognition over disclosure in financial statements. The aim of this chapter, which focuses on lease accounting by the lessees, is to give an overview of the proposed new approach and to provide some commentary on it.

**Keywords**: accounting, finance lease, lessee, operating lease, right-of-use.

## 1. Introduction

According to Coase (1937), a corporation can be viewed as a contracting intermediary, inserted between factor owners and consumers, to minimise contracting costs. All parties contracting with a firm have a specific (in the sense given by Alchian (1984)) investment in it, equal to at least their contracting costs. It follows that all parties contracting or contemplating contracting with the firm demand information about the firm's ability to meet its contractual obligations. Firms therefore agree to incur the costs of supplying information; in return they receive better terms of trade from factor owners and customers (Ball, 2001, pp. 131–132).

We could say that accounting is a service activity. Its function is to provide quantitative information (primarily financial in nature) about economic entities, that is intended to be useful in making economic decisions and in making reasoned choices among alternative courses of action (APB, 1970, paragraph (hereinafter para.) 40; cited in Alexander and Nobes, 2001, p. 4). Thus, accounting is a means to assist a wide variety of parties in making economic decisions. Accounting may be further divided into financial accounting and management (or managerial) accounting. Financial accounting is the branch of accounting that provides economic and financial information for external decision makers such as investors, creditors (bankers, bondholders, suppliers), and other third parties, who do not have ready access to an entity's financial records or accountants. Management accounting, in contrast, is the branch of accounting that provides economic and financial information for decision makers inside the reporting entity, such as managers, employees and other internal users.

In the setting of accounting theory, the discussion of accounting usually revolves around financial accounting and financial reporting. The former relates to the generation of accounting data for external reporting, while the latter is the communication of this data to interested parties outside the reporting entity[1] (Higson, 2003, p. 19). Financial statements are the principal means of communication of financial information to external decision makers (Raiborn and Watson, 2003, p. 7).

## 2. Accounting Regulation and Users of Accounting Information

Accounting regulation could be defined as the imposition of constraints upon the preparation, content and the form of external reports by bodies other than the pre-

1 Actually, financial reporting has both an internal and an external aspect. Managers are interested in information about assets, liabilities, earnings and related elements as external users and, among its other requirements, generally need the same kind of information about those elements as external users. Thus, management is a major user of the same information that is provided by external financial reporting. However, management's primary role in external financial reporting is that of communicating information for use by others. For that reason, it has a direct interest in the cost, adequacy, and understandability of external financial reporting (FASB, 1978, para. 29). For convenience, the term 'financial reporting' is usually used in place of the term 'general purpose external financial reporting'.

parers of the reports, or the organisations and the individuals for which the reports are prepared (Taylor and Turley, 1986, p. 1; cited in Higson, 2003, p. 61). Financial reporting could be regulated by accounting standards, which could be identified as a feature of the Anglo-Saxon approach to accounting; or by laws, as in France, Germany, Italy and Japan.[2]

The fundamental economic function of accounting regulation is to provide agreement on how important commercial transactions are to be implemented (Ball, 1995, p. 19; in Ball, 2006, p. 6). For example, if lenders agree to lend to a company under the condition that its debt financing will not exceed 60% of tangible assets, it helps to have an agreement on how to count the company's tangible assets as well as its debts. Specifying the accounting methods to be followed constitutes an agreement as to how to implement important financial and legal concepts such as leverage (gearing) and earning (profit). Accounting methods thus are an integral component of the contracting between firms and other parties, including lenders, shareholders, managers, suppliers and customers (Ball, 2006, p. 7).

Accounting standards such as International Financial Reporting Standards (hereinafter IFRS), which are issued by the International Accounting Standards Board (hereinafter IASB),[3] or accounting standards issued by the Financial Accounting Standards Board (hereinafter FASB) in the USA,[4] are designed to apply to the

2 Although the internationalisation of financial reporting induced a trend of establishing private sector standard setters, as for example in France, Germany, Italy and Japan (Delvaille et al., 2005; Nobes, 2003, p. 100), which could suggest the transition from public-sector to private-sector financial reporting regulation, in some countries purely private-sector standard setting has never really been achieved. For example, the private-sector German Accounting Standards Board (GASB) did not replace the German parliament as the main financial reporting regulator. Its standard-setting authority is restricted to developing mere recommendations on those few aspects of consolidated financial reporting unregulated in the German Commercial Code. Its pronouncements, the German Accounting Standards (GAS), are subordinated to laws and thus can not contradict Commercial Code rules (Sellhorn and Gornik-Tomaszewski, 2006, p. 193).

3 On June 7, 2002, after the European Parliament had approved the text, the European Council adopted European Commission's proposal for a regulation on the application of the of International Accounting Standards (IAS), with which for each financial year starting on or after 1 January 2005, companies governed by the law of a member state whose securities are admitted to trading on a regulated market in the European Union (EU), must prepare their consolidated financial statements in conformity with the IAS, i.e., IFRS, endorsed by the EU (van Hulle, 2004, pp. 363–364).

4 Both accounting standards could be labelled as the Anglo-Saxon or common law accounting standards. Ball (2006, pp. 43–44) writes that the IASB and its promulgated standards historically have enjoyed – and currently do enjoy – a strong 'common law' orientation.

general purpose financial statements[5] and other financial reporting of all profit-oriented entities (IASB, 2009b, para. BC49).

Although there is no extant academic theory of accounting or standard setting, both of the world's most important standards setters, i.e., FASB and IASB, articulate their theory of accounting and standard setting in their Conceptual Frameworks[6] (Barth et al., 2001, p. 78).

Financial reporting should 'provide information that is useful to present and potential investors and creditors and other users in making rational investment, credit and similar decisions' (SFAC 1,[7] para. 34), while paragraph 12 of the IASB's Framework states that 'the objectives of financial statements is to provide information about the financial position, performance and changes in the financial position of an entity that is useful to a wide range of users in making economic decisions'.

Even though both Conceptual Frameworks consider a wide range of users, they all seem to give priority to accounting reports that aid reasonably informed investors,

Nobes (2003, p. 103) writes that it might be helpful to move from such labels towards such descriptors as investor-/decision- (oriented) accounting (standards). Anglo-Saxon accounting is oriented towards decision-making by investors; it plays down the measurement of taxable income and distributable income, is less worried about prudence and is more willing to go beyond superficial legal forms (Nobes, 2003, p. 99).

5 Three kinds of financial statements may be prepared (Riahi-Belkaoui, 2004, p. 134):
- General-purpose financial statements meeting the common needs of the users. In the designing of the financial statements presented in most annual reports, accountants assume that the reports will meet the common needs of users.
- Specific-purpose financial statements meeting the needs of specific user groups, for example, for the purpose of determining taxable income.
- Differential disclosures present different figures for the users to select.

6 A conceptual framework could be seen as an attempt to operationalise the accounting theory either by individuals or standard-setters (Higson, 2003, p. 62). Davies et al. (1999, p. 53; cited in Higson, 2003, p. 63) define the conceptual framework as a statement of generally accepted theoretical principles that form the frame of reference for a particular field of enquiry. In terms of financial reporting, these theoretical principles provide the basis both for the development of new reporting practices and the evaluation of the existing ones. The IASB's current one is officially labelled Framework for the Preparation and Presentation of Financial Statements ('Framework'), while the FASB's consists of six Statements of Financial Reporting Concepts (SFACs). Solomon's (1986, p.116; cited in McKernan, 2007, p. 173) identifies defence against politicisation as one of the key functions of conceptual framework for financial reporting.

7 Statements of Financial Reporting Concepts (SFAC) No. 1 *Objectives of Financial Reporting by Business Enterprises, issued in November 1978.*

usually coupled with creditors,[8] who are willing to study information with sound diligence (Bromwich, 2004, p. 34).

# 3. Current Lease Accounting Approach

A lease is a contractual obligation that allows assets owned by one party (the lessor) to be used by another party (the lessee), for specified periods of time, in return for a payment or series of payments. Assets that are commonly leased include automobiles, airplanes, buildings and other real estate, machinery, computer equipment, and many other tangible assets (SEC, 2005, p. 60).

Historically, the leasing industry has developed products designed to satisfy economic needs. The principal economic reasons for the existence of leasing include (Monson, 2001, p. 279):
to intermediate the risk of owning property;

- to finance the acquisition of property, plant, and equipment;
- to enable users of property to conserve working capital as compared to more traditional financing arrangements;
- to intermediate credit risk between sub-prime credits and traditional lending institutions;
- to intermediate the transfer of income tax benefits associated with owning property from low marginal-rate tax payers to higher-rate tax payers; and
- to outsource significant activities related to the maintenance and administration of property, plant, and equipment to specialists.

Leasing is a very important source of finance for European businesses. In 2006, new leasing volumes amounted €297.5 billion and the leasing volumes outstanding amounted €630.7 billion. The European leasing industry thus financed almost 20% of all new European investments. Moreover, it has been estimated that more than half of Europe's SMEs have made use of leasing or rental (Leaseurope and KPMG, 2007, p. 1). In 2007, U.S. rental and leasing services companies accounted for $123 billion of revenue (U.S. Census Bureau, 2010).

---

8 In the exposure draft (ED) *Conceptual Framework for Financial Reporting: The Objective of Financial Reporting and Qualitative Characteristics and Constraints of Decision-Useful Financial Reporting Information* (Phase A ED) issued in May 2008, the Boards confirmed that present and potential capital providers are the most prominent users of an entity's financial statements. The Boards also concluded that by serving the information needs of capital providers, financial statements would serve the needs of a wide range of users.

Existing lease accounting standards from both world's most important standards setters (IASB and FASB) – International Accounting Standard (IAS) 17 *Leases* under IFRS and Statement of Financial Accounting Standard (SFAS) 13 *Accounting for Leases* under U.S. generally accepted accounting principles (U.S. GAAP)[9] – require lessees to classify their lease contracts as either finance (capital)[10] leases or operating leases. Finance leases are defined as those leases that transfer to the lessee all the risks and rewards incidental to ownership of the leased asset. All other leases are operating leases (IASB, 2009a, para. 1.3). It should be emphasised that the focus of this paper is the lease accounting by lessees.

Currently under the finance leases, if 'most' of the risks and rewards of ownership are transferred to an issuer leasing an asset (the lessee), the lease is treated as a sale of the entire asset by the owner (the lessor) and a purchase of an asset financed with debt by the issuer using the asset. In these cases, the lessor removes the cost of the asset from its balance sheet[11] and reports a sale of the asset for proceeds equal to the present value of the required lease payments, plus the expected remaining value of the leased asset at the end of the lease term. The lessee using the asset records the (underlying) asset and a related liability for the present value of the required lease payments on its balance sheet (SEC, 2005, p. 60). The lessee subsequently records in the income statement interest expense on the liability and depreciation expense on the asset.

If the lease does not transfer sufficient risks and rewards to the lessee to be treated as a sale and purchase, the lease is classified as an operating lease and is then treated like a rental contract. In this case, the owner of the asset (the lessor) retains the asset on its balance sheet and records lease rental revenue (as well as depreciation, property taxes etc.) in its income statement on a period-by-period basis. The entity using the asset (the lessee) does not record the asset, or a related liability for the future contractual rental payments, on its balance sheet, but records leasing expense in its income statement, normally on a straight-line period-by-period basis over the lease term (SEC, 2005, p. 60).

9 U.S. generally accepted accounting principles (GAAP) are legally imposed on only that small proportion of companies registered with the Securities and Exchange Commission (SEC) (Nobes, 1998, p. 165).

10 U.S. generally accepted accounting principles (GAAP) uses the term 'capital' lease rather than 'finance' lease. To avoid repetition, the term 'finance' lease is used in this paper.

11 It is worth noting that in the revised version of IAS 1 *Presentation of Financial Statements*, which was issued in 2007, the title 'balance sheet' was replaced by the title 'statement of financial position', mainly because the new title reflects more closely the function of the statement as described in the IASB's Framework. Despite this fact, it has been decided to use the term 'balance sheet' in our chapter, mainly due to its familiarity to readers.

The objective of the current lease accounting approach is thus to treat the leases that are economically equivalent to sales and purchases as sales and purchases, and to treat other leases similarly to service contracts. As a consequence of this approach, which could be labelled as an 'all-or-nothing' approach from the point-of-view of the lessee's balance sheet, the lessee leasing the asset will either recognise the entire leased asset on its books and a liability for all of its contractually required payments, or it will recognise no asset and no liability. This approach thus basically claims that some leases give rise to assets and liabilities and others do not, despite the fact that during the deliberations that preceded the SFAS 13 (issued in 1976), some argued that all lease commitments create obligations that should be reflected as liabilities in the balance sheets of lessees (Monson, 2001, p. 276). In the June 2005 report on off-balance-sheet activity commissioned by U.S. Congress as part of the Sarbanes-Oxley Act of 2002, the U.S. Securities and Exchange Commission (SEC) staff argued that this approach does not allow the balance sheet to show the fact that, in almost every lease, both parties have some interest in the asset, as well as some interest in one or more financial receivables or payables.

To faithfully represent the arrangement, the classification whether a lease is a finance lease or an operating lease should depend on the substance of the transaction rather than the form of the contract. However under the SFAS 13, lease classification is made according to the 'bright-line tests',[12] while the IAS 17 uses a princi-

12 SFAS 13 (para. 13.7) specifies that a lease is a capital lease if:

- The lease transfers ownership to the issuer (the lessee) using the asset by the end of the lease term; or
- The lease contains an option whereby the issuer can purchase the leased property at a price sufficiently lower than the expected fair value of the leased property at the end of the lease term (bargain purchase option); or
- The term of the lease is equal to or greater than 75% of the estimated economic life of the leased property; or
- The present value of the minimum lease payments to be made by the issuer is equal to or greater than 90% of the fair value of the leased property.

The 'all-or-nothing' nature of the guidance means that economically similar arrangements may receive different accounting if they are just to one side or the other of the 'bright-line' test. Conversely, economically different transactions may be treated similarly (SEC, 2005, pp. 62-63). Alexander and Jermakowicz (2006, p. 150) also argue that the application of specific rules may require economically different situations to be accounted for identically and thus create a pseudo-comparability. Wüstermann and Wüstermann (2010, p. 17) provide the following example: consider a rule prescribing that liabilities shall only be recognised if the probability of the outflow of resources is higher than 50% (see IAS 37.23 for a similar rule). In the case of a pending law suit, consider a company that expects to be ordered to pay damages with a 5% probability, and another company that expects to have to pay damages

ples-based approach and provides only the list of examples and indicators that would normally lead to a lease being classified as a finance lease. Of course, these classifications are very important, as they can completely change the accounting for the lease and thus have very different balance sheet applications.

The accounting guidance for leases also includes extensive disclosure requirements for the notes of the financial statements. These requirements vary according to the type of lease and whether the entity is the lessor or lessee. This paper focuses on the lease accounting by lessees. Thus, as already mentioned, under the operating lease, the lessee does not recognise any lease asset or liability in the balance sheet, but is, in contrast, obliged to disclose in the notes (IAS 17, para. 35):

- the total of future minimum lease payments under non-cancellable operating leases for each of the following periods:
    - not later than one year;
    - later than one year and not later than five years;
    - later than five years.[13]
- the total of future minimum sublease payments expected to be received under non-cancellable subleases at the end of the reporting period.
- lease and sublease payments recognised as an expense in the period, with separate amounts for minimum lease payments, contingent rents, and sublease payments.
- a general description of the lessee's significant leasing arrangements.

On average, lessees seem to prefer operating lease accounting, and much of the empirical research investigates the implications of unrecorded lease commitments, i.e., obligations (Lipe, 2001, p. 299).

Lindsey (2006, pp. 1–2) found that at the end of 2004, total rental commitments by U.S. firms from off-balance sheet operating leases equalled $1.05 trillion. Had these operating lease rental commitments been capitalised, the estimated as-if capitalised operating lease liabilities for U.S. firms at the end of 2004 would have exceeded $625 billion. In comparison, long-term debt for U.S. firms totalled more

with a 45% probability. Neither, according to this rule, would require the potential outflow of resources being shown as a liability. Hence, both companies show the same amount of income in the accounts even though their economic situation is different.

13 For operating leases having initial or remaining non-cancellable lease terms in excess of one year, the following information shall be disclosed (SFAS 13, para. 16b): future minimum rental payments required as of the date of the latest balance sheet presented, in the aggregate and for each of the five succeeding fiscal years, and the aggregate for the periods beyond five year. The usefulness of only a lump-sum amount disclosure beyond five years is indeed probably questionable.

than $6.5 trillion at the end of 2004. Accordingly, operating lease rental commitments that remain off the balance sheet account for approximately nine percent of corporate debt. The magnitude of leasing undertaken as operating leases dwarfs that undertaken as finance leases. At the end of 2004, the total amount of finance lease liabilities recognised by U.S. publicly-traded firms was $89.8 billion or $16.2 million per firm. A simple comparison of the relative magnitudes of operating and finance lease activity reveals that approximately 85 percent of leasing obligations occur under leases that avoid the lease capitalisation criteria of SFAS 13.

Similarly, in its June 2005 report the SEC's staff estimated that the standards allow U.S. publicly traded companies to keep an undiscounted $1.25 trillion in future cash operating lease obligations off their balance sheets. The staff also noted that the ratio of the total cash flows related to non-cancellable operating leases to finance leases is more than 12 to 1 within the sample and is estimated to be more than 25 to 1 for the population.

In addition, there is evidence that managers in the USA use operating leases to achieve off-balance sheet financing,[14] thus avoiding the lease capitalisation criteria, i.e., taking advantage of the 'bright-line' nature of the lease classification guidance of the SFAS 13 (El-Gazzar et al. 1986, Imhoff et al. 1988).

Furthermore, in a June 2005 report, the SEC's staff was of the opinion that problems with the 'all-or-nothing' character of the existing lease accounting (under SFAS 13) have been magnified because many issuers involved in leases, taking advantage of the 'bright-line' nature of the lease classification guidance, structure their lease arrangements to achieve whatever accounting (finance or operating) is desired. These issuers have been aided in these endeavours by a large number of attorneys, lenders, investment banks, accountants, insurers, industry advocates, and other advisers. Indeed, lease structuring to meet various accounting, tax, and other goals, has become an industry unto itself in the last 30 years (SEC, 2005, p. 63).

Unfortunately, we could not find any data on the magnitude of operating leasing under the IFRS in Europe. Nevertheless, it is probably reasonable to expect that there is proportionately less operating leasing in Europe than in the USA, because under the IFRS it is probably more difficult to structure a lease to be an operating lease given the IAS 17's principles based approach.

---

14 A commonly cited motivation for off-balance sheet financing is a reduction of book (balance sheet) leverage (Lim et al., 2003, p. 1).

# 4. Recognition vs. Disclosure in the Notes Dilemma for Leases

Recognition is the process of formally recording or incorporating an item into the financial statements of an entity as an asset, liability, revenue, expense, or the like. Recognition includes the depiction of an item in both words and numbers, with the amount included in the totals of the financial statements (SFAC 5,[15] para. 6). The IASB's Framework (para. 82) provides a very similar definition of recognition: 'Recognition is the process of incorporating in the balance sheet or income statement an item that meets the definition of an element and satisfies the criteria for recognition. It involves the depiction of the item in words and by a monetary amount and the inclusion of that amount in the balance sheet or income statement totals.'

It is worth noting that while recognition is specifically defined in SFAC 5 and in the Framework, disclosure in the notes to primary financial statements is not. In addition to defining and describing recognised items, both state that disclosure is not a substitute for recognition (SFAC 5, para. 9; Framework, para. 82) and provide recognition criteria: the item must meet the definition of a financial statement element; it must have a relevant measurement attribute with sufficient reliability; and the information must be both relevant and reliable. (SFAC 5, para. 63). The IASB's Framework (para. 83) provides very similar recognition criteria: 'An item that meets the definition of an element should be recognised if:

- it is probable that any future economic benefit associated with the item will flow to or from the entity; and
- the item has a cost or value that can be measured with reliability.'

In contrast to the detailed treatment of recognition, Conceptual Frameworks merely discuss disclosures (without defining them) and provide some examples.[16] That discussion is not definitive with respect to the question of what disclosures

15 Statements of Financial Reporting Concepts (SFAC) No. 5 *Recognition and Measurement in Financial Statements of Business Enterprises, issued in December 1984.*

16 For example, the current IASB Framework in paragraph 21 states that the financial statements also contain notes and supplementary schedules and other information. For example, they may contain additional information that is relevant to the needs of users about the items in the balance sheet and income statement. They may include disclosures about the risks and uncertainties affecting the entity and any rights and obligations not recognised in the balance sheet (such as mineral reserves). Information about geographical and industry segments and the effect on the entity of changing prices may also be provided in the form of supplementary information.

are, conceptually, expected to achieve in the communication of decision-useful information. However, interpreting the discussion in Conceptual Frameworks as indicating that recognition is a special case of disclosure, restricted to items that meet certain criteria (that is, disclosures (in the notes) differ from recognised items because disclosed items fail one or more of the recognition criteria) does yield two inferences. First, because recognition is subject to special criteria, and because both Conceptual Frameworks state that disclosure and recognition are not substitutes, it is evident that disclosure and recognition are not financial reporting alternatives, i.e., they are not intended to serve the same purpose. Second, items that meet the definitions of financial statement elements but fail one or more of the recognition criteria should be disclosed, and the most likely criterion to matter for this distinction is reliability. It seems implausible that a standard setter would not require the recognition of highly reliable items unless those items do not meet the definitions of financial statement elements (Schipper, 2007, p. 304).

Under this rationale, reliability can determine information location. However, standards setters may determine information location for other reasons (Bernard and Schipper, 1994). Former FASB members have indicated that the decision to allow disclosure rather than recognition has been driven by political pressure in some cases (e.g., Beresford, 1996). This suggests that information location decisions can be influenced by considerations other than those described in the Conceptual Frameworks. However, it is worth noting that the U.S. standard SFAS 13 *Lease Accounting* was issued (1976) before any of the FASB's Conceptual Framework pronouncements (SFAC 1 in 1978).

Monson (2001, p. 275) notes that standards setters, academics, auditors, users, and preparers of financial statements have long debated whether or when assets and liabilities result from lease contracts. In a very real sense, a workable method of reporting leases in the financial statements of lessees has been the most eagerly sought goal of accounting standards setters in the USA for at least 40 years. Neither the Accounting Research Committee of the AICPA[17] nor the Accounting Principles Board (both predecessor standard-setting bodies to FASB) were able to build a consensus for doing anything substantive with this issue. The FASB, which was formed in 1973, took up the subject of accounting for leases as one of its first priorities. Monson (2001, p. 276) claims that focus of these efforts, SFAS 13 *Accounting for Leases*, clearly represents progress when compared to all previous attempts at developing lease accounting standards, despite the fact that by

17 American Institute of Certified Public Accountants is the national professional association of accountants in the USA, with more than 360,000 members. (Source: http://www.aicpa.org/ABOUT/MISSIONANDHISTORY/Pages/MissionHistory.aspx).

preserving in SFAS 13 the distinction between operating and finance leases previously articulated in Accounting Principles Board Opinion No. 5, the FASB agreed that some leases give rise to assets and liabilities (finance leases) and others do not (operating leases).

Hence, it is quite likely, in our opinion, that at that time the pragmatic improvements to lease accounting standards were deemed more important and less problematic than conceptual consistency.

## 4.1 Recognition vs. Disclosure and Efficient Market Theory

The question is whether share prices reflect amounts disclosed in the notes to the financial statements and those recognised in the primary financial statements similarly, as would be expected in efficient markets, is of interest to regulators, account preparers and auditors. In this, standards setters clearly prioritise recognition over disclosure.

The efficient market theory (EFM) suggests that the markets adopt a substance-over-form approach and incorporate all publicly available information, irrespective of the mode of disclosure, i.e., whether the amount is disclosed on the face of the primary financial statements or in the notes.

But some value relevance[18] academic empirical research suggests that under certain conditions note disclosures are less strongly associated with market values (of equity, i.e., share prices), as for example Bernard and Schipper (1994), Davis-Friday et al. (1999) and Ahmed et al. (2006). One of these conditions is if investors inappropriately undervalue disclosed amounts either through lack of expertise or due to the cost of processing note information (see next section). Furthermore, recognition may imply greater relevance or reliability, in which users correctly

18 Value relevance research assesses how well accounting amounts reflect information used by equity investors (Barth et al., 2001, p. 86). Value relevance as defined in the academic literature is not a stated criterion of the standard-setting. Value relevance is an empirical operationalisation of the FASB's (and IASB's) stated criteria of relevance and reliability because an accounting amount will be value relevant, i.e., have a predicted significant relation with share prices, only if the amount reflects information relevant to investors in valuing the firm and is measured reliably enough to be reflected in share prices. Only if an accounting amount is relevant to a financial statement user can it be capable of making a difference to that user's decisions (Barth et al., 2001, p. 82). Note also that the concepts of value relevance and decision relevance differ. In particular, accounting information can be value relevant but not decision relevant if it is superseded by more timely information (Barth et al., 2001, p. 82).

assign lower weight to disclosed amounts. For example, auditors or management may require more stringent standards for recognised values (Jifri and Citron, 2009, p. 124).

In contrast, the recent empirical results[19] of Jifri and Citron (2009) suggest that, for particular classes of firms (firms engaged in R&D), the market perceives recognised and disclosed amounts equivalently, which is consistent with the efficient market hypothesis (EMH).

We can thus conclude that the empirical evidence on the value-relevance of note disclosures is mixed. In order to contribute to the recognition vs. disclosure debate in the standard-setting context, we support Jifri and Citron's (2009, p. 123) conclusion that further research should investigate the extent to which market assessment of recognised vs. disclosed amounts depends on the accounting item in question, its method of valuation and processing through books of account as well as the characteristics of the firm.

## 4.2 Possible Reasons for Perceived Market Inefficiencies

Hirshleifer and Teoh's (2003) paper represents a step towards bridging what appears to be an increasingly wide gap between the views of many accounting and finance researchers (specifically, the views of 'hard core' believers in market efficiency) and the views of just about everyone else in the world with respect to the perceived efficiency of capital markets (Lambert, 2003, pp. 387).

Their approach departs from theories in assuming that investors have limited attention and processing power. Limited attention is a necessary consequence of the vast amount of information available in the environment, and of limits to information processing power. Attention must be selective and requires effort (Hirshleifer and Teoh, 2003, p. 339).

In their model, owing to the limits to investor attention, the information that is presented in a prominent, easily processed form is assumed to be absorbed more easily than the information that is less prominent, or that is only implicit in the

19 The paper exploits the unique UK regulatory framework in which accounting for goodwill moved from note disclosure to balance sheet recognition. According to Jifri and Citron (2009, p. 125) the paper adds to the literature in a number of ways. Firstly, it studies the recognition vs. disclosure issue in a new context: that of goodwill accounting. Secondly, it investigates whether the relative importance of recognised and disclosed amounts varies by type of firm, specifically whether or not a firm engages in R&D.

public information set. Thus, (some) investors neglect relevant aspects of the economic environments they face.[20]

Lambert's paper develops a theoretical model in which a nontrivial fraction of investors are 'inattentive' (unsophisticated) and either miss important information disclosures entirely or systematically misinterpret their implications. In such a situation, accounting measurement rules, earnings management activities, and discretionary disclosures have an impact on stock prices, even when these features bear no relation to the underlying cash flows of the firm.[21] The model is applied to three topical accounting controversies: expensing stock options, pro forma earnings disclosures, and segmental reporting (Lambert, 2003, pp. 387–388).

One of the conclusions Hirshleifer and Teoh (2003, p. 380) make is that limited attention may help explain why investors are insufficiently sceptical of firms that are positioned to conceal liabilities, such as off-balance sheet contractual provisions, e.g., example operating leases.

Lambert (2003, p. 399) agrees that individual investors cannot possibly process everything or even pay attention to everything that is of potential relevance to the valuation of the firm. However, he also argues that we know that the market has at least some ability to process information in a sophisticated fashion. He notes that we have witnessed over one hundred accounting standards enacted in recent several decades, and the stock price reactions were analysed for many of them. We have rarely observed a major fall in stock prices when new accounting standards resulted in significant changes to companies' balance sheets and income statements. For example, when firms had to recognise capital leases, or pension obligations, or post-retirement health care benefits, stock prices did not systematically fall. Similarly, when firms stopped amortising goodwill, prices did not shoot up. In many instances, stock prices react to events before the accounting statements

20 Although inattention perhaps seems foolish because such investors lose money by ignoring aspects of the economic environment, if time and attention are costly, such behaviour may be reasonable.

21 One interpretation of the model of inattentive investors is that they are actually 'fully rational' decision makers who bear extremely high information collection costs for certain types of signals. It is also possible to interpret them as decision makers who psychologically anchor on a value (zero) or who have limited information processing capabilities (due to lack of training or education). There are certainly other psychologically based assumptions about how individuals process information that might have been analysed, such as over-reaction or under-reaction to information. It would be interesting to examine how the results would change under these alternative assumptions (Lambert, 2003, pp. 390–391).

reflect these events. Thus, in his opinion, the question is: where on the continuum between total inattentiveness and total attentiveness are we?

Barth et al.'s paper (2003) focuses on the effect of recognition and disclosure on capital market performance, i.e., market prices. Analysis of their model reveals that the price informativeness depends on the qualities of three sources of information available to investors: (a) the recognised amount, (b) the disclosed information, and (c) the information revealed by the security prices; and interaction with expertise acquisition.

They assume that investors decide whether to acquire accounting expertise. In doing so, investors trade off the cost of expertise acquisition against informational benefits they obtain from understanding disclosures. They assume that expertise acquisition is costly because understanding disclosures requires accounting expertise beyond that needed to understand recognised amounts.

Barth et al. (2003) compare disclosure with three types of recognition: aggregate recognition with disclosure, separate recognition, and aggregate recognition without disclosure. If information is disclosed only in the notes, users of financial statements have to expend time and effort to become sufficiently expert in accounting to know (a) that there are items that are not recognised in the financial statements, (b) that there is information about those items in the notes, and (c) how to assess the note disclosures. Because gaining such expertise comes at a cost, and not all users of financial statements will become accounting experts, information that is merely disclosed may not be fully reflected in share prices.

When comparing the disclosure regime with the separate recognition regime, they find that recognition always increases price informativeness. This is because in this regime recognition results in the disclosed amount being freely available to all investors. However, when aggregation is a part of recognition, as it is in the aggregate recognition with or without disclosure regimes, the results are more complex. In particular, in the aggregate recognition with disclosure regime, they find that recognition of an accounting component that results in a higher (lower) quality recognised amount does not always result in greater (lower) price informativeness.

In the context of leases, according to Ge et al. (2008, p. 2), users' off-balance sheet operating lease adjustments to accounting measures of risk (i.e., debt-to-asset ratio) are based on two different estimation methods: the multiples method and the discounted cash flow (DCF) method. As the name suggests, the multiples approach uses a multiple of rent expense (recognised in the income statement) as an approximation of the unrecognised operating lease asset and liability. The multiples approach ignores the future cash flow information in notes to financial statements. In contrast, the DCF method mimics finance lease accounting in that both the leasehold amount and the lease obligation are based on the present value of the future minimum lease payments disclosed in the notes. However, use of the DCF method for operating leases requires making assumptions regarding the interest rate and the duration of the lump sum cash payments beyond five years into the future (among other things). Still, the DCF method is grounded in theory, while the multiples method is ad hoc.[22]

In addition, Ge et al. (2008, p. 5) imply that investors do not appear to use the DCF method (i.e., the more accurate approach) in a consistent manner to incorporate the effects of operating lease adjustments on accounting measures of risk and performance. Building on the earlier studies by Imhoff et al. (1993) and Ely (1995), their results suggest that, even after more than a decade, investors do not appear to have become more sophisticated in using the operating lease information disclosed in the notes to financial statements. That fact could be, in our opinion, explained by the cognitive activities of the investors described in this section.

# 5. Criticism of the Current Lease Accounting Approach

The existing accounting approach for leases has been criticised for failing to meet the needs of users of financial statements. In particular (IASB, 2009a, para. 1.12):

- Many users think that operating leases give rise to assets and liabilities that should be recognised in the financial statements of lessees. Consequently, users routinely attempt to adjust the recognised amounts in the financial statements.[23] However, the information available to users in the notes to the financial statements is insufficient for them to make reliable adjustments.

22 'Financial analysts also treat non-cancellable leases like debt with the nature of the analysis becoming more sophisticated over time. For example, until recently Standard & Poor's debt rating analysis estimated the operating lease liability by multiplying the annual rent by a factor of 8 and adding the result to balance sheet debt. Cottle et al. (1988) state that this rule-of-thumb procedure is consistent with the approach of many security analysts. Currently, Standard & Poor's (2000) converts all operating leases to capital leases as described below: The debt-equivalent value of operating leases is determined by calculating the present value of minimum operating lease obligations as reported in the annual report's footnotes. The lease amount beyond five years is assumed to mature at a rate approximating the minimum payment due in year five' (Ryan et al., 2001, p. 291).

23 Operating lease adjustments could affect investment decisions in two dimensions: investors' assessment of firm equity risk and operating performance (Ge et al., 2008, p. 4).

- The existence of two very different accounting models for leases (the finance lease model and the operating lease model) means that similar transactions can be accounted for very differently. This reduces comparability for users.
- The existing standards provide opportunities to structure transactions so as to achieve a particular lease classification. If the lease is classified as an operating lease, the lessee obtains a source of unrecognised financing that can be difficult for users to understand.

Preparers and auditors have criticised the complexity of the existing accounting approach for leases. In particular, it has proved difficult to define the dividing line between finance leases and operating leases in a principled way. Consequently, the standards use a mixture of subjective judgements (IAS 17 *Leases*) and 'bright-line' tests (SFAS 13 *Accounting for Leases*) that can be difficult to apply (IASB, 2009a, para. 1.13).

Some have also argued that the existing accounting approach is conceptually flawed. In particular (IASB, 2009a, para. 1.14):

- on entering a lease contract, the lessee obtains a valuable right (the right to use the leased item). This right meets the FASB's and the IASB's definitions of an asset. Similarly, the lessee assumes an obligation (the obligation to pay rentals) that meets the Boards' definitions of a liability. However, if the lessee classifies the lease as an operating lease, that right and obligation are not recognised.
- there are significant and growing differences between the accounting approach for leases and other contractual arrangements. This has led to inconsistent accounting for arrangements that meet the definition of a lease and similar arrangements that do not.

In the already-mentioned June 2005 report on off-balance-sheet activity commissioned by the U.S. Congress as part of the Sarbanes-Oxley Act of 2002, the SEC staff recognised the inadequacies of the existing lease accounting standards and recommended that the FASB undertake a project to reconsider the leasing standards, preferably as a joint project with the IASB.

# 6. The Proposed New Approach to Lease Accounting

## 6.1 General Idea behind the Approach

As already mentioned, the focus of this paper is lease accounting by the lessees. The lease accounting project is being undertaken jointly by the FASB and IASB (hereinafter the Boards) and is a part of the Memorandum of Understanding.[24] The objective is to create common lease accounting requirements to ensure that the assets and liabilities arising from lease contracts are recognised in the balance sheet. A discussion paper (DP) *Leases: Preliminary Views* was issued on 19 March 2009 with a comment deadline of four months. The next step was publication of an exposure draft (ED) *Leases* on 17 August 2010 with a comment deadline of four months. The current project plan (as of 30 June 2011) envisages either the re-exposure or the review draft in the third quarter of 2011 and a final standard in the first half of 2012.[25]

In the DP, the Boards decided on an overall approach that would apply the existing finance lease model, adapted where necessary, to all leases. The Boards decided to focus only on lessee accounting and defer the development of a new lessor accounting model until a later time. However, the Boards decided to include in the DP a high-level discussion of lessor accounting issues.

The Boards identified the following rights and obligations in a simple lease (IASB, 2009a, para. 1.13):

- right to use the asset for the lease term,
- obligation to pay rentals, and
- obligation to return the asset at the end of the lease term.

---

24 In September 2002, the IASB and the FASB agreed to work together to remove the differences between IFRS and U.S. GAAP. This decision was embodied in a Memorandum of Understanding (MoU) between the Boards known as the Norwalk Agreement. The Boards' commitment was further strengthened in 2006, when the IASB and FASB set specific milestones to be reached by 2008 (A roadmap for convergence 2006–2008). In 2008, the two Boards issued an update to the MoU, which identified a series of priorities and milestones to complete the remaining major joint projects by 2011, emphasising the goal of joint projects to produce common, principle-based standards. In 2009, the Group of 20 Leaders (G20) called for standard-setters to re-double their efforts to complete convergence in global accounting standards by June 2011. Following this request, in November 2009, the IASB and the FASB published a progress report describing an intensification of their work programme, including the hosting of monthly joint board meetings and to provide quarterly updates on their progress on convergence projects (IASB, 2010a).

25 The IASB's standard-setting process comprises six stages (IASCF, 2008, pp. 7–14): 1) setting the agenda; 2) project planning; 3) development and publication of a discussion paper; – although a discussion paper is not a mandatory step in its due process, the IASB normally publishes a discussion paper as its first publication on any major new topic as a vehicle to explain the issue and solicit early comment from constituents; 4) development and publication of an exposure draft; 5) development and publication of an IFRS; and 6) procedures after an IFRS is issued.

Having identified the rights and obligations arising in this simple lease, the Boards then considered whether those rights and obligations meet the definitions of assets and liabilities. Although the wording of the existing IASB and FASB asset definitions are different, the basic concepts underpinning them are the same (IASB, 2009a, para. 3.12–13).

The Boards have tentatively concluded that the lessee's right to use a leased item for the lease term meets the definitions of an asset in the IASB's Framework and the FASB's Concepts Statement No. 6 *Elements of Financial Statements* (SFAC 6) and that the lessee's obligation to pay rentals meets the definitions of a liability (IASB, 2009a, para. 3.17 and 3.21).

However, the Boards decided that the obligation to return the leased item does not result in an outflow of economic benefits from the lessee and does not meet the definitions of a liability. They reasoned that although the lessee has physical possession of the leased item, it has no right to use the item once the lease term expires and that the position of the lessee at the end of the lease term is like that of an asset custodian. The lessee is holding an asset on behalf of a third party but has no right to the economic benefits embodied in that asset (IASB, 2009a, para. 3.23 and 3.24).

On the basis of their analyses, the Boards tentatively decided to develop a new approach to accounting for leases[26] that would result in the recognition of the assets and liabilities identified as arising in a lease contract. Rather than treating some lease contracts like a purchase of the leased item (finance leases) and others as executory contracts (operating leases), the new approach would treat all lease con-

26 In 1996, the G4+1 group of standard-setters (from Australia, Canada, New Zealand, the UK, the USA and International Accounting Standards Committee (IASC), the predecessor body of the IASB) published a discussion paper (*Accounting for Leases: A New Approach — Recognition by Lessees of Assets and Liabilities Arising under Lease Contracts).* The paper proposed an approach to lease accounting that would abolish the requirement to classify leases as operating leases or finance leases. Under that approach, a lessee would similarly recognise as assets and liabilities all material rights and obligations arising in a lease contract. The G4+1 published another discussion paper in 2000 (*Leases: Implementation of a New Approach*). That paper set out proposals for how the approach described in the 1996 paper might be made to work, i.e., be reflected in accounting standards, and deals more extensively with lessor accounting (Nailor and Lennard, 2000, p. 7). Similarly SEC's Pozen Committee Report (SEC, 2008a, p. 42) argues that an entity should fully recognise its rights to use an asset, rather than the physical asset itself. In these cases, regardless of whether the lease is considered to be operating or finance (based on today's dichotomy), all entities would record amounts in the financial statements to the extent of their involvement in the related business activities.

tracts as the acquisition of a right to use the leased item for the lease term. Thus, the lessee would recognise the following (IASB, 2009a, para. 3.26):

- an asset representing its right to use the leased item for the lease term (the right-of-use asset),
- a liability for its obligation to pay rentals.

As regards lease accounting by the lessees, we can conclude that the Boards followed the basic accounting concept according to which items that meet the definition of an element (asset, liability etc.) and satisfy the recognition criteria should be included in the primary financial statements, i.e., recognised (see also the IASB's Framework, para. 82–88). The failure to recognise such items is not rectified by disclosure of the accounting policies used nor by notes or explanatory material.[27]

That was another argument against the existing operating lease treatment of some of the lease contacts, in which the lessee does not need to recognise any lease asset or liability in the balance sheet despite the fact that the recognition criteria are met. Instead, certain disclosures in the notes are deemed sufficient.

The Boards also tentatively decided not to recognise the components of a lease contract separately (such as options to renew, purchase options, contingent rental arrangements or residual value guarantees). Instead, the Boards tentatively decided that the lessee should recognise (IASB, 2009a, IN7):

- a single right-of-use asset that includes rights acquired under options; and
- a single obligation to pay rentals that includes obligations arising under contingent rental arrangements and residual value guarantees.

At the October 2009 joint meeting, i.e., in the deliberations after the DP was issued, the Boards tentatively decided to exclude from the scope of the proposed new leases guidance contracts that represent the purchase (lessee) or sale (lessor) of the underlying asset. A contract is a purchase or a sale if at the end of the contract, the contract transfers:

- control of the underlying asset,
- all but a trivial amount of the risks and benefits associated with the underlying asset.

The Boards also developed criteria to determine whether a transaction is in fact a purchase or sale of the whole underlying asset and thus should be excluded from

27 Some disclosed items in financial reports are not recognised – and likely never will be – because they cannot be expressed in numbers or, more narrowly, in currency units. Examples include the qualitative description of accounting policies, a summary of inputs to the calculation of a recognised number, and a sensitivity analysis (Schipper, 2007, p. 301).

the scope of the leases guidance.[28] It should be noted that the accounting proposed for lessees is very similar (but not identical) to (instalment) purchase accounting, but not of the underlying asset itself, but rather of the right-of use of the underlying asset. However, the accounting proposed for lessors is very different to sales accounting. Consequently, this is a much more significant issue for lessors than for lessees; thus, since our paper focuses on lessee accounting, we will not go into the details on this issue.

Therefore, the lessee recognises a (single) right-of-use asset and a (single) obligation to pay rentals in the case of the lease not qualifying as a sale/purchase of the underlying asset. We could thus conclude that the objective of the proposed lease accounting approach is to treat the leases that are economically equivalent to sales and purchases of the underlying assets as sales and purchases, and to treat other leases as the acquisition of the right-of-use.

## 6.2 Measurement of Lessee's Obligation and Asset

The lessee's obligation to pay rentals meets the definition of a financial liability in IAS 32 *Financial Instruments: Presentation*. IAS 39 *Financial Instruments: Recognition and Measurement* requires financial instruments to be measured initially at fair value, but excludes lease liabilities from its scope. The Boards discussed whether to require the lessee to measure the obligation to pay rentals initially at fair value and noted that in most lease contracts it is not possible to observe the fair value of the obligation to pay rentals directly. Consequently, discounted cash flow techniques will be used to determine the initial measurement of the obligation to pay rentals (IASB, 2009a, para. 4.4–7). Therefore, the Boards tentatively decided to initially measure the lessee's obligation to pay rentals at the present value of the lease payments, discounted using the lessee's incremental borrowing rate.[29] The Boards noted that in most leases the present value of the lease payments

28 Control of the underlying asset has generally been transferred/obtained in the following situations:
- Contracts in which the title of the underlying asset transfers to the lessee automatically
- Contracts that include a bargain purchase option if it is reasonably certain that the options will be exercised
- Contracts in which the return that the lessor receives is fixed
- Contracts in which it is reasonably certain that the contract will cover the expected useful life of the asset and any risks or benefits associated with the underlying asset retained by the lessor at the end of the contract are expected to be not more than trivial.

29 The IAS 17 (para. 4) definition of the lessee's incremental borrowing rate is 'the rate of interest the lessee would have to pay on a similar lease or, if that is not determinable, the rate that,

discounted using the lessee's incremental borrowing rate will be a reasonable approximation to fair value. Consequently, requiring lessees to measure the obligation to pay rentals using this approach would provide users of financial statements with information similar to measuring the obligation at fair value. In addition, this approach would be simpler for lessees to apply than a requirement to measure the obligation to pay rentals at fair value (IASB, 2009a, para. 4.15–17).

The lessee's right-of-use asset is a non-financial asset. Most non-financial assets are initially measured at cost. For example, IAS 16 *Property, Plant and Equipment* and IAS 38 *Intangible Assets* require initial measurement at cost rather than at fair value. Similarly, US GAAP requires the initial (and subsequent) measurement of assets at cost under ARB 43 Chapter 9 *Depreciation* and SFAS 142 *Goodwill and Other Intangible Assets*. Consequently, in discussing a cost-based measurement for the right-of-use asset, the Boards concluded that cost would equal the present value of the lease payments discounted using the lessee's incremental borrowing rate (IASB, 2009a, para. 4.18–23). In a lease, there is a link between the obligation to pay rentals and the right-of-use asset. They arise from the same contract and do not normally exist independently of each other. The Boards' decisions on initial measurement thus reflect this linkage (IASB, 2009a, para. 5.5).

The lease (right-of-use) asset is subsequently to be amortised over the shorter of the lease term and the economic life of the leased asset,[30] and the lease liability is to be reduced by the part of the principal of the lease payment calculated based on the discount rate, which determines the present value of the lease payments[31] (Sakai, 2010, p. 4). The Boards thus tentatively decided to adopt an amortised cost-based approach to subsequent measurement of the obligation to pay rentals, which is consistent with the way many other non-derivative financial liabilities are measured and under which the lessee would accrue interest on the outstanding obligation to pay rentals (IASB, 2009a, para. 5.17–20). Consequently, no rental expenses would be recognised, interest expenses on obligation to pay rentals would decrease from period to period, while the right-of-use asset would most likely be

at the inception of the lease, the lessee would incur to borrow over a similar term, and with a similar security, the funds necessary to purchase the asset.' Consequently, the incremental borrowing rate takes account of: (a) the credit standing of the lessee, (b) the length of the lease and (c) the nature and quality of the security provided (i.e., the leased item).

30 The lessee's right-of-use asset would be considered for impairment by referring to existing applicable standards for impairment. A lessee preparing financial statements in accordance with IFRS would follow IAS 36, *Impairment of Assets*. A lessee applying U.S. GAAP would follow Topic 350, Intangibles - Goodwill and Other of the *FASB Accounting Standards Codification*™.

31 On initial recognition the effective interest rate equals the incremental borrowing rate.

amortised on the straight-line basis, resulting in the higher expenses in the early years of the lease, which is quite a different expense pattern than under operating leases today (please see Appendix 1).

It should be noted that the Boards' public meeting in January 2010 resulted in a tentative decision to permit lessees to use a simplified form of lease accounting for those leases that have a maximum possible lease term of less than 12 months. Under that simplified accounting, lessees would recognise (undiscounted) gross amounts payable and a corresponding right-of-use asset in the balance sheet. Nonetheless, we are of the opinion that the impact of discounting of short-term liabilities (and corresponding short-term right-of-use assets) is often not significant and consequently the simplification proposed might not offer much relief in practice.

## 6.3 Leases with Options

Lease contracts often grant the lessee the right (but not the obligation) to extend the lease beyond the initial lease period or the right to terminate a lease before the end of the lease period. While options to extend or terminate a lease may meet the definition of an asset, as discussed previously, the Boards tentatively decided to adopt a single asset and liability approach to lease contracts (IASB, 2009a, para. 6.1 and 6.8). To address the uncertainty of the lease term introduced by these options, two different approaches were considered by the Boards in the DP (IASB, 2009a, para. 6.9):

- The lessee recognises the uncertainty of the lease term through measurement, e.g., one of the possible lease terms is selected and the accounting is based on that lease term.
- The lessee recognises the uncertainty of the lease term through recognition.

Under the first approach, an entity would use a probability-weighted lease term. For example, assume a lease had an initial lease term of 10 years with a single five-year renewal period. If the probability that the renewal would be exercised was 80 per cent, the lease would be measured using a 14 year lease term (20% × 10 years + 80% × 15 years = 2 years + 12 years). Under the second approach and using the same example, an entity would determine if the lease was either a 10- or a 15-year lease. The DP indicates advantages and disadvantages of each approach. The first approach better reflects the existence of the option, but may result in a lease obligation that does not match any possible outcome. In the example above, the lease can only be a 10- or a 15-year lease, not a 14-year lease. The second approach reflects the 'binary' nature of the recognition decision. However, that second approach might effectively ignore the existence of the option if the 'most likely' lease term is 10 years and thus the lease is determined as a 10-year lease (IASB, 2009a, para. 6.11–21).

At the DP stage, the Boards tentatively decided to adopt the second approach that would require an entity to recognise an obligation to pay rentals for a specified lease term. That is, in a 10-year lease with an option to extend for five years, the lessee must decide whether it should recognise an obligation to pay 10 years of rental payments or 15 years of rental payments. The Boards noted that additional disclosures in the notes may be required to enable users to differentiate between leases that include options and leases that do not (IASB, 2009a, para. 6.22–23).

We note that the approach tentatively decided by the Boards is consistent with the management intent approach. However, one has to wonder whether there may be an unintended consequence of using a binary approach, because some lease agreements may be structured so that the initial term of the lease is of a short duration, e.g., one year, with fourteen renewal option periods. No single possible lease term might be considered the 'most likely' and the amount recognised as a lease obligation may result in a minor amount as well as be significantly different from a probability-weighted approach. The Boards acknowledged the potential problems with the 'most likely' notion and thus, at the November 2009 meeting, tentatively decided that the recognised lease term would be the longest possible lease term that is more likely than not to occur and that in determining the lease term, the lessee would consider all relevant factors.

Let us assume that a lessee enters into a five-year lease of a machine. The lease includes an option to terminate the lease at the end of each year. The assessed probabilities of each of the lease terms are shown in Table 1.

*Table 1: Example of the longest lease term that is more likely than not to occur*

| Term | Probability | Probability that the lease will cover the term |
|---|---|---|
| 1 year | 35% | 100% (25% +30% + 5% + 5% + 35%) |
| 2 years | 5% | 65% (25% +30% + 5% + 5%) |
| 3 years | 5% | 60% (25% + 30% + 5%) |
| 4 years | 30% | 55% (25% + 30%) |
| 5 years | 25% | 25% |

*Source: IASB, 2009d, p. 12.*

The most likely lease term is one year (the term with the highest probability), while the single longest term that is more likely than not to occur is four years.

We also emphasise that some of the comment letters the Boards received challenged this proposal in the DP on the grounds that it requires lessees to recognise amounts that are not liabilities as liabilities (because they are not enforceable obligations until the lessee decides to exercise an option to renew/terminate) and that it misrepresents a lessee's financial position (particularly the flexibility inherent in that position).

The IAS 17 does not require reassessment of the lease term unless certain conditions are met. The Boards discussed whether reassessment of the lease term should be required after initial recognition and the effect that reassessment would have on the recognised lease assets and lease obligation. The Boards tentatively decided to require a reassessment of the lease term at each reporting date because it is likely to provide users with more relevant information. The Boards also decided that changes in the lease obligation from a reassessment in the lease term should be recognised through an adjustment to the carrying amount of the right-of-use asset (IASB, 2009a, para. 6.42–53). We agree that the change in the expected lease obligation has a direct link to the expected value of the leased asset. If a lease obligation is, for example, remeasured from a four-year obligation to a five-year obligation, the entity is expected to derive higher economic benefit from the right-of-use asset due to the extended period time in which the entity expects to use the underlying asset.

## 6.4 Contingent Rentals

Lease contracts often contain contingent rental terms that cause payments to vary because of future events or changes in factors after the inception of the lease. Contingent rentals can be based on index or price changes, lessee performance or usage. The Boards considered whether recognition of contingent rentals should be the same as under existing IAS 17, i.e., generally expensed as incurred, or whether the contingent rental should be reflected in measurement of the lease obligation.

Those supporting the current approach argue that there is no obligation to pay contingent rentals until the future event requiring the payment occurs, and recognition prior to the event overstates the liability. The DP lists disadvantages with this approach, including potential understatement of leased assets, inconsistency with the Boards' preliminary views on recognition of options to renew or terminate a lease, and the creation of an incentive to structure lease arrangements. Others support an approach that views the lease obligation as a single liability that includes both a fixed and a variable component. Under that approach, the contingent component would be reflected in the measurement of the liability. The DP also lists the advantages of this approach. The Boards tentatively decided that assets and liabilities recognised by the lessee should reflect the obligation to make contingent rental payments. The Boards reasoned that while the amount of the payment might be conditional on future events, the obligation to make the payment should the event occur is unconditional[32] (IASB, 2009a, para. 7.5–12).

Different measurement approaches were considered in the DP for the initial measurement of contingent rentals including the advantages and disadvantages with each approach. The approaches included (IASB, 2009a, para. 7.13):

- a probability-weighted estimate of the rental payable, and
- the most likely rental payment.

The IASB tentatively decided that a probability-weighted approach of expected outcomes of contingencies should be used to measure the lease obligation. The IASB believes that measurement provides the most useful information to users.[33] In contrast, the FASB tentatively arrived at a different conclusion: that a lessee should measure contingent rentals on the basis of the most likely rental payments. A lessee would determine the most likely amount by considering the range of possible outcomes (IASB, 2009a, para. 7.21–22). At the December 2009 joint meeting, the Boards tentatively decided for a probability-weighted approach with the final wording and an example indicating that not every possible scenario has to be considered in the measurement.

32 Like contingent rental payments, payments under residual value guarantees are conditional on future events. However, the obligation to make a payment if the specified future events occur is unconditional. Consequently, the Boards have tentatively decided to treat residual value guarantees the same as contingent rental payments in all respects. Therefore, a lessee's obligation should include payments to be made under a residual value guarantee and the residual value guarantee should be included as part of a measurement reassessment (IASB, 2009a, para. 7.46).

33 The probability-weighted approach considers a range of outcomes and their probabilities of occurring. This approach is consistent with measurement methods used for some other liabilities that have an element of uncertainty, e.g., provisions involving a large population, in accordance with IAS 37 *Provisions, Contingent Liabilities and Contingent Assets*. This measurement approach includes the uncertainty in the measurement rather than predicting a specific outcome. However, the approach is more complex and in some cases can reflect an outcome that will never happen.

Since the Boards tentatively decided for the reassessment of the expected contingent rental payments, the accounting for that change also needs to be addressed. The Boards considered whether the change should be accounted for through profit or loss or whether the change should be accounted for as an adjustment to the carrying amount of the leased asset.

The IASB believed changes in the obligation to pay rentals are effectively changes to the original assessed cost of the right-of-use asset and tentatively decided to require changes in the measurement of lease obligation due to changes in an estimated contingency be recognised as an adjustment to the carrying amount of the related right-of-use asset. The IASB stated that this is consistent with its tentative decision for changes in the estimated lease term. However, the FASB arrived at a different tentative decision. The FASB believed changes in the measurement of lease obligation due to changes in an estimated contingency should be recognised in profit and loss, because it is both easier for users to understand and less complex for preparers (IASB, 2009a, para. 7.22–32).

We believe that the fact concerning the change in a reassessed lease obligation is being either better recognised as an adjustment to the carrying amount of the right-of-use asset or recognised in profit or loss may depend on whether the contingent rental is based on a price or index change, the lessee's performance, or usage. We agree with Nailor and Lennard (2000, p. 79) that leases with contingent rentals that vary with usage give rise to the similar issues as with leases that contain renewal options. The similarity is that both kinds of leases give the lessee the option to 'purchase' more of the right-of-use asset and thus both should have the same accounting treatment, i.e., the change in a reassessed lease obligation should be recognised through an adjustment to the carrying amount of the right-of-use asset.

However, if for example, a lease obligation was remeasured for contingent rental payment associated with an interest rate increase, the increase in the lease obligation would not necessarily be indicative of a new and better measurement of the right-of-use asset.

It should be noted that, at the public meeting in February 2010, the Boards acknowledged a different nature of contingent rental arrangements and tentatively decided that changes in amounts payable under contingent rental arrangements arising from current or prior periods should be recognised by the lessees in profit or loss. All other changes should be recognised as an adjustment to the lessee's right-of-use asset.

# 7. Conclusion

The existing lease accounting approach, which could be characterised as a 'risk-and-rewards' approach, has received criticism, and the Boards believe the improvements are needed to ensure that financial statements provide useful, transparent and complete information about leasing transactions to investors and other users of financial statements. Therefore, in March 2009 the Boards issued a discussion paper (DP) *Leases: Preliminary Views*, which focuses almost exclusively on lease accounting by lessees, with a comment deadline of four months. In this paper, a new approach for the recognition of assets and liabilities arising under lease contracts was developed. According to this approach, usually referred to as a 'right-of-use' approach, all lease contracts would be treated as the acquisition of a right to use the leased item for the lease term and, consequently, the capitalisation, i.e., the recognition of lease assets and liabilities for all lease contracts, would be required for lessees.

The Boards received a total of 290 comment letters on the DP. Approximately half of the respondents supported the overall principles and objectives as set out in the DP while approximately one-third of the respondents did not support the Boards' preliminary views (IASB, 2009c, pp. 1–2).

The majority of the respondents who supported the right-of-use approach in principle generally expressed concerns over the complexity of the approach. They claimed that the implementation and the ongoing compliance would be costly and would require significant effort. In particular, they were concerned about the complexity of the proposed accounting for lease options and contingent payments. Some of those respondents questioned whether the costs of the proposed approach would outweigh the benefits (IASB, 2009c, p. 3).

The publication of the exposure draft (ED) Leases on 17 August 2010 confirmed the Boards' determination to follow the 'right-of-use' approach (please see Appendix 2 for the comparison of the existing and proposed new lease accounting requirements). The Boards received a total of 760 comment letters on the ED. There was general support for the Boards' efforts to address criticisms of the current 'bright-lines' that exist in the current lease accounting guidance and the objective of improving information provided to users of the financial statements by providing greater transparency and comparability. In this regard, most respondents supported the recognition of lease obligations and related assets on the lessee's balance sheet. However, significant concerns were expressed relating to the complexity and cost of implementing the proposals, specifically the initial and subsequent measurement of lease assets and liabilities and to reduced comparability arising from the level of estimation and judgement required by the proposals (e.g. determination of lease term and calculation of variable lease payments) (IASB, 2011, pp. 1-6). Nevertheless we are highly confident that the 'right-of-use' approach will be kept in the new standard itself.

To address some concerns expressed in the comment letters, the Boards tentatively decided that for short-term leases (leases that have a maximum possible lease term of less than 12 months) a lessee need not recognise lease assets or lease liabilities. For those leases, the lessee should recognise lease payments in profit or loss on a straight-line basis over the lease term, unless another systematic and rational basis is more representative of the time pattern in which use is derived from the underlying asset. The Boards also tentatively decided that a lessee may elect to apply the recognition and measurement requirements in the leases guidance to short-term leases (FASB, 2011).

We note that one of the main objectives of developing the proposed 'right-of-use' approach was to eliminate the operating lease accounting treatment and thus the off-balance sheet financing, accompanied with only limited disclosure in the notes to financial statements, which complicates external evaluation of the effective amounts of the off-balance sheet obligations. However, the same accounting effect could be achieved if the contact is structured as a service arrangement rather than a (finance) lease. Therefore, we agree with EFRAG[34] that applying the 'right-of-use' approach to all leases will make the distinction between leases and service arrangements even more important than it is currently the case. We also agree that it would be particularly unfortunate if the result of the new lease accounting standard was simply to replace one difficult border, i.e., the one between operating and finance leases, with another, i.e., the one between service arrangements and leases. It will therefore be important to make sure there is a clear, principle-based boundary between the two.

It also should be noted that despite the fact that standards setters prioritise financial recognition over disclosure, the academic value relevance empirical research does not give a clear answer about the superiority of recognition over disclosure in the financial statements.

---

34 EFRAG (The European Financial Reporting Advisory Group) was set up in 2001 to assist the European Commission in the endorsement of International Financial Reporting Standards (IFRS), as issued by the International Accounting Standards Board (IASB) by providing advice on the technical quality of IFRS.

Given the complexity of the subject matter and the inter-relationships between the leases project and some of the Boards' other ongoing projects, the Boards should take, in our opinion, all necessary time to ensure that all lease accounting issues are thoroughly examined, including the lessor accounting part, which was deferred due to the time constraints. As already mentioned, this project is a joint Memorandum of Understanding project, which was supposed to be finished in the second quarter of 2011 with the issuance of the new standard. This deadline corresponded with the announced timing of the U.S. Securities and Exchange Commission's decision on whether the mandatory use of the IFRS by the U.S. issuers under the scrutiny of SEC would benefit investors and would be in the public interest. Despite various important time imperatives, we believe the quality of the final standard should not be compromised and thus the decisions, which will affect so many entities which are currently lessees or/and lessors, should not be rushed. This is especially significant since the fundamental changes in the lease accounting standards are not made very often; for example, the SFAS 13 was issued in 1976 and the IAS 17 in 1997. Therefore we support the announced postponement of the publication of the new standard to the first half of 2012.

## References

Ahmed, A. S., Kilic, E., Lobo, G. J. (2006): Does recognition versus disclosure matter? Evidence from value-relevance of banks' recognised and disclosed derivative financial instruments, *The Accounting Review*, Vol. 81, No. 3, pp. 567–588.

Altamuro, J. (2006): *The economic, financial accounting and governance determinants of synthetic lease financing*. Working Paper (December), Massachusetts Institute of Technology.

APB - Accounting Principles Board (1970): *Statement of the Accounting Principles Board No. 4 Basic Concepts and Accounting Principles Underlying Financial Statements of Business Enterprises*, American Institute of Certified Public Accountants, New York.

Alchian, A. (1984): Specificity, specialization, and coalitions, *Journal of Institutional and Theoretical Economics*, No. 140, pp. 34–49.

Alexander, D., Jermakowicz, E. (2006): A true and fair view of the principles/rules debate, *Abacus*, Vol. 42, No. 2, pp. 132–164.

Alexander, D., Nobes, C. (2001): *Financial accounting – an international introduction*, Pearson Education Limited, Harlow.

Ball, R. (1995): Making accounting more international: why, how, and how far will it go?, *Journal of Applied Corporate Finance*, Vol. 8, Fall, pp. 19–29.

Ball, R. (2001): *Infrastructure requirements for an economically efficient system of public financial reporting and disclosure*, Brookings-Wharton papers on Financial Services, 2001, pp. 127–169.

Ball, R. (2006): International Financial Reporting Standards (IFRS): pros and cons for investors, *Accounting and Business Research*, International Accounting Policy Forum, pp. 5–27.

Barth, M. E., Beaver, W., Landsman, W. R. (2001): The Relevance of the value relevance literature for financial accounting standard-setting: another view, *Journal of Accounting and Economics*, Vol. 31, No. 1–3, pp. 77–104.

Barth, M. E., Clinch, G., and Shibano, T. (2003): Market effects of recognition and disclosure, *Journal of Accounting Research*, No. 41, pp. 581–609.

Beresford, D. R. (1996): What did we learn from the stock compensation project? *Accounting Horizons*, Vol. 10, No. 1, pp. 125–130.

Bernard, V., Schipper, C. (1994): *Recognition and disclosure in financial reporting*. Working paper (November), University of Michigan and University of Chicago.

Bromwich, R. (2004): *Aspects of the future in accounting: the use of market prices and 'fair values' in financial reports*. The Economics and Politics of Accounting, pp. 103–143, C. Leuz, D. Pfaff and A. Hopwood, (Editors), Oxford University Press, Oxford.

Coase, R. H. (1937): The nature of the firm, *Economica*, Vol. 4, November, pp. 386–405.

Davis-Friday, P. Y., Folani, L. B., Liu, C. S. and Mittelstaedt, H. F. (1999). The value relevance of financial statement recognition vs. disclosure: evidence from SFAS No. 106, *The Accounting Review*, No. 74 (October), pp. 403–423.

Delvaille, P., Ebbers, G., Saccon, C. (2005): International financial reporting convergence: evidence from three Continental European countries, *Accounting in Europe*, Vol. 2, pp. 137–164.

Demski, J. S., Fellingham, J.C., Iljiri, Y. and Sunder, S. (2002): Some thoughts on the intellectual foundations of accounting, *Accounting Horizons*, Vol. 16, No. 2, pp. 157–168.

EFRAG (2009): EFRAG's comment letter on the DP Leases. http://www.efrag.org/projects/detail.asp?id=108 (Accessed 18 March 2010).

El-Gazzar, S., Lilien, S., Pastena, V. (1986): Accounting for leases by lessees. *Journal of Accounting and Economics,* October, pp. 217–237.

Ely, K. (1995): Operating lease accounting and the market's assessment of equity risk. *Journal of Accounting Research*, Autumn, pp. 397–415.

FASB - Financial Accounting Standards Board (1978): *Statement of Financial Accounting Concepts No. 1 (SFAC 1) Objectives of Financial Reporting by Business Enterprises*, FASB, Stamford.

FASB - Financial Accounting Standards Board (1980): *Statement of Financial Accounting Concepts No. 2 (SFAC 2) Qualitative Characteristics of Accounting Information*, FASB, Stamford.

FASB - Financial Accounting Standards Board (1984): *Statements of Financial Reporting Concepts No. 5 (SFAC 5) Recognition and Measurement in Financial Statements of Business Enterprises,* FASB, Stamford

FASB - Financial Accounting Standards Board (1985): *Statement of Financial Accounting Concepts No. 6 (SFAC 6) Elements of Financial Statements*, FASB, Stamford.

FASB - Financial Accounting Standards Board (1976): *Statement of Financial Accounting Standard No. 13 Accounting for Leases*, FASB, Stamford (used the version of the standard as of 2008).

FASB - Financial Accounting Standards Board (2011): Leases – project update as of 23 June 2011. http://www.fasb.org/cs/ContentServer?c=FASBContent_C&pagename=FASB%2FFASBContent_C%2FProjectUpdatePage&cid=900000011123 (Accessed 12 July 2011).

Ge, W., Imhoff, G., Lee, F. L. (2008): *Investment decisions and off-balance sheet leases: Do we really need further rule change?* Working Paper (September), University of Michigan.

Higson, A. (2003): *Corporate financial reporting – theory & practice*, SAGE Publications, London.

Hirshleifer, D., Teoh, S. H. (2003): Limited attention, information disclosure, and financial reporting, *Journal of Accounting and Economics*, No. 36, pp. 337–386.

IASB - International Accounting Standards Board (2009): Discussion Paper Leases: Preliminary Views. http://www.iasb.org/Current+Projects/IASB+Projects/Leases/Discussion+Paper+and+Comment+Letters/Discussion+Paper+and+Comment+Letters.htm (Accessed 10 March 2010).

IASB - International Accounting Standards Board (2009): *IFRS for SMEs*, International Accounting Standards Committee Foundation (IASC), London.

IASB - International Accounting Standards Board (2009): Leases: comment letter summary. Agenda paper 6A for the September 2009 joint IASB-FASB meeting. http://www.iasb.org/Current+Projects/IASB+Projects/Leases/Meeting+Summaries+and+Observer+Notes/IASB+September+2009.htm (Accessed 14 July 2010).

IASB - International Accounting Standards Board (2009): Leases: lessee accounting – leases with option. Agenda paper 5D for the November 2009 joint IASB-FASB meeting. http://www.ifrs.org/Current+Projects/IASB+Projects/Leases/Meeting+Summaries+and+Observer+Notes/IASB+November+2009.htm (Accessed 14 July 2010).

IASB - International Accounting Standards Board (2010): *Convergence between IFRSs and US GAAP.* http://www.iasb.org/Use+around+the+world/Global+convergence/Convergence+with+US+GAAP/Convergence +with+US+GAAP.htm (Accessed 12 July 2010).

IASB - International Accounting Standards Board (2010): *IFRS 2010*, International Accounting Standards Committee Foundation (IASC), London.

IASB - International Accounting Standards Board (2010): Exposure Draft Leases. http://www.ifrs.org/Current+Projects/IASB+Projects/Leases/ed10/Ed.htm (Accessed 17 August 2010).

IASB - International Accounting Standards Board (2011): Leases: comment letter summary – main issues. Agenda paper 5A for the January 2011 joint IASB-FASB meeting. http://www.ifrs.org/Current+Projects/IASB+Projects/Leases/Meeting+Summaries+and+Observer+Notes/IASB+January+2011.htm (Accessed 12 July 2011).

IASCF - International Accounting Standards Committee Foundation (2008): *Due process handbook for the IASB.* http://www.iasb.org/How+we+develop+standards/How+we+develop+standards.htm [Accessed 8 March 2010].

Imhoff, E. A., Lipe, R. C., Wright, D. W. (1993): The effects of recognition versus disclosure on shareholder risk and executive compensation, *Journal of Accounting Auditing & Finance*, Vol. 8, No. 4, pp. 335–368.

Imhoff, E. A., Thomas J. K. (1988): Economic consequences of accounting standards: the lease disclosure rule change, *Journal of Accounting and Economics*, No. 10, pp. 277–310.

Jifri, K. A., Citron, D. (2009): The value relevance of financial statement recognition versus note disclosure: evidence from goodwill accounting, *European Accounting Review*, Vol. 18, No. 1, pp. 123–140.

Lambert, R. A. (2003): Discussion of 'limited attention, information disclosure, and financial reporting', *Journal of Accounting and Economics*, No. 36, pp. 337–386.

Leaseurope, KPMG (2007): *European leasing*, Leaseurope, Brussels.

Lim, S. C, Mann, S. C., Mihov, V. T. (2003): *Market evaluation of off-balance sheet financing: you can run but you can't hide*. Working Paper (December), Texas Christian University.

Lindsey, B. P. (2006): *A Value Relevance Examination of Current Leasing Standard*, Dissertation paper, University of North Carolina.

Lipe, R. (2001): Lease accounting research and the G4+1 proposal, *Accounting Horizons*, Vol. 15, No. 3, pp. 299–310.

McKernan, J. F., (2007): Objectivity in accounting, Accounting, *Organisations and Society*, Vol. 32, No.2, pp. 155–180.

Monson, D. (2001): The conceptual framework and accounting for leases, *Accounting Horizons*, Vol. 32, No. 3, pp. 275–287.

Nailor, H., Lennard, A, (2000): *Leases: Implementation of a New Approach*, Accounting Standards Board (ASB), London.

Nobes, C. W. (1998): Towards a general model of the reasons for international differences in financial reporting, *Abacus*, Vol. 34, No. 2, pp. 162–187.

Nobes, C. W. (2003): On the myth of 'Anglo-Saxon' financial accounting: a comment, *The International Journal of Accounting*, Vol. 38, No. 1, pp. 539–557.

Raiborn, C. A., Watson, S. F. (2003): *Core Concepts of Accounting*, John Wiley & Sons, Inc, Hoboken.

Riahi-Belkaoui, A. (2004): *Accounting Theory*, Thomson Learning, London.

Ryan, S. G., Herz, R. H., Iannaconi, T. E., Maines, L. A., Palepu, K. G., Schipper, K., Schrand, C. M., Skinner, D. J, Vincent, L. (2001): Evaluation of the lease accounting proposed in the G4+1 special report, *Accounting Horizons*, Vol. 32, No. 3, pp. 289–298.

Sellhorn, T., Gornik-Tomaszewski, S. (2006): Implication of the 'IAS regulation' for research into the international differences in accounting systems, *Accounting in Europe*, Vol. 3, pp. 187–217.

Sakai, E. (2010*): Comparison of the Value Relevance between the Purchase and Rental Treatment of Leases*. Working Paper (February 3), Musashi University.

Schipper, C. (2007): Required disclosures in financial reports, *The Accounting Review*, Vol. 82, No. 2, pp. 301–326.

SEC - U.S. Securities and Exchange Commission (2005): *Report and recommendations pursuant to Section 401(c) of the Sarbanes-Oxley Act of 2002 on arrangements with off balance sheet implications, special purpose entities, and transparency of filings by issuers*, June 15, SEC, Washington, D.C.

SEC - U.S. Securities and Exchange Commission (2008): *Final Report of the Advisory Committee on Improvements to Financial Reporting to the United States Securities and Exchange Commission* (Pozen Committee Report), August 1, SEC, Washington, D.C.

SEC - U.S. Securities and Exchange Commission (2008): *Roadmap for the potential use of financial statements prepared in accordance with International Financial Reporting Standards by U.S. issuers*, Proposed rule, Release No. 33-8982, November 14, SEC, Washington, D.C.

Solomons, D. (1986): The FASB's conceptual framework: an evaluation, *Journal of Accountancy*, June, pp. 114–124.

U.S. Census Bureau (2010) The 2010 statistical abstract. http://www.census.gov/compendia/statab/cats/banking_finance_insurance/_real-estate_rental_and_leasing.html (Accessed 18 July 2010).

Van Hulle, K. (2004): *From Accounting Directives to International Accounting Standards. The Economics and Politics of Accounting*, pp. 350–375, C. Leuz, D. Pfaff and A. Hopwood, (Editors), Oxford University Press, Oxford.

Wüstermann, J., Wüstermann, S. (2010): Why consistency of accounting standards matters: a contribution to the rules-versus-principles debate in financial reporting, *Abacus*, Vol. 46, No. 1, pp. 1–27.

## About the Author

**Aleš Novak** is an assistant professor of Accounting and Business Economics at the Faculty of Organizational Sciences, University of Maribor. He studied Economics at the University of Maribor and Accounting at the University of Maribor and the University in Ljubljana, both in Slovenia. In 2008/2009, he was employed at the European Financial Reporting Advisory Group (EFRAG) in Brussels (Belgium). His fields of research are Financial Reporting, Controlling and Pensions.

## Appendix 1 – Numerical Example of the Differences between Operating Lease-Lessee Accounting and Lessee Accounting under the Proposed 'Right-of-Use' Approach

A machine is leased for a fixed term of three years; the expected life of the machine is 10 years. The lease is non-cancellable, and there are no rights to extend the lease term or to purchase the machine at the end of the term and no guarantees of its value at that point. Lease payments are due at regular intervals at the end of the year over the lease term after the machine has been delivered, in the amount of 10,000 EUR. These are fixed amounts that are specified in the original agreement. No maintenance or other arrangements are entered into.

### Existing operating lease accounting by lessees

| Balance sheet | Initial | Year 1 | Year 2 | Year 3 |
|---|---|---|---|---|
| Equipment | 0 | 0 | 0 | 0 |
| Lease obligation | 0 | 0 | 0 | 0 |
| | | | | |
| **Income statement** | | | | |
| Rent expense | - | 10,000 | 10,000 | 10,000 |
| Depreciation/ amortisation | - | 0 | 0 | 0 |
| Interest expense | - | 0 | 0 | 0 |
| Total lease expenses | - | 10,000 | 10,000 | 10,000 |

### Lease accounting by lessees under the proposed right-of-use approach

| Balance sheet | Initial | Year 1 | Year 2 | Year 3 |
|---|---|---|---|---|
| Right-of-use asset | 25,770.97* | 17,180.65 | 8,590.33 | 0 |
| Lease obligation | 25,770.97* | 17,832.65 | 9,259.26 | 0 |
| | | | | |
| **Income statement** | | | | |
| Rent expense | - | 0 | 0 | 0 |
| Amortisation | - | 8,590.32 | 8,590.32 | 8,590.32 |
| Interest expense | - | 2,061.68 | 1,426.61 | 740.74 |
| Total lease expenses | | 10,652.00 | 10,016.93 | 9,331.06 |

*Assumptions: incremental borrowing rate of 8%, straight-line amortisation.*
**25,770.97 = present value of the 3-year ordinary annuity of 10,000.*

## Appendix 2 – Comparison of the Lessee Accounting Requirements under IAS 17, Discussion Paper (DP) *Leases: Preliminary Views* and Exposure Draft (ED) *Leases*

| Lease accounting for lessees | | | |
|---|---|---|---|
| **Issue** | **Existing IAS 17 for finance leases** | **Proposals in the DP** | **Proposals in the ED** |
| Timing of initial recognition | Initial recognition occurs at the date of commencement of the lease. | The DP stated that before the commencement date the lessee may obtain rights and the Board should consider the issue. | Assets and liabilities arise when a contract is signed. Between contract signing and delivery, the unit of account is the contract as a whole, and the contract position would be presented net. |
| Assets and liabilities recognised | The lessee recognises the leased asset and a finance lease liability. | The lessee recognises a right of use of the underlying asset and a finance lease liability for all agreements in scope. | The lessee recognises a right of use of the underlying asset and a finance lease liability for all agreements in scope. |
| Initial measurement of assets | At the lower of the fair value of the leased asset and the minimum lease payments determined at inception. | At cost, being the present value of the lease payments. | At cost, where cost is the present value of the lease payments plus any initial direct costs incurred by the lessee. |
| Initial measurement of liabilities | At the same amount as the leased asset. | At the present value of the lease payments. | At the present value of the lease payments. |
| Initial measurement – discount rate | The implicit rate in the lease or (if not determinable) the lessee's incremental borrowing rate. | The discount rate is the lessee's incremental borrowing rate. | The discount rate is lessee's incremental borrowing rate (the rate implicit in lease will often be equal). |
| Options to extend / terminate the lease | An option to extend impacts the determination of the lease term to the extent that it is reasonably certain to be exercised at inception date. | The measurement of the liability should be based on the most likely lease term. | The measurement of the liability should be based on the longest lease term that is more likely than not to occur. |

| | | | |
|---|---|---|---|
| Purchase options | A bargain purchase option impacts the classification of the lease and the determination of the minimum lease payments. | The measurement of the liability should include purchase options when they are likely to be exercised. | Both lessees and lessors should account for purchase options only when they are exercised. |
| Contingent rentals | Contingent rentals should not be included in the minimum lease payments and are charged as expenses when incurred. | The liability should include contingent rentals and residual value guarantees based on the weighted average outcome. | The liability should include contingent rentals and residual value guarantees based on the weighted average outcome. |
| Residual value guarantees | Residual value guarantees should be included in the minimum lease payments when they are extended by the lessee or its related parties. | | |
| Subsequent measurement of assets | Cost less cumulative depreciation and impairment. | Cost less cumulative depreciation and impairment. | Cost less cumulative depreciation and impairment. IFRS preparers would be permitted to revalue their right-of-use assets using the less restrictive version of the revaluation model in IAS 38, *Intangible Assets.* U.S. GAAP preparers would not be permitted to revalue their right-of-use assets unless required to do so to recognise an impairment loss. |
| Subsequent measurement of liabilities | Lease payments should be apportioned between finance charges and repayment of the liability to obtain a constant return. | Amortised cost. | Amortised cost. |

| | | | |
|---|---|---|---|
| Subsequent measurement – discount rate | The initial discount rate is not remeasured. | The obligation to pay rentals should be remeasured for changes in the lessee's incremental borrowing rate. | The obligation to pay rentals would not be revised for any changes in the lessee's incremental borrowing rate |
| Subsequent measurement – options to extend | Reassessment of contingent and optional payments cannot trigger a change in classification of the lease. Existing IAS 17 does not require remeasurement unless the lease terms are changed. | Entities should reassess the most likely lease term and contingent payments on the basis of new facts and circumstances.<br><br>Changes in the obligations arising from a reassessment of options, contingent rentals and residual value guarantees adjust the right-of-use (FASB's position on changes in the measurement of lease obligation due to changes in an estimated contingency - recognition in profit and loss). | Entities should reassess the longest lease term that is more likely than not to occur and contingent payments on the basis of new facts and circumstances.<br><br>Detailed examination of every lease would not be required unless there is a change in facts or circumstances that indicate that the lease term may need to be revised.<br><br>Changes in the obligations arising from a reassessment of options and residual value guarantees should be accounted for as an adjustment to the right-of-use asset. Changes in amounts payable under contingent rental arrangements arising from current or prior periods should be recognised by the lessees in profit or loss. All other changes should be recognised as an adjustment to the lessee's right-of-use asset. |
| Subsequent measurement – purchase options | | | |
| Subsequent measurement – contingent rentals | | | |
| Subsequent measurement – residual value guarantees | | | |

# Multi-Attribute Decision Model for Evaluating ERP Project Implementations Success by Using the Global Efficiency Factors Approach

***Ksenča Bokovec***

*ksenca.bokovec@sapphir.si*

***Talib Damij***

*talib.damij@ef.uni-lj.si*

***Uroš Rajkovič***

*uros.rajkovic@fov.uni-mb.si*

## Abstract

The implementation of ERP systems in global corporations is a highly complex activity, in which companies are experiencing many project failures: projects are greatly exceeding their time and budget frameworks and/or are not rendering the expected results. Therefore, it is important to understand critical success factors that companies should take into account in any ERP project. This chapter presents the 'global efficiency factors approach', which can be viewed as an upgrade of critical success factors for application in a global context. This ensures efficient and productive roll-out implementations in all subsequent companies of the group. Global efficiency factors allow us to manage the complexity of the ERP implementation projects more efficiently and more effectively. An evaluation of ERP implementation based on global efficiency factors is explained step-by-step with an example of five case studies (companies) of an international corporation implementing a compatible ERP solution, which relies on a global concept of the whole ERP system.

**Keywords**: ERP system implementation, global efficiency factors, critical success

# 1. Introduction

Enterprise resource planning (ERP) systems are powerful software packages that support and integrate a variety of business processes and disparate business functions. They also form the foundation for many e-commerce-based processes, thus integrating global business environments and inter-organisation communication and collaboration. As best practice models, they support different industry branches (these are so-called ERP industry solutions). The ERP implementation projects also serve companies in carrying out partial or complete business process re-engineering and/or process optimisation. This is due to the fact that ERP systems incorporate best-practice solutions, which companies prefer to adopt to be able to use the standardised features of such systems. ERP implementations in multi-site or global environments are especially complex and require a global approach to business process and the standardisation and unification of organisational structures. Thus, there is a need for a carefully designed methodology for the implementation of ERP systems in global environments, which takes into account the requirements of the corporation and aligns them with the features and structure of the ERP system. The methodology presented in this paper was developed for global ERP implementations based on simultaneous business process re-engineering (Moon, 2007).

The implementation of an integrated ERP system in an international multi-site environment is a highly complex activity. Since ERP systems are a developing field of research, the objective is to provide a global ERP implementation methodology in the field of multi-site ERP implementation projects. Due to the vast evidence that the overwhelming majority of ERP implementations exceed their budget and time allocations or face severe difficulties (Krasner, 2000; Calisir, 2004; Zhang et al., 2005), thus affecting the company's market value (Bharadwaj et al., 2009), researchers began to analyze ERP implementations in case studies in order to provide an implementation framework that maximises their efficiencies (Parr et al., 2000). Several authors addressed these issues by defining critical success factors (CSFs) which influence ERP implementation projects. In the literature, CSF models apply to project management problems (Slevin et al., 1987; Holland et al., 1999; Davidenkoff et al., 2008; Dezdar et al., 2009), manufacturing system implementation (Lockett et al., 1991), as well as process re-engineering (Bashein et al., 1994; Grover et al., 1998; Urh et al., 2008). Some authors also address global and local views of the ERP implementations in multinational companies with an emphasis on requirements definition (Kirsch et al., 2006; Pozzebon et al., 2005). However, global efficiency factors (GEFs) have been proven to best form the basis for global implementation methodology. The methodology based on these factors and supported by a multi-attribute decision support system would help us leverage the ERP maturity curve throughout the implementation project life cycle.

The implementation methodology based on GEFs and the multi-attribute decision support system can be used as a methodological approach for implementing multi-site ERP systems. It focuses primarily on the organisational and functional aspects of the ERP systems, and not as much on the standard project management CSFs, as addressed by other authors. Brown et al. (2003) define the systems project success as an up-and-running system with agreed upon requirements delivered within schedule and budget. The major benefits of this methodology are the reduction of project complexity, the simplification of roll-out and step-by-step projects, the avoidance of conceptual mistakes with regard to time and achievement of better results, thus, keeping projects on time and within budgets.

## 2. The use of Global Efficiency Factors for Managing ERP Implementation Projects

Case studies in the following study are based on five anonymous companies of a multi-national corporation, which implemented SAP ERP in the retail business. Based on the project life cycle phases, among them (I) project planning, (II) project concept definition, (III) design and development, (IV) implementation and realisation, (V) going live and close-out, we defined the global efficiency factors, which in our professional experience support system implementation from the functional and organisational perspective rather than the project management perspective. This means that the focus was on the contextual definition of the basic ERP elements: organisational structures, master data and process definition from the logical point of view. The role of GEFs is primarily the development of the content of the system. Therefore, the GEFs should be distinguished from the CSFs, which in turn contribute more to the management of the project. Figure 1 shows how selected GEFs correspond to project phases. The following five GEFs were applied:

- Business process re-engineering based on ERP system requirements,
- Legacy systems,
- System configuration,
- Alignment with the corporate level,
- Project synergy.

*Figure 1: GEFs through project phases*

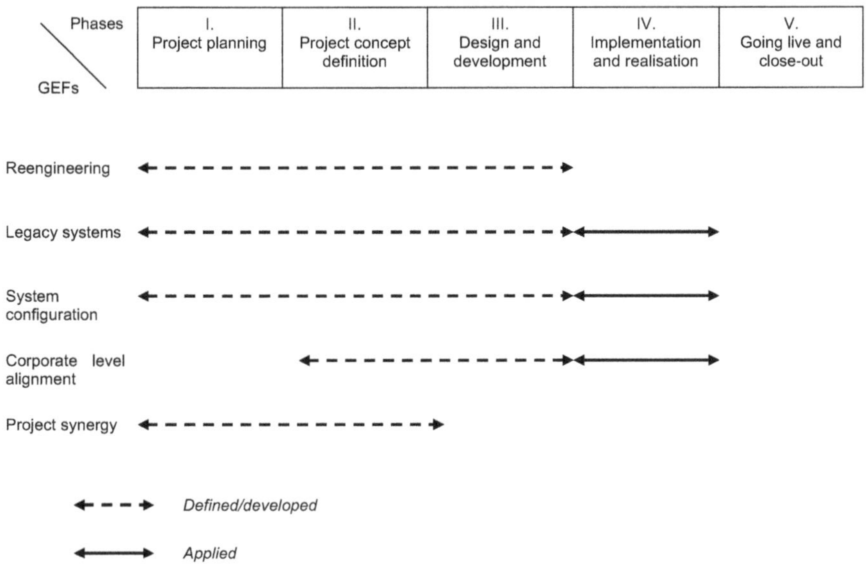


The implementation of a new ERP system is an opportunity to take a closer look at the company's processes and adjust them to fit the best-practice processes and requirements of the ERP system. Business process re-engineering based on business requirements requires a clear definition of business needs, processes that would cover these requirements, and potential gaps. Business requirements are therefore transformed into business processes, which in turn will be carried out by means of the ERP modules and functionalities (Bingi et al., 1999; Holland et al., 1999; Esteves-Sousa et al., 2000; Welti, 1999; Somers et al., 2001; Fui-Hoon Nah, et al., 2001; Brown et al., 2003). This GEF has to be fully developed through the first three project phases.

Legacy systems contain the processes, organisational structure, culture, and information technology of a company (Holland et al., 1999; Esteves-Sousa et al., 2000; Fui-Hoon Nah et al., 2001). Some authors (e.g., Holland et al., 1999) emphasise that they offer a clearer picture of the information system that will be implemented, as well as of potential problems. However, legacy systems influence the strategy of the ERP implementation. We represent legacy systems as a GEF in terms of the migration to the new system, which has a major impact on the conceptual design of the new system. This GEF has to be developed through the first three project phases and applied in the implementation and realisation phase.

System configuration was also defined as a critical success factor by certain authors (Holland et al., 1999; Esteves-Sousa et al., 2000). It represents the global implementation of the system content in terms of business processes and all their dependent elements, which were defined in the framework of the business process re-engineering based on the ERP system requirements. It encompasses not only customised but also non-standard solutions, testing, data transfer, reporting system and documentation. This GEF is important in the implementation and realisation phase.

The factor 'alignment with the corporate level' has not previously been recognised and given attention. It appears to be an important element in global ERP implementations. One of the most critical tasks when planning and implementing IT is the reconciliation of global business and IT strategies (Yip, 1992; Palvia, 1998; Jarvenpaa et al., 1992; Roche, 1992). When implementing ERP systems in different branches or sectors of the corporation, we usually reengineer and standardise the business processes that are mainly used in each branch. On a higher level, we also have to bring sector specific business processes and entities in line with the corporate guidelines, standards and structures in order to use common corporate-wide organisational structures and cross-branch processes. This GEF had to be defined in the second and third project phases after the basic business processes, organisational structures and IT infrastructure were defined. It proved to be very important for the alignment of the ERP implementations in different sectors of the corporation, since it ensured global information conformity and efficient enterprise performance management throughout the corporation.

Project synergy is another factor that has not yet found its way into the existing literature. However, when implementing ERP systems in global corporations, we have to take into account two different lines of parallel projects in the corporation: (1) ERP projects in other sectors of the corporation and (2) other non-ERP projects with potential influence on the respective ERP project. The impact of parallel projects can be attributed to time priorities and content definition. Therefore, this GEF should be analyzed in the project planning and project definition phases.

In the following section, we present on the example of the five case studies on how the GEFs can be used in the multi-attribute decision support system with the intention of determining the state of the art of all five case study projects.

## 2.1 A Multi-Attribute Decision Model for Evaluating ERP Projects

Retail companies of a large international corporation with diversified industry sectors were implementing SAP ERP to support their back office, logistics and administration functions as well as POS interfacing in different countries of the world. We used the model for the evaluation of ERP implementation projects in five retail companies (RTC), on which we based our case studies. They were carried out in five anonymous retail companies of a US-based corporation with different business divisions in almost 200 countries around the world. The RTC companies are based in all the countries where the corporation has its subsidiaries. They are managed regionally. Retail is only one of its business segments in addition to different kinds of manufacturing and trade. Since the ERP implementation project was ongoing in the retail sector, this was the focus of our research.

The criteria representing the GEFs were organised into a tree structure, and assigned attributes. We included the following criteria in the decision tree:

GEF re-engineering:

- Enterprise model: This model includes the organisational structure, the master data model and other entities, such as units of measures and currencies. The enterprise model is represented twice in the decision tree: (1) as the model of the corporate branch, where the ERP system is being implemented, and (2) in terms of its alignment with the corporate-wide standards and regulations.
- Business processes: These are cross-functional processes, like purchase-to-pay, sales-to-cash, plan-to-stock etc., which form part of the business process re-engineering based on the ERP system requirements and best practice. Business processes are shown twice in the decision tree: (1) as business processes of the corporate branch, where the ERP system is being implemented, and (2) in terms of their alignment with the corporate-wide standards and regulations as well as common application of the cross-branch global processes.
- Gaps: These are business requirements that cannot be implemented in the standard ERP system. Additional development or external applications have to be used in order to compensate for the missing functionality.

GEF corporate level alignment:

- Enterprise model: A model as defined according to the industry and aligned with the corporate standards, encompassing organisational structures, attributes of central data, currencies etc., as it enables joint reporting.
- Business processes: business processes in their entirety or in part, most of all those not specified in the industry, are aligned for all the companies within the

system. Definition of the business processes can be adopted from the corporate level.

- Infrastructure: This criterion represents business requirements in terms of re-engineering and standardisation of the computer and peripheral systems as well as networks and their maintenance. It is shown twice in the decision tree: (1) in terms of the infrastructure alignment with corporate standards and (2) in terms of migration from the legacy systems (unification and modernisation of the IT infrastructure).

GEF legacy systems:

- Migration strategy: This includes the strategy used to migrate to the new system (e.g., big bang, step-by-step migration, roll-out projects etc.), delimitation of functions in the legacy and the new systems as well as migration scenarios which support the desired type of migration strategy.
- Infrastructure: Strategies and scenarios for a transfer to a new system are defined. If the infrastructure is unified and the transfer strategy is globally planned, then more unified steps and tools can be defined.

GEF system configuration:

- Development: This includes custom solutions, programmes and reports, which cover the gaps. They can be part of the ERP system (programmed in its original language) or external applications from third party suppliers, which have to be interfaced with the new system.
- Code changes: They represent the way in which the ERP system is being implemented. This can be a so-called vanilla approach, where we set up the business processes exclusively by customising (use of best-practice scenarios), where no code changes are allowed, or we allow a certain extent of code changes to align the system with the existing business processes in the company.
- Testing: This includes functional, integration and regression tests as well as quality assurance tests.
- Customisation: This includes setting up the parameters and coding user exits (these are parts in the standard code, where the users can incorporate their own programming logic to enhance standard functionalities).
- Version: The version of the ERP system represents the level of innovations that were updated in the system by the system provider. All companies sharing the same system should use the same version.
- Industrial solution: The providers of the ERP systems develop industrial solutions for different industries or business branches. They are based on the best-

practice processes used in a certain industry or branch. Companies from the same group can use one or several different industrial solutions.
- Modules: These are application areas with certain functionalities in the ERP system (e.g., Sales & Distribution, Finance, Materials Management etc.). Modules that are to be used in a certain implementation have to be selected according to the business processes used in the company.

GEF project synergy:
- Other ERP projects: These are ERP projects in other segments or branches of the corporation. In terms of timing, they can be more or less aligned with the current ERP project.
- Other projects: These are non-ERP projects that are not directly linked to the current ERP project. Nevertheless, they can have direct impact on the implementation of the current ERP project (e.g., in case they influence the content of the business processes).

## 2.2 Structuring Criteria in the Decision Support Tree

Based on the criteria that we extracted from the GEFs, we developed a decision-support tree (see Figure 2). The GEFs are shown on the intermediate levels and are decomposed into individual elements, i.e., criteria that are important for the evaluation and represent the branches of the tree. Attributes were assigned to each of the leaves. The attributes are connected by utility functions that evaluate each criterion with respect to their immediate descendants in the hierarchy. They can be represented by numbers or words. In this case, words were used to describe soft, fuzzy criteria, which we evaluated by means of qualitative methods. A multi-attribute decision support model using the DEXi software was developed (Bohanec, 2009).

The role of a utility function is to define a mapping from the lower level attributes' values to a higher level aggregate attribute value. In DEXi, the utility function of every aggregate attribute is precisely presented as a table defined by an expert group, in which rows can be read as logical expressions. For example, in Figure 2 in the second table, row number 4 can be read as: if the value of the re-engineering attribute is between 'acceptable' and 'good' and corporate-wide has the value 'acceptable', the aggregated attribute re-engineering-corporate-wide is estimated as 'acceptable'.

Certain exclusion criteria are included in the model. Every evaluation case in the model has to have the same version and the same industry solution of the ERP system as well as the same set of modules selected. These are the prerequisites that allow for a common, global concept of the ERP system and underlying IT infrastructure.

*Figure 2: Criteria attributes*

**DEXi**
**Criteria attributes**

| Criteria | Attributes |
|---|---|
| **Project grade** | unacceptable; **acceptable; good;** excellent |
| **Reengineering-corporate wide** | unacceptable; **acceptable; good;** excellent |
| **Reengineering** | unacceptable; **acceptable; good;** excellent |
| Enterprise model-reengineering | local; **partially global;** global |
| Business processes-reengineering | local; **partially global;** global |
| Gaps-reengineering | local; **partially global;** global |
| **Corporate wide** | unacceptable; **acceptable; good;** excellent |
| Enterprise model-corporate wide | non-aligned; partially aligned; aligned |
| Business processes-corporate wide | non-aligned; partially aligned; aligned |
| Infrastructure-corporate wide | non-aligned; partially aligned; aligned |
| **LCP** | unacceptable; **acceptable; good;** excellent |
| **Legacy systems** | non-unified; **partially unified;** unified |
| Migration strategy | local; **partially global;** global |
| Infrastructure-legacy systems | local; **partially global;** global |
| **Configuration** | unacceptable; **less acceptable; acceptable;** good |
| **Work** | unacceptable; **less acceptable; acceptable;** good |
| Development | local; **partially global;** global |
| Code changes | large; **medium; small;** null |
| Testing | local; **partially global;** global |
| Customizing | local; **partially global;** global |
| **Tecnical** | non-aligned; partially aligned; aligned |
| Version | different; **unique-old;** unique-new |
| Industrial solution | different-inconsistent; **different-consistent;** equal |
| Modules | very different; **less different;** equal |
| **Project synergy** | low; **medium;** high |
| Other ERP projects in the corporation | non-considered; **partially considered;** considered |
| Other non-ERP projects | non-considered; **partially considered;** considered |

Figure 3 represents an example of the utility functions, e.g., three levels of utility functions. The third level shows the weights of the criteria inside 're-engineering', where the business processes have by far the highest weight (62%) and the strongest influence on the overall result for the criterion 're-engineering'. On the next two levels above, we can see how the results of the lower level utility functions impact the criterion 're-engineering/corporate-wide', and this in turn the project grade.

The other two important criteria are the 'migration strategy' and the 'infrastructure', with which we want to ensure a conceptually unified migration and common IT infrastructure. A uniform IT infrastructure allows a unified migration strategy. There are two criteria that have less important weights than the others. These are 'other ERP projects in the corporation' and 'other non-ERP projects'. Both criteria nevertheless have to be evaluated in terms of their impact on the content and time priorities of the current ERP implementation. The global concept does not depend on these two criteria, but they should be taken into account in order to transfer the existing knowledge and incorporate any potential business process changes before the realisation phase or going live, if necessary.

Based on the above-described facts, we have defined utility functions, which give us an adequate answer to the subject of evaluation: 'Is the project on track in terms of time and costs and, if not, which corrective measures do we have to undertake to bring it back on track?'

*Figure 3: Utility functions*

DEXi

Utility functions

| | Reengineering-corporate wide | LCP | Project grade |
|---|---|---|---|
| | 50% | 50% | |
| 1 | unacceptable | * | unacceptable |
| 2 | * | unacceptable | unacceptable |
| 3 | acceptable | >=acceptable | acceptable |
| 4 | >=acceptable | acceptable | acceptable |
| 5 | excellent | excellent | excellent |

| | Reengineering | Corporate-wide | Reengineering-corporate-wide |
|---|---|---|---|
| | 55% | 45% | |
| 1 | unacceptable | * | unacceptable |
| 2 | * | unacceptable | unacceptable |
| 3 | acceptable | >=acceptable | acceptable |
| 4 | acceptable; good | acceptable | acceptable |
| 5 | excellent | acceptable; good | good |
| 6 | excellent | excellent | excellent |

| | Enterprise model-rengineering | Business processes-rengineering | Gaps-rengineering | Rengineering |
|---|---|---|---|---|
| | 33% | 62% | 5% | |
| 1 | local | <=partially global | * | unacceptable |
| 2 | * | local | * | unacceptable |
| 3 | <=partially global | global | * | acceptable |
| 4 | acceptable; good | >=partially global | * | acceptable |
| 5 | >=partially global | partially global | * | acceptable |
| 6 | global | global | <=partially global | good |
| 7 | global | global | global | excellent |

# 3. Application of the Decision Support Model

The RTC companies decided to implement a new ERP system that would efficiently support their key processes in the back office and stores as well as the management and administration by means of flexible financial and management accounting and reporting. The goal of the implementation was to reduce the stock in stores to a minimum and to ensure the right assortment, to tightly control cash and other payment media management, to improve management accounting practice, to increase profitability of the stores, to efficiently connect the POS system with the back office system, and to ensure automatic integration with the wholesale companies' ERP system as well as the corporate consolidated reporting system.

SAP was selected as the ERP system with the industrial solution 'Retail'. Wholesale companies had already implemented SAP but only as a standard package without any industry-specific solution. The project was based on a roll-out approach, in which a model is built in one company or at one location and is then rolled out to other companies/locations (Welti, 1999). In terms of selected functionality, the big bang approach was used, with all the modules being implemented at once (purchasing, sales, finance and controlling), including a pilot store. In this way, we used the roll-out approach on two levels: (1) as a roll-out of the ERP reference retail company template, designed on the basis of the GEFs, and (2) as a roll-out of the pilot store to other stores in each RTC company.

In RTC 1, the GEFs were not taken into account during design and implementation, since the implementation was based only on a local approach. Project RTC 2 was implemented in a similar way. In contrast, RTC 4, as well as RTC 3 and 5, were implemented on the basis of the GEFs model. Therefore, all the elements of GEFs were defined globally.

## 3.1 Evaluation and Analysis of the Implementation Projects

The projects were evaluated retroactively in order to test the evaluation model. The same method was used as for current projects. First, we reviewed all the project plans and project documentation by studying how the elements of the GEFs were defined in each project phase. We noted which elements were defined or designed according to the GEFs model, and which were defined locally. Figure 4 shows the evaluation of the variants by criteria.

- The evaluation of the variants was carried out based on:
- Analysis of project plans,
- Comparison of the variances of each project from the global template,
- Comparison of the settings in each project,
- Status of each 'live' system given by the users (the number and types of errors and problems),
- Review of the reporting procedures in the retail sector as well as in the corporate consolidated system,
- Requests by the process owners for business process changes,
- Time and costs of each implementation.

Figure 4 shows that the first two projects, RTC 1 and 2, which were defined and designed locally, received unacceptable grades; meanwhile, the other three projects were evaluated with positive grades. The comparison of variants shows that local projects are unacceptable from the point of view of global implementation. The evaluation gradually improved from project RTC 3 (acceptable) to project

RTC 5 (excellent) with each subsequent implementation. The reason is that the GEFs model was first used in the project RTC 3, where the global template was also initially defined and then refined in the due course of this project. The model was fully developed before starting the implementation in RTC 4. Therefore, the variants RTC 4 and 5 were evaluated with higher grades.

*Figure 4: Evaluation of the variants by criteria*

| Variants | RTC1 | RTC2 | RTC3 | RTC4 | RTC5 |
|---|---|---|---|---|---|
| Project grade | unacceptable | unacceptable | acceptable | good | excellent |
| Reengineering-corporate wide | unacceptable | acceptable | acceptable | excellent | excellent |
| Reengineering | unacceptable | acceptable | good | excellent | excellent |
| Enterprise model-reengineering | local | partially global | global | global | global |
| Business processes-reengineering | local | partially global | global | global | global |
| Gaps-reengineering | local | local | partially global | global | global |
| Corporate wide | unacceptable | acceptable | acceptable | excellent | excellent |
| Enterprise model-corporate wide | non-aligned | partially aligned | partially aligned | aligned | aligned |
| Business processes-corporate wide | non-aligned | partially aligned | partially aligned | aligned | aligned |
| Infrastructure-corporate wide | non-aligned | partially aligned | aligned | aligned | aligned |
| LCP | unacceptable | unacceptable | acceptable | good | excellent |
| Legacy systems | non-unified | non-unified | partially unified | unified | unified |
| Migration strategy | local | local | partially global | global | global |
| Infrastructure-legacy systems | local | partially global | global | global | global |
| Configuration | unacceptable | unacceptable | less acceptable | good | good |
| Work | unacceptable | unacceptable | acceptable | good | good |
| Development | local | local | partially global | global | global |
| Code changes | medium | small | null | null | null |
| Testing | local | local | partially global | global | global |
| Customizing | local | local | global | global | global |
| Tecnical | non-aligned | aligned | aligned | aligned | aligned |
| Version | different | unique-new | unique-new | unique-new | unique-new |
| Industrial solution | equal | equal | equal | equal | equal |
| Modules | equal | equal | equal | equal | equal |
| Project synergy | low | low | low | medium | high |
| Other ERP projects in the corporation | non-considered | non-considered | partially considered | partially considered | considered |
| Other non-ERP projects | non-considered | non-considered | non-considered | partially considered | considered |

Criteria with the highest weights are 're-engineering' and 'corporate-wide' as well as 'configuration'. 'Re-engineering' and 'corporate-wide' have to be globally defined during the first three project phases in order to be used efficiently in the realisation and implementation phase as the basis for configuration and system migration.

Configuration depends on the business process re-engineering, since we carry out configuration in the realisation and implementation phase. Business processes have to be re-engineered in the first three project phases, where the blueprint for the configuration is formed. In Figure 5, we can see that configuration became global with a slight delay in relation to the definition of the business processes, enterprise model and gaps definition. This is due to the fact that global configuration, which is the basis for all roll-out projects, is a relatively complex task. It can have a significant impact on the system integration within and across the enterprises configured in the same system. Global customising also requires global development and testing.

*Figure 5: Comparison of the criteria 'Business process re-engineering' and 'Configuration' in projects RTC 2, RTC 3, RTC 4 and RTC 5*

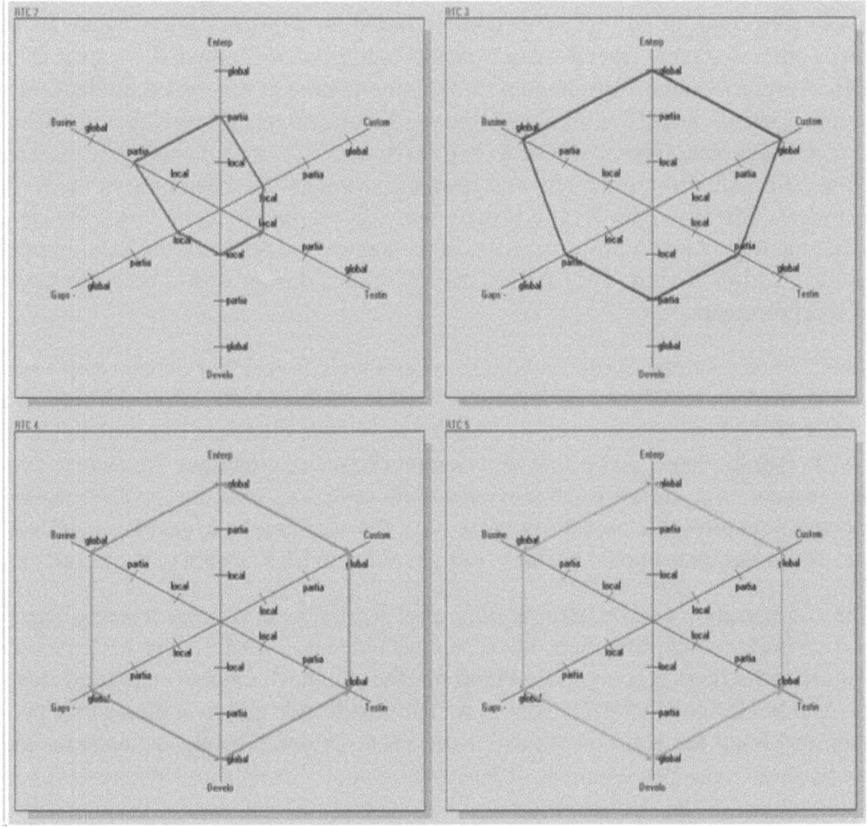

The project RTC 1 is not relevant in this comparison, since it was running on a different version of the ERP system (disqualifying criterion). Figure 5 clearly shows that only projects RTC 4 and 5 introduced entirely global configurations (copy of the RTC G template), which was in line with the global business process re-engineering.

The projects were evaluated as follows:
1. RTC 5: Excellent
2. RTC 4: Good
3. RTC 3: Acceptable
4. RTC 2: Unacceptable
5. RTC 1: Unacceptable

The projects RTC 1 and 2 were implemented without a real global project plan. These were two ad hoc implementations based on external factors (year 2000, euro conversion) that forced the companies to migrate to a new ERP system. The RTC 3 project can be considered a turning point, since it was based on the GEFs design. During the RTC 3 implementation, the project group developed the RTC G global template, which served as the basis for all future roll-out projects. The global template was completely designed and refined at the beginning of the RTC 4 project. Therefore, the RTC 3 project was still marked by certain deficiencies, while the RTC 4 and 5 projects received the highest grades in all the most important evaluation criteria. They reflect the real global design with a very low level of local elements.

Several interrelations of the evaluation criteria were revealed. Business processes in a branch can be aligned with corporate-wide standards only after unifying and standardising business processes within the respective branch in line with the ERP system requirements. To be able to reengineer business processes, we have to first design a common enterprise model with all the necessary elements such as organisational structures, the model of master data, the currencies and accounting model etc. These elements impact business processes in the ERP system to a great extent.

The configuration can be optimal only after the business process re-engineering and corporate-wide alignment have been established based on the ERP system requirements (best practice) in a blueprint document. The global migration strategy can be designed after the common IT infrastructure and its maintenance procedures for all the roll-out projects have been defined. Testing depends on the configuration and development. It has to be globally designed. This, however, is only possible if the configuration and development of the custom programs and interfaces have been globally defined. In every roll-out project, we have to simultaneously test global and local settings to trace potential interference among global and local elements.

# 4. Conclusion

A GEF model contributes to the development of an ERP evaluation model, which can be used in each project phase to evaluate the current progress of the project. Therefore, we can bring the project back on track in time without major additional costs.

Project or roll-out projects that were implemented according to the GEFs model demonstrated several benefits, which we divided into those of measurable and non-measurable natures. The measurable benefits proved to be:

- The reduction of the implementation time,
- The reduction of project costs due to shorter implementation time and fewer expert consultants needed for the roll-out projects (the most important role of the experts is in the global template design),
- The reduction of opportunity costs, which could be lowered by transferring the existing knowledge and solutions from other projects in the corporation.

However, there are even more non-measurable benefits:

- The possibility of implementing roll-out projects in parallel, which considerably reduces the whole implementation time span;
- The unification and alignment of business standards and strategies in all parts of the corporation, which ensures a standardised usage of the business processes, organisational structures and IT infrastructure;
- The knowledge exchange in the corporation, which brings the knowledge from the top of the corporation to its companies and vice versa, thus encapsulating the broadest view of the business;
- Direct controllability, consistency and reliability of data and information flows in the organisation,
- Benefits from the synergy of individual projects and project programs in the corporation,
- The usage of best practices by minimising custom development and code modifications,
- The project's complexity reduction, which ensures easier and more effective project management;
- Faster and better achievement of expected business improvements and benefits.

A model based on GEFs can be used for any kind of ERP implementation projects, independently of the project sise or implementation strategy. The GEFs model has been proven to encompass the most basic content elements of each ERP implementation. Therefore, it can be used as a generic model in any company or industry where an ERP system is being implemented. Such models can be extended from core ERP modules to broader solutions like CRM (Customer Relationship Management), SCM (Supplier Chain Management), SRM (Supplier Relationship Management), PLM (Product Lifecycle Management), and BI (Business Intelligence). These solutions bring together many companies from different corporations into one single business environment, thus enabling an efficient exchange of information and knowledge by linking together their ERP systems. This is, moreover, an opportunity for upgrading the GEFs model and consequently the evaluation model in order to develop a tool for managing the next wave of ERP projects efficiently and effectively.

## References

Bashein B. J., Markus L. M., Riley P. (1994): Preconditions for BPR Success: And How to Prevent Failures, *Information Systems Management* (11:2), Spring, pp. 7–13

Bharadwaj, A. Keil M., Maehring M. (2009): Effects of information technology failures on the market value of firms, *Journal of Strategic Information Systems* 18, pp. 66–79

Bingi P. Sharma M. K., Godla J. K. (1999): Critical Issues Affecting an ERP Implementation, *Information Systems Management*, Vol. 16, No. 3, Summer, pp. 7–14

Bohanec M. (2009): *DSS Resources*: http://www.ai.ijs.si/MarkoBohanec/dss.html, (Accessed on 11.12.2009)

Brown C. V., Vessey I. (2003): Managing the Next Wave of Enterprise Systems: Leveraging Lessons from ERP, *MIS Quarterly Executive*, Vol. 2, No. 1/ March, pp. 65–77

Calisir F. (2004): The relation of interface usability characteristics, perceived usefulness, and perceived ease of use to end-user satisfaction with enterprise resource planning (ERP) systems, *Computers in Human Behaviour* Vol. 20, pp. 505–515

Davidenkoff A., Werner D. (2008): *Global SAP Systems – Design and Architecture*, Boston Galileo Press Inc.

Esteves-Sousa J., Pastor-Collado J. (2000): *Towards the Unification of Critical Success Factors for ERP Implementations*, URL: http://www.lsi.upc.es/~jesteves/BIT/2000.htm, (Accessed 24 September, 2002).

Fui-Hoon Nah F., Lee-Shang Lau J., Kuang J. (2001): Critical Factors for Successful Implementation of Enterprise Systems, MCB University Press: *Business Process Management Journal*, Vol 7, No. 3, pp. 285–296

Grover V., Jeong Seung R., Teng J. T. (1998): Survey of Re-engineering Challenges, *Information Systems Management*. Spring, pp. 53–59

Holland C. P., Gibson N., Light B. (1999): *Enterprise Resource Planning: A Business Approach to Systems Development*, Proceedings of the 32nd Hawaii International Conference on Systems Sciences. Vol. VII, CD-ROM

Jarvenpaa S. L., Ives B. (1992): Organising for Global Competition: The Fit of Information Technology, *Decision Sciences*, Vol. 24, No. 3, pp. 547–573

Jereb E., Rajkovič U., Rajkovič V. (2005): A Hierarchical Multi-Attribute System Approach to Personnel Selection, *International Journal of Selection and Assessment*, Vol. 13, No. 3, pp. 198–205

Kirsch L. J., Haney M. H. (2006): Requirements determination for common systems: turning a global vision into a local reality, *Journal of Strategic Information Systems* 15, pp. 79–104

Krasner, H.(2000): Ensuring e-business success by learning from ERP failures, *IT Professional*, Vol. 2, Issue 1, Jan/Feb, pp. 22–27

Lockett A.G., Barrar P.R.N., Polding M.E. (1991): *MRPII Systems: Success Factors in the Process of Implementation*, In: Production Research: Approaching the 21st Century M. Pridham and C. O'Brien (eds.), Taylor and Francis

Moon, Y.B. (2007): Enterprise Resource Planning (ERP): A Review of the Literature, *International Journal of Management and Enterprise Development*, Vol. 4, No. 3, pp. 235–264

Palvia P. C. (1998): Research Issues in Global Information Technology Management, *Information Resources Management Journal*, Spring, Vol. 11, No. 2, pp. 27–36

Parr A. N., Shanks G. (2000): *A Taxonomy of ERP Implementation Approaches*, Proceedings of the 33rd Hawaii International Conference on System Sciences, pp. 1–10

Pozzebon M., Pinsonneault A. (2005): Global-local negotiations for implementing configurable packages: The power of initial organizational decisions, *Journal of Strategic Information Systems* 14, pp. 121–145

Roche E. M. (1992): *Managing Information Technology in Multinational Corporations*, Macmillan Publishing Company, New York, N.Y.

Slevin D. P., Pinto J. K. (1987): Balancing Strategy and Tactics in Project Implementation, *Sloan Management Review*, Fall, pp. 33-44

Somers T., Nelson K. (2001): *The Impact of Critical Success Factors across the Stages of Enterprise Resource Planning Implementations*, Proceedings of the 34th Hawaii International Conference on System Sciences, CD-ROM

Urh B., Kern T., Roblek M. (2008): *Business Process Modification Management*, In: Putnik G. (ed.) Encyclopaedia of Networked and Virtual Organizations. Hershey: Information Science Reference; pp. 112–120

Welti N. (1999): *Successful SAP R/3 Implementation: Practical Management of ERP Projects*, Addison-Wesley, Harlow, England

Yip G. S. (1992): *Total Global Strategy: Managing for Worldwide Competitive Advantage*, Prentice Hall, Englewood Cliffs, NJ

Zhang Z., Lee,M. K. O., Huang P., Zhang L., Huang X. (2005): A framework of ERP systems implementation success in China: an empirical study, *International Journal of Production Economics* Vol. 98, pp. 56–80.

## About the Authors

**Ksenča Bokovec** received her PhD in Information-Management Science from the Faculty of Economics at University of Ljubljana in 2009. She is currently employed as a CEO in Sapphir, a consulting company for IT and management consulting services. Her major field of operation and research interests include global ERP implementation methodologies and business process re-engineering in global corporations.

**Talib Damij** is a full professor of Management Information Systems at the Faculty of Economics, University of Ljubljana, Slovenia. Prof. Damij's research interests include information systems development methodologies, information systems project management, business process improvement and innovation.

**Uroš Rajkovič** acquired his PhD from the Faculty of Organizational Sciences, University of Maribor in 2010, where he is employed as an assistant professor. His main research field is information systems.

# Awareness of Existence and Use of Open Source Software in Slovene Micro-Enterprises

***Borut Werber***

*borut.werber@fov.uni-mb.si*

***Anja Žnidaršič***

*anja.znidarsic@fov.uni-mb.si*

## Abstract

This chapter presents the partial results of an investigation conducted in Slovenia between May and December 2009 in 134 Slovene micro-enterprises. We used a structured questionnaire with some demographic questions about the business computerisation, owner's characteristics and some questions about the level of awareness and use of available free software and open source software (OSS). We discovered that micro-enterprises do not know much about it and also do not use OSS as they could. We discovered that owners' formal education is in correlation with amount of OSS used. We also discovered that in the limited liability companies the amount of OSS used is higher than in companies owned by individual private entrepreneurs. The results in our study indicate that the availability of adequate training, courses and literature is one of the main weaknesses of OSS. Based on the survey results, we can conclude that OSS will not soon replace existing commercial software.

**Keywords**: small enterprises, micro-enterprises, open source software, free software, information system, information technology

# 1. Introduction

Why we are interested in micro-enterprises? In Slovenia, there were 105,272 enterprises registered in sections of activities C-K of the Standard Classification of Activities (NACE) in 2007; 92.8% of them were micro-enterprises, 5.7% were small enterprises and 1.5% were medium-sized and large enterprises (Matek and Butalič, 2007). The overall share of individual private entrepreneurs was 58.1% and of limited liability companies 35.9%. Enterprises organised in other organisational forms represented only 6.0% of all enterprises. Despite the large difference in the number of enterprises between micro-enterprises (1–9 total employees), small (10–49 total employees) and medium-sized enterprises (50–249), each of these three size classes generated around one fifth of total turnover. Among them, most persons were employed in micro-enterprises (27.4%), followed by medium-sized (20.8%) and small enterprises (18.0%) (Matek and Butalič, 2007).

No generally accepted definition of a micro-enterprise can be found in the research literature. The most common criterion for a micro-enterprise is the total number of employees, often combined with some financial indicators, such as the firm's annual turnover and assets. In the absence of a precise definition, micro-enterprises are defined in different contexts in various business cultures. Sometimes, the definition of a micro-enterprise depends on the industry (Jungwoo, 2004).

In an investigation in Slovenia in 1999 (Werber and Zupančič, 2005) the computerisation of small businesses were analysed. From 122 included firms with 1 to 50 employees, the average number of total employees was only 5.7.

On 6 May 2003, the Commission of the European Communities (2003) adopted Recommendation 2003/361/EC regarding the definition of micro-, small and medium-sized enterprises (SMS) in Community policies applied within the Community and the European Economic Area. Within the SME category, a micro-enterprise is defined as an enterprise that employs fewer than 10 persons and whose annual turnover and/or annual balance sheet total does not exceed EUR 2 million (Neuberger and Räthke, 2009). Slovenia as Member State of EU accepted this Recommendation which replaced Recommendation 96/280/EC from 1 January 2005 onward.

Due the results of the investigation in 1999 (Werber and Zupančič, 2005), recent Slovene statistical data and present legislation, in 2009 we decided to focus our attention on micro-enterprises.

# 2. Background

## 2.1 Micro-Enterprises and Computerisation

Micro-enterprises cannot be treated as downscaled versions of large companies (Rohde, 2004), due to differences in organisation, management style, business practice and information systems (IS). However, the available evidence on the size-efficiency relation seems to strongly indicate that there is a positive association between firm size and technical efficiency, and that there are also substantial and persistent productivity differences between SMEs and large firms (Yang and Chen, 2009). The role of small and medium-sized enterprises (SMEs) in economic development and economic growth for both developed and developing countries has been increasingly recognised (Yang and Chen, 2009).

The decision-making process is often more intuitive than based on reliable, precise and unambiguous information. In particular, innovative business ideas require people to make decisions based on very little evidence (Koellinger, 2008, Andersson and Florén, 2008). Small firms generally lag behind medium and large companies in adopting and implementing computerisation (Lee et al., 2009, Jungwoo, 2004). This is due to severe constraints on financial resources, lack of in-house expertise, and a short-term management perspective imposed by a volatile competitive environment.

In contrast, micro-enterprises demonstrate a high level of ability to adapt to changes in the environment. They use IT for automation of existing processes, rather then for decision support, or to increase the flexibility of the firm and thereby gain competitive advantage. While large firms are typically capital and equipment intensive, labour-intensive micro-enterprises may be able to increase productivity and provide value-added services through increased computerisation and digitisation (Lee et al., 2009).

## 2.2 Micro-Enterprises and Open Source Software

Several investigations about use of open source software (OSS) have been published (Williams van Rooij, 2009, Carillo and Okoli, 2008, Goode, 2005, Garand, 2009). Mostly they deal with use of OSS in higher education (Williams van Rooij, 2009), in small and medium-sized enterprises (SME) (Garand, 2009), and in large firms (Goode, 2005). We did not find much about the use of OSS in micro-enterprises and, to our knowledge, no such research has been carried out in Slovenia yet.

Open source software (OSS) is defined as computer software for which the source code and certain other rights normally reserved for copyright holders are provided under a software license that meets the Open Source Definition or that is in the public domain. This permits users to use, change, and improve the software, and to redistribute it in modified or unmodified forms. The term 'open source software' originated as part of a marketing campaign for free software (http://en.wikipedia.org/wiki/ Open_source_software).

Under the open source model, groups of enthusiasts develop software applications which are, depending on the license, available free of charge for private or commercial use (Goode, 2005).

Open source software and free software are different terms for software that comes with certain rights, or freedoms, for the user. They describe two approaches and philosophies towards free software. Open source and free software (or 'software libre') both describe software which is free from onerous licensing restrictions. It may be used, copied, studied, modified and redistributed without restriction. Free software is not the same as freeware, i.e., software available with no price. For instance CourseLab is a powerful, yet easy-to-use, e-learning authoring tool. CourseLab is OSS that we can use for free, but if we want to import Microsoft PowerPoint presentations we must buy an import pack licence for $99 per user (www.courselab.com).

The best known open source software (used in several state organisations) is OpenOffice.org. It is the leading open-source office software suite for word processing, spreadsheets, presentations, graphics, databases and more. It is available in many languages and works on all common computers. It can be downloaded and used completely free of charge for any purpose.

These and several other reasons encouraged us to conduct research on the awareness of the existence of and the use of open source software in Slovene micro-enterprises.

## 3. Research Approach

After having reviewed the literature on small enterprises and OSS, a structured interview framework was developed to help address the research objectives. We expected that the use of OSS and free software would depend upon the characteristic of the business (Yang and Chen, 2009, Lee et al. 2009, Jungwoo, 2004, Rodhe, 2004), the characteristics of the owner (Koellinger, 2008, Andersson and Florén, 2008, Jeon, 2006) and the annual turnover of the firm (Jangwoo, 2004, Wiklund et al. 2009).

The main research questions were:

- Are Slovene micro-enterprises aware of the existence of OSS?
- Are Slovene micro-enterprises familiar with OSS?
- What kind of OSS is used in Slovene micro-enterprises?
- What kind of Slovene micro-enterprises uses OSS?
- Is the use of OSS in correlation with any other factors found in enterprises?

Based on this premise, we proposed the following null hypotheses:

H1: *There are no differences in the average amount of OSS used between individual private entrepreneurs, limited liability companies and other organisational forms.*

H2: *There is no correlation between the average amount of OSS used and enterprises' annual turnover.*

H3: *There is no correlation between the average amount of OSS used and owners' computer knowledge.*

H4: *There are no differences in the average amount of OSS used between enterprises with the positions of different respondents (owner, manager, relative, other).*

H5: *There are no differences in the average amount of OSS used and the level of owner's formal education.*

H6: *There are no differences in the average amount of OSS known between individual private entrepreneurs, limited liability companies and other organisational forms.*

H7: *There are no differences in average annual HW investments between enterprises that use or do not use OSS.*

H8: *There are no differences in average annual SW investments between enterprises that use or do not use OSS.*

The study was conducted in two stages: the preliminary pilot interviews and the main study. The interview was tested in 36 selected small and micro-enterprises. Repeated contact with respondents helped to improve the accuracy and relevance of the interviews. Interviews were conducted between June and July 2009 by second year part-time master's-level students at the University of Maribor. Out of the total of 36 interviews, only 16 met the criteria for inclusion in the main study.

Data for the main study were collected via structured interviews with owners or top managers of micro-enterprises between October and December 2009. Several other studies (e.g., Wiklund et al., 2009; Lee et al., 2009, Koellinger, 2008; Jeon, 2006) showed that this group plays a dominant role in decision-making in small enterprises. In the interview, mostly closed-response questions were asked. Except for demographic data, respondents either rated statements on scale of 1 to 5, or responded to multiple choice questions. In total, 123 interviews were conducted. Five of them were not usable because the interviewed businesses did not meet the criteria for a micro-company in different areas (annual turnover, business type etc.), or because of too many questions left unanswered. With the combining of 16 interviews from preliminary study our sample consisted of 134 micro-enterprises.

# 4. Results

## 4.1 Characteristics of the Enterprises Participating in the Study

Respondents who supplied data came from a wide variety of business backgrounds and sizes. The overall share of individual private entrepreneurs was 56% and of limited liability companies 40%. Enterprises organized in other organisational forms represented only 4% of the sample. Among 134 enterprises, 44% were family owned. The average number of total employees was 3.4, including the owner of the enterprise. In the micro-enterprises analysed three years ago, average number of total employees was 3.2. The largest share of enterprises came from service sector (16%), manufacturing (13%), construction (13%) and retail (10%). Others were from tourism (8%), agriculture (7%), wholesale (6%), transportation (4%) and other (23%). The average existence time of micro-enterprises was 12.3 years. Most small enterprises (24%) reported annual turnover (Figure 1) of between €21,000 and €68,000. Annual turnover of more than €209,000 was reported in 22% of micro-enterprises.

*Figure 1: Micro-enterprises according to annual turnover*

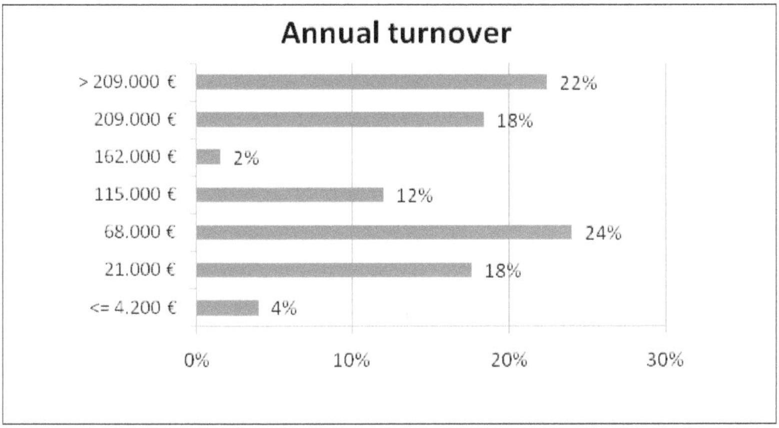


The majority of enterprises (80%) outsourced accounting and bookkeeping to an external partner who specialised in selling accounting services to small companies.

## 4.2 Characteristics of the Respondents

The majority of respondents (76%) were the owners of their businesses, 10% were executive directors, 7% owner-relatives and 7% were some other employees. The age of most of them (45%) was between 31 and 45 years, 34% between 46 and 55, 10% were older than 55 years (Figure 2). Only 2% were between 21 and 25 and 9% between 26 and 30 years.

*Figure 2: Respondents' age*

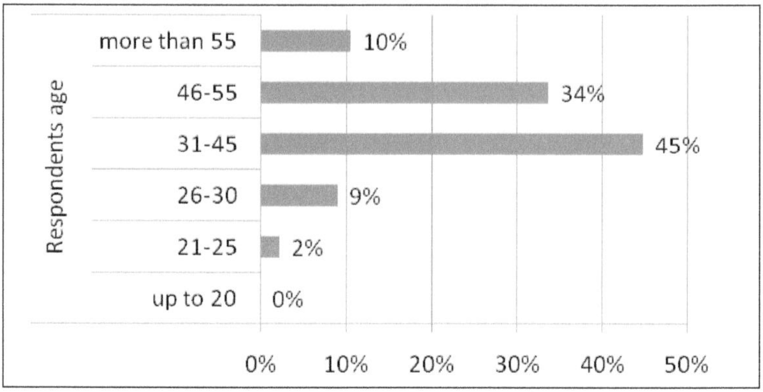


There were 72% male and 28% female respondents. In most cases, their formal education was secondary school (50%), 12% vocational level, 11% higher, 23% graduate and 4% postgraduate. The majority of respondents (40%) self-estimated their computer knowledge (Figure 3) as neither good, nor bad. Thirty-one percent of respondents estimated their computer knowledge as poor or very poor.

Among 134 included owners or managers, 4% do not use a computer, 26% use it passively, only for private purposes, and to supervise employers work on computer. Employees were, on average, at computer-related courses for only 9.89 hours in last three years.

*Figure 3: Self-estimated computer knowledge of the owner*

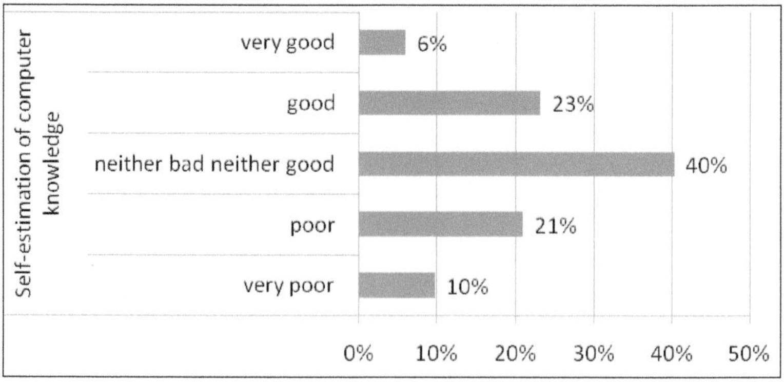

## 4.3 Computer Hardware and Software

The average number of laptops per company was 2.6, desktops 1.5, workstations 0.2 and network servers 0.4. In total, companies from our sample had 4.7 computers per organisation (1.4 computers per employee). Micro-enterprises in our sample had on average 8.9 years of computer experience. On average, micro-enterprises invest €1,539 per year in computer hardware or computer hardware services and €880 in software or software licences. Almost all (98.5%) of the enterprises had an internet connection.

Most enterprises (95%) use some version of the Windows operating system (XP, Vista, NT). Of the various other operating systems, 5% of the enterprises use Linux. In 93% of all companies (Figure 4), general programs (word processor, spreadsheets, databases etc.) were installed, but only a few of them used them to analyze data from their databases or to prepare customised reports. These tools were mostly bought together with the computers, which may explain why they were not often used. Insufficient computer knowledge and skills of the owners/managers and employees may be a possible explanation for the non-use of software tools. The relatively low self-assessment of computer knowledge and skills found in our study (Figure 3) supports this assumption.

*Figure 4: Type of software used by micro-enterprises*

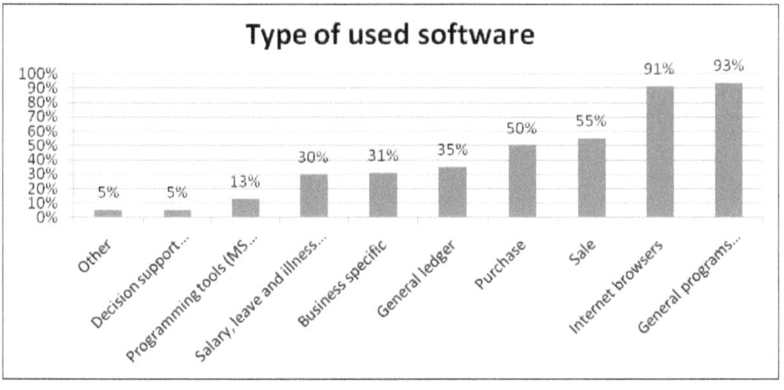


Only 13% of businesses used some type of package for application development (MS Access, Visual Basic etc.), and 5% had applications for decision support.

Almost half (48.9%) of enterprises use some kind of software without a license. This is one of the reasons we proposed the use of OSS to them when we conducted our interviews.

## 4.4 Use of OSS

Almost half (48%) of included micro-enterprises use no OSS, 27% use one OSS or free SW (Figure 5). We can assume that most of them use Mozilla Firefox since 52% of micro-enterprises that use OSS majority (82%) use Mozilla Firefox. Mozilla Firefox is also most popular internet browser in Slovenia after the commercial MS Internet Explorer. Only 11% of micro-enterprises use two types of OSS or free SW. According to Figure 5, we can conclude that the second most-used OSS or free SW is some kind of computer virus protection program (26%) such as Avast (5.2%) or AVG Free, (3.7%).

*Figure 5: Number of OSS and free SW used by micro-enterprises*

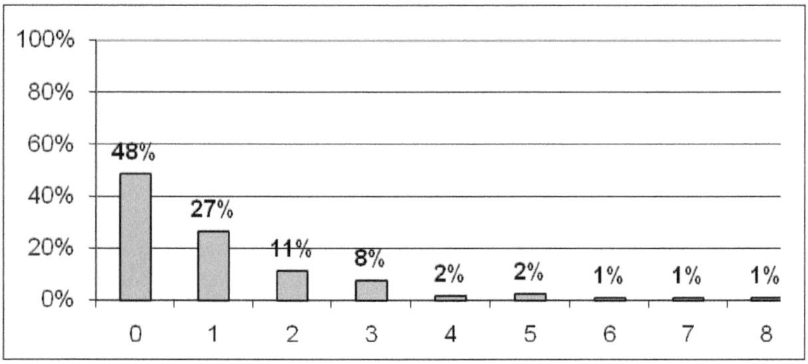


Eight percent of enterprises use three types of OSS or free SW. Among them we can expect Open Office, which is in 14% of enterprises.

If we picture a typical Slovene micro-enterprise (Table 1) they would have at least one computer with some Windows XP operating system, with MS Office (71%), MS Outlook mail program (70%), MS Internet Explorer (88%), some commercial antivirus program (60%) and MS Windows Media Player (48%). The probable reason for this is that most micro-enterprises purchase computers with preinstalled SW. WinZip is used in 37% of enterprises; others use WinRar (11%) or 7-Zip (5.2%). Surprisingly, Photoshop is used in 19.4% of the surveyed companies.

*Table 1: Percentage of SW used by micro-enterprises*

| **Commercial SW** | | **OSS and free SW** | |
|---|---|---|---|
| NT | 14.9% | | |
| Vista | 17% | SuSe | 0.7% |
| XP | 78% | Linux | 4% |
| Internet Explorer | 88% | Mozilla Firefox | 42.5% |
| | | Google Chrome | 2.2% |
| MSOffice | 71% | Open Office | 14% |
| Photoshop | 19.4% | GIMP | 1.5% |
| MS Windows Server | 7.5% | Apache Server | 2.9% |
| Symatec Anti Virus | 4.4% | AVG Free | 3.7% |
| Other commercial | 60% | AVAST<br>Other free | 5.2%<br>26.1% |
| MS SQL Server | 5% | MySQL | 4.4% |
| Oracle | 0.7% | Postgre SQL | 0.7% |
| | | Firebird | 3.7% |
| Outlook | 70% | Mozilla Thunderbird | 6% |
| MS Exchange Server 2003 | 1.5% | Sendmail | 0.7% |
| | | PostFix | 0.7% |
| MS Visual Studio .NET Ent. | 2.9% | ECLIPSE | 0.7% |
| Windows Media player | 47% | VLC Media Player | 4.5% |
| | | GomPlayer, Bsplayer | 2.9% |
| ASP Net | 2.2% | PHP | 0.7% |
| DREAMWARE | 0.7% | JSP | 0.7% |
| WinZip | 37% | 7-zip | 5.2% |
| | | WinRar | 11% |
| Oracle | 0.7% | OpenBravo | 0.7% |
| Siebel | 0.7% | SugarCRM | 0.7% |
| MS Money | 2,9% | | |
| MS Project | 3,7% | | |
| Cognos | 0,7% | | |

## 4.5 Awareness of OSS

One of questions associated with OSS was also: Which of the listed OSS programs do you know? Figure 6 show results of this question. More then one third (34%) of respondents do not know any OSS, 19% know one OSS. We can assume this is Mozilla Firefox. Seven percent of respondent know two OSS programs and 7% know three of them.

*Figure 6: Number of knowing OSS by micro-enterprises (31 possibilities)*

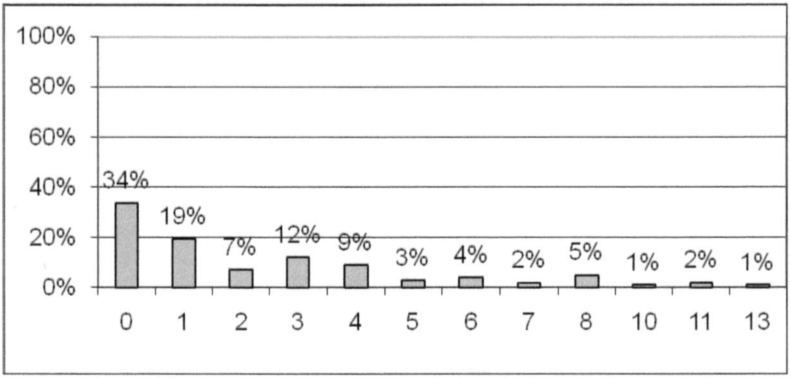


Respondents were asked about importance of OSS characteristics (Figure 7). As expected, lower cost is main reason an owner or manager would use OSS. The main reason of non-use or the lowest estimated characteristics was the very limited possibility of training for OSS. We believe that this is the main reason for the low market share of OSS.

*Figure 7: Importance of OSS characteristics*

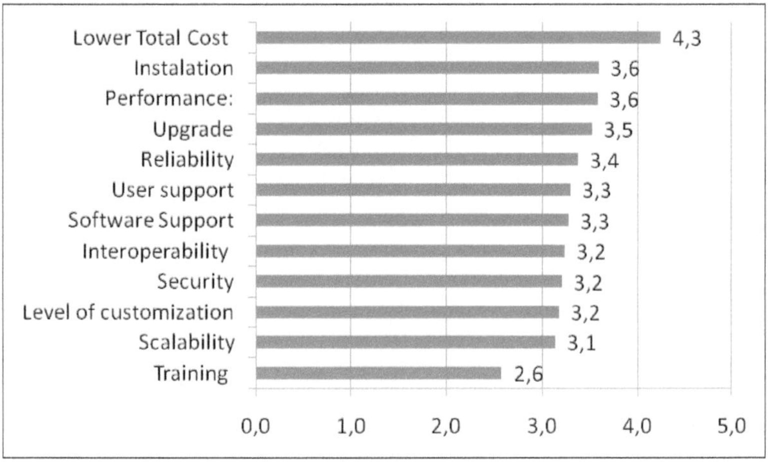

## 4.6 Results of Hypothesis Test

The t-test, analysis of variance (ANOVA) and correlations tests were used in hypothesis testing. Tests were performed using SPSS Statistics version 17.0. With an analysis of the data from 134 micro-enterprises in the sample, we found that:

(1) The first null hypothesis (H1) was tested with an analysis of variance. The descriptive statistics are shown in Table 2. The average number of used OSS programs is statistically different among enterprises with different organisational forms (F=4.991, p-value is 0.008<0.01), so we reject null hypothesis H1 at 1% significance level. Micro-enterprises organised as limited liability companies have on average a higher use of OSS (1.47) than enterprises organised as individual private entrepreneurs (0.7). The highest average numbers of used OSS (1.8) are in enterprises that describe their organisation as 'other type of organisation'. In most cases, those enterprises are associations, clubs or societies; i.e., their existence and activities depends on membership fees or donations. A possible explanation for this is that they do not have enough money to invest in commercial software, so they are required to use free software or OSS.

*Table 2: Descriptive statistics of used/known OSS and organisational form of an enterprise*

| **Organisational form** | **Number of used OSS** | | | | | **Number of known OSS** | | | | |
|---|---|---|---|---|---|---|---|---|---|---|
| | N | Mean | Std. Dev | Min | Max | N | Mean | Std. Dev | Min | Max |
| Individual private entrepreneurs | 74 | 0.7 | 1.144 | 0 | 5 | 59 | 1.83 | 2.422 | 0 | 10 |
| Limited liability companies | 53 | 1.47 | 1.772 | 0 | 8 | 35 | 3.46 | 3.467 | 0 | 13 |
| Other organisational forms | 5 | 1.8 | 1.924 | 0 | 5 | 4 | 3.50 | 3.317 | 0 | 8 |
| Total | 132 | 1.05 | 1.500 | 0 | 8 | 98 | 2.48 | 2.951 | 0 | 13 |

(2) Correlation between the average annual turnover and enterprises number of used OSS is statistically significantly positive (Pearson correlation coefficient is 0.184, p-value is 0.036, and it is significant at 5% level; so we can reject the null hypothesis H2), which means that enterprises with higher number of used OSS also have higher annual turnover (Table 3).

(3) The correlation between the self-estimated owner computer knowledge and the amount of OSS used (Table 3) is statistically significantly positive (Pearson correlation coefficient is 0.270, p-value is 0.002, and it is significant at the 1% level; so we can reject the null hypothesis H3). In enterprises where the owner has more computer knowledge, on average they use more OSS.

*Table 3: Use of OSS with annual turnover and owner computer knowledge*

| | | Use of OSS | Annual turnover | Owner computer knowledge |
|---|---|---|---|---|
| Use of OSS | Pearson Corr. | 1 | .184* | .270** |
| | Sig. (2-tailed) | | .036 | .002 |
| | N | 132 | 131 | 132 |
| Annual turnover | Pearson Corr. | .184* | 1 | .224** |
| | Sig. (2-tailed) | .036 | | .009 |
| | N | 131 | 133 | 133 |
| Owner's computer knowl-edge | Pearson Corr. | .270** | .224** | 1 |
| | Sig. (2-tailed) | .002 | .009 | |
| | N | 132 | 133 | 134 |

(4) There are statistically significant differences in the average number of used OSS between enterprises with different respondent position (ANOVA: F=5,496, p-value is 0.001<0.01; so the null hypothesis H4 can be rejected at the 1% significance level). We continued with multiple comparisons (LSD test) and discovered that there are statistically significant differences in average use of OSS in enterprises where respondents were managers in comparison to enterprises where respondents were owners or relatives. On average, the number of used OSS was 2.31 (Table 4) in enterprises where the respondents were managers in comparison to owners of enterprises, where the average amount of used OSS programs was only 0.84.

In the enterprises where the respondents were relatives, the average number of OSS used was even lower (0.63). Multiple comparisons also indicated that there were no statistically significant differences in the average amounts of OSS used between enterprises where respondents were managers or relatives.

*Table 4: Descriptive statistics of used/known OSS and respondent position*

| **Respondent position** | **Number of used OSS** | | | | | **Number of known OSS** | | | | |
|---|---|---|---|---|---|---|---|---|---|---|
| | N | Mean | Std. Dev | Min | Max | N | Mean | Std. Dev | Min | Max |
| Owner | 101 | 0.84 | 1.376 | 0 | 8 | 75 | 2.51 | 2.733 | 0 | 12 |
| Manager | 13 | 2.31 | 1.702 | 0 | 7 | 12 | 4.58 | 3.118 | 0 | 10 |
| Relative of owner | 8 | 0.63 | .916 | 0 | 2 | 3 | 6.33 | 4.041 | 4 | 11 |
| Other | 10 | 1.90 | 1.853 | 0 | 5 | 8 | 7.25 | 3.694 | 3 | 13 |
| Total | 132 | 1.05 | 1.500 | 0 | 8 | 98 | 3.27 | 3.222 | 0 | 13 |

(5) The null hypothesis H5 was tested with an analysis of variance. There are statistically significant differences in the average number of OSS programs used between different levels of formal education of the owners (F=9.504, p-value is 0.000<0.01; so the null hypothesis H5 can be rejected at 1% significance level). We continued with multiple comparisons and discovered that only in the enterprises where the owner/manager's level of formal education is postgraduate is the number of OSS programs used statistically significant higher (4.6) than in other enterprises where the average number of OSS programs used was between 0.8 and 1.20.

(6) Similar to hypothesis H1, there are statistically significant differences in average number of OSS programs known between different organisational forms of the enterprise (ANOVA: F=3.794, p-value is 0.026<0.05; so we reject null hypothesis H6 at the 5% significance level). We continued with multiple comparisons and discovered that average number of known OSS programs (Table 2) between individual private entrepreneurs (1.83) and limited liability companies (3.46) is statistically significantly different.

(7) We performed the mean difference test (the t-test) among groups of enterprises (Table 5) that use OSS or not, and we discovered that there is a statistically significant positive effect of use of OSS on average annual HW investments (t = -2.174, p-value is 0.031<0.05; so we can reject the null hypothesis H7 at the 5% significance level). The enterprises that use OSS on average annually invest €1,935.60 for HW in comparison to those that do not use OSS and on average annually invest €1135.62.

(8) Similar to hypothesis H7, we discovered (Table 5) that there are statistically significant differences in the average annual SW investments between enterprises that use OSS or not (t = -2.166, p-value is 0.031<0.05; so we can reject the null hypothesis H8 at the 5% significance level). The enterprises that use OSS invest

annual in average €1,253.03 for SW in comparison to those that do not use OSS and invest in average only €496.16.

*Table 5: Descriptive statistics of use/non-use of OSS and annual HW and SW investments*

| Use/non-use of OSS | Average annual HW investments | | | Average annual SW investments | | |
|---|---|---|---|---|---|---|
| | N | Mean | Std. Dev | N | Mean | Std. Dev |
| Non-use of OSS | 66 | 1135.62 | 1920.547 | 64 | 496.16 | 750.358 |
| Use of OSS | 67 | 1935.60 | 2302.138 | 66 | 1253.03 | 2695.611 |

# 5. Conclusion

Almost half of included micro-enterprises in our research use some kind of software without licence. Since OSS seems to be cheaper and in most cases adequate substitute for commercial software, why then Slovene micro-enterprises do not use free OSS?

Our research results show that 34% of micro-business enterprise owners or managers do not know any of OSS. An additional 18% of owners or managers only know one OSS. Lack of knowledge and information about OSS is one of the main issues that should be overcome in the coming years if we wish to increase the amount of used OSS.

As concluded in Lee et al. (2009), our results also show that it is imperative for micro-enterprises to adopt computerisation to achieve improvements in business performance. Micro-enterprises in Slovenia are relatively well equipped with information and communication technology (1.4 computers per employee), but they are rather far from exploiting its full potential. Similar to Wiklund et al. (2009) and Jungwoo (2004), our investigation showed that owner/managers' personal attitudes directly and/or indirectly influence their businesses' use of OSS. Implementation and successful operation of computerised business and use of OSS is strongly related to the characteristics of the owner/manager (formal education, computer knowledge and skills). Micro-enterprise owners/managers in general recognise and value IT, but they use it mainly to support daily operations of the business rather than to support decision-making and are mostly not aware of its strategic and organisational impact. The results in our study confirmed relation between number of used OSS and higher annual turnover. We also discovered that investments in HW and SW are in correlation with use of OSS. All that indicates that use of OSS also depends on business success.

According to our findings and those reported by Riemenschneider and Mykytyn, (2000), in order to take full advantage of the existing technology, current owners and managers of micro-enterprises are aware that they should increase the level of their computer skills and knowledge, stay informed about new trends, developments in the IT and communications areas, and acquire technical and managerial competences needed to effectively manage the IS. Among respondents, 21% estimated their computer knowledge and skills as 'poor' and 10% as 'very poor'. If their computer knowledge is poor, how they can use computer software and OSS?

The results of our study indicate that the possibility of getting adequate training, courses and literature is one of the main weaknesses of OSS. The same conclusion can be found in Gardan (2009), where that possibility of training for OSS was also evaluated as lowest of twelve listed OSS characteristics. Similar findings can be found in Goode's (2005) study of 500 top Australian managers. They reject OSS because of a perceived lack of reliable ongoing technical support and substantial learning costs. Because of that, investments in education and training for OSS are unavoidable.

Aside from the expected learning costs, there is no doubt about lower costs when using OSS. Participants in our research indicate the costs of OSS as the most important factor for OSS use. In his study, Garand (2009) focuses on customer perception of OSS among SME and investigates why the level of OSS market share is so low. He compares cost calculations for new hardware with Microsoft and OSS-Linux Standard or Enterprise solutions. He discovered that the costs are lower from 20 to 51% depending Linux solution used. We can find examples of best practice in the use of OSS among several large state organisations (Munich, Germany, Mannheim, Germany, Bristol City Council, UK etc.). If Slovene government organisations would take the same path in replacing Microsoft software with OSS, then micro-enterprises could also follow them. Considerable savings could be achieved by doing so.

## References

Andersson, S. and Florén, H., (2008): Exploring managerial behaviour in small international firms, *Journal of Small Business and Enterprise Development*, Vol. 15 No. 1, pp. 31–50.

Burke, E.A., Fitzroy, R.F. and Nolan, A.M., (2008): What makes a die-hard entrepreneur? Beyond the 'employee or entrepreneur' dichotomy, *Small Bus Econ*, Vol. 31: pp. 93–11.

Carillo, K., Okoli, C., (2008): The Open Source movement: a revolution in software development, *The Journal of Computer Information Systems*; Vol. 49, No. 2, pp. 1–9.

Goode, S., (2005): Something for nothing: management rejection of open source software in Australia's top firms, *Information & Management*, Vol. 42, pp. 669–681.

Garand, B., (2009): *Open Source Software: The customer perception from SME and SMI?*, Group ESC Rouen School of Business, Rouen Normandy MBA 07–08, pp. 1–40.

Jeon, B., Han, K. and Lee, M., (2006): Determining factors for the adoption of e-business: the case of SMEs in Korea, *Applied Economics*, Vol. 38, pp. 1905–1916.

Jungwoo, L., (2004): Discriminant analysis of technology adoption behaviour: a case of Internet technologies in small businesses, *The Journal of Computer Information Systems*, pp. 1–9.

Koellinger, P., (2008): Why are some entrepreneurs more innovative than others?, *Small Bus Econ* Vol. 31: pp.21–37.

Matek, M., Butalič, S., (2007): Rapid reports, No. 6/2009, 14 *BUSINESS ENTITIES* No 1, Statistical office of the Republic of Slovenia, pp. 1–12.

Neuberger, D. and Räthke, S., (2009): Microenterprises and multiple bank relationships: The case of professionals, *Small Bus Econ*, Vol.32: pp. 207–229.

Lee, S.M., Kim, J., Choi, Y., Lee, S.G., (2009): Effects of IT knowledge and media selection on operational performance of small firms, *Small Bus Econ* , Vol. 32, pp. 241–257.

Riemenschneider, C. and Mykytyn, P., (2000): What small business executives have learned about managing information technology, *Information & Management*, Vol. 37, pp. 257–269.

Rohde, F., (2004): IS/IT outsourcing practices of small- and medium sized manufacturers, *International Journal of Accounting Information Systems*, Vol. 5. pp. 429–451.

The commission of the European Communities, (2003): Commission recommendation of 6 May 2003 concerning the definition of micro, small and medium-sized enterprises, *Official Journal of the European Union*, L124, pp. 36–41.

Yang, C.H. , Chen, K.H., (2009): Are small firms less efficient? *Small Bus Econ*, Vol. 32: pp. 375–395.

Werber, B. and Zupančič, J., (2005): *Information system adoption in small companies - model of key issues*. In: Jašková, Mária (ed.). ECON '05: [selected research papers], (Research works proceedings, Vol. 12, Ostrava: Technical University of Ostrava, Faculty of Economics, pp. 355–367.

Wiklund, J., Patzelt, H., Shepherd, A.D., (2009): Building an integrative model of small business growth, *Small Bus Econ*, Vol. 32, pp. 351–374.

Williams van Rooij, S., (2009): Adopting Open-Source Software Applications in U.S. Higher Education: A Cross-Disciplinary Review of the Literature, *Review of Educational Research*; Vol. 79, No 2, pp. 682–701.

## About the Authors

**Borut Werber** graduated in Information Systems from the Faculty of Organizational Sciences, University of Maribor, Slovenia. At the same faculty in 2001, he became a senior university teacher of Information Systems. His fields of research are computerisation of small and micro-enterprises, computing and knowledge and skills of MIS professionals.

**Anja Žnidaršič** has a diploma in Mathematics from the University of Ljubljana. In 2007, she became a teaching assistant at the Faculty of Organizational Sciences, University of Maribor, Slovenia. She is currently working on her doctoral thesis in statistics where she explores social networks and blockmodeling. Her field of research also includes micro-enterprises.

www.ingramcontent.com/pod-product-compliance
Ingram Content Group UK Ltd.
Pitfield, Milton Keynes, MK11 3LW, UK
UKHW041822031026
15587UKWH00002B/511

9 783631 621134